Praise for
Human Scale Revisited

"Like Schumacher's *Small Is Beautiful* but packed with countless examples and careful theory on how to create a truly democratic community from the bottom up, Sale's charming update of his classic *Human Scale* is the best single book on how to build a localist world. A must read!"

—**Gar Alperovitz**, author of *What Then Must We Do?*;
cofounder, The Democracy Collaborative

"*Human Scale* was once ahead of its time, but this updated edition is just in time. While the mainstream assumes that the worldwide grassroots repudiation of globalization will mean war, racism, and poverty, Kirkpatrick Sale's classic book shows how true localization can lay the foundation for peace, harmony, and prosperity. This is indispensable reading for anyone who cares about replacing Big Brother with small-scale democracy."

—**Michael H. Shuman**,
author of *The Local Economy Solution*

"Is it possible to improve a classic? Kirkpatrick Sale has done so with this erudite, provocative, and, ultimately, *hopeful* exploration of human-scale alternatives to soul-deadening Bigness in agriculture, architecture, business, education, government. . . . You name it, Sale knows it."

—**Bill Kauffman**, author of *Bye-Bye, Miss American Empire*
and *Dispatches from the Muckdog Gazette*

Also by Kirkpatrick Sale

The Land and People of Ghana (1963, 1972)

SDS (1973)

Power Shift:
The Rise of the Southern Rim and
Its Challenge to the Eastern Establishment (1975)

Dwellers in the Land:
The Bioregional Vision (1985)

The Conquest of Paradise:
Christopher Columbus and the Columbian Legacy (1990)

The Green Revolution:
The American Environmental Movement, 1962–1992 (1993)

Rebels Against the Future:
The Luddites and Their War on the Industrial Revolution (1995)

The Fire of His Genius:
Robert Fulton and the American Dream (2001)

Why the Sea Is Salt:
Poems of Love and Loss (2001)

After Eden:
The Evolution of Human Domination (2006)

Emancipation Hell:
The Tragedy Wrought by the
Emancipation Proclamation (2012)

HUMAN
SCALE
REVISITED

HUMAN SCALE

=== REVISITED ===

A New Look at the Classic Case

for a Decentralist Future

KIRKPATRICK SALE

Chelsea Green Publishing

White River Junction, Vermont

This book is an updated and revised edition of a work originally published in 1980 by Coward, McCann & Geoghegan.

The author gratefully acknowledges the following for granting permission to quote from copyrighted materials: Houghton Mifflin Co. for an excerpt from "America Was Promises" from *New & Collected Poems, 1917–1976* by Archibald MacLeish, by permission of Houghton Mifflin Co., copyright © 1976 by Archibald MacLeish; Rutgers University Press for an excerpt from "The Size of Song" by John Ciardi from *Person to Person*, by permission of Rutgers University Press, © 1964 by Rutgers The State University of New Jersey.

Project Manager: Patricia Stone
Project Editor: Joni Praded
Copy Editor: Polly Zetterberg
Indexer: Shana Milkie
Designer: Melissa Jacobson

Printed in the United States of America.
First printing April 2017.
10 9 8 7 6 5 4 3 2 1   17 18 19 20 21

Our Commitment to Green Publishing
Chelsea Green sees publishing as a tool for cultural change and ecological stewardship. We strive to align our book manufacturing practices with our editorial mission and to reduce the impact of our business enterprise in the environment. We print our books and catalogs on chlorine-free recycled paper, using vegetable-based inks whenever possible. This book may cost slightly more because it was printed on paper that contains recycled fiber, and we hope you'll agree that it's worth it. Chelsea Green is a member of the Green Press Initiative (www.greenpressinitiative.org), a nonprofit coalition of publishers, manufacturers, and authors working to protect the world's endangered forests and conserve natural resources. *Human Scale Revisited* was printed on paper supplied by McNaughton & Gunn that contains 100% postconsumer recycled fiber.

Library of Congress Cataloging-in-Publication Data is available upon request.

Chelsea Green Publishing
85 North Main Street, Suite 120
White River Junction, VT 05001
(802) 295-6300
www.chelseagreen.com

Dedicated to Leopold Kohr,
1909–1994
great man, good friend

CONTENTS

PART ONE

TOWARD THE HUMAN SCALE

Units of measure are the first condition of all. The builder takes as his measure what is easiest and most constant: his pace, his foot, his elbow, his finger. He has created a unit which regulates the whole work. . . . It is in harmony with him. That is the main point.

—LE CORBUSIER, Towards a New Architecture, 1958

The proper size of a bedroom has not changed in thousands of years. Neither has the proper size of a door nor the proper size of a community. . . .

Scale: by that we mean that buildings and their components are related harmoniously to each other and to human beings. In urban design we also mean that a city and its parts are interrelated and also related to people and their abilities to comprehend their surroundings.

—PAUL D. SPREIREGEN, Urban Design:
The Architecture of Towns and Cities, 1965

The most important balance of all the elements in space is that of the human scale.

—CONSTANTINE DOXIADIS, Ekistiks, 1968

1

Parthenothanatos

F or more than two thousand years the Parthenon has stood atop the Acropolis, an enduring monument to the imagination and craft of humankind and to the complex civilization that gave it birth.

Artfully placed against the backdrop of two dramatic mountains, on a large stone outcrop 500 feet above the Aegean's Saronic Gulf, it was purposefully built at an angle to the entrance gate so that you see it first not head on but in perspective, the columns receding in order and harmony, their delicately fluted lines etching a series of shadows in the Attic light against the bright, creamy stone. As you approach, the temple seems almost to float, massive and assertive though it is, for it rests on a slight hill and it was crafted without any true verticals whatsoever, the columns bending inward from base to capital with infinite subtlety and precision, the flutes so carefully measured that each one had to be carved individually like a jewel, the whole effect pulling the eye imperceptibly upward. It asserts, directly though not stridently, the glory that was Greece, or more properly, Athens.

Close up, the human measure is pronounced in the building's decorations and relationships. The exterior sculptures, at least in original form, though many have decayed, display an extraordinary concern for the varieties of the human form, in motion and at rest, clothed and naked, while the friezes of the Panathenaic procession convey the energy and centrality of the workaday civic life of the city below. Within, the sense of the human measure is again reflected in the dimensions of the columns and remnant forms, and the rational, humanistic spirit that originally informed it is unmistakable still.

Indeed, for all its outsized grandeur and magnitude, it is a building carefully gracefully designed on the human scale, measured by the human thumb and pace and body, created in its every detail with the principle, to be articulated by Protagoras only a few decades later, of "man the measure of all things." The height of the average ancient Greek man, known to be shorter than a modern European, I have calculated to be about 5 feet 7½ inches, a figure confirmed by the fact that, allowing for minuscule variations in the original construction and in the settlement of the building over the years, it is in exact multiples of this measure to which the major dimensions were built. The full height is 540.12 inches, that unit by 8, the width is 1,215.3 inches, that unit by 18, and the length is 2,734.3 inches, that unit by 40.5. The interior columns at 202.5 inches reflect that unit by 3, the distance between the architraves is 405 inches, that unit by 6, and the statue of Athena herself, the goddess to whom the city and temple were consecrated, may have been around 12 meters, or 473 inches tall, exactly 7 times that unit. It is a monument to the human scale, only natural in a land whose cities were ordered according to the human scale, whose society, economic relations, and government were all constructed with regard to the human scale.

To architects a model, to archeologists a treasure, to classicists a palimpsest, to historians a time chamber, to humanists an inspiration, the Parthenon has no equal, on any continent, from any age. "Earth proudly wears the Parthenon," Emerson wrote, "as the best gem upon her zone." It has been the object of pilgrimages for many peoples of the world, but for the West it is even more: the seat of the civilization that has done more than any other to shape our own, our arts and sciences, our politics and governments, our culture and our most basic perceptions of the world. During the course of twenty-four centuries—longer than any single civilization has lasted since the dawn of time—the Parthenon has stood as the embodiment of our heritage. It has suffered much, to be sure, in the course of human warfare and human greed, but it always endured, always seemed to be possessed, as Plutarch wrote, of "a living and incorruptible breath, a spirit impervious to age."

Not exactly impervious. Over the centuries it has been looted and damaged by various hands, but the worst were those of Lord Elgin in the nineteenth century, who removed sculptures from the entire building, including about 60 percent of the iconic friezes, and sent them to England, where they still reside. But it took the twentieth century to begin its nearly final collapse through the poison of pollution, particularly acid rain, from the ubiquitous automobiles of Athens and the coal-burning electrical plants and factories (together producing as much as 5,500 tons per day by the

4

1970s), literally melting the marble stones of the Parthenon. By the 1970s the faces of relief sculptures along the metopes had begun to erode and some hands and arms and horses' legs were missing, the sculptures were becoming indistinguishable blobs, and the columnar flutes were fading. Scholars and authorities associated with the Acropolis realized that something had to be done. In the words of UNESCO Director General Amadou-Mahtar M'Bow, called in to try to rescue the Attic buildings, "After resisting the onslaughts of weather and human assailants for 2,400 years, this magnificent monument is threatened with destruction as a result of the damage which industrial civilization has increasingly inflicted on it."

For 25 years, experts of all kinds from all around the world worked to protect, restore, and preserve what was left of the Parthenon, and what they finally decided to do was open a new $165 million Acropolis Museum in 2008—a giant modern building, only 300 yards down the Acropolis, that has been said to look like a parking garage. Much of the Parthenon itself was in effect taken apart and put back together, with titanium bars and ties to strengthen the marble blocks, new marble used to patch holes and replace chips, and the blocks and columns were cleaned by laser beams of infrared and ultraviolet rays. No one is allowed to go close to the columns or go inside the building, however, because foot traffic of 6 million tourists a year was jarring the floor and deep paths across it; visitors are made to stay behind barriers 25 feet away and forbidden to experience the interior as the original Greeks would have. All the remaining frieze sculptures were removed, taken into the museum and installed on a replica of the metopes, and replaced by copies made of what is called "artificial stone." Together with freestanding sculptures, the museum now houses nearly 4,000 pieces of original art, the Parthenon above displays copies.

As a genuine artifact of Hellenic civilization, the Parthenon is no more. What remains after the ravages of the modern world is a genuine artifact of industrial civilization. The monument that was—the shrine that even in its imperfect shape excited for centuries—will never exist again, and at best the restorers can transform the temple into a kind of picture postcard, its sculptures no more than "authentic reproductions," as the museum world's contradiction has it, its interior barred to public experience. Pilgrimages have not been made these many centuries so that the inheritors of the classic Greeks could stand off in mid-distance and gaze at the wonders of artificial stone.

Nor is this awesome devastation confined to the Parthenon, or Greece, or Europe. The monuments of the world's civilizations, in almost every country, are being degraded and obliterated by the misfortune of being located in modern industrial car-polluted cities, in the path of acid rain or other airborne pollutants, or in the middle of wars and rebellions. UNESCO originally identified some 500 important buildings in peril throughout the world in 1976, and subsequently has produced an annual list of World Heritage Sites that face some kind of danger and destruction, standing at 779 in 2015. In some cases, the monuments are undergoing processes of protection or reproduction, but all those are expensive, makeshift, and ultimately futile fingers in dikes. Industrial civilization, overbuilt, overextended, and overpowerful, feeds on the human imperilment of the earth, its resources and its species, heedless of the ruination in its wake and powerless to cease or even control its calamitous pace.

But the Parthenon stands out for two reasons.

First, as a fitting symbol of Western civilization, it acts as a symbol of the crisis to which that civilization has come. This is not some temporary aberration but rather a fixed condition, and it cannot be stopped even if ameliorated here and there by the devices of modern technology, which almost always bring along additional problems of their own. I am tempted to say that it is too late to try to bring a halt to this crisis, even if we had the perception and the will to change our priorities, rethink our values, reorganize our systems, and abandon the false gods of the seven deadly sins. But if it is not too late, our only hope would be to reorder and rework our habitats and environments, our lives and civilizations, along such lines as the original Parthenon would suggest, a building built on the principles of the human scale. Or, if that call is not heeded, and the collapse is inescapable, then I would suggest that it will be only by following the human scale will any successful human society be rebuilt and regenerated after that collapse.

And second, unlike the peoples of the preceding empires—Babylonia, Mesopotamia, Assyria, Egypt—the Greeks did not worship omnipotent gods, did not serve almighty kings, did not cluster themselves into faceless urban multitudes. They evolved, for the first time, philosophies and organizations built on the quite remarkable notion of the freeborn citizen, an individual with an inalienable equality within the community or *polis*,

6

who was expected to participate in its arts, sciences, athletics, politics, discourses, and games for the betterment not only of the self but for that of the entire population.

In Athens, daily life evidenced that human principle. In the *agora*, the public square that was at once the marketplace and the meeting place, there would be an amorphous and spontaneous movement of people and goods and ideas from dawn to sunset, a social axis on which the rest of the city's life spun. In the *ecclesia*, the democratic assembly of the citizens, the freemen (though not, alas, women) would meet to formulate the decisions of the community on the principles of open participation and individual right, and the offices of the city would be held by various of them chosen by lot throughout the year. In the sports-grounds and parks, and at the periodic games and dances, the human body would be celebrated with an almost pagan zeal, and at the schools and *gymnasia* a similar passion, at least among those who had the leisure, was devoted to the development of the human mind—*mens sana in corpore sana*, as the Romans would later say, something we loosely translate to *sound mind, sound body*. And though there would be toil for many, Athenian life was meant, and the day was organized as much as possible, for the individual's intellectual, aesthetic, sexual, social, and civic satisfaction.

In short, Athens was, in the words of the great urban historian Lewis Mumford, a city "cut closer to the human measure."

———

The perils and the promise, then, coexist in the singular shrine that is the Parthenon. Its present plight makes manifest the crises, its past glories suggest the direction of our remedies.

What follows is an extrapolation from that duality. In this book's first two parts, I point out the processes and institutions that have brought us to our crisis, and explain that there is an overarching cause that is, quite simply, the excesses in all aspects of our lives that have gone beyond human scale. Bigness, in short, is at the heart of our predicament.

That given, then the next three sections of the book deal with the appropriate-scaled remedies that are known and available for the three main sectors of our lives—our society, economy, and polity—and show how smaller and more people-sized institutions and arrangements are not simply necessary and desirable, but—despite the myopic critics—are possible. I use a plethora of examples from other cultures, other ages, and this culture and this age to show that we have the means to achieve a desirable future as soon as we can apply the will.

It takes some time to pursue all of this, and you will not have failed to notice that this, a book about the virtues of the small and human-measured, is fairly large. The easy answer is that, in books as in other artifacts or systems, I am no advocate of the needlessly small, rather only of the appropriate size, given ecological and human limits—or as E. F. Schumacher once said, "I called my book *Small Is Beautiful* not because everything small is beautiful but because everything else is too BIG." The more elaborate answer is that I have found that to present so many ideas running against mainstream and current thought, not only ideas of our era but those of the past few centuries, and to survey the workable alternatives that have been tried and proven throughout history, has inevitably taken a goodly number of pages—as it has of researches, and years.

I do not ask that you agree with me as we begin. Only that you keep an open mind and heart, and remember the awful fate of the Acropolis: Parthenothanatos.

2

Crises of Civilization

The crises symbolized by the Parthenon are so palpable and pervading that it almost seems superfluous to list and describe them, but since they are illustrative of a serious, encompassing truth of surpassing importance, I feel that I am obliged to touch on them. That truth is that now, well into the twenty-first century, particularly in advanced industrial countries, *the world is enduring a series of plights and predicaments beyond any yet experienced in the procession of civilized societies.*

That could be taken as hyperbole, but there is enough evidence around us, and affirmations from enough different kinds of people in enough different disciplines, to prove that these crises are quite real and quite unique.

There is, to begin with the most serious, an imperiled global ecology, with the irremediable pollution of atmosphere, oceans, and soils, the unprecedented extinction of species, the melting of ice sheets at the poles, the alteration of climate, the exhaustion of fisheries, the slow elimination of forests, the spread of deserts, the depletion of resources, especially groundwater, the increase in production of untested chemicals, the creation of environmental diseases, and the overpopulation and overdomination of one single bipedal species. In the words of a landmark Millennium Ecosystem Assessment issued by 1,360 scientists in March 2005, the most comprehensive environmental review ever done, nearly two-thirds of the natural world that supports life on earth is being degraded by human pressure, and "human activity is putting such a strain on the natural functions of Earth that the ability of the planet's ecosystems to sustain future generations can no longer be taken for granted."

There is as well an imperiled social ecology, with a breakdown of family and community throughout the industrial world, an increasing dependence on the uncontrolled internet and "social" media, international cyberwarfare, unchecked and spreading slave and sex trades worldwide;

in the United States, an erosion of religious commitment, contempt for law and law enforcement, increasing alienation and distrust of established institutions (throughout the end of the twentieth century and for all of the twenty-first, the General Social Survey of the University of Chicago determined that public confidence in all American institutions is below 30 percent), cultural ignorance and confusion, ethical and moral deterioration, a growth of suicide, mental illness, alcoholism, prescription and nonprescription drug addiction, alienation, poverty, domestic and racial violence, broken and divorced families, and unwed motherhood (from 4 percent to 40 since 1950, 93 percent of mothers under 20 in 2015), an inability to establish racial harmony or justice, and increasing rates of mass incarceration by an order of four since the 1970s.

The political order, at every level, has deteriorated as well, with some 65 countries fighting wars in 2015, plus no fewer than another 638 conflicts between various insurgent and separatist militias (with the United States engaged in 134 of them and selling arms to the great majority), uncontrolled migration from within broken states in Africa and Asia resulting in displaced populations of more than 500 million people, a steady increase in dictatorships and authoritarian regimes and what Freedom House calls "a growing disdain for democratic standards in nearly all regions of the world," worldwide government corruption with a large majority of nations (107 out of 174) ranked below average in 2014, multiple failures and increasing irrelevance of the United Nations. And, in this country, a democracy only in name, the evidence of government corruption, waste, incompetence, and inefficiency, maintenance of empire through more than 725 overseas bases costing trillions of dollars a year, government-corporate cronyism, money control of elections, and sheer ineptitude leading to widespread disaffiliation and virtual collapse of the two-party system, government stagnation, inability to deal with mounting debt (an unimaginable $19 trillion in 2016), insolvency of entitlement programs, uncheckable defense and space budgets, repeated administration lying and deceit, revelations of government overreach, and invasions of privacy without regulation or limitation.

All of which is reflected in economic disarray and stagnation throughout the West, caught in the chaos and calamity of a globalization in service to the largest corporations and banks, with a stagnant dollar and a weak uncertain euro, increasing poverty through much of the world and increasing inequity of wealth in the rest, continuing international corruption, as with the FIFA World Cup fiasco, dependence on ever-less-secure and ever-more-complex internet communication, in this country a failing economy despite rampant growth-based consumerism, high unemployment (despite misleading official statistics), a real-estate bank scandal that led to the 2008 Great Recession, continued multibillion-dollar Wall Street fraud, mortgage market manipulation, stock market algorithm shenanigans, ever-increasing income differences and a shrinking middle class, ineradicable poverty (the population below the median income in 2014 was 70.6 million, or 23 percent, unchanged in 50 years), personal debt of almost $12 trillion in 2015 (increasing 3 percent annually), credit card fraud and identity theft, shoddy manufacturing leading to record product recalls (as, for example, with air bags), continuing trillion-dollar debt to the Chinese and Japanese governments, and a crumbling infrastructure (particularly bridges).

Now it can be fairly objected that every age has its crises and so far the ingenuity of the human brain or the capacity of human society has been able to solve, or appear to solve, most of them. No matter how problems have grown in the past they have not interfered with the sort of growth that has characterized Western civilization in the modern period. But that lesson from the past disguises one important fact of the present: our crises now proceed, like the very growth of our systems, *exponentially*. "During the past two centuries," in the words of M. King Hubbert, the prescient geophysicist with the United States Geological Survey, "we have known nothing but exponential growth, and we have evolved what amounts to an exponential growth culture, a culture so heavily dependent upon the continuance of exponential growth for its stability that it is incapable of reckoning with problems of non-growth."

What that means is best shown by the fable of an Indian rajah who offered to give a subject who had made a beautiful chessboard for him any gift he desired. The humble subject asked only for some grains of wheat on a chessboard, one grain on the first square, two on the second, four on the third, and so on, doubling each time until all the squares are filled. Naturally the ruler was willing to comply with this modest request and the granary managers were called forth to begin distributing. Much to everyone's amazement there wasn't enough wheat in the entire country to supply the subject. Before they reached the thirty-third square he was owed 8,000 bushels of wheat, by the fiftieth square 1 billion bushels (half the 2012 output of the United States), and by the sixty-fourth square some 7.4 trillion bushels, roughly 300 times the production of the entire world. That's exponential growth.

In 1965, at the very beginning of the computer revolution, Gordon E. Moore of the Intel Corporation formulated Moore's Law, which said that the number of transistors, and thus the power, memory, sensors, and much else, would double every two years. His prediction of exponential growth in the computer world has come true exactly, and the enhanced impact of digital electronics on the global economy—increased productivity, innovation, and development—has transformed it and much of the rest of society in barely half a century. The lives of almost everyone in the developed world, West and East, and of many countless others, have been transformed in that time, a time span that no one could have predicted. That's exponential growth.

I say no one could have predicted, but that's not precisely true. Back in 1972 an outfit called the Club of Rome published an analysis called *Limits of Growth*, whose principal authors, Donella and Dennis Meadows, showed by computer models what exponential growth would do. It concluded that "if the present growth trends in world population, industrialization, pollution, food production, and resource depletion continue unchanged, the limits to growth on this planet will be reached sometime within the next one hundred years. The most probable result will be a rather sudden and uncontrollable decline in both population and industrial capacity," in fact "overshoot and collapse" in all dimensions with a tipping point around 2020–30. A second study in 2000 by an international banker named Matthew R. Simmons found that, while some minor predictions that had not been as dire as the Meadows expected, "there was nothing that I could find in the book which has so far been even vaguely invalidated. To the contrary, the chilling warnings of how powerful exponential growth rate can be are right on track." An update of the *Limits* book in 2004 found much the same thing, and a subsequent analysis by University of Melbourne scholar Graham Turner in 2014 came to the conclusion that resource depletion, overpopulation, economic decline, industrial slowdown, and environmental collapse were following almost exactly the lines of the 1972 forecast.

In simplest terms, this means we are now living through a time that is markedly different from that of the past. Our crises are not only different in degree, they are also, because of that, different in kind. Never before have nations grown so large, never have corporations become so powerful, never have banks and brokerages been so influential and intrusive, never before have governments swollen to such unmanageable sizes, never have the systems, the factories, the technologies been so huge—hence, never before have the crises been so acute.

Obviously the solutions to these crises, even when they are identified and tried, have done nothing to diminish the impact of exponential growth, and indeed the solutions turn out to be problems, or generate unforeseen problems, as often as not. That is why it is necessary to turn in a totally different direction with a totally different mind-set and expectation—a way, as I will show you, to the human scale.

3

The Human–Scale Future

I t is now obvious that the way we have been going, particularly for the last 25 years, has plunged us into these multiple crises, and going on in that direction invites, if it does not guarantee, civilization's collapse within the next 25. That is no exaggeration: as Pope Francis said in his June 2015 encyclical, "Doomsday predictions can no longer be met with irony or disdain."

So to save our planet and its civilizations we must move in an opposite direction, we must work toward the decentralization of institutions, the devolution of power, and the dismantling of all large-scale systems that have created or perpetuated the current crises. In their place, smaller, more controllable, more efficient, more sensitive, people-sized units, rooted in local environments and guided by local citizens. That is the human-scale alternative.

In the search for the proper order of things and societies, a search that has inspired humankind since its earliest sentient days, no better guide has been found than the human form, no better measure than the human scale. "Man the measure"—has that not been the standard, or at least the goal, for the greatest number of human societies for the last 5,000 years, though lost from ours for more than a century? And still today, though many are deluded into a giantism dependent on technology, the guide to any desirable future, for the ways in which tools, building, communities, cities, homes, shops, offices, factories, forums, and legislatures should be constructed; I see no reason to go beyond the simple rule: they should be built to human scale.

Human scale was originally an architectural term, used to describe the components of a building in relation to the people who use it. A cottage door, for example, is necessarily built to human scale, high enough and wide enough so that a body can move through it comfortably, located at a

15

place convenient for the body to use it, in some harmonious relation with the other elements of the building. A hangar door, by contrast, is not, for it has nothing to do with the human form, and is outsized and disproportionate to the human body. From earliest times until quite recent eras, most conscious building has been a reflection of human scale, for in every society the measurements most convenient and most constant were those of the finger, the hand, the arm, the stride, and the height of the builder—a tradition we honor today in the English system in which an inch is based on the length of the first joint of the thumb, the foot on the length of the forearm, and the yard on the length of a normal pace or an extended arm from fingers to nose. (It is vastly preferable to the metric system, based not on anything human at all but on a meter that the French Convention in 1799, in its zeal to do away with all tradition and rely on what it regarded as rational thinking, chose quite arbitrarily by taking one ten-millionth of the meridian of the earth from the North Pole to the Equator.) Even buildings intended to evoke awe and inspiration, such as the Parthenon and Peking's Temple of Heaven, were, when successful, built on these human measures.

But the idea of human scale can also be used to govern the design of communities and towns, indeed of whole cities. As we shall see in some detail later, it means buildings that can be easily taken in by the human eye, in harmonious relations that do not engulf or dwarf the individual; streets that can be comfortably walked, parks and arenas for habitual human contact, places for work and play and sleep within easy distance of each other; the natural world brought into daily life, with grass and trees and flowers in every part, open spaces to experience scenery by day and the starts by night, woods and farms and grazing ground somewhere within walking distance. And all of this of such a size as can be comprehended by a single individual, known at least by acquaintance to all others, where the problems of life are thus kept to manageable proportions, and where security is the natural outcome of association. Cities, too, with their overlays of urbanity, can arise from an amalgam of such communities, with interlocking networks and cross-neighborhood relationships of all kinds, providing only that the cities themselves do not lose the human scale, either in their buildings or their total size, and do not smother their separate parts.

And if buildings and communities can be built to the human scale, then it is not so difficult to imagine all the other aspects of human life, by extension, governed by the same principle. I mean social arrangements, economic conditions, and political structures could all be designed so that individuals can take in their experience whole and coherently, relate with other people freely and honestly, comprehend all that goes on in their working and civic lives, share in the decisions that make it all function, and not feel intimidated or impotent because there are any large hidden forces beyond their control or reckoning. What it takes is a scale at which individuals become neighbors and lovers instead of just acquaintances and ciphers, makers and creators instead of just users and consumers, participants and protagonists instead of just observers and taxpayers.

This alternative future would certainly not be without its problems, some considerable perhaps, and would likely face crises of its own in the course of its enactment, which in any case might take several decades, unless the will to escape the impending doom serves to vivify populations worldwide. But it would, at a minimum, provide relief from the imperilment brought on by the large-scale institutions of the present. Such an age would not be congenial to centralized bureaucracies or high-tech conglomerates, would not permit multibillion-dollar investments in nuclear plants or military adventures or useless space stations. It would not allow the production of 89 million polluting motor vehicles (2014) every year, or countrywide fracking that fouls drinking water and creates earthquakes, or metropolitan areas of 24 million people, or a cabinet department (Homeland Security) formed out of 22 agencies with 216,000 bureaucrats, or the manufacture of 387 cereal brands in America, or a Code of Federal Regulations that at 175,496 pages in 2014 was 117 times as big as the Bible, or a single World Trade Organization, governed by a secret court, regulating 90 percent of international trading.

At the moment such a world might seem a utopian dream, and it will not come easily, but there are several reasons to imagine it possible.

For one, it accords with some of the deepest instincts of the human animal, possibly encoded in our DNA, such as the need for tribal and community sustenance, for harmony with the natural world, for companionship and cooperation. It accords with the experience of by far the greatest part of human history, from the earliest settlements to most of the world today, in which people lived in compact villages and self-contained towns, crafting and hunting (and later farming and herding) for themselves, before some of them evolved into cities and empires. And it accords with much that is rooted in the American experience, such as the traditions of cooperation and self-sufficiency that grew up in the early settlements, the town-meeting democracies that extended at one time from New England to Virginia, the agrarian and anti-authoritarian values of the Founding Fathers, the Jeffersonian understanding of scale and distrust of centralism, the drive for self-sufficiency and independence that for generations led people from the cities to the frontier.

For another, we have had the advantage of knowing the ills and errors of high technology in these past decades, the one ironic benefit of its super-rapid exponential growth. I say "we" though it might better be said "a few," and those of the quasi-Luddistic bent who realize that machines must be differentiated so that those that are of human scale—small, safe, simple, manageable by a single individual, along the lines suggested by E. F. Schumacher's "alternative technology"—are not confused with all those that tie people into large, dangerous, complex, and uncontrollable systems and webs. The Luddites, as a matter of fact, made those distinctions, for they were very comfortable with certain small-scale looms and stocking machines they used every day, only opposed to the belching factories that replaced them, "machinery hurtful to the commonality" as they said in one threatening letter. Thus a human-scale world would have the advantage of knowing not to depend on technology that involved expensive and manipulable machines within large, widespread, even global complexes that would have no regard for the individual village, the community, the family.

And finally, the evidence continues to mount, despite certain trends to the contrary, that such a human-scale future is, at least in many tenets, doable. Models for almost every part of such a future already exist now, or have existed in the knowable past, in many parts of the world, including our own: worker-owned businesses, intentional communities, cooperative movements and banks; generations-old independent communes—like the twenty-three Bruderhof communities around the world and the seven Amana villages in Iowa—Quaker meetings governed by consensual democracy, coast to coast; independent city-states, basic to life in ancient Greece, common in medieval Italy, recurrent in modern times and extant today in many places, including Singapore, Monaco, San Marino, and the Vatican; societies without a state, from the million years of tribes in Africa, Indian tribes in both North and South America, settlements in Polynesia and other South Pacific islands, New England villages in the US colonial period, and countless others. Most of these entities have lived within the shadows of larger institutions and states, it is true, but that is only a testament to the fundamental, and apparently eternal, tenacity of the idea of the empowered community. And if it *has* been done, it *can* be done.

Inuit children are given a puzzle at a fairly early age that asks them if, given a square of nine dots, how can you connect all the dots with only four straight lines, never taking your pencil off the paper?

```
•    •    •

•    •    •

•    •    •
```

Most Inuit have no difficulty in solving this after a few minutes, but even sophisticated children in other parts of the world have failed to solve it, and it stumps most adults as well. Those who fail are accustomed by their culture to certain quite unconscious ways of thinking that are difficult to break out of, but Inuit children, living as they do in wide-open Arctic spaces, naturally have a different sense of space. With that sense they find nothing difficult in the idea of extending the straight lines beyond the nine-dot square, thus:

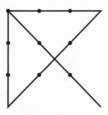

In the same way, there is much about the human-scale alternative that at first seems impossible, undoable. But that is largely because our culture has conditioned us in myriad ways over the last several centuries to thinking of certain kinds of solutions and disregarding—in fact not being aware of—others.

But they are there.

PART TWO

THE BURDEN OF BIGNESS

Everywhere Nature works true to scale, and everything has its proper size accordingly. Men and trees, birds and fishes, stars and star-systems, have their appropriate dimensions, and their more or less narrow range of absolute magnitudes.

—D'ARCY WENTWORTH THOMPSON,
On Growth and Form, 1915

On a small scale, everything becomes flexible, healthy, manageable, and delightful, even a baby's ferocious bite. On a large scale, on the other hand, everything becomes unstable and assumes the proportions of terror.

—LEOPOLD KOHR, The Breakdown of Nations, 1957

*Some rule of birds kills off the song
in any that begin to grow
much larger than a fist or so.
What happens as they move along
to power and size? Something goes wrong.*

—JOHN CIARDI, "The Size of Song," 1964

4

The Beanstalk Principle

I t occurred to me one day, looking at the drawings in a book of fairy tales I was reading to one of my children, that the giant in "Jack and the Beanstalk" looked somehow more *fragile* than menacing, as if he weren't put together quite right. I sat down and made a few calculations. If the giant was, as he looked in the picture, about five times as big as Jack—five times taller, five times wider, five times thicker—then he would have to weigh not just five times as much but *five-to-the-third-power* times as much, five times in each direction—just as the volume of a box of five square feet is not just five times bigger than a box of one square foot, but five-to-the-third-power times as big, or 125 cubic feet. Naturally lugging around all that weight would be something of a problem, an immensely greater problem than the human form has been developed for. Particularly so because the giant's leg bones, though indeed they were 125 times as big as Jack's in all, were only 25 times as big in the dimensions where it counts in carrying weight, that is, in a cross section through the bone that takes in only width and breadth. In short, the giant would have been trying to support 125 times the weight on bones only 25 times as strong—like an average man trying to carry a ton of bricks—and he would have cracked his legs in two and fallen flat on his face if he were even to stand up, much less try to chase after Jack. No wonder he didn't seem very menacing.

Some time later I happened upon a forgotten essay by the British biologist J. B. S. Haldane entitled "On Being the Right Size," quite a delightful little exercise in comparative anatomy. And there, sure enough, Haldane had made the same sorts of computations I had, though he had figured them out from a copy of *Pilgrim's Progress* showing Giant Pope and Giant Pagan towering over tiny Christian, and had come to the same conclusions: "As the human thigh bone breaks under about ten times the human weight, Pope and Pagan would have broken their thighs every time they took a step. This is doubtless why they were sitting down in the picture I remember." But he went beyond Bunyan's morality tale to show the importance of size in the entire biological world.

Haldane shows, for example, that size matters when you consider the fate of various animals when they fall any distance. Since smaller animals tend to have greater surfaces proportional to their weight than larger ones, their air resistance is greater; at the same time, having less weight, their gravitational impulse is smaller. So if a mouse were to fall from a ten-story building, it would be only slightly bruised, get up, and scamper away. A rat would be temporarily stunned and dazed, but probably not seriously hurt. A man would be killed, a horse splattered.

Size matters, too, he shows, in the form an animal takes. A gazelle, for example, could not become larger without putting so much weight on its skinny little legs that they would shatter—unless it adapted like two other members of the same general family: "It may make its legs short and thick, like the rhinoceros, so that every pound of weight has still about the same area of bone to support it. Or it can compress its body and stretch out its legs obliquely to gain stability like the giraffe." Similarly, a human being cannot ever be able to fly because he would need a totally different form to supply enough power to keep his body continually in the air. Thus the notion of an angel—or at least a human-shaped angel—is patently ridiculous: "An angel whose muscles developed no more power, weight for weight, than those of an eagle or a pigeon would require a breast projecting for about four feet to house the muscles engaged in working its wings, while to econ-omize in weight, its legs would have to be reduced to mere stilts."

Haldane limits his brief inquiry mostly to animals, but he is not unmindful of the broader conclusion, one with implications important for our own inquiry: "Just as there is a best size for every animal," he says, "so the same is true for every human institution." And, of course, giants.

There are countless examples of how size matters, but let's look at just two.

A committee meeting has—or rather should have—a certain optimum size. We all know what it is like to be in interminable meetings, and it generally happens that the greater the number of participants, the more talking, the longer the meeting—and usually the less decided. There are several effects of size here, but the basic one is that the number of signals between participants increases exponentially once you get past a certain very small number. For example:

Primus is seated at the committee-room table, next to Secundus. He has only one other person with whom to relate, one other source of signals, words, expressions, gestures, body language, all that goes into the communication by which to arrive at intelligent decisions, and the same is true for Secundus. When they are joined by Tertius, there are suddenly *nine* possible ways of sending and receiving signals—from Primus to Secundus or Tertius (2), from Secundus to Primus or Tertius (4), from Tertius to Primus or Secundus (6), and from each one of them to any other pair (9). Now when Quadrius joins them, the elemental signals are multiplied again, this time to twenty-eight, since each participant then has three other individuals, three possible pairs, and one trio to relate to ($7 \times 4 = 28$). This exponential process continues with each additional person (the formula is $N [2^{n-1} - 1] = x$) and by the time ten people are sitting around the table, not an unusual number for a committee meeting, there are a total of 5,110 ways for all the participants to relate to each other.*

No wonder that a committee often takes so long to achieve anything at all, and that's usually only when most of the participants are so worn down that they cease to participate or give off any signals whatsoever. (Incidentally, the optimum size, as we shall see later, generally seems to be five, when each person deals with no more than fifteen signals, perhaps the limit of the human brain's capacity.)

Take another and more complex example, the American university. Obviously it is possible to build such an institution to any size one wants (as many of our present state universities seem determined to demonstrate), providing only that you make the buildings large enough and the amplification systems loud enough. (And online it is possible to go even larger, as the so-called University of Phoenix had 600,000 students in 2010, down to 155,000 in 2016, but that's a completely fraudulent idea of "university.") There are university systems with a quarter of a million students in them and single campuses with as many as 50,000 students. But just as obviously there is a size beyond which real *teaching* and *learning* can no longer take place, except in isolated and happenstantial cases. A

---

* It works this way: 2 people, 2 signals; 3 people, 9 signals; 4 people, 28 signals; 5 people, 75 signals; 6 people, 186 signals; 7 people, 441 signals; 8 people, 1,016 signals; 9 people, 2,295 signals; 10 people, 5,110 signals.

university of 40,000 students, say, of which there were seven in the United States in 2015, in which students daily go to classes of 300 and 400 people (and some universities have introductory classes of 700 people) and have only minimal contact with their professors—such a place is hardly a university at all, in the sense that knowledge is imparted from the wise, and minds are developed and higher learning and true education are undertaken. As Cardinal Newman pointed out more than a century ago, long before institutions of this size were even imagined, "A university is an Alma Mater, knowing her children one by one, not a foundry, or a mint, or a treadmill."

The simplest way to indict the large American university for the crime of miseducation and intellectual malfeasance is to look at the rankings, as put out annually by *U.S. News*, of the largest institutions. The largest of those listed in 2013, University of Central Florida with 51,000 students, ranks 173rd nationally. DeVry, with 49,000, is unranked in the bottom fourth; Liberty, with 47,000, is 80th in the Southern region; Texas A&M, with 44,000, is 68th nationally; Ohio State, with 44,000, is 54th. None of the largest is above 50. As to those ranked highest, Princeton has 5,323 students, Harvard 6,722, Yale 5,430. None of the rest of the top 10 has more than 10,000, and the average overall is 6,650. And I would add to that indictment another charge: student tuition has increased at five times the rate of inflation, from an average of $10,273 a year in 1974–75 to $31,231 in 2014–15 at private four-year universities ($2,469 to $9,169 for in-state students at public universities), and the faculties and administrations have increased enormously, from 447,000 faculty members and 269,000 administrators in 1970 to 675,000 faculty members and 756,000 administrators in 2005, and 1.2 million and 1.1 million in 2011; yet the graduation rates have been stagnant at around 50–60 percent for years. A big university, a big expense, a big administration, and half the students fail.

As long as what matters is "efficiency"—giving the maximum number of degrees to the maximum number of students in the minimum amount of time and with the minimum amount of expense—then American universities have certainly performed their function over the last two decades. But if it is *education* that's wanted, or the creation of acquisitive and logical minds, or even the production of well-read and well-equipped individuals, then the large institutions that characterize this country may be said for the most part to have failed. "The growth of the campus in size," observed the definitive *Higher Education in America* as long ago as the 1970s, "inhibits the education of the individual."

It's really quite simple. When the intimate teacher-student relationship is distended and broken, the student can no longer be individually probed and guided and nurtured and stretched, nor does the teacher have much incentive to do so. Studies confirm the point. One project in the 1960s found "a negative relationship between size, and individual participation, involvement, and satisfaction": "As schools increase in size, the number of persons increases much faster than either the number of learning settings or the varieties of settings. . . . Students in small schools were involved in more activities than those in large schools and had more satisfying experiences related to developing competence, being challenged, and engaging in important activities." Alison R. Bernstein, one of the few educators to have confronted this issue, similarly has concluded that "the massive size of a great many institutions stifles not only student development but the entire process of innovation." "The process of change itself is often hindered at large institutions," she found, and even communication, the very basis of an education system, becomes "a massive problem in logistics." And the faculty is generally "more cynical" at large universities, senses its powerlessness, and feels little sense of loyalty, and at big institutions "the frustrations, cynicism, and alienation of the faculty are reflected in the students."

———

So size matters, in human institutions as well as human forms, and it has its limits. We may formulate this more precisely as a principle—let's call it the Beanstalk Principle in honor of the medium that after all brought Jack and the Giant to the point of comparison—that holds:

> *For every animal, object, institution, or system, there is an optimal limit beyond which it ought not to grow.*

To which might be added the Beanstalk Corollary:

> *Beyond this optimal size, all other elements of an animal, object, institution, or system will be affected adversely.*

I am not saying that size—and its companion notion of scale, or sizes in relation to each other—is the *only* measurement to make in judging something. But it does make sense that it should be the first, and the central, consideration, inasmuch as it is likely to affect, in one degree or another, all other considerations.

As the biologist knows. If an earthworm were ten times bigger, its weight would be a thousand times greater and its need for air a thousand times greater, but the surface area through which it absorbs oxygen would be only a hundred times greater, so it would get only a tenth of the air it needed and would immediately die.

As the architect knows. To build a skyscraper 110 stories tall, you have to make special allowances for sinkage, wind stress, tensile strength, and movement, and work out special problems of heating and cooling, lighting, plumbing, transportation, congestion, and maintenance that are completely different from those when you are doing a building of two or three stories.

As the city planner knows. Doubling a city's population means vastly increasing its area—since as a population increases arithmetically its space tends to increase geometrically—and it means completely reorganizing its systems—since as population grows, urban services become increasingly complex, interdependent, rigid, and vulnerable, while levels of citizen participation and bureaucratic job performance decline.

As we all know. A big mansion is not simply a bungalow with more rooms, a big party is not simply an intimate dinner with more people, a big metropolitan hospital is not simply a clinic with more beds and more doctors, a big corporation is not simply a family firm with more employees and products, a big government is not simply a town council with more branches.

Size, indeed, might well be regarded as *the* crucial variable in anything. More important than, say, ideology—for a large disciplined party like the Communist Party in China is much like a large undisciplined one like the Democratic Party in the United States, unwieldy, unrepresentative, undemocratic, inefficient, and often unable to carry out policies enacted, not because of the politics but because of the party size. Size is more important than, say, public or private governance—for a large public system like the Veterans Administration is just as chaotic, wasteful, unfixable, and unwieldy as a large private one like General Motors. Size is more

28

important even than wealth—for a rich city like Chicago is no more capable of ending poverty and school segregation than a poor city like Newark, and all of the huge, immensely wealthy New York banks the early 2000s produced could not control the chaotic housing market, and all suffered in its collapse in 2008 because they were too big and distended to operate efficiently in crisis.

As the rest of part 2 will prove, *size matters*, and big size matters most. That is what the Beanstalk Principle is all about.

5
___

The Condition
of Bigness

B igness is pervasive in America as nowhere else in the world. It is as
much a part of the American system, the American way of thinking,
and the parts of the world that America has touched, as the capillaries are
a part of the vascular system. Consider:

- In the United States there are 13 olive sizes, ranging from bullets
  and fine to large, jumbo, extra jumbo, giant, colossal, super colossal, mammoth, and super mammoth.
- The producer of the Easter extravaganza at New York's Radio City
  Music Hall once declared the theater to be "the greatest theater in
  the history of the world." Not because it has produced art of any
  distinction, nor contributed in any serious way to a culture in the
  way that the Dionysian theater of Athens or the Globe Theatre of
  London did—but for the reason that it is the largest indoor theater in the world, with the largest stage curtain in the world, and
  has had more customers, some 300 million, than any previously
  known theatrical building.
- Big cars have been so quintessentially American—Europeans
  find it baffling—that even after periods of rising fuel prices they
  continue to make up more than half the annual automotive market. Big sedans began the trend, but sport utility vehicles, huge
  truck-like cars introduced in the 1980s, quickly became popular
  and today, with pickups and vans, have captured nearly half the
  market and are continuing to be the top sellers—the Ford F-Series
  pickup became the single best-selling vehicle in the country in
  1981 and has remained so to 2014 (when 754,000 were sold) and

beyond. But not just big, increasingly gigantic: between 1980 and 2013 the average car weight rose 26 percent, and a Honda Civic, for example, that weighed 1,500 pounds in 1973 was bloated to 2,800 pounds by 2012, and the average midsized SUV gained 474 pounds in that period as well as growing 10 inches longer and 4 inches wider. There are no social values to large vehicles other than implied superiority, since they cost more, pollute more, and are more deadly in accidents. "A 1,000-pound increase in a striking vehicle weight," said the National Traffic Safety Administration in 2013, "raises the probability of fatalities by 47 percent," with SUVs and pickups "significantly more likely to cause fatalities." The ultimate cost to the public, it said, was $136 billion a year.

- A survey of 300 American chefs found that most are serving up food portions two to four times what the government recommends, the Obesity Society was told in 2007. The government says *two-thirds* of Americans now rank as overweight or obese, defined as being more than 30 pounds beyond their healthy weight.

- The average American home has almost doubled in size since 1973, from 1,500 square feet then to 2,657 square feet in 2015, and the number with four or more bedrooms went from 27 percent in 1978 to 51 percent in 2013.

- Texans, as everyone knows, typify American bigness. As John Bainbridge explains it in his account of *The Super-Americans*:

> *It really means something to Texans that their San Jacinto Monument, just outside Houston, is a little higher than the Washington Monument and that their Capitol, in Austin, has a similar edge on the Capitol in Washington, DC. They also take satisfaction in knowing that of all the states, Texas has the most farms, the most churches per capita, the biggest state fair, the most airports, the most insurance companies, the most species of birds, the most banks, the most football teams, and the most holidays, among other things.*

It also claims the largest herd of whitetail deer and the largest circus museum, the largest and most expensive high school football stadium, and it has a forest called Big Thicket and some canyons called Big Bend. Amazon sells shirts and sweatshirts emblazoned with the motto, "Everything's Bigger in Texas," in 39 models and styles.

- The largest restaurant operator in the world, and the largest single-brand restaurant chain, is Subway, headquartered in Milford, Connecticut, with 43,981 restaurants in 110 countries and territories as of June 2015.
- American advertising expresses its most important messages in superlatives about size: supersize your lashes . . . dream bigger with Thermador . . . the biggest sale we've ever held . . . big in nutrition . . . jumbo: jets/muffin pans/red straws/peanut butter/piggy banks . . . super-sized: coin jars/clock hands/scrapbooks/base cabinets/bib overalls . . . the largest condominiums in Florida . . . we're growing bigger every day . . . Big Macs, Whoppers, Big Catch, Giant Sub, Grande, Superlongs . . .

It has become part of the American character not only to accept bigness but actually to admire, respect, revere, glorify it. Size is the measure of excellence: in cars, tomatoes, houses, breasts, audiences, salaries, skyscrapers, muscles, penises, and fish. Where but in America could a con man like P. T. Barnum actually get people to pay money to see someone he billed as "The Biggest Midget in America" (a perfectly normal-sized man, as you found out after you paid your nickel)? Or could people successfully sell a cigarette called simply "More" or a tennis racket called "The Giant"? Or, in a national art form known as the tall story, could a giant lumberman with a big blue ox be considered an admirable folk hero? Every outsider from Tocqueville to Jean-Francois Revel has noted this peculiarity in the American psyche; the French writer Raoul de Roussy de Sales was bemused by the whole thing:

> When I listen to Americans talking on shipboard, or in a Paris restaurant, or here in New York, it is only a question of time before someone will come out with that favorite boast of yours — "the biggest in the world!" The New York skyline, or the Washington Monument, or the Chicago Merchandise Mart — the biggest in the world. You say it without thinking what it means.

Or as one nineteenth-century German journalist summed it up: "To say that something is large, massive, gigantic, is in America not a mere statement of fact but the highest commendation."

———

Part of the reason for this has to do with American uniqueness.

To begin with, we inhabited such a gigantic continent that we didn't even know quite how big it really was until the Lewis and Clark expedition some 175 years after we began settling the place. Generations of settlers just assumed it was *there*, land to move to, to build on, whenever anyone wanted to; a kind of infinitude settled into our national psyche. And of course we did not have much else—no aristocracy, no fine castles, no institutions, no cathedrals, no traditions, no titled families, in short no History—so it was natural enough, as a young country, to emphasize what we *did* have: size. When the United States began, even though it was a quarter of the size it is today, it was already far bigger than any European country, indeed larger than any other nation in the world except Russia, India, and China.

Gradually, too, blessed as we were by the riches that this vast territory conferred on us, we came to use its resources with a prodigious energy, proving to the people back in Europe that we were doing all right, thanks, and could build our buildings taller, our cities bigger, our roads farther, our fields wider. And for more than three centuries we grew accustomed to living in an ever-expanding boom society, with free land, rich soil, abundant timber, animals for hunting and trapping, gold and iron ore and coal and oil there for the taking, all in an abundance quite unlike anything known to the world before.

The pace with which all this happened also had its effect. America became instantly rich, within a few generations of its first settlement, and established its independence only a century and a half later, hardly much time at all in the eyes of Europeans—the Greeks, say, who had to wait 2,000 years for their independence. The speed with which the country grew in the nineteenth century surpassed even that of Britain, which was at the time the most powerful nation on earth, and the rate of growth by the end of that century, particularly in the economic realm, was truly dizzying. Remarkably, that pace accelerated in the twentieth century, so much that as early as 1970 Alvin Toffler could write a book describing

Future Shock as that condition arising from "too much change in too short a time." And that was before the computer revolution, in which growth moved from mathematical to exponential and shows no sign of slowing much in this century.

The effect of this rapid change is that Americans have tended to notice and admire that which is easily perceptible and most obvious—which is to say, bigness. When there is no time to pause and judge, to reflect, to measure, *quantitative* values must replace *qualitative* values—as sociologist Margaret Mead once said, when a speeding car rushes past us it is only the size that we can judge; we have no way of knowing how well the engine works.

Finally, the fact that the United States has been the most exemplary capitalist nation during most of this modern era has contributed to its love of bigness as well. Capitalism is a system that depends, quite simply, on growth: minor cycles of boom and bust there may be, but overall there must be expanding markets, and therefore greater production, and therefore greater income and more expansion, and therefore more workers and more salaries, and therefore expanding markets and more consumption. When capitalism does not grow it does not work, a lesson that Lord Keynes forcefully bore in upon the politicians of our time in persuading them that something always had to be priming the pumps and stoking the furnaces of the economy, and that if business couldn't do it the government must. Long schooling in this system of continual growth has taught nothing so well as the lesson that more is better, size is value, and big is beautiful.

———

Bigness is the condition of America also because, especially since World War II, it has been the function of the national government—fulfilling, it is presumed, the will of the people—to foster and promote it.

The phenomenon is seen everywhere, as the following indicate. The creation of the internet was largely due to Department of Defense awards in the 1960s and National Science Foundation's sponsoring the Computer Science Network from 1981 on, creating all the giant computer-based corporations that dominate the economy today. The Interstate Highway System created by the federal government in the 1950s with an initial $26 billion (the largest and most expensive public works project ever undertaken to that date) destroyed many small towns and Main Street commerce, drove through cities creating instant slums, disemboweled railroad systems nationwide, pre-empted funds for vital urban mass transit, made nearby land so expensive only big, usually nationwide businesses could afford it, and permitted nationwide commerce only big companies could take advantage of. Federal policies permitted the creation of big banks, especially after the repeal of the already weakened Glass-Steagall Act in 1999 created entities understood to be "too big to fail," though they grew even larger after the selective bailouts in 2008–09. American farm subsidies from the federal government since the 1930s, and growing every year, now amount to about $20 billion a year, most of which goes to big, rich farmers growing a few staple monopoly crops, following Secretary of Agriculture Earl Butz's mandate in the 1970s, "get big or get out." And national defense spending, which has gone from an average of $458 billion through the Cold War years to nearly $829 billion in 2016, has created an enormous "military-industrial complex" dominated by large defense and space corporations that make up by far the largest military economy in the world.

And still, the largest beneficiary of the government, creating the largest and most expensive corporations and plants, is the US nuclear industry — which is, surprisingly, the world's largest and equal to that of France and Japan, the next largest, put together. The entire nuclear food chain, from research and development and fuel supply services to liability insurance, waste disposal, and eventual decommissioning, has been backed by government policies and financing since the 1940s, and it has had the largest section of the Department of Energy devoted to it since 1977. No plants would have been built without government subsidies since the market saw too much risk and too little need, and for most of the time the government has exceeded the presumed market price by 140 to 200 percent, even when it became clear that the cost well exceeded the value of the energy produced every time. Bailouts alone to keep nuclear plants going when no one with any financial sense would back them amounted to some $300 billion from 1947 to 1999, and perhaps another $400 billion in the years since then as aging power plants developed costly troubles in recent years. Madness the whole thing, and madder still that no one yet has been able to solve the problem of what to do with its toxic waste.

Examples could be multiplied, but the point is clear enough. In the words of onetime Michigan State economist Walter Adams: "As I read the industrial history of the United States, I find that the trend toward concentration of economic power is not a response to natural law or inexorable technological imperatives. Rather it is the result of institutional forces which are subject to control, change, and reversal . . . ; the inadequacy of existing antitrust laws and/or the desultory performance of the enforcement agencies; and the unwise, man-made, discriminatory, privilege-creating actions of Big Government."

In other words, the business of America is Big Business. Politicians see to it that it can only grow, and Big Business sees to it that they are well rewarded.

———

But perhaps you are wondering if there is anything wrong with America's commitment to bigness. Aren't there things, you might say, that are better or more efficient when they are bigger—say a symphony orchestra, or a telescope, or a computer manufacturer?

Well, yes, that might be true sometimes. The Beanstalk Principle after all says only that there is a certain limit beyond which things ought not to grow, not that everything must be miniature. Each group or function or object will have its own most desirable size, and some are bound to be bigger than others.

To begin with, there is no necessary connection between size and worth in most instances. Just because a hospital is large does not mean that it is efficient or well run or competent or has a good rating. Just because a library is big does not mean that it has a wide range of books or any meaningful rare-book collection or a helpful staff. Just because a supermarket is large does not mean that it is well stocked or well managed or has fair prices. And so on. Size, where pertinent at all, is often simply an ancillary, not an essential, component of worth.

Also, when benefits are produced by size they are almost always accompanied—and in many cases outweighed—by drawbacks. This is very often true of the bigger institutions in our society, where inefficiencies are increased, personal attention is diminished, system breakdowns are more frequent. Large parks do have more sights and more playgrounds, but the larger they get the greater the risks of mugging and robbery, the more despoliation, the more litter. It is certainly true of a variety of large machines—nuclear-power plants, oil supertankers, jumbo jets—where

37

the purported benefits of size are well overbalanced by the manifold dangers, not to mention the cost of maintaining complex systems. And it is even true of giant cities of the world, where the presumed advantages of size—greater diversity, anonymity, cultural opportunity—are more and more overshadowed by the accreted disadvantages—pollution, noise, congestion, crime, stress, higher prices and taxes.

Moreover, it has to be remembered that many big institutions and systems are large not because they are better or more efficient that way, but simply because they happened to grow that way for reasons other than need or value. Government bureaucracies are an obvious case in point, as Parkinson's Laws remind us: "Work expands so as to fill the time available for its completion" and the number employed in a bureaucracy will rise by 5–7 percent per year "irrespective of any variation in the amount of work (if any) to be done." Parkinson's chief evidence was the British Admiralty office, which expanded its staff by no less than 768 percent between 1914 and 1967, although the actual number of ships decreased by 475 percent in that period, with the result that "over 33,000 civil servants are barely sufficient to administer the navy we no longer possess." In the United States, there has been a similar pointless expansion not only in the Navy Department but throughout government in ways that have become so egregious that scholars of all stripes have written about them with increasing alarm. Cato Institute economist Chris Edwards summed it up in 2014: "As the government has grown larger, leaders have become overloaded. They do not have enough time to understand programs, to oversee them, or to fix them. The more programs there are, the harder it is to efficiently allocate resources, and the more likely it is that programs will work at cross purposes." Worst of all, "Within departments, red tape has multiplied, information is getting bottled up under layers of management, and decision-making is becoming more difficult because more people are involved." As evidence of this, Paul Light of the Brookings Institution found that the number of layers in the typical agency has jumped from 7 to 18 since the 1960s, including such offices as "principal associate deputy undersecretary," so that information from the bottom almost never reaches the top, or does so in so distorted a form as to make it worthless.

Finally, the virtues of size, as we have been taught to regard them, are mostly illusory. We may be told that foot-long carrots and 15-pound radishes are better than the ordinary kind—there are several dozen giant vegetables now, from peas to pumpkins, that you can get seeds for—but that is reckoning without our taste buds. Captains of commerce often assert that the American economic system is the most successful in the world, but in fact of the top 20 nations ranked by Gross Domestic Product per capita in 2014, the United States ranks tenth after Liechtenstein, Qatar, Luxemburg, Bermuda, Norway, Kuwait, Jersey, Singapore, and Brunei. (And notice that large size is not an advantage here.) Pharmaceutical firms may argue that they need to get big and bigger to provide research on new cures for myriad diseases, but if that were true most of those diseases would have been cured by now and we wouldn't be paying astronomical prices for drugs that don't do that job.

One class of myths, perhaps the most common of all, has to do with the supposed superiority of large American corporations. It is a complex matter and we will have occasion to touch on it again when weighing the virtues of human-scale economic units, but for the moment it may suffice to examine a few of these myths. For example, there is the one that big corporations are more productive than small ones—but in fact, as Barry A. Stein, the leading scale economist, has shown, "studies of productivity, as measured by value of shipments per manufacturing employee, show that the highest efficiencies tend to occur not in the largest size plant, but in those of moderate size," that is, *with fewer than forty-five people*. There is the myth that big companies make more profit than small ones—but in fact Stein's figures show that "there is a declining relationship between profitability and size," that "smaller firms are more efficient users of capital," and that as firms grow bigger they show a "decreasing efficiency of asset use." There is the myth that big companies can sell their goods more cheaply than small ones, which is why consumers benefit from the American system—but in fact, because of increased inefficiency, accident rates, strikes, sabotage, absenteeism, storage facilities, distribution networks, transportation costs, advertising, promotion, and product differentiation, large firms actually must charge more for their products. It seems to be, in sum, that many of the "advantages" of big business, as we have been taught them, have all the substantiality of the big housing bubble in 2008.

With those four cautionary points, then, we can conclude at the very least that what's wrong with infatuation with bigness is that it leads us to assumptions that are often unsupportable and hence to practices and policies that are often detrimental. Bigness may have its place here and there, but it is the pervasiveness of it that is so alarming. Because bigness as a virtue is by now so rooted in our culture, we have not really ever come to grips with the questions of size, of scale, of quantity, of extent, for our individual dwellings, our organizations and workplaces, for our cities and systems. Because we do not really know how much is enough, we assume that bigger is better.

The danger in that should be evident, made all the more ominous by the sobering judgment of the great twentieth-century genius, Lewis Mumford, after a lifetime of studying history: "In the repeated decay and breakdown of one civilization after another, after it has achieved power and centralized control, one may read the failure to reach an organic solution of the problems of quantity."

6

Beanstalk Violations

A lmost 60 years ago a little book called *The Breakdown of Nations* was published in England. It was written by Leopold Kohr, an Austrian-born economist who was a recognized expert in international customs unions, and who had taught economics at several prominent universities in America, but its thesis went far beyond run-of-the-mill economic matters, indeed beyond run-of-the-mill matters of any kind. It offered one of the most extraordinarily provocative arguments of contemporary political philosophy, right from its opening lines:

> As the physicists of our time have tried to elaborate an integrated
> single theory, capable of explaining not only some but all phenomena
> of the physical universe, so I have tried on a different plane to develop
> a single theory through which not only some but all phenomena of the
> social universe can be reduced to a common denominator. The result
> is a new and unified political philosophy centering in the theory of
> size. It suggests that there seems only one cause behind all forms of
> social misery: bigness. Oversimplified as this may seem, we shall find
> the idea more easily acceptable if we consider that bigness, or oversize,
> is really much more than just a social problem. It appears to be the
> one and only problem permeating all creation. Wherever something is
> wrong, something is too big.

So far as I can tell, this remarkable thesis was almost totally ignored at the time, though its pertinence then, in the aftermath of a second world-wide war and the rise of the giant superpowers, would seem to have been obvious. Its relevance today, in a world ever more plagued by bigness, is clearer still. For today we are surrounded by countless examples of diffi-culties and crises brought about by one form or another of overgrowth, excess, distention, enormity, or expansion, for which we are seemingly unable to contrive any solutions at all. As Kohr notes:

> Social problems have the unfortunate tendency to grow at a geometric ratio with the growth of the organism of which they are a part, while the ability of man to cope with them, if it can be extended at all, grows only at an arithmetic ratio. Which means that if a society grows beyond its optimum size, its problems must eventually outrun the growth of those human faculties which are necessary for dealing with them.

In short, we are a society plagued by violations of the Beanstalk Principle, the victim of institutions and systems grown beyond their optimal size to the point where they are literally out of control.

We have already seen some of them, but to make the point I want to look especially at the government that has become the largest and most powerful in the world, our own United States.

In general, it can be said that as governments become centralized and enlarged beyond a certain limited range they not only cease to solve problems, they actually begin to create them. Regardless of any other attribute, beyond a modest size a government cannot be expected to perform optimally, and the larger it gets the more likely it is that it will be increasingly inefficient, autocratic, wasteful, corrupt, and harmful. The United States is, regrettably, an excellent case in point.

First, it is necessary to apprehend the enormous size of the American federal government. It is charged with, or has taken unto itself, the job of overseeing much of the lives of some 326 million people—more than any government, except China, before the twentieth century had ever thought of trying to administer to; with guiding the destiny of the mightiest industrial economy ever fashioned, within an imperial arrangement that affects at least half of the 7 billion people on the globe; and with operating public systems of unprecedented scope and detail that stretch for nearly 5,000 miles and cover 3.6 million square miles of territory. For this task the United States employs more people than any other government but China, almost 4.2 million people in 2014, 2.6 million in the executive branch, 1.3 in the military, and 63,000 in the other two branches, to which should be added another 1 million who work for the government in private aerospace and defense industries. These are spread through 15 federal departments (each of which has several sub-departments), 8 executive offices, and 456 agencies (2009 figure) from coast to coast, only about one-sixth of them in or around Washington, DC—plus more than 1,000 federal advisory committees, boards, commissions, councils, conferences, panels, and task forces.

But that's not all. For the government actually outsources tasks to a great many outside contractors, who do government work for government pay but are not strictly government employees—state and local government workers, for-profit business contractors, and nonprofit organization grantees who administer federal policies, programs, and regulations. In 2015 a professor of politics at University of Pennsylvania, John J. Dilulio, Jr., analyzed this outsourcing and said that today, more than two dozen federal departments and agencies spend a combined total of over $600 billion a year on more than 200 intergovernmental grant programs for state and local governments, spend over $500 billion a year on contracts with for-profit firms, and spend more than $2 trillion on the nonprofit sector, amounting to a third of its annual revenues. And he noted that the Department of Defense has 800,000 civilian employees but 700,000 contract workers, the ones (like the infamous Blackwater USA) who did and are doing much of the fighting and security work in Iraq and Afghanistan. Such workers are well paid, too: $250 billion of the $800 billion "stimulus" act in 2009 went to 80,000 federal deals outsourced to state governments and contract employees.

Then it is necessary to appreciate not only the size but the reach of this government. Particularly since the Rooseveltian ascendency in the 1930s, and especially with magnified presidential powers since Lyndon Johnson (creating what many have called the "imperial presidency"), the government apparatus has been charged with the task of overseeing and regulating the lives of the citizens literally from cradle (hospitals participating in Medicare are federally regulated) to grave (there are nine lengthy regulations under part 453 of the federal code relating to "Funeral Industry Practices"). Guided by a liberal mania that government is able to solve all problems, Washington's reach extends into virtually every nook of the society; where it does not control, it influences, where it does not dictate by virtue of law, it persuades by reason of power.

As long ago as 1974 a Washington veteran, Richard Goodwin, could observe:

> The central government has added more to its reach over the last few decades than during the previous century and a half of our history. In this respect, we are more distant from Herbert Hoover than he was from George Washington. Sovereignty withdrawn from states has gone to augment the immense, continuing, unimpeded accumulation of authority within the central government, especially its executive branch. The result is an Executive vested with almost exclusive power to take substantial initiatives; with a virtually unappealable veto over the actions of states and Congress, particularly in economic matters; and with the almost sole management of government bureaucracies that infringe upon the economic process at every strategic point.

Since then four vast departments have been added—Education, Energy, Veterans Affairs, and Homeland Security—and presidents since Reagan have increasingly used such maneuvers as "presidential signing statements" accompanying the signing of a law with which the chief executives arbitrarily reserve the right to ignore provisions they do not want to obey. (George H. W. Bush, for example, used such statements 232 times, Clinton 140, George W. Bush 161, and Obama at least 30 times.)

It is necessary to add that despite the enormous size and reach of the federal apparatus, it is not particularly efficient at anything it does, except prolonging its own life. Inefficiency in this case might be seen as a blessing.

The reason for this inefficiency, of course, comes down to one word: bureaucracy.

All bureaucracies since Napoleon, when formal state structures became solidified, have had deficiencies, but governmental ones have the most—particularly those, like the American, that enjoy civil-service protection, a large public purse, and weak legislative review. I don't want to linger long over these failings—I assume there is no citizen who has not encountered them in one form or another—but among the most obvious may be listed the following.

Bureaucracy is *inflexible*, operating by rules that cannot be altered "because it's always been done that way." It is *unproductive*, mired in regulations and overwhelmed with paperwork, and totally unaccountable. It is *self-protective*, rewarding loyalty and subservience and punishing whistle-blowing (despite laws to protect it). And it is of course *inefficient*, because there is no premium put on efficiency—and no competition—and much hierarchic machinery to prevent it.

Considering how technologically advanced and rich this country is, one might think those defects would be completely minimized by the twenty-first century. But no: let me mention a few memorable bureaucratic snafus from just the past few years. Let's start with the Secret Service at the heart of it all, which, in addition to having two scandals with prostitutes, was unable to stop two drones, one of which crashed on the South Lawn, or, in September 2014, a man armed with a knife who made it well into the White House without being detected. Then there's the IRS, which was caught in a blatantly political dirty trick when in 2010, in the two years before a national election, it put mostly right-wing groups seeking tax exemption as nonprofits under such scrutiny that it made them spend time and money repeatedly submitting documents, and managed to approve only one of 290 applications. The Federal Emergency Management Agency became notorious for its complete inability to help the people of New Orleans after Hurricane Katrina in 2005 devastated the city—thanks to another bureaucracy, the Army Corps of Engineers, which did not build or maintain the levees properly—and did not do much better to New York and New Jersey after Superstorm Sandy in 2013, unable to handle the hundreds of homeowners seeking help. The National Security Agency, operating in secret, decided sometime after 2001 to collect telephone records of all American citizens every day, without legal warrants, and conducted 60,000 illegal hacking operations throughout the world. The Veterans Administration was found in 2013 to have more than 600,000 disability claims that it took more than four months—sometimes a lot longer—to address, and in two years could do no better than to get that down to 100,000; its "Choice" program to fix that in 2015 was a complete, expensive failure. And even the Office of Personnel Management in 2015, failing to correct known disabilities in its information security defenses, admitted that it had been hacked and the data on 21.5 million government employees, and their contacts, had been stolen; it was then learned that attacks on all government agencies, where security was lax and antiquated computers remained unfixed, had grown elevenfold since 2005, amounting to more than 67,000 attacks compromising cybersecurity.

Given all that it is perhaps not surprising that the *Washington Times* offered a reason for such failures in a report in February 2015 that "government employees in multiple agencies and departments, including the Federal Communications Commission and the Commerce Department, have been caught viewing pornography on the job, blaming in part the lack of work and boredom."

There is a story sometimes told in Washington by the civil servants themselves, usually at the end of one of those days of bureaucratic business, or boredom, that seem to require alcoholic restoration. It seems that three men, a doctor, an architect, and a bureaucrat, were arguing among themselves one night as to which of them had the oldest profession.

"Why, mine's the oldest," claimed the doctor. "Didn't God operate on Adam and remove a rib to make Eve?"

"Yes," replied the architect, "but mine's older still. After all, right at the beginning God constructed the universe out of chaos."

The bureaucrat sat back and looked at them both. "And who do you think," he said, "made *that*?"

7

Prytaneogenesis

Leopold Kohr tells the story of the *Treuga Dei*, the Truce of God, which was first propounded in AD 1041 and in successive decades slowly became the dominant code in European warfare. Originally simply a measure to limit the costliness of the battles that were fought from time to time among the cities, principalities, and duchies of central Europe, it held that all battles had to end on Saturday noon and could not resume until Monday morning, thus assuring that the Sabbath was undisturbed as a day of peace. Gradually more and more territories adopted the code and gradually too it extended its reach: battles should not be fought in churches or in working grain fields, should not involve women and children, should not continue after sundown or begin before dawn. In time the truce was extended even further, with Friday being declared a day of peace, in honor of the day of the Crucifixion, and Thursday, too, in honor of the day of the Last Supper, and all day Monday as well, in honor of the day of the Resurrection. For nearly four centuries the *Treuga Dei* was observed throughout much of central Europe, particularly where the influence of the Catholic Church was strongest, not by every local ruler and state but by a goodly number, not in every contestation but in a surprising number. For four centuries, the warfare of Europe was significantly moderated by a principle that seemed to work to the benefit of the many disparate states and cities. There were wars, to be sure, and some bloody battles, even among the adherent polities, but they were usually on a modest scale and not terribly destructive at their worst; and the severest and bloodiest campaigns were waged by those not aligned to the truce (most notably the nascent states of France, England, and Russia) or those who chose to forsake it.

But finally, with the emergence of more centralized states in the sixteenth century, the piecemeal application of the Truce of God and its apparent sanction of midweek warfare came under fire. Maximilian I, who took the title of emperor of the Holy Roman Empire in 1508, began the process of making the truce permanent and all-encompassing under his royal auspices. If no warfare for five days a week, he reasoned, why not make it seven? If no warfare in churches and fields, why not include streets and towns and forests as well? If no killing of women and children, why not add all innocents, including men, into the bargain? Thus, he argued, instead of intermittent warfare there would be total and perpetual peace—and he set his empire and his armies in service of this noble goal. His success was limited, but after him came others, within the Holy Roman Empire and the budding nation-states of central Europe, who used their growing, centralized powers to enforce the idea of making the partial into the whole, the limited into the absolute, the small into the grand.

The result, as Kohr notes, was a period of unprecedented slaughter and brutality leading to the catastrophic Thirty Years War and beyond, a period of all-out warfare fought every single day of the week, Sundays included, of battles on every piece of ground including churches and fields, of the killing not only of men but of women and children as well. And so it has gone down to the present, with increasing brutality and mounting casualties as big nations have continued to proclaim their devotion to everlasting peace, until the twentieth century ushered in warfare fought right around the clock, with the regular and indiscriminate killing of all human beings, and the experience of war extended to every part of the land and sea, and in the air besides.

Something had become total and perpetual, but it was not peace.

In this little tale we may see the Beanstalk Principle at work in the political realm. As we might expect, when governments become centralized and enlarged beyond a certain limited range, they not only cease to *solve* problems, they actually begin to *create* them.

It matters not the nationality of the government, nor the ideology, nor the governing system. Simply as a result of the inefficiencies and inequities of their size, and quite often without intending to, big governments tend to set in motion forces that they are unable to control, or understand, with consequences they are unable to foresee. Regardless of any other attribute, beyond a modest size a government cannot be expected to perform optimally, and the larger it gets, and the more distended the policy, the more likely it is that it will be increasingly inefficient, autocratic, wasteful, corrupt, and harmful. And the more likely it is that it will do irremediable harm to the smaller polities on which it acts or into which it intrudes, and that includes states, regions, cities, towns, even neighborhoods.

Government laws and policies attempting to prohibit the sale of alcohol and remove the scourge of alcoholism served to create a vast network of organized crime that set such firm roots that it still thrives to this day. Government laws and crackdowns designed to control the drug traffic and wipe out addiction have driven the trade underground, fattened the coffers of criminal gangs, generated billions of dollars of burglary and street crime, created an aura of challenge and danger that attracts the young, and failed to stem an increase in the estimated addict population from 50,000 to 560,000 in the last thirty years. Government tax policies designed to stimulate economic growth in underdeveloped sections of the country helped to create the pell-mell chaos of the Sunbelt in the last three decades and drain industries and populations from the ailing older regions of the Northeast.

And, most telling of all, intrusive government regulations passed or promulgated with good intentions, though very little forethought— worker safety, consumer protection, environmental protection, and the like—have come at immense costs, most of them hidden—costs to the manufacturer or producer, costs to the consumer, costs to the state, county, city, school district, and neighborhood for compliance, and costs to Washington for the time and (often considerable) personnel it takes to enforce them. And these regulations involve every aspect, including the most intimate, of the average American's life: toilets, mattresses, food, lightbulbs, showerheads, clothes, diapers, washing machines and dryers, refrigerators, bicycles, television sets, and of course cars. There is no official tabulation of these costs—the government would prefer to keep them hidden and uncalculated—but a respected economist at the Competitive Enterprise Institute, Wayne Crews, estimated in 2015 that government regulations would cost the economy $1.882 *trillion* in that year, a figure that is greater than the GDP of all but eleven countries in the world and is one-ninth of the entire American GNP. Whatever the benefits, it's hard to believe that they can be worth that much.

This process of unfortunate government enlargement, and subsequent malfunction and malignancy, seems to deserve a name. Following the model from medicine, in which the term *iatrogenesis* refers to illnesses actually generated by a doctor (*iatro*, healer), we may derive another Greek coinage, *prytaneogenesis*—from the Greek word *prytaneum* for the seat of government—to refer to damage actually generated by the state. Wherever we locate a problem and find there some governmental law, policy, regulation, statute, code, or decree at its root, there we witness the operation of *prytaneogenesis*.

Let me illustrate the process with a short look at the awful urban phenomenon of the modern slum, particularly the South Bronx in New York City.

To some a slum may seem as natural and inevitable as a desert. But deserts are not in the main caused by natural shifts toward hotter and drier climates (though global warming may contribute) or some sudden drying up of rains and rivers. They are caused by human governments, through ignorance or intention, that overregulate, overmeddle, overrule, and overpower the city neighborhoods, weakening the human culture necessary for the protection of the community.

The South Bronx, that 12-square-mile section of New York City that has become synonymous with urban devastation, is a good case in point.

Today it is a place of such ruin—buildings burned out for block after block, their black windows staring pitilessly on the rubbled streets—that almost every visitor compares it to the bombed-out cities of Europe in the wake of World War II. Many sections are home only to derelicts and a few desperate welfare families; in others you find clusters of sad and determined people still working to keep up their homes while garbage piles up along the sidewalk, rats skitter through the vacant lots, and nearby buildings are gutted by fire after fire; three-quarters of the occupied buildings do not meet New York's legal minimum standards for health and safety. Hopelessness and fear are present everywhere: the crime rate is the highest in the city; more than a hundred youth gangs roam their turfs; heroin addicts cluster in every neighborhood and are serviced openly; arson-related fires gut buildings almost every single night of the year. The area is poor—the poorest in all New York, worse than even Harlem or Brownsville, with a median family income of $18,000—and unhealthy— with a quarter of all the city's known cases of malnutrition and an infant mortality rate almost twice the New York State average. It has been

50

called—and there are few even among the local residents who are inclined to disagree—"perhaps the most wretched slum in America" and "a social sinkhole in which civilization has all but vanished."

But it wasn't always that way. It wasn't that way even fifty years ago. It became that way mostly because of specific actions by large and sadly uncomprehending governments.

Fifty years ago the South Bronx was not exactly a Gold Coast or a Georgetown, but it was a solid, safe, and stable community, primarily blue-collar white, with Italians, Poles, Jews, some Irish and Germans, only a sprinkle of blue-collar blacks and a dot here and there of the well-to-do, some with roots going back to the earliest years of the country. It had its tenements, six or eight stories, brick, dull, with fire escapes on the front, not always very sightly to be sure, though well built, substantial enough, and usually safe; but on many streets there were clusters of two-story row houses, owner-occupied, neat and brightly painted, with tree-lined sidewalks and little gardens; and in a dozen different neighborhoods there were large, handsome apartment buildings, with ornate carved cornices and friezes done by the first-generation craftsmen, lobbies of Italian marble, high-ceilinged and spacious rooms, home for one or another tightly knit and upwardly mobile ethnic community. A good deal of the industrial plant in the area was old and some of it obsolescent, but there were plenty of factories and warehouses operating all over—food processors and a piano manufacturer, some garment factories and small furniture manufacturers—and the area had an economic vitality still. And there were always the Yankees, who played in the stadium on the western edge of the South Bronx, and in the 1930s and '40s they were champions.

Then came the deluge.

After World War II—and then in every housing act and in most tax bills for the next thirty years—the federal government intervened in the housing markets with schemes that continuously induced people to move out of older neighborhoods like the South Bronx and into newer developments in the suburbs. Low-interest mortgages, tax credits, and government guarantees made it advantageous to buy the single-family homes being put up in rings around the central city, and uneconomical to try to repair and rehabilitate existing urban housing: a family that wanted to buy a new, jerry-built $40,000 house in the suburbs could get it for about $2,000 down after all the credits and tax breaks, but a family that wanted to buy an old, solidly built $40,000 house in the city would have to put down about $13,000, assume a high-interest mortgage, and pay full rates for repairs. Naturally, most of those who could afford it chose the suburban alternative, and the backbones of communities like the South Bronx began to crumble. As the Urban Institute put it in its recondite way somewhat later:

> Directly or indirectly, provisions of the federal tax code have tilted the terms of economic competition in favor of suburban development and development of new regions of the country, thereby accelerating the abandonment of central city housing, contributing to the deterioration of the existing urban capital infrastructure, and precipitating decline of the central city tax base.

Other similar federal tax policies also encouraged businesses—particularly the kinds of small manufacturing and warehouse businesses that had been the mainstay of the South Bronx—to relocate to new premises in suburban "industrial parks" or the growing Sunbelt states. Slowly, the jobs, and the economic ripple effect they produce in the attendant service industries, began to vanish.

And then came the interstate highway scheme. For the South Bronx, the unintended effects were almost extirpatory: it pre-empted funds for mass transit, the key to the region's economy; it encouraged the flight to Westchester and Long Island of still more businesspeople and homeowners; and it mandated the destruction of several stable neighborhoods so that freeways like the Major Deegan and the Bruckner could extrude their concrete sepulchers on top of them.

The federal hand did not stop there. As it was drawing the more affluent (and often white) citizens out of the cities, it was forcing the poorer (and often black) citizens into them. Federal tax policies and subsidies helped to establish the agribusiness industry in the postwar years, particularly in the Sunbelt states, one effect of which was to mechanize and expand larger holdings at the expense of the poorer and more marginal farmers and farmhands, who then generally came to Northern cities in droves to look for work. At the same time, federal welfare money, funneled largely through states and cities in the North, also attracted impoverished newcomers by giving them a way to live even if they couldn't find jobs, drawing millions of unskilled workers into those cities, like New York, that agreed to participate, and into those regions, like the South Bronx, that were already in fluctuation.

By the 1960s, as a result of all this, the South Bronx was teetering on disaster. Enlightened policies—or, better, none at all—might have saved it. But that was not to be. Another outsized government, in this case New York City's, had its own contributions to make. City rent regulations discouraged the rehabilitation of marginal buildings by wrapping the whole process in complicated red tape, administered by sinecured bureaucrats and approved by not-always-honest inspectors. City rent-control laws allowed landlords to raise their rents with each new tenant, in effect encouraging them toward high turnovers and minimal repairs. City taxes rose steadily as city services expanded beyond those of any comparable municipality in the Western world, placing an increasing burden on the property owners, especially those with marginal rental housing. City welfare programs, severely overburdened, distributed clients wherever housing was cheapest, slowly pouring them into the deteriorating tenements of the inner city, creating a whole inbred welfare ghetto where the dispirited fed on the despairing amid the decaying. And thus, gradually, whole blocks of buildings began to sink into disrepair, landlords choosing to give up rather than resuscitate, tenants choosing to desecrate rather than maintain, and within just a few years the domino effect of abandonment began to topple its way down the South Bronx streets, gathering momentum as it went: between 1970 and 1975 at least 45,000 buildings were left to rot or burn. It was not long before an arsonist's racket grew up, teenagers being paid to burn down still-occupied but decrepit buildings so that the landlords could abscond with the insurance money—tax-free, thanks to federal policies.

The flurry of federal money thrown into the South Bronx in the 1960s and '70s paradoxically worked to destroy the area even further. Federal housing programs paid for more than 10,000 dwelling units there, all of them in depressing high-rise projects whose sterile and anti-human buildings had the look of east European penitentiaries and served as little more than crude detention centers for the poor and elderly. "Model cities" projects were pasted together without thought for controls or safeguards, inviting massive frauds and scalawaggeries every year. The vast array of "war on poverty" programs, though clearly well intentioned and well financed, were similarly misguided. The grants actually went to paper agencies controlled by machine politicians and their henchmen who were able to build up "anti-poverty empires" to siphon off funds for their own purposes and leave very little behind for the people who needed help. Federal agencies remote from the South Bronx streets and honeycombed with overlapping bureaucracies had little idea where their funds were really going and in general cared more about satisfying their regulations than satisfying their clients. It took HEW, for example, three years to find out that one local satrap in the South Bronx was bilking the agency out of more than a million dollars, so lax were its financial controls—and even then it couldn't find enough hard evidence to prosecute the man, because he had easily covered his tracks months before. At least $500 million, perhaps $1 billion, was wasted on the South Bronx in this way, as useless as if it had been burned in the gutters.

The ripple effect of this federal squandering was even worse. When money went to machine satrapies, it was not available for genuine community groups and neighborhood associations, and they slowly lost the allegiance of the populace and began to wither. People with no popular base other than their personal retinues and friends at City Hall came to exercise enormous power, and it was hardly surprising that many of them went whole hog into corruption, extortion, thievery, and other crimes; one boss, to pick a particularly callous example, took $312,000 from the New York State Education Department to give out free summer lunches to malnourished children and simply dumped the lunches in vacant lots to save the cost of dispensing them. Much of the money pouring into the area, which neither federal nor city agencies were able or willing to keep track of, found its way into crime, particularly the heroin trade that flourished in the South Bronx from 1967 on and the police bribery that made it possible, giving the region not only one of the highest crime rates in the nation but one of the most corrupt police forces as well—as Frank Serpico found out when he was stationed in that very precinct and discovered nearly everyone but he was "on the pad."

One might find dozens of other examples of government actions that hastened the slide of the South Bronx into its present perdition. New York City came up with a Yankee Stadium "renovation" project that theoretically was to create new jobs and rehabilitate streets and shops in the stadium area, but managed to usurp more than $100 million of city funds away from far more needy Bronx projects without adding one permanent job or rehabilitating a single street. New York State financed the huge Co-op City apartment complex, designing it specifically for "middle-income" people (mostly white) and siting it off in the northeastern corner of the Bronx, thus effectively drawing most of the last remaining middle-echelon families out of the South Bronx and making it darker and poorer at a single stroke. And the federal government provided the 1966 Banking Act, which permitted savings-and-loan banks, heretofore restricted to making most loans in the neighborhoods where they were located, to send their investments to any part of the country, thereby instantly drawing money out of the South Bronx, where investments might be risky, to the booming real-estate regions of the suburbs and the Sunbelt, beginning a process of "redlining" that effectively dried up all loans and mortgages in the area within two years. Given all this, it is perhaps fortunate that the grand multimillion-dollar schemes started by the federal and city governments after Jimmy Carter's much-publicized visit to the South Bronx in 1977 fell into such a morass of red tape and polit-ical bickering—there was a New York City office of sixty people that spent $4 million a year simply to get the programs organized—that only a third of the promised money ever got administered.

After the turn of the century nothing much changed in the area, though there was a slight increase in population, mostly Hispanic, and a steady decline in crime, eventually in 2014 declining by 91 percent from 1980 lev-els, largely because there was no money left there: as of 2010, the South Bronx Congressional District was the poorest in the nation, with almost 40 percent of the people below the poverty level and 75 percent of the children in extreme poverty. Partly as a result of that, and the decline in housing prices while real-estate fees went through the ceiling in the other boroughs, a trickle of gentrification began around that time, with some whites moving into the Grand Concourse neighborhood for the first time in a generation.

Still, the South Bronx is a slum today, sixty-five years after the federal government began its first tilting of the tax code in favor of the suburbs, and change, if it comes in the next few years, will be slow and for some time longer it will be essentially a slum. It didn't have to be, but we have seen that it was *made* that way.

But the specific governmental measures are less important than their relentless cumulative effect: to bleed the life, slowly and painfully, from the South Bronx and similar communities in older cities across the land. In the South Bronx, or other ravaged areas, it does not lessen the tragedy to know that the legislatures that created the measures of destruction often intended to be benevolent, that the bureaucrats who carried them out often were able and well meaning, or that the judiciary that upheld them often was sensitive and reasonable. The bare and unappealing fact remains that it was the hand of big government and not any accident of nature that wrought the tragedy.

Prytaneogenesis.

———————

The sad story of the South Bronx points not only to the creation of problems by governments grown beyond their efficient size but to the essential reason why this should be so: namely, that big governments tend to weaken and ultimately destroy the very organizations that might be capable of solving the problems, the local agencies, block associations, and community groups who know most about them. It seems that political power is finite and inelastic: when one instrument absorbs it, it no longer exists elsewhere. When the federal government takes effective power into its own hands, it simultaneously removes that power from local and intermediate governments, and the more power it absorbs, the weaker the local agencies become.

This is a pattern that is familiar to any historian of the nation-state over the past five centuries. As the state has grown in power, it has done so at the expense of the villages and cities that once were sovereign, of the duchies and principalities that once were independent, until ultimately the only permissible governmental organization of power has become the state. The process took several hundred years, but it was quite ruthless and quite methodical. The powerful families that set themselves up as royal houses and sought to build a large-scale apparatus around them worked systematically to deny to the smaller units power that they had had from the time of the Roman Empire. Gradually, over decades, these nascent states passed laws against town meetings and folkmote government, they warred against the medieval "free cities," they outlawed local guilds and municipal unions, they took away communal farmlands and common grazing grounds, they established central control over independent universities, they replaced local coinage with royal banks, they abolished local tolls in favor of "King's Highways," they superseded municipal taxation with nationwide tax systems, and they sent their own agents and operatives to direct local affairs following directives from the central capital. They were often resisted, sometimes ignored, and in a few instances thwarted—but eventually, over the long sweep of centuries, these royal families succeeded in enlarging their powers, established ready allies among a few they were pleased to designate as nobility, amassed armies and fortunes to ensure their dominance, fostered bureaucratic machines to minister to their wishes, and ultimately forged what we recognize today as nations over most of the map of Europe. This was in its way an impressive achievement, but as Lewis Mumford tells us:

> *The consolidation of power in the political capital was accompanied by a loss of power and initiative in the smaller centers: national prestige meant the death of local municipal freedom. The national territory itself became the connecting link between diverse groups, corporations, cities: the nation was an all-embracing society one entered at birth. The new theorists of law . . . were driven to deny that local communities and corporate bodies had an existence of their own: the family was the sole group, outside the state, whose existence was looked upon as self-validated, the only group that did not need the gracious permission of the sovereign to exercise its natural functions.*

What happens with this consolidation of national power is that the state *makes itself necessary* by destroying the other organizations that were supplying public services to the citizenry before it came along. When the guild system operated in medieval cities it was generally guided by the *conjuratio*, the oath of mutual help by which each guild brother and his family would pledge responsibility for the welfare of other guild members and rally to them in time of need. But when the guild organization was destroyed by royal decree as being contrary to the interests of national mercantilism, there was no one to take care of the sick workman but his own small family, and more often than not it proved inadequate. At that point the state stepped forward and said, look, this poor man is sick and friendless, we must build a state hospital for him, he will surely die if left to himself—and, look, does that not prove the necessity of the state?

It happened all over, and it went on for centuries. As the size of the state increased and its control over localities grew, the instruments of self-sufficiency and cooperation by which these communities had come to live began to wither. As they withered, the state took upon itself the task of intervening to supply those services left undone, thereby justifying its existence by remedying the problems that its existence caused. Simple, circular—and devastating.

———

We have seen this same prytaneogenic process in the growth of the United States, of course.

In the earliest days when there was no government other than a chartered colony, the settlers had to do most things for themselves and thought nothing of it; official governments were so unimportant that the colony of Pennsylvania in the seventeenth century went without a governor or legislative council for twenty years, without anyone visibly worse for it. The entire Revolutionary War was fought with nothing more than a temporary and intermittent "Continental" Congress, whose powers were restricted in practice to the raising and support of an army, and much the same system worked for the first eight years of the new nation's life under the Articles of Confederation, during which time local governments of only modest potency were easily the most important influence in the citizens' lives.

Then, for a variety of complicated reasons, some of the powers of the land decided that a more centralized state would be more beneficial for such enterprises as carving out the wilderness, exploiting the natural riches, fostering manufactures, and protecting international trade. Thus arose the Constitution of 1787 and the Hamiltonian principles of federal power, with the adoption of which the United States embarked on the same kind of path the earlier royal houses of Europe had traveled in consolidating the nation-state at the expense of local governments.

That process was a long and complex one, but two disparate examples may serve to illustrate it: government control of the postal service and government dominance of education. Today we generally assume both to fall within the province of the state. It was not always that way.

In the earliest settlements, mail service was a matter of simple cooperation: letter packets would be off-loaded from ships at some dockside tavern or shop, townspeople would come in to collect their mail, and the few letters going into the hinterland would naturally be entrusted to the occasional traveler. Colonial governors set up systems of their own from time to time—a monthly service was begun between New York and Boston in 1672, another between Philadelphia and Delaware in 1683—and army units typically had their own couriers, but private citizens generally relied on travelers, friends, and neighborhood boys. Many settlements also depended upon some sort of informal cooperative arrangement along the lines that the Virginia colony made official in 1657, by which each plantation was expected to deliver the mail packet to the next outlying one, and so on from coast to hinterland. Private mail-service businesses also developed early on, charging rates according to distance, and this was dependable enough so that one William Goddard, a Baltimore printer, was able to run a service among thirty colonial cities at a steady profit. Even when the British crown took over the operation of official posts in the eighteenth century, such private services continued to be tolerated, but the government soon took the expedient of buying them out when they became too successful and threatened the income from official mails.

With the creation of the new nation, one of the first acts was to create an official postal organization (1789), under the constitutional provision that "the Congress shall have power to establish post-offices and post roads"; it ran, naturally, at a deficit. Over the next few decades, it was authorized by Congress to extend its control over more and more territory, gradually displacing more informal methods of delivery, but somehow it never seemed to be able to match the private systems in either service or profitability. By the 1840s these private systems were so numerous and so successful—at least 200 of them in the Boston area alone—that the government decided to launch a frontal attack. Congress protected the government service with the 1845 postal act that explicitly prohibited "any private express" between cities running "by regular trips or at stated periods," and the Justice Department vigorously prosecuted competitors, such as Lysander Spooner's American Letter Mail Company operating along the East Coast.

Thereafter the government set about determinedly to protect its monopoly over the postal business—not because it was so good at mail service, one hastens to note, but precisely because it was so poor at it. Occasional private services were tolerated in the Western territories—the Pony Express, for example, in the 1860s—but in the states, federal laws required compulsory prepayment in 1855, the use of official stamps in

1856, the use of federal equipment on rail routes in 1864, the elimination of all private carriers within cities (and even buildings) in 1872, and the exclusive patronage of official couriers for rural delivery in 1896. By the twentieth century, the postal service was a clear and powerful monopoly, its reign absolute over all classes of mail (with the exception of some types of parcel and third-class). Today the United States Postal Service (USPS) maintains its tax-free monopoly, and though express services like FedEx and United Parcel Service (UPS) have arisen that deliver packages legally, it is a crime for any private service to engage in dispatch of first-class mail, unless it is "extremely urgent" and costs at least twice the USPS's cost; home mailboxes are specifically designated as government property and are forbidden to anyone else, paperboy or neighbor or political candidate or advertiser; and letters delivered by any person anywhere, even from your daughter to her classmates inviting them to a birthday party, are legally required to be put in a postbox and have US stamps on them.

And in Rochester, New York, in 1976, Patricia and Paul Brennan were sued by the federal postal service to keep them from continuing their thriving private first-class mail system, which guaranteed same-day delivery at a cost three cents under the federal rate. The courts, naturally, upheld the suit. The *New York Times* declared: "The Brennans may have been enterprising, but they were also behaving like vigilantes—benign vigilantes, to be sure, but still taking a government prerogative into their own hands. There are some enterprises that can't be free, that must be monopolized by government." How far has the country come.

So the state justifies its existence by arguing that it is after all necessary to deliver the mails. That this service has seriously deteriorated in recent decades, running up deficits of hundreds of millions of dollars every year but one since 1945 (1979 was a temporary exception, following rate increases of 15 to 25 percent), while the quantity and quality of services have shrunk, suggests that in fact the state may not be a very good instrument for performing this task. That private parcel services have increased their business since 1960 from a few million packages to more than a billion a year, making a tidy profit out of that section of the mails in which they are allowed to compete, *and* providing better service, suggests that indeed the original system may have made the most sense after all.

Education represents another area where government intervention has worked to undermine effective local power, steadily and surely.

For more than a hundred years, schooling in the United States was a matter for the home, the local public school, and the church or private school, with state and federal governments remaining largely in the background. From the first New England township schools in the eighteenth century and down through the public school movement of the late nineteenth century, education was in the hands of local school boards, usually elected by members of the school district and empowered to raise their money through local taxation. Then at the beginning of the twentieth century, state governments began to intrude themselves, first setting standards and examinations for all classes of schools, then organizing teachers' colleges and certifications, then finally mandating the textbooks, classroom equipment, and types of instruction that would be used; and as funding to these ends came from state financing, local boards had to agree to state demands.

The federal government similarly has increased its role, beginning with grants for agricultural and vocational education during World War I and the GI Bill after World War II. In 1958 Washington got directly into the action with the National Defense Education Act (the "Sputnik Bill"), intended to create enough little scientists and engineers to win the Cold War, followed by the Elementary and Secondary Education Act in 1965 providing money for certain school programs, intended to expire after five years but in fact renewed every five years since then. On one of those renewals in 2001, pushed by President George W. Bush, Congress enacted the No Child Left Behind Act, tripling federal money for education with the express aim of eliminating all local variations in schools across the country and in theory creating common tests to which all children would be taught. Despite the fact that this met with a good deal of resistance from teachers and parents who hated the idea of a school year substantially devoted to learning how to pass a test, President Obama went the same direction in 2009 by approving and funding state-generated "Common Core" standards to establish a uniform curriculum across the nation, followed by a "Race to the Top" grant of $4.3 billion to states that would agree to follow along.

The result of all this is that now local boards, though still empowered to *raise* money at the local level, are practically powerless to *spend* it as they

61

see fit, since from 90 to 99 percent of all expenditures now are mandated by state and federal requirements. The sad complaint of a president of a suburban school board association on Long Island can be heard almost from coast to coast: "We no longer have much control over finances because of the mandates, and we no longer have control over whom we can dismiss because of the unions and the courts. There has been a severe, accelerated erosion of local control."

And with it a decline in the quality of education in the broadest sense, and though there is a great deal of federal money in the trough—federal expenditure has gone (in constant dollars) from $138 per student in 1961 to $563 in 1981 to $993 in 2005—there is a consensus that American public education is pretty terrible, confirmed by various polls such as the Pearson survey in 2015 that ranked the United States 14th in the world, behind Ireland and Poland. It's no mystery. Where the control of education is taken out of the hands of the family and the community, and schooling gets further and further away from the people who have a direct stake in it, the quality suffers.

Prytaneogenesis.

8

The Law of Government Size

I t is an interesting fact that when the peoples of Germany were divided into dozens of little principalities and duchies and kingdoms and sovereign cities—from about the twelfth century to the nineteenth—they engaged in fewer wars than any other peoples of Europe. During this period, according to the estimates in Quincy Wright's massive *A Study of War*, the Germans participated in only thirteen wars—whereas Denmark participated in fifteen, Sweden in twenty-four, Austria and Russia in forty, France in forty-two, Britain in forty-four, and Spain in forty-eight. From 1600 on, when modern warfare developed in Europe, the German states (even with the rise of Prussia) spent fewer years at war than any other nations except Denmark and Sweden, engaged in fewer battles, and suffered fewer casualties. Generally, it seems, the various small polities saw no particular advantage in trying to assemble unified forces for warfare, so attacks *by* them were few; and the outside powers saw very little advantage in trying to conquer and govern a bunch of disparate entities, so attacks *upon* them were few. Not that there was total peace, nothing so otherworldly as that. But there were long stretches without war, and those (mostly internecine) wars that did erupt tended not to be so intense or so lasting as those on the rest of the continent.

All that changed, of course, with the unification of Germany and the establishment of one government over 25 million people and 70,000 square miles. Then, within only a few decades, the German state embarked on major wars against Denmark, Austria, and France, conquered territories in Africa and the Pacific, and ultimately instigated two devastating world wars within the space of thirty years.

I find that quite suggestive. Nothing conclusive, of course, but it stands for me as a symbol of what large nations and governments so very often do, because of their size and power, that smaller ones usually do not.

And that same phenomenon is one that I find recurrent in history since Sargon's first empire in the second millennium before Christ. Governments, whether meaning to or not, always seem to create more havoc as they grow larger, and the largest of them historically have tended to be the most disruptive and bellicose. Some almost tangible quantity of power seems to accumulate in large-scale governments, boiling and seething until it has to find an outlet, sometimes emerging as domestic upheaval, often enough of the economic kind, sometimes as international warfare—and frequently as both. Indeed, so regularly does one encounter this phenomenon in the reading of history that I am emboldened to advance this as a full-blown maxim, what we may call the Law of Government Size:

> *Economic and social misery increases in direct proportion to the size and power of the central government of a nation or state.*

Let us examine that through a brief overview of the historical record.

As to the proof of this law in the ages before the rise of modern Europe, I can think of nothing better than the conclusions of Arnold Toynbee, whose masterful study of human civilizations is replete with evidence that any student may subject to microscopic examination. Time after time he shows that civilizations begin to decay shortly after they are unified and centralized under a single large-scale government, and he posits that the next-to-last stage of *any* society, leading directly to its final stage of collapse, is "its forcible political unification in a universal [by which he means united and centralized] state":

> *For a Western student the classic example is the Roman Empire into which the Hellenic Society was forcibly gathered up in the penultimate chapter of its history. If we now glance at each of the living civilisations, other than our own, we notice that the main body of Orthodox Christendom has already been through a universal state in the Ottoman, . . . that the Hindu Civilisation has had its universal state in the Mughal Empire and its successor, the British Raj; the main body of the Far Eastern Civilisation in the Mongol Empire and its resuscitation at the hands of the Manchus; and the Japanese*

offshoot of the Far Eastern Civilisation in the shape of the Tokugawa Shogunate.

There is, Toynbee concludes, "the slow and steady fire of a universal state where we shall in due course be reduced to dust and ashes."

Lewis Mumford, from a different perspective, has reached these same kinds of conclusions. Throughout history, he has shown, the consolidation of nations and the rise of governments have gone hand in hand with the development of slavery, the creation of empires, the division of citizens into classes, the recurrence of civil protests and disorders, the erection of useless monuments, the despoliation of the land, and the waging of larger and ever-larger wars.

Of early cities, Mumford writes:

> *Once the city came into existence, with its collective increase in power in every department, [its] whole situation underwent a change. Instead of raids and sallies for single victims, mass extermination and mass destruction came to prevail. What had once been a magic sacrifice to insure fertility and abundant crops . . . was turned into the exhibition of the power of one community, under its wrathful god and priest-king, to control, subdue, or totally wipe out another community.*

Such consolidated cities, the nuclei of growing states, succeeded by undermining "the positive symbiosis of the Neolithic village community . . . by a negative symbiosis resting on war, exploitation, enslavement, parasitism. . . . The very means of achieving this growth oriented the community to sacrifice, constriction of life, and premature destruction and death." Whether in Sumer, Babylonia, Egypt, Assyria, or Persia, for all their differences these imperial metropolises all fell into the same pattern when they experienced successful consolidation: "Specialization, division, compulsion, and depersonalization produced an inner tension within the city. This resulted throughout history in an undercurrent of covert resentment and outright rebellion."

Later on, Mumford tells us, when the once-independent city-states of Greece were joined together into the successive Hellenistic empires, the same misuse of power, the same economic and political dislocations arose:

These new states squandered human vitality and economic wealth on the arts of war [and] would often crown their success in commanding slave power and garnering tribute by lavishing money on costly public works of every kind. Democracies are often too stingy in spending money for public purposes, for its citizens feel that the money is theirs. Monarchies and tyrannies can be generous, because they dip their hands freely into other people's pockets.

And still later, in the empire that was to pride itself on central power and imperial control, "all the magnitudes [were] stretched . . . not least the magnitude of debasement and evil." The Roman Empire, Mumford writes, suffered from a failure

to make either the towns or the provinces more democratically self-governing and more self-sufficient: for too much of their surplus was destined to flow back to the center, through the very leaky channels of tax-gatherers and military governors. The cities were often given some degree of independence within this scheme; but what was needed was a method of encouraging their interdependence and of giving their regions effective representation at the center. This possibility seems to have been beyond the Roman imagination.

The result of such extreme centralization was "a parasitic economy and a predatory political system," both based in the Roman capital and "built on a savage exploitation and suppression." Incessant warfare, the extremes of poverty, torture, and extermination, the devastation of the land—this was the life of Rome as it developed, in Mumfordian terms, from "parasitopolis" to "pathopolis," thence to "tyrannopolis" and finally "necropolis":

Rome remains a significant lesson of what to avoid: its history presents a series of classic danger signals to warn one when life is moving in the wrong direction. Wherever crowds gather in suffocating numbers, wherever rents rise steeply and housing conditions deteriorate, wherever one-sided exploitation of distant territories removes the pressure to achieve balance and harmony near at hand, there the precedents of Roman building almost automatically revive, as they have come back today.

The glories that were Rome? Such as they were, they must have been produced at an awful price.

———————

So much—at least in overview—for the earlier examples of the Law of Government Size. For it to be truly valid, however, it must be shown to operate particularly during those periods that saw the emergence and consolidation of the most powerful governments yet known in the world, the nation-states of Europe. And, since we deal here with more documentable history, it must make some direct and specific correlations between those periods of growth and the economic and political upheavals that are known to have taken place in Europe.

Dealing with amorphous categories like these, of course, one must treat with caution any attempt at too great a precision. Historical fluctuations are never exact, and movements do not usually fit nicely into those precise periods historians proffer us. Nonetheless, it is possible to ascertain certain broad trends over long historical reaches, certain valleys and peaks, and one can make some reasonable generalizations about patterns and correspondences. Or else what's a history for?

In the post-Roman era of Europe that saw the establishment of the modern nation-state—a process that altogether went on for eight hundred years or more—there have been, by common agreement, only four periods of marked solidification of governmental power: the dynastic era of the twelfth century, the absolutist era of the sixteenth century, the Napoleonic era of the nineteenth century, and the totalitarian era of the twentieth century. And thanks to the extraordinary work of some contemporary scholars, we are able with some accuracy to compare those periods with the times of most extreme economic and political turmoil over the same centuries.

The most precise economic evaluation comes from two Oxford University scholars, E. H. Phelps Brown and Sheila V. Hopkins, supplemented by material from the American business magazine *Forbes*. Together they have constructed a price index for all the years since AD 1000, based on the probable amount of money an English working family (and presumably a family on the continent as well) would have spent for basic necessities as they were reckoned at any given time. This index shows with some clarity the periods in European history when prices were rising the fastest and the resulting inflation and economic dislocations were the greatest, as well as the periods of relative stability and tranquility in between. For political evidence, the most accurate measure of dislocation comes from statistics on the nature and extent of warfare, much of which has been painstakingly compiled by Pitirim Sorokin, the Harvard historian whose masterful *Social and Cultural Dynamics* is a most detailed examination of the full sweep of post-medieval European history. Supplemented by the work of other military scholars, particularly Quincy Wright, these findings give a similar picture of the periods when European powers were most often convulsed by civil and international strife, and when they enjoyed times of relative peacefulness.

Remarkably, the economic and political indicators tend to coincide with great fidelity. More remarkably still, they coincide with the eras of governmental consolidation with almost uncanny historical precision. It is worth a somewhat more extended look.

The first period, from about 1150 to 1300, was the time in which royal dynasties were established and royal cities began to emerge in those parts of Europe where the medieval municipal traditions were weakest—particularly England, Aquitaine, Sicily, Aragon, and Castile. Sometimes under pressure from outside invaders such as the Mongols and the Turks, sometimes with the connivance of the Catholic Church looking for temporal power, baronies and principalities chose to unite under a single ruling family, which, though still with only limited power, worked to assert its control over wider and wider areas. Some of these dynasties were able to cause the creation of permanent royal centers now for the first time, with permanent archives, offices, courts, and bureaucracies. It was then that simple towns like London, Paris, Moscow, and Vienna begin to grow into true royal capitals, then that systems of delegated central authority and hierarchical administration begin to replace the loose pattern of mobile supervision, characteristic of the earlier baronies.

This centralizing process is associated with the reigns of Philip Augustus (1180–1223) in France, Frederick II (1198–1250) in Sicily, and Henry II (1154–89) in England, and the rise of the house of Hapsburg (from 1273) in Austria; but the English example typifies them all. Henry succeeded ably in subduing the rival barons and establishing his control over much of the countryside from his royal town of Westminster, and his fight with

Thomas à Becket—which Henry won, you may remember—was precisely a struggle about whether the state or the church would have control over ecclesiastical law. As one British historian has noted, "By Henry II's reign, the English king had centralized so much authority under his immediate jurisdiction that all men of substance had frequent occasion to seek justice or to request favors at court." Though this centralizing process was partially curtailed by the greatly overrated Magna Carta, it was quickly re-established by Henry III (1216–72) and his doctrines of absolutism and then extended by Edward I (1272–1307), victor over the nobility in the Barons' War, and his all-embracing legal system, the Statutes of Westminster. After this Edwardian consolidation, England went through a long period of internal dissension, on-again-off-again warfare, baronial revolt, and finally the chaotic War of the Roses before royal power was reasserted some two centuries later.

This centralizing coincided with a period of rampant inflation unlike anything Europe had ever known during the early medieval ages—or perhaps ever before. This explosive epoch—economic historians call it the Commercial Revolution—disrupted the long-stable practices of medieval commerce and gradually eroded the self-sufficient free cities that had been the backbone of the earlier economy. Now, with newly powerful dynasties in the lead, the new economic order emphasized inter-city trade and court-protected trading routes, and introduced cash money and "ghost money" (credit) backed by the emerging royal houses and their favored banking houses and entrepots. The result was that for almost all of this century and a half, prices soared decade by decade, ultimately increasing by nearly 400 percent before leveling off in the early fourteenth century, a dizzying and devastating economic climb.

Over these same years, the political turmoil of accelerated warfare also increased, both internally as the royal consolidations met with baronial resistance, and externally as the dynasties tried to extend their territories, trade routes, and sources of wealth wherever they could. The period was particularly marked by those chaotic campaigns that go under the name of the Crusades (1095–1291), whose effect was to create far more serious dislocations in the European countryside than in the Palestinian: the First Crusade, for example, involved the massacre of Jews in the Rhineland and civil wars in Bulgaria and Hungary; the Fourth Crusade was devoted entirely to carrying out Venice's plan for the sack of the Christian city of

Zara in Dalmatia; the Children's Crusade degenerated into the selling of tens of thousands of children into slavery—and none of the bloody campaigns ever came close to succeeding in freeing the Holy Lands from the Muslims. Not until the end of the Crusades, and shortly thereafter with the decimation of the Black Plague, did European warfare enter a period of relative quietude that was to last for the next two centuries.

The second period of marked governmental growth, from about 1525 to 1650, saw the introduction of standing armies, forced taxation, centralized bureaucracies, national tariffs, royal customs collections, and extended territorial control. During this century the established orders that remained to challenge the royal houses—the church and the nobility—were pretty much vanquished, peasant uprisings in opposition to national control were quite brutally crushed, and sovereign cities that till then had resisted state dominance were brought to heel. The doctrines of absolutism became widespread, the notion of the "divine right" of kings was advanced and codified (particularly in France and England), and at the end of the period there appeared one of the most forceful of all justifications for the total sovereignty of the state. Thomas Hobbes's *Leviathan*—according to which the citizens "confer all their power and strength upon one man, or upon one assembly of men, that may reduce all their wills, by plurality of voices, unto one will." In England this is the time of the powerful Tudor rulers, the establishment of the state's own sanctioned form of religion (Church of England), the reunification of the country and its rise to international prominence under Elizabeth I, and the extension of state power into matters of currency, manufacturing, mail, labor conditions, agriculture, and the like, which had theretofore been private or communal affairs. In France, likewise, this is the time of the emergence of the House of Bourbon (from 1589) and the solidification of its administrative dominance under Richelieu and Mazarin (1624–61), and the ascendance of the man who came to embody absolute monarchy, Louis XIV, the "Sun King." "Throughout Europe," concludes Gerald Nash, a leading historian of government administration, "the absolute rulers created new institutions, such as efficient bureaucracies, to extend their powers into many aspects of the economic and social life of the nation."

In such a period, providing for the mere trappings of governmental power was bound to create economic strains, and sustaining the substance beneath them would have to cause unprecedented financial turmoil. It did. Starting about 1525, after two centuries of relative economic stability, prices shot up steadily in an almost unending spiral, increasing by an unprecedented 700 percent in all, before leveling off in the middle of the seventeenth century. Accompanying this unchecked spiral was the economic transformation known as the Capitalist Revolution, during which the primary mechanisms of capitalism came to be adopted throughout Europe, fueled by the newfound riches in, and colonization of, the New World. Then came, too, a whole new stratum of mercantile adventurers, fusing into what Karl Marx was later to call the bourgeoisie and marking the end of what remained of the communitarian economic arrangements of the medieval period: "good goods at a fair price" gave way to "what the market will bear," *res publica* to *caveat emptor*.

At about this same time, Europe was also wracked on an unprecedented scale by the civil wars that the attempts to consolidate government power made inevitable, particularly the bloody Wars of Religion in France (1562–98), the Puritan Revolution in England (1642–49), and the ongoing internecine struggles of the city-states in Italy. More important, it suffered the single most destructive epoch of warfare between the ninth and the eighteenth centuries, the calamitous Thirty Years War (1618–48). That war, the first truly all-European war, fought from the Pyrenees to the Danube, from the Baltic to the Mediterranean, resulted in something on the order of 2 million casualties—twice as many as had been caused in the entire previous two centuries—and a "war intensity" that Sorokin marks as *seven times* as great as anything experienced in Europe before. Something was there that was absolute during this era, but it was not peace.

The third period of state consolidation, from about 1775 to 1815, comes with the adoption of what we would now think of as the modern system of government (and its rationale) over most of Europe. First through the American Revolution and then more drastically through the French Revolution, the existence of the nation-state was established as being even more absolute, more compelling, than that of the crown, or the mother country, or any subcategory of citizens within it: "The State alone has the duty to watch over the interests of all citizens," maintained the French Convention in 1793 to some workers on strike. "By striking, you are forming a coalition, you are creating a State within the State. So—death!" True national chauvinism was born in this era (indeed, it was a Napoleonic soldier, Nicolas Chauvin, who gave his name to it), with the accompanying fanaticism, zealousness, and flag-waving on behalf of the state that becomes part of modern patriotism.

The Napoleonic despotism that followed—not alone in France but in much of Europe—gave organizational form to such doctrines. Ancient provinces were officially abolished and replaced with new administrative units tied directly to the capital; newly empowered bureaucracies of increasing size took provenance over almost every human function; a Bank of France was created; a national police force was established (under Joseph Fouche, often called the father of the modern police state) for the first time in European history; national armies were drawn by conscription for the first time since the Pharaohs; and an all-encompassing *Code Napoleon* was promulgated, the first national code embracing all activities within the state since the Roman Empire. Napoleon's was a monumental creation of governmental power that, as Tocqueville himself remarked well after Napoleon had departed, was bound to outlive the Emperor:

> *Centralization was built up anew, and in the process all that had once kept it within bounds was carefully eliminated. . . . Napoleon fell, but the more solid parts of his achievement lasted on; his government died, but his administration survived, and every time that an attempt is made to do away with absolutism the most that could be done has been to graft the head of Liberty onto a servile body.*

Accompanying this achievement in almost every corner of Europe were the final blows to what, so persistently, remained of the communal villages and independent cities. France abolished the commune meeting, confiscated the remaining communal lands, and attempted to assign village mayors from Paris; England passed a flurry of Enclosure Acts from 1760 on, more than at any time before, effectively driving the villagers to the urban factories; and in Belgium, Prussia, Italy, Spain, Austria, and Russia, every royal house with sufficient power confiscated communal grazing and farming territories for its royal holdings or for division among the favored aristocracy.

The economic dislocations that accompanied all of this were, of course, severe. The inflationary curve shot upward during these four decades by more than 250 percent, breaking out of an equilibrium that had lasted for a full century, and at its peak in 1815 it stood higher than at any point in the past—indeed at any point in the future until the wild inflationary decade of the 1920s. This inflation and upheaval signaled the advent of the Industrial Revolution, particularly in England, during which the remaining agricultural and commercial economies were subsumed under the factory and wage-labor economies, with all their attendant maladies. The Industrial Revolution was to continue well beyond this period, of course, but it was during these first decades that the most intense dislocations took place, especially in western Europe, and the patterns of rural ruination and urban overcrowding were established.

It was during these decades of the late eighteenth and early nineteenth centuries that political turmoil and warfare reverberated throughout Europe, and through much of the Americas as well. The American and French Revolutions were easily the most violent and disruptive of any revolutions until the Russian in the twentieth century, the French being a particularly bloody and terrifying cataclysm that resonated in Belgium and Holland, in Ireland and England, in Spain and Italy, and as far east as Austria and Prussia. These were followed immediately by the French Revolutionary and Napoleonic Wars (1792–1815), which engulfed the entire European continent in total warfare for the first time since the Thirty Years War of the early seventeenth century, and involved more nations in more battles (an estimated 713) than in any previous thirty-year period in European history, more battles indeed than took place during the awful carnage of World War I; there were twice as many casualties for England and France alone as those countries had experienced at any comparable time since 1630.

———

The final period, the one most familiar to us, encompasses most of the decades of the last century, roughly from 1910 to 2010. This has been an era of unprecedented governmental growth that in almost every society, even the most liberal and benign, has meant large bureaucracies, universal conscription, compulsory taxation, state police forces, restrictions on individual freedom, and executive powers essentially remote from popular control. All European states have greatly extended the role of government through wide-reaching social legislation and attendant taxation, and most of them have nationalized a great number of the industries and services of the land—in some cases, as with the Soviet Union, *all* (until the collapse). The phenomenon of total power in the hands of the state, not only in Europe but today in remote American, Asian, and African lands as well, has even come to have a twentieth-century name: totalitarianism.

One indication of the extent of this progression is its effect on even such a nominally decentralized and traditionally anti-authoritarian country as the United States. In those ten decades, the US government has gathered powers to it that the Founding Fathers would have found unthinkable—gathered legitimately, as it were, because sanctioned for one branch of government by the other two—until it has become one of the strongest national governments in history. The process was slow and piecemeal—with the establishment of a national bank (1913), compulsory income taxes (1913), regulation of trade (1914), general conscription (1917), regulation of private power companies (1920), a national police force (1925), regulation of wages and working conditions (1935–38), an espionage organization (1942), and since World War II with a dizzying array of provisions covering almost all aspects of individual and political life, the creation of the Departments of Defense (1947), Health and Human Services (1953), Housing and Urban Development (1965), Transportation (1966), Energy (1977), Education (1979), Veterans Affairs (1989), and, most centripetal of all, Homeland Security (2002). After this century there could be no mistaking the overall transformation that the American government had undergone in the direction of consolidated state power.

During these decades, the world has also experienced economic turmoil of a kind and a degree unknown before. The period began with an international depression in the 1930s beyond anything previously known, followed by prices rising inexorably every decade of the twentieth century ($100 in 1910 was equal to $2,110 in 2007), creating a rampant worldwide inflation that eroded people's earnings faster than they could compile them—until another worldwide crash in 2008. Again, these economic dislocations have been directly associated with the growth of government, since the federal government's treatment for the Depression was an enormous expansion of federal programs and then a world war, and its treatment for the Recession was an injection of trillions of dollars into the economy, doubling of the federal debt, and all power given the Federal Reserve. In between, Keynesian-minded governments poured money into all kinds of projects and services, and enormously expanded "the public sector," people working not in the production of goods but for the newly enlarged governments themselves.

As to political turmoil, it is probably sufficient to point to the two most ruinous wars in all of human history within the space of just thirty of these years. But one might also add the innumerable second-rank wars that were far more destructive than most of those that had preceded them — particularly the Russian Civil War, the Spanish Civil War, the Korean War, the Vietnam War, and then the two miry misadventures in Afghanistan and Iraq. By every measure — the number of troops engaged, firepower, duration of battles, military casualties, civilian deaths, destruction of property, and devastation of the countryside — this last has been the most violent era in human history.

If one were to attempt the enormously difficult task of quantifying all this — the long process of history over more than eight centuries — the figures for price inflations and war casualties would provide, at the very least, a suggestive basis. These may not be precise — though they are compilations of diligent and thorough researchers — but they offer a general picture as few other statistics can. And when plotted on a graph, as on the Inflation and War Chart shown here, they give telling confirmation to the Law of Government Size. Again, I must caution that what we see in this graph is only an approximation, and it is based on statistics that must be considered open to modification and refinement. Nonetheless, the pattern that emerges does seem quite unmistakable and the correlations do seem to hold true with remarkable consistency: as government increases in size, it generates economic and political dislocations, and the bigger the governments, the bigger those dislocations.

I recognize that the *coincidence* of these three phenomena does not necessarily prove *causation*: one might make a claim that war needs big governments and drives up prices, or that inflation necessitates the diversion of war and increased government control. But obviously the initial

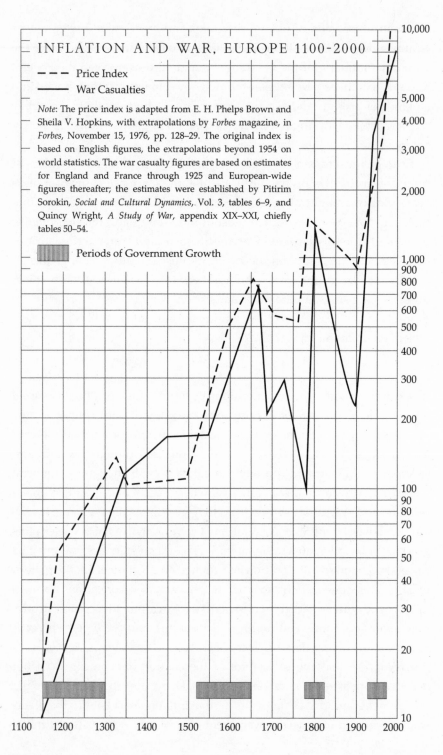

INFLATION AND WAR, EUROPE 1100-2000

- - - Price Index
——— War Casualties

Note: The price index is adapted from E. H. Phelps Brown and Sheila V. Hopkins, with extrapolations by *Forbes* magazine, in *Forbes*, November 15, 1976, pp. 128–29. The original index is based on English figures, the extrapolations beyond 1954 on world statistics. The war casualty figures are based on estimates for England and France through 1925 and European-wide figures thereafter; the estimates were established by Pitirim Sorokin, *Social and Cultural Dynamics*, Vol. 3, tables 6–9, and Quincy Wright, *A Study of War*, appendix XIX–XXI, chiefly tables 50–54.

▨ Periods of Government Growth

causative element in the process has to be the government. It alone can set in motion the forces that lead to conflict, it alone declares and wages war, it alone sets the conditions for economic expansion or contraction, it alone determines the national protections and international opportunities within which the economy operates. Much happens without military reckoning, much without business considerations, but very little, particularly when the states accrue increasing powers with each passing century, happens without national governments.

The processes are not mysterious. As a government grows, it must expand both its civilian and its military might, generally by extending the bureaucracy's influence in domestic affairs and the armed services' influence in external ones. New money must be found to pay for this expansion, and the greater the expansion the greater is the need for money. One way to raise money is through taxation—and that inevitably translates into inflation because businesses will always pass on their taxes to consumers in the form of higher prices, and higher prices mean inflation; result—as Mr. Micawber might say—social misery. Another way to raise money is by increasing the money supply, for example through central bank loans, measures of credit, guaranteed royal companies, or government-sponsored trade arrangements. More money means inflation. Result: again, social misery.

With the need for money to pay for government expansion so important, a state will also naturally seek to increase its spheres of influence, and to enlarge its take of spoils, through warfare. And one government's expansion naturally runs up against another government's expansion more and more often, with more and more conflicts of greater and greater intensity, and greater and greater consequences to the social harmony. At the same time, war proves invaluable for fostering the spirit of nationalism that justifies the government psychologically to its people, and thereby for inducing them further to wage wars on its behalf. With warfare, too, goes additional government expansion and solidification: "War," as Tocqueville points out, "must invariably and immeasurably increase the powers of civil government; it must almost compulsorily concentrate the direction of all men and the management of all things in the hands of the administration." Result: more social misery, and oftentimes stark social tragedy.

The process is circular, neat, and powerful. If it were not, it would not have lasted so long. It is not by accident that it has produced the most powerful governments known to human history. And, for nearly a thousand years, the most severe economic and political turmoil.

––––––––––

And so we have come, not by accident, back to the Beanstalk Principle: for everything—even a nation—there is an optimal size beyond which it ought not to grow, for at that point the critical mass of power accumulates to the point that demands an outlet, and thus is everything in that nation affected adversely. Or as Aristotle put it, anticipating the Law of Government Size two thousand years ago: "To the size of states there is a limit, as there is to other things, plants, animals, implements, for none of these retain their natural power when they are too large or too small."

There must be an alternative to nations grown too big, to governments grown too dangerous, to bureaucracies grown too inflated, to systems grown too complex, to enterprises grown too unwieldy, to corporations grown too immense, to production grown too massive, to cities grown too crowded, to buildings grown too vast, to tools grown too complicated, to relations grown too distended.

There is: human scale.

PART THREE

SOCIETY ON A HUMAN SCALE

I think that it will ultimately be proved that scale *is a key factor in planning towns, neighborhoods, and housing developments. While very little is known about something as abstract as scale, I am convinced that it represents a facet of the human requirement that man is ultimately going to have to understand.*

—EDWARD T. HALL, The Hidden Dimension, 1966

Recovery of human scale is at the root of every enlightened concept of the city of our age.

—ARTHUR B. GALLION *and* SIMON EISNER,
The Urban Pattern, 1965

If humanity is to use the principles needed to manage an ecosystem, the basic communal unit of social life must itself become an ecosystem —an eco-community. It too must become diversified, balanced and well-rounded. By no means is this concept of community motivated exclusively by the need for a lasting balance between man and the natural world; it also accords with the utopian ideal of the rounded man, the individual whose sensibilities, range of experience and lifestyle are nourished by a wide range of stimuli, by a diversity of activities, and by a social scale that always remains within the comprehension of a single human being.

—MURRAY BOOKCHIN, Post-Scarcity Anarchism, 1971

9
___

Ecological Hubris,
Ecological Harmony

In the 1950s, the World Health Organization (WHO), following its long-standing mandate, began to try to eliminate malaria in the Malay Peninsula by spreading DDT. Within a year or so there was a marked decline in the instances of malaria, but other problems cropped up, particularly an alarming increase in the rat population. It seems that the DDT, while killing some of the malarial mosquitoes, also poisoned roaches and other insects, which poisoned the gecko lizards who fed on the insects, which poisoned the cats who fed on the geckos, which ultimately reduced the number of predators for the rats and allowed them to increase in prodigious amounts. The rat boom was a particular problem because the rats seemed to be carrying lice, and the lice in turn were carrying plague. The various governments of the area were about to embark on the natural and approved techno-fix solution—spraying rat poison over the country—when a couple of WHO ecologists rushed forward to intervene. Kill the rats, they explained, and you will merely force the lice and their diseases to find *another* carrier, most likely humans, and the plague that you want to avoid will come for sure. Their own proffered solution was decidedly non-techno-fix: bring in more cats, get the cat population up to previous levels, and they will eat the rats, lice and plague and all. This was naturally regarded with some disdain and condescension by the governmental authorities of the region, but there being no appropriately expensive, large-scale, and high-technology alternative, they eventually agreed. WHO was permitted to parachute hordes of cats over the countryside, and within a few months they had carried out their instinctive feline duties, decimated the rat population, and averted the threat of plague.

And the malaria? That was not so easily solved. As in most other countries around the world where the WHO DDT campaign was waged, the incidence of malaria showed a dramatic decrease for several years and then suddenly began to creep up again as the malaria mosquitoes developed resistance to the insecticide. Eventually the continued spraying of DDT was shown to have no measurable effect on the mosquitoes, and malarial rates were back to what they had been before the campaign, although the number of human miscarriages and malformations seemed to be on the increase.

The number of cases continued to increase in the 1980s and '90s because of immunities to successive insecticides until the Malaysian government embarked on a serious grassroots process of developing a national health system with doctors and volunteers trained in diagnosis and treatment and mandatory reporting of cases, which cut the number sharply by the late 1990s and into the twenty-first century. This process was supplemented in places by the use of treated mosquito nets and some interior spraying, but the use of widespread insecticides like DDT was abandoned.

So it proved to be another case of the failure of elaborate techno-fix and the substitution of simple down-home medical methods. As a matter of fact, it has been known for some years—a 1972 article in *Environment* magazine presented the data—that the only permanent and effective cure for malaria comes not from some chemical techno-fix but simply from an improvement in the diet and general health of the affected population. The reason there is no malaria in the United States, for example, is not that there are no anopheles mosquitoes in this country, but rather that there are no malarial protozoa in our blood for the mosquitoes to pass along, and the reason for that is that the protozoa simply didn't find a sufficient number of hospitable—i.e., weak—hosts; to take California as a case in point, it has been shown that malaria was eliminated there as a serious disease by 1930, long before the use of DDT, simply through improvements in the social and economic conditions of the majority of the inhabitants.

So much for the vaunted modern society. Here is a case once again of human technology, applied in ignorance of the natural ecosystems, not only failing to improve, but in serious ways threatening to damage, human ecology.

———

Much is made of that concept "ecology," and, for a long time, so little was understood about it. Yet it is quite simple. Ecology is that grand system of the interaction of all elements of the natural world—plant, mineral, animal, human—and a healthy ecology is one in which all of these are in such harmony that none dominates or destroys the others. The challenge for humankind today lies precisely in finding the scale at which it can live in that sort of harmony with nature—not eternally buffeted by it, defenseless and cowering, nor yet continually perverting it, altering and deforming it, as the industrialized nations so often do today. In fact, it is just this challenge—establishing the balance between the human mode and the natural, in which human comforts are secured without ecological disruption—that should stand as one of the central occupations of any rational society.

You can figure it this way. The human animal is always outnumbered. Biologists who calculate these things once found that for every human in a one-acre patch of forest in North Carolina there were more than 125 million other animals. That included about 50,000 vertebrates—toads, turtles, snakes, and other reptiles; rodents, coatis, possums, raccoons, and other mammals; robins, sparrows, woodpeckers, crows, and other birds; plus, fish and frogs and assorted amphibians. In addition, there were some 124 million other animals—invertebrates—sharing that same turf, including 89 million mites, 28 million collembolans, 662,000 ants, 388,000 millipedes, 372,000 spiders, 90,000 earthworms, 45,000 termites, 19,000 snails, and a large number of various other crawling things, not including protozoa. And that says nothing about the vegetable life that may be found within that acre, from the pine trees and kudzu vines to the bacteria, molds, and actinomycetes, altogether amounting to some 5,000 pounds' worth of plant life, roughly thirty-seven times the weight of the average human individual.

If all that suggests the need for some enterprise and ingenuity on the part of the lone human animal, it also suggests caution and a certain outnumbered modesty as well. Which is not to say that humans do not have their rightful place within that acre and are not as entitled to carve out their existence there—fishing with the earthworms, trapping the rodents, swatting the insects—as the rest of the creatures. One must not, after all, confuse the ecological ideal of living *within* nature with the somewhat more Eastern notion of living *under* it. It is only to say that humans do not have the right to create major imbalances there and wreak destruction upon either natural or animal configurations, for they will imperil themselves as well as the other species if they do so. And they certainly do not have the right to exterminate their fellow creatures, as human beings in fact have done in recent decades at a rate some now estimate to be dozens a day—perhaps 9,000 a year—and, according to the Center for Biological Diversity in 2009, "the worst spate of species die-off since the loss of the dinosaurs 65 million years ago."

A society guided by the human scale must begin right there, with an ecological consciousness that reminds us that we are only one animal among many, and one species among millions, that continually seeks the balance between the human animal and human arrangements on the one hand, and the natural world and natural arrangements on the other. Hans Selye describes a process he calls "intercellular altruism," the natural interdependence of the parts of the body so as to create a healthy organism; that is the obvious model for the wider world as well, an "interspeciate altruism" that interconnects all parts of the firmament so as to create a healthy ecology.

In the 1980s and '90s a movement grew up called *bioregionalism,* so compelling and so meaningful that many of its adherents, and all of its principles, are alive and well even today. It tried to implant that ecological consciousness in a wide circle of people through the concept of a living territory, defined by its life-forms, its topography and hydrology, its flora and fauna, where nature, not a legislature, made the boundaries. In writing about it then, I came across a book called *The Interpreters* that expressed the core idea of bioregionalism best, decades before the term was even coined.

In the book, written at the height of the Irish revolution by the Irish author known as AE, there is a passage in which a group of prisoners, a disparate lot, sit around discussing what the ideal new world should look like. One of them, a philosopher, advances the now-familiar vision of a unitary world order with a global, scientific, cosmopolitan culture. Another, the poet Lavelle, argues fervently against this conception, trying to show that the more the world develops its technological superstructure and global reach, the farther it gets from its natural roots. "If all wisdom was acquired from without," he says, "it might be politic for us to make our culture cosmopolitan. But I believe our best wisdom does not come from without, but arises in the soul and is an emanation of the Earth spirit, a voice speaking directly to us dwellers in the land."

That is the bioregional admonition: it calls us to become "dwellers in the land." Much as the ancient Greeks were, who comprehended the earth as a living creature and contrived the goddess of the earth, Gaia, in English Gaea. We must try to learn that she is, in a very real sense, sacred, and that therefore there is a holy way to confront her and her works, a way of awe and admiration and respect and veneration that simply will not permit despoliation or abuse. We must try to understand ourselves as participants in and not masters over her biotic community —a "reinvention of the human at the species level," in the philosopher Thomas Berry's telling phrase—and take to heart Mark Twain's remark that humans are different from other animals only in that they are able to blush—or need to.

But to become dwellers in the land, the all-encompassing task is to understand place, the immediate specific place where we live. The kinds of soils and rocks under our feet, the source of the waters we drink, the particular cycles of the seasons, the times to plant and harvest and forage, and especially the common insects, birds, mammals, plants, and trees that live where we live—these are the things that are necessary to know. The limits of its resources, the carrying capacities of its lands and waters, the places where it must not be stressed, the places where its bounties can best be developed, the treasures it holds and the treasures it withholds—these are the things that must be understood. And the cultures of the people, of the populations native to the land and of those who have grown up with it, the human social and economic arrangements shaped by and adapted to the geomorphic ones, in both urban and rural settings—these are the things that must be appreciated.

That, in essence, is bioregionalism. And it is human-scale ecology because it limits human influence to one particular known and understood part of the world, with the task of keeping it healthy and functioning and productive for all its habitants, and the wisdom not to extend its influence in any baleful way beyond its boundaries. Especially does it allow humans to flourish, in harmony with the other elements of their surroundings.

———

The historical record is replete with evidence of the consequences of human societies disregarding ecological harmony, always to their ultimate ruination. Two examples may suffice.

The Roman Empire from the middle of the first century BC grew so extensively that it demanded an ever-larger army to secure its borders and an ever-larger bureaucracy to see to its imperial affairs; at the same time, it permitted the accumulation of ever-larger numbers of people in its major cities, particularly Rome, which grew from perhaps 50,000 in the first century BC to more than 300,000 by the first century AD. The feeding of these large non-agricultural—essentially non-productive—populations over the decades made severe demands upon the farmlands of Italy and eventually upon the conquered agricultural areas of Europe and North Africa as well. First Latium, then the Apennines, Campania, Sicily, and Sardinia, then Spain, parts of Gaul, Illyria, and finally Hispania, Macedonia, and all of northern Africa were turned into granaries for the insatiable populations of the empire, with little or no regard to the effect that this process might have upon the natural systems. Overgrazing of animals depleted the grass covers and compacted the soils, with the result that the ground was able to hold less and less water and more and more of the topsoil was carried away by runoffs during the rains; overharvesting of crops led to an exhaustion of the soil's fertility and thus to a relentless deforestation of hills and mountains in the quest for new farmlands, with the result that whole regions were very quickly depleted and laid bare.

Ultimately this human rapaciousness led to the desertification of millions of acres around the Mediterranean, particularly in North Africa where the Sahara, once only a minor wasteland, soon became a desert from the interior to the sea. (It is easy to forget how recently this now-barren region must have been a reasonably thriving forest—this is, after all, where Hannibal got his elephants for the crossing of the Alps in 218 BC.) Ultimately, too, it led to the creation of swamplands in impoverished and abandoned valleys throughout the Italian peninsula and around the Adriatic, and the mosquitoes that inevitably bred there soon carried malaria throughout the empire. And though the immediate causes of the downfall of the Roman Empire were myriad, one need look no farther for the underlying causes than right here: what strength remained after the widespread starvation that marked the third and fourth centuries—and the consequent unrest and rebellion brought about by the increasing deficiencies of food—was surely sapped by the widespread ravages of malaria and other mosquito-borne diseases.

Across the world and several centuries later, a similar ecological vengeance took place in the Valley of Teotihuacan, on the central plateau of Mexico, not far from the present-day Mexico City. There an autocratic priesthood and an ostentatious aristocracy rose to power sometime around the sixth century AD—it has been called the New World's earliest "superpower"—and determined that their temporal glory could be satisfied only with massive accumulations of cement blocks in the form of temples and citadels and monuments. They thus created the sacred city of Teotihuacan, which at its height covered more than eight square miles, with thousands of religious buildings from one edge to the other, including a citadel with a cement courtyard of 1.7 million square feet and the gigantic Pyramid of the Sun, 750 feet long and 216 feet high, the equivalent of a twenty-story building spread over two city blocks.

However, in the process of achieving all this monumentality they slowly depleted the surrounding countryside of all its forest cover. Not only did most of the buildings require beams and rafters made of wood, but the cement for the building blocks themselves was made from quicklime in a process that required continuous fires and huge quantities of wood, about ten times as much as the resultant lime. At the same time, the capital city became swollen with people, perhaps as many as 150,000, and to feed this population more and more farmland had to be wrested from the surrounding hills, usually by the ruinous slash-and-burn method of cutting down forest areas and burning them clear just before planting. As the forests gradually disappeared to satisfy the continuing demands of empire, the unchecked rains began to erode croplands, unimpeded winds swept away fertile topsoils, underground springs lost their normal water supply, and the low-lying rivers that once irrigated the fields began to fill up with silt. Deforestation on this sort of scale, moreover, eventually affects the climate itself, diminishing the amount of water in both the ground and air and leading to a sharp decline in rainfall over quite large areas.

The resultant failure of the crops, attested to by archaeological evidence in the valley, and the ultimate starvation deaths of tens of thousands of people were undoubtedly the primary reason for the collapse of Teotihuacan sometime at the end of the eighth century and its later conquest by the rising Toltec kingdom. The bald hills around the ruins of Teotihuacan even today bear testimony to the fate of its imperial arrogance.

87

Obviously what we have here are striking violations, in ecological terms, of the Beanstalk Principle: for every state there is a size beyond which it cannot grow without disrupting its natural surroundings and eventually producing its own destruction. In fact, it seems that throughout history it has always been the largest states that have been the most extreme in their ruthlessness toward, in effect their denial of, nature, and always eventually to their own detriment. From the Babylonians through the Byzantines, from the Bourbons to the British, we confront time and again in history the imperial passion for monumental construction, the maltreatment of the elements of nature, the dissipation of irretrievable resources, the subjugation of unwilling populations, the exhaustion of fertile lands, and the dislocation of ecological harmony. It is as if the natural world itself were held in some careful equilibrium, the violation of which by states grown overlarge and overconfident inevitably ends in their self-immolation.

A certain satisfaction may be had from these examples, perhaps, and we of a more sophisticated era may be inclined to an indulgent chuckle or deprecatory smile. Yet what is one to make of the brutal disregard for the ecosystem that characterizes our own period and our own nation? It is not simply the pollution that we scatter into the ionosphere, or the chemicals we spread upon the soils, or the nuclear wastes that we leave to radiate for the next 250,000 years, or the poisons that we scatter into our rivers and oceans, or the millions of acres of forests that we eliminate every year, or the animal species we obliterate in increasing numbers, though those are serious assaults indeed upon our ecology. It goes deeper than that. It is interwoven into all parts of our daily lives, into the institutions, the settlements, the habits and attitudes and religions, the laws and the history and the myths.

We are assured by Genesis—the opening lines of the West's single most important book—that we shall have "dominion over" all the earth: "Be fruitful, and multiply, and replenish the earth, and subdue it: and have dominion over the fish of the sea, and over the fowl of the air, and over every living thing that moveth upon the earth."

We are confirmed by the anthropocentric ideology of the Renaissance that the natural world is meant to be in service to the human: "It may be master'd, managed, and used in the Services of humane Life," as Joseph Glanvill put it in the seventeenth century.

We are persuaded by the evident triumph of capitalism that the resources of the earth are less to be contemplated and preserved than extracted and consumed for the betterment of our particular species, following the dictum of Adam Smith that "consumption is the sole end and purpose of production."

We are taught by the special progress of American history that a ruthless battle against the natural world is not only necessary for survival but in the long run beneficial in producing agricultural and mineral wealth for those who conquer the frontiers: "America is promises to / Us / To take them / Brutally," writes Archibald MacLeish, "With love but / Take them. / Oh believe this!"

We are convinced by the undoubted accomplishments of modern industrial technology that it is manifestly right to extend human control over the non-human world, believing, as Chauncey Starr, who founded the Electric Power Research Institute, once put it, "science and technology are powerful and unlimited resources for bettering man's condition [and] have continually relieved the limitations on man's ability to live in the circumstances provided by nature."

We are encouraged by certain laws of our nation, and by the example of the Army Corps of Engineers for more than two centuries, in the belief that we may divert any stream, develop any seashore, fill any swampland, farm any hillside, dam any river, and build on any surface with impunity. We are even authorized by the deliberate provisions of federal statutes to disregard the consequences of building at seashores or steep hillsides or fire-prone forests since the Federal Disaster Act of 1950 and its successors provide full compensation to individuals whose building follies contribute to natural disasters: "Our response to hazard, from colonial days to the present," investigator Wesley Marx has noted, "has made an about-face from an early policy of controlling hazardous development to one of controlling the hazard itself."

The Greeks had a word for it: *hubris*. It was the sin that most often brought down the figures in the Greek tragedies and wrought troubles upon their states. In its modern form it continues to do the same.

The principal example of ecological hubris in the world, with dire effects sure to befall the United States in the near future, is the destruction of the earth's atmosphere by what is benignly called "climate change." Since 1988 the United Nations body studying this, the Intergovernmental Panel on Climate Change, has issued repeated warnings of what will happen if the world does not rein in polluting gases, principally carbon dioxide and methane. In its latest assessment in 2014, it warned of "severe, pervasive, and irreversible impacts" in coming decades and warned of "extreme weather events" and "high risk levels" for increasing diseases in Africa, the spread of wildfires in North America (2015 was the worst ever), and decreased food production in South America.

This was followed in 2015 by a scientific paper from former National Aeronautics and Space Administration (NASA) scientist James Hansen and sixteen colleagues that said there is an accelerating loss of ice, especially in West Antarctica and Greenland, caused by a rise in world temperature, which is certain to increase if there is no global comprehensive movement to stop atmospheric pollution. The team figured that going on the way we are would cause the ocean levels to rise at least 15 feet in the next 50 to 100 years, with obvious disastrous effects on coastlines everywhere. And an increase in cold water of that degree would significantly change ocean circulation, changing weather patterns everywhere, and likely causing severe cold in Europe and other parts of the Northern Hemisphere.

The hubris behind this accelerating destruction of the atmosphere is very powerful, nothing less than the capitalist system itself. Capitalism, based as noted above on resource extraction and personal consumption, is the engine of the world's economy, and it is *totally* dependent on processes that cause polluting gases to enter the atmosphere, from combustion engines to coal-fired electric plants to cattle farming, and it demands that these processes grow regularly. It is further based on the assumption, or blind faith, that these processes are perfectly normal and nothing that the earth can't take in stride, or adjust to with sufficiently clever technology.

Pope Francis, in his 2015 encyclical, has called this hubris nothing less than a sin: "The harmony between the Creator, humanity, and creation as a whole was disrupted by our presuming to take the place of God and refusing to acknowledge our creaturely limitations." Christians therefore "must forcefully reject the notion that our being created in God's image and given dominion over the earth justifies absolute domination over other creatures." And he is of no doubt as to what is causing this disruption: global warming "caused by huge consumption on the part of some rich countries," "extreme and selective consumerism," and "the logic of violence, exploitation, and selfishness."

That pretty well nails it. What he failed to add, however, and this he might well have anticipated, was that among the sins is a willful obliviousness to any criticism that goes to the heart of a system that has made many rich beyond the dreams of kings. The encyclical was cheered by some leftists and a few liberals, more or less ignored by the climate-change deniers, and went without comment whatsoever by the capitalist powers-that-be. The old interfering bleeding-heart can say what he wants to say, but it's going to be business as usual.

Until, of course, the oceans rise fifteen feet and farmlands go dry.

All in all, given such sinful hubris, it seems likely that the accumulated ecological disasters of the modern industrial nations will easily surpass those of Rome and Teotihuacan. An increasing number of scientific voices have gone so far as to echo the sober thoughts of G. Evelyn Hutchinson, who wrote in *Scientific American* as long ago as 1970 that things have come to the point where it is possible "that the length of life of the biosphere as an inhabitable region is to be measured in a matter of decades rather than thousands of millions of years," and then added: "It would not seem unlikely that we are approaching a crisis that is comparable to the one that occurred when free oxygen began to accumulate in the atmosphere."

It begins to appear that what separates the human animal from the lower orders is not a sense of humor or the ability to blush (although it is clear enough why it is that we had especial need to develop both of those), but rather a fully developed conceit, the conceit that declares us to be the rulers and shapers of the world and all its workings. Of course we could continue to indulge that conceit in a continuing and relentless battle with nature, for indeed we are armed with a considerable array of most effective technology and may be able to destroy many of the most basic elements of nature. But, as Fritz Schumacher used to say, if we win that battle we will be on the losing side.

It is perhaps wiser to contemplate a contrary course, the course of establishing a society based upon ecological harmony. Such a course is uncharted, to be sure, and until recently few have attempted to determine just what might be the limits of an ecologically balanced world. But guided by the principle of the human scale and the matrix of the human form, I think it is possible to draw the rough outlines of what it must look like. Specifically, we might be able to determine the sort of technology that an ecological society would require; the limits at which an ecological society would construct its buildings, its communities, its cities; the kinds of social functions—energy, transportation, education, and the like—an ecological society would require and the scale at which they would be best supplied. Such is the enterprise upon which this section embarks.

In 1946, flush with its success in winning a war, Britain decided it could solve at least part of its domestic problems with the same kind of technological development and administrative concentration that had defeated the Germans. With guidance from the multimillion-dollar United Africa Company and upon the advice of its best technical minds, it established the British Overseas Food Corporation and proceeded on a massive plan for growing groundnuts (peanuts) in the East African territory of Tanganyika. And thus began one of the greatest ecological follies of the twentieth century.

Postwar Britain suffered from a shortage of cooking oil—essential for fish-and-chips, among other things—and it seemed natural enough to envision planting millions of acres of some tropical colony with the kind of crop that could supply such oil. The managing director of the United Africa Company, flying over the bare red-dirt scrubland of Tanganyika one day in 1946, figured that he had found the perfect spot, and he persuaded the British government to send out a team of experts to survey the area. The Wakefield Mission spent nine weeks in the field, testing the soil, checking rainfall charts, talking to local British administrators, and eventually it issued an enthusiastic report recommending the clearing of 3.2 million acres, proposing the planting of groundnuts within two years, and forecasting a harvest of at least 600,000 tons by 1951. The British government welcomed the scheme, allocated an initial $60 million, and dispatched 2,000 technicians to oversee 30,000 Africans on the job. No one doubted that a nation that could build the "Pluto" pipeline across the English Channel under fire, or checkmate the Japanese army throughout Asia, could tame the soils of Africa for the tables of Britain.

Nature is not so easily trifled with.

Hundreds of tons of earthmoving equipment were shipped into Tanganyika, and the huge operation of clearing the brush began. But the scrub roots and baobab trees were so tough and tenacious that they frequently broke the plows and blades used to clear them; that, coupled with the punishing climate, put at least three-quarters of the equipment out of order in the first three years. Then after the roots were removed, the soil, without anything to bind it, began to fall apart and turn to dust, rolling up in great clouds of dirt as the bulldozers moved through and dissipating the thin layers of fertile topsoil over the countryside. In some places the heavy treads of the earthmovers created tracks and gulleys in the fields that filled with water when the rains came, hastening the erosion further; in other places the equipment packed down the earth so solidly that it could not be worked or planted.

And after the scrub cover was cleared, the soil simply baked and withered in the African sun, its nutrients slowly drying up. One common weed that was eradicated early in the operation was later found to have been crucial for mobilizing the soil phosphates, without which the soil could not be healthy. The rainfall did not come as neatly as the charts had predicted: during the rainy season the soil, which turned out to have an unexpectedly high clay content, became sticky and unworkable, and during the dry season it cracked and shrank, imprisoning and choking off the roots of the groundnuts that did manage to get planted.

It was about that time that someone in the British Food Corporation pointed out that it was actually *West* Africa, a far different climatic area, that had been successful for many decades in groundnut production.

Shortly after the first crops were planted, on an inevitably reduced scale, late in 1948, the planners of the groundnut scheme began to worry about the overdependence on a single crop, the creation of an unstable "monoculture" unhealthy to any agricultural area. So they tried American soybeans, tobacco, cotton, even sorghum: none of it took. Finally, they hit upon sunflowers, which grow practically anywhere and also produce a valuable oil. It was after planting acres of them, however, that they realized something was wrong: almost all of the bees necessary to pollinate the flowers had been driven away when the brush was cleared two years earlier. So at great expense they shipped out appropriate sunflower bees from Britain and Italy, only to discover that many of them could not survive in the harsh new ecosystem of East Africa. At least a third of the original sunflower crop had to be scrapped.

In 1954 the Great Groundnut Scheme was at last abandoned, a sorry tale of human hubris come full circle. Some 300,000 acres had been cleared by then, less than a tenth of what had been envisioned. Production amounted to about 9,000 tons a year, compared with the 600,000 tons that had been planned for. Total costs came to at least $80 million, about $1.6 million for every ton produced—roughly a dollar a peanut. It was as clear as any proof could be of the faultiness of the assumption, in the words of the great British Africanist Lord Hailey, "that mechanization would overcome the climatic and other defects of the notoriously unsuitable area." Or, as British scientist Ritchie Calder was later to remark, it was "a warning of the things you cannot do to nature and get away with." And he added, in a most telling comment: "On a small scale it would have been a matter for adjustment; on a large scale it was a chronic crisis."

Human–Scale Technology

T here is no such thing as a society without technology. *Homo erectus* and *Homo sapiens* for nearly two million years had the hand-axe, a small, simple, beautiful, and extremely useful tool that could butcher animal carcasses, slice off the meat, and crack open the bone for the nutritious marrow. (The fact that it remained essentially unchanged for all this time suggests that, unlike our own, these societies had a settled social order, were highly cohesive and cooperative, and did not feel any individualistic need to innovate, change for the sake of change.)

The question is not of eliminating technology but of deciding what kind of technology should prevail, which of society's values should it express. For there is no such thing as neutral technology—rather it comes with an inevitable logic, bearing the purposes and priorities of the economic and political systems that spawn it. Thus a reporter for *Automation* at the dawn of the computer age could praise a computer system as "significant" because it assures that "decision-making" is "removed from the operator [and] gives maximum control of the machine to management"—a system, that is, that turns the user into a soulless factotum without any power and assures that management retains power to itself, quite what our manufacturing world desires.

A violent empire guided by the principles of capitalism will surely develop technologies that heedlessly wrench resources from the earth in service to a few corporate and financial interests that are protected and nurtured by the political systems that they have commandeered to their ends. It seems fairly clear by now, as we have seen, that these technologies—more powerful and more rapacious than the world has ever known—will end by extracting and consuming so much of those resources, so altering the systems of atmospheric balance and oceanic tolerances, that it will diminish or destroy most of the surface and many of the marine species within the near future. These technologies have been developed to permit the human species to devote itself to every deadly sin but sloth, particularly pride, and it has done so with great skill, ingenuity, and speed. An alternative technology is clearly necessary, one based upon the human scale, in the sense both of being designed for and controlled by the individual and of being harmonious with the individual's role in the ecosphere.

——————

In an important but generally unnoticed phenomenon, just such a movement has arisen in the last fifty years, starting only in the 1960s and still evolving today, and it has created, tested, and proven an amazing array of soft technologies. Called variously "appropriate," "green," "intermediate," or "alternative," it satisfies the basic criteria of a human-scale technology as set out by the wise Kentucky essayist Wendell Berry in the 1980s: a new tool, he says, should be cheaper, smaller, and better than the one it replaces, should use less energy (and that renewable), be repairable, come from a small local shop, and "should not replace or disrupt anything good that already exists, and this includes family and community relationships." To which need be added only two other crucial standards—that those family and community relationships embrace all the other species, plants and animals alike, and the living ecosystems on which they depend, and that they be considered, as the Irokwa nation has expressed it, with the interest of the next seven generations in mind.

There is one other good way of assessing human-scale technology, as expressed in a sage axiom of the British philosopher Herbert Read: "Only a people serving an apprenticeship to nature can be trusted with machines." Far from serving an apprenticeship, modern industrial society works to enslave nature, for the benefit of humanity (or some small part of it), and regards mastery over it as ordained.

Since technology is generally, by its very essence, artificial—that is to say, not natural, a human construct not otherwise found in nature—it tends to distance humans from their environment and set them in opposition to it. "The artificial world," says Jacques Ellul, the French philosopher, is "radically different from the natural world," with "different imperatives, different directives, and different laws" such that it "destroys, eliminates, or subordinates the natural world." In order to avoid the catastrophe that this has brought us to, it is necessary to embed technology with a due regard for the natural world, with a sense of humans as a species and the individual as an animal, needing its elements for successful survival, including healthy land and air, decent food and shelter, intact communities and nurturing families. Only then, suggests Read, can we start monkeying around with artifacts.

––––––––––

Most of the technology along these precepts has already been developed over the last fifty years. It is now possible to find instruction in multiple books and pamphlets and magazines on—to take just a few—how to build underground houses and aquaculture greenhouses, how to design windmills and solar-powered bicycles, how to grow food by organic, hydroponic, or French-intensive methods, how to establish urban-homesteading projects and eco-villages, how to set up land trusts, food co-ops, and self-examination clinics, and how to construct practically anything you want out of earth, adobe, canvas, wood, stone, hemp, skins, logs, bamboo, or pneumatic balloons. And all of this creativity has been achieved in the face of the dominant, computer-driven technology, which argues that it has some serious durability and sufficiently ardent, widespread support.

Human-scale technology is not some dream or illusion: it exists. And that makes the present age unique. We now know that it is possible to achieve a technology for a wide range of human actions and still be kept within human dimensions and human control, without doing violence to the planet's resources or ecosystems. We are on the brink of a truly alternative technological paradigm and can enter if we but choose to.

––––––––––

One further point. It should be obvious that there is no necessary contradiction between sophisticated technology and human-scale technology. Rational technologies of the future would not *discard* everything about contemporary systems but rather *evolve* from them, leaving aside the dangerous and destructive aspects, absorbing the humanistic and communitarian ones. Obviously there is much in current high technology that is anti-human and brutalizing, but there is also part of it that, however it has managed to slip in, is potentially liberating. In fact in the last twenty years or so there has been a strong trend in the direction of smaller and more decentralized operations: miniaturization has brought about the silicon chip and the proliferation of sophisticated machines available to any home or office; the creation of machines that perform a multiplicity of functions, allowing a wide range of products to be built in a single plant, has opened the way for communities to have an increasing number of goods manufactured locally; and the development of solar energy has pointed the way to the time, not far off, when we can have a completely localized power source no longer dependent on centralized plants.

In an age of high authoritarianism and bureaucratic control in both governmental and corporate realms, the dominant technology tends to reinforce those characteristics—ours is not an age of the assembly line and the nuclear plant by accident. Nonetheless, it must be recognized that there are always many other technological variations of roughly equal sophistication that are created but *not* developed, that lie ignored at the patent office or unfinished in the backyard because there are no special reasons for the dominant system to pick them up.

For example, sometime before the birth of Christ, Hero of Alexandria designed (and probably built) a steam engine: a fire created boiling water in a cauldron and the steam from it was sent along a tube into a hollow metal ball; two other tubes on opposite sides of the ball expelled the steam, forcing the ball to turn steadily and creating motion that could then be harnessed. The trouble was that neither the rulers of Alexandria nor any other powers in the Mediterranean world had any particular need for such a device, since the muscle power of slaves seemed perfectly adequate and the economic advantages of such a machine were quite unappreciated. It was not until the eighteenth century, in an England of entrepreneurial capitalism, where slavery was outlawed and cheap labor unreliable, that the virtues of steam power were sufficiently appreciated to enlist whole ranks of inventors and investors, many of whom set about unknowingly reinventing Hero's machine.

Or again. By the late eighteenth century there were two kinds of machines capable of sophisticated textile production in England. One was a cottage-based, one-person machine built around the spinning jenny, perfected as early as the 1760s; the other was a factory-based, steam-driven machine based upon the Watts engine and the Arkwright frame, introduced in the 1770s. The choice of which machine was to survive and proliferate was made not upon the merits of the machines themselves nor upon any technological grounds at all but upon the wishes of the dominant political and economic sectors of English society at the time. The cottage-centered machines, ingenious though they were, did not permit textile merchants the same kind of control over the workforce nor the same regularity of production as did the factory-based machines. Gradually, therefore, they were eliminated, their manufacturers squeezed by being denied raw materials and financing, their operators suppressed by laws that, on various pretexts, made home production illegal. It is interesting that it was against this technological tyranny that the Luddites in the early nineteenth century actually acted: they were not engaged in the destruction of all machines, as they are usually blamed for, but only those factory-centered machines that threatened to destroy their cottage-based textile industry.

In other words, each politico-economic system selects out of the available range of artifacts those that fit in best with its own particular ends. In our own time, we have seen the great development of machinery that displaces labor (and hence does away with labor problems), but there is a vast array of machinery, as the alternative technologists have proved, that is of equal sophistication and effectiveness but is labor-intensive. A human-scale system would select and develop the latter kinds of machinery, at no especial sacrifice in efficiency but with considerable enhancement of individual worth and ecological well-being.

———————

One day in 1973, Ridgway Banks, then 39, a backyard inventor and amateur musician employed as a technician at the Lawrence Laboratories in Berkeley, came across a metal called nitinol that he discovered to have almost magical properties. A blend of nickel and titanium, nitinol, he found, was capable of changing its shape rapidly and contracting under heat and then springing quickly back to its original shape again when cooled—and then reverting to exactly the same contracted shape when reheated. This, Banks figured out, was exactly what he needed to make a practical steam engine run by solar power.

Working with a machinist colleague, Banks constructed a simple solar collector on a rooftop and used the hot water that it produced to fill up half of a small circular cylinder—about the size of a cookie tin—while the other half was filled with cold water. He then constructed a flywheel holding a series of nitinol-wire loops and set it into the cylinder. Because the nitinol loops contracted powerfully and straightened out as they went through the hot water—with a force somewhere around 67,000 pounds per square inch—they were able to turn the flywheel, and then because they quickly assumed their original shape in the cold-water bath they were able to exert their force again when they hit the hot-water side. The wheel thus could run continually, providing energy of up to about 70 RPM and capable of generating about a half a watt of electricity.

The first test run was on August 8, 1973. Five years and tens of millions of cycles later the machine was still running, without adjustment or hitch, with no sign of fatigue or failure—and even, for some unknown reason, running 50 percent faster than it had originally. It was by any measure a success: simple, sophisticated, effective, safe, cheap, nonpolluting, small-scale, easy to make, operated by renewable energy, and built of simple materials (both nickel and titanium, though nonrenewable, are fairly abundant). Human-scale technology at its best. Banks got a patent for it in 1984.

And the reason you've never heard of the Banks machine is that nobody is interested in developing it. The National Science Foundation put $113,000 into trying to develop a huge version of the machine and then gave up when the prototype didn't work properly; no one else, neither corporate nor military nor governmental, has expressed any interest at all. But the technology is proven and it is possible to find several working model versions on the internet as of 2015. And his daughter Zoe produced a short video on Banks, easily available, called *The Individualist*, which won the Audience Award for best documentary at the San Francisco DocFest in 2010.

One of Banks's friends, Bob Trupin, also a nitinol enthusiast, was quoted several years ago in *CoEvolution Quarterly* summing up, with a touch of bitterness, the fate of the Banks engine:

> *Isn't it amazing? There's no money in this country, despite all the talk about the energy crisis, for a project that could end our dependency on oil. They don't intend to scrap any of their existing technology. And there's no way for the big utility companies to cash in on nitinol. It lends itself to a small rooftop unit where the sun can heat up a pan of water.*
>
> *You look at this wire and you see an engine that's* small. *I guess small is what they really hate. Only big is good.*

But the engine, like hundreds and hundreds of other kinds of alternative hardware, is *there*, and probably still spinning as of this moment. Should we choose to want it.

We Shape Our Buildings

"We shape our buildings," Winston Churchill is often quoted as having said, "thereafter our buildings shape us." He was talking about the rebuilding of the House of Commons, which had been damaged during World War II, and he was pointing out the way that the special oblong character of the Commons room had naturally led to a system of two distinct and oppositional political parties, both directed by a row of leaders rather than a single head, and—he might have added—whose debates and electoral styles were characterized by confrontation and challenge rather than cooperation and harmony. (A similar point might be made about the chambers of the US Congress, though in that case the semicircular rooms and radiating aisles led to blurred lines of distinction between parties, a lack of face-to-face debate, a sense of spectatorship as in a theater, and individualistic rather than communal political styles.) But his remark applies with equal force to all buildings, everywhere, indeed to all built environments of any kind: one way or another they affect us, the good ones with pleasure and serenity, the bad ones with stress and disquiet.

Other examples make the same point.

- Green buildings, which are increasingly common now, especially those LEED (Leadership in Energy and Environmental Design) certified, bring more sunlight to the workplace, regularly proved to increase health, productivity, and "psychological and physical well-being," as one study in 2010 put it, with declining rates of turnover and absenteeism, and of course they save on energy costs.
- One group of researchers examined a graduate student apartment project at MIT—a series of large U-shaped courts, the open end

facing the street—and found that the people who lived at the upper points of the U, with their front doors facing the street, had on average half as many friends as those living within the court itself—not, obviously, because those living within the court were more gregarious and charming but simply because they lived in a more communal setting. (As sociologist William Whyte once wrote, "The court, like the double bed, enforces intimacy.")

- A team in St. Louis spent three years interviewing residents of the infamous Pruitt-Igoe housing project and concluded that the chief reason for the obvious social collapse there—crime, vandalism, litter, property destruction, hostility among residents, isolation, anomie—was that the buildings were designed without any semi-public places either inside or out, where small groups of neighbors could gather informally and accidentally during the course of their daily activities. Never getting together with others, residents retreated into their own apartments and did not evolve the kinds of small networks that develop in normal neighborhoods, even slum neighborhoods, to provide social cohesion and exert social control. No wonder it was demolished in the 1970s, only two decades after it had been built.

- Another study showed that men living in large open army barracks were able to identify, and usually selected for friendship, a far wider group of men than those living in walled-off, cubicle-style barracks; and though the cubicle soldiers tended to develop more intense and cohesive groups, they also were more likely to have disruptive fights with their companions.

Daily experience provides other examples. Airport waiting rooms, designed always with seats in long rows and with wide aisles between them, effectively prohibit any conversations except those between people sitting right next to one another—and it's none too easy for them since the seats don't move for face-to-face contact. Office buildings with enormous doors and archways, leading into tabernacular lobbies, succeed, perhaps not accidentally, in creating a sense of insignificance and powerlessness among the people herded there. Boardrooms that are long and rectangular, with elongated tables and space for a single individual at the head, discourage discussion and open decision making, while those ad-agency "creativity" rooms with circular tables and muted furnishings do in fact encourage give-and-take (for whatever pernicious ends) and collective judgments. Apartment blocks built in small clusters, two to three stories high and enclosing comfortable courtyards, create what Oscar Newman has called "defensible space," in which it has been shown that residents naturally identify with, supervise, and protect their own areas and neighbors. Government buildings in Washington, massive and hulking ponderosities, dwarf those who work within them: "They are designed," as *New York Times* columnist Russell Baker once pointed out, "to make man feel negligible, to intimidate him, to overwhelm him with evidence that he is a cipher, a trivial nuisance in the great institutional scheme of things," perhaps not too healthy a condition for those who theoretically guide our lives.

Now if we were to operate on the Churchillian principle, it would seem logical to construct our buildings so as to discourage certain kinds of behavior, and to stimulate other kinds. One may not be able to change human nature, exactly, but one might well be able to bring out its better side; as C. M. Deasy has put it in his provocative *Design for Human Affairs*, "The chances of redesigning a checkout line to make line-jumping impossible are much better than the chance of reforming pushy people in the world." (As a matter of fact, a few supermarkets have had success operating with a single feeder-line system such as that used in larger banks.) What it would take is simply an appreciation of the effect of buildings on people—what *their* lifetimes do to *our* lifetimes—and the creation of architecture that would enhance the activities and ennoble the sensibilities of the people who actually would be using them. It would take the conscious design of buildings to the human scale.

The idea of "human scale" is an old one in architecture, perhaps primordially old. We know that most pre-literate tribes build homes wittingly with the size of the human form and the activities of the human family in mind, and some tribes, like the Dogon of West Africa, according to anthropologist Daryll Forde, go so far as to build their huts in deliberate imitation of the human body. In the towns and cities of most pre-Hellenic civilizations—as we know from the archaeological remains of such cities as Catal Hiiyiik in Turkey and Mohenjo-Daro in India—buildings generally

103

were quite small and houses were divided according to family and social functions; even the few larger structures, such as the huge community center and public bath in Mohenjo-Daro, were well within the limits of what we would feel to be a human *public* scale. (There were of course exceptions—the Pyramids, the Tower of Babel, the temple at Eridu in Mesopotamia—but they were rare and always occurred in those empires that purposefully shunned the human scale and sought to create larger-than-life monuments.) With the Greeks particularly, the human body was taken as the central module by which all the built environment was measured—as one can see today in the Parthenon, in the buildings at Delphi, the temple at Bassae, the theater of Dionysus in Athens, indeed, one way or another, in practically all the known buildings of that civilization: "Man," as Protagoras often said, "is the measure of all things." And if the Romans for the most part ignored concepts of human scale in their major works—not to mention in the eight- and ten-story apartment buildings they put up in downtown Rome during its period of "grandeur"—it was not for want of being instructed: the first-century-BC-architect Vitruvius showed time and again how both individual buildings and public squares ought to be designed within the specific limits of normal human sight and mobility. Medieval European cities grew up with conscious human limits—houses of no more than three or four stories, regular public spaces throughout for markets and celebrations, the whole kept by walls and fortifications within an area whose boundaries could be easily walked in half a day; a surviving print of the layout of the city of Bern, for example, shows what must have been a conscious imitation of the human form, with a main cathedral and fortified bridge at the head, radiating arm-like stretches of parks, the market and public square in the genital region, and buttressed fortifications splayed out like feet at the farthest end. And then with the Renaissance, when the human body was studied and celebrated as perhaps never before in history, architects built consistently in imitation of the figure, following such maxims as Luca Pacioli's, in his *De Divina Proportione*, "From the human body derive all measures and their denominations and in it is to be found all and every ratio and proportion by which God reveals the innermost secrets of nature"; one may still see it in the countless Christian churches built across Europe from the fourteenth century on, laid out deliberately in imitation of the body of Christ, sometimes with details in the apse to mimic mouth and eyes.

But the idea of human scale began to be lost somewhere in the early industrial era, around the time, not coincidentally, of the beginnings of the nation-state. With the rise of government-sanctioned science and the solidification of architecture into royal academies in the eighteenth-century "Enlightenment," the idea of objective, "scientific" rules came to supersede subjective, "humanistic" ones; this is when we get long, abstract building shapes like Wren's Naval College at Greenwich, and absurdly rectangular formal gardens like those of Le Notre's Tuileries in Paris. Then with the rise of industrialism and the triumph of engineering in the nineteenth century, mechanical considerations came to outweigh visual and aesthetic ones and the "utility" of a building became its prime consideration; hence the look of those red-brick factory towns in industrial New England and of many squat and squalid prison and military installations still standing today. Ultimately, with the rise of technological prowess and modern architecture in the twentieth century, the buildings took on a form of their own, quite unrelated to human or even social perceptions, where the objects and buildings are to let the materials simply perform to their utmost—thus the triumph of steel in the Seagram Building, of glass in Lever House, of cement in the Guggenheim Museum, and so on—and to let technology provide, God help us, "a machine to live in."*

What happened in this long process, over nearly three centuries, was that gradually the *user* of the buildings was forgotten: the human scale was discarded. Yes, there was continual talk about it—hardly any great architects of this century have failed to declare their fealty to it—but usually they paid homage the way Mies van der Rohe did when he designed the Illinois Institute of Technology: he claimed he was building to the human scale because his windows were of human height, but in fact he put those windows in unappetizing rows along long, abstract boxes that look most like machine-made toys for giants, a perfect celebration not of the human form but the geometric. As Italian architect Bruno Zevi has noted, that is *not* what human scale means: "Scale means dimension with respect to man's visual apprehension, scale means dimension with respect

---

* The words are Le Corbusier's, as were many of the deeds: such anti-human machines may be seen in his Unite d'Habitation in Marseilles and in his plan for the ideal city, the Ville Radieuse.

to man's physical size." And he adds, "In the last hundred years, however, enormous crimes have been perpetrated against it."

In fact, the standard modern building, particularly the downtown office block, is *scaleless*—literally without any sense of human dimensions or perceptions either in its size, volume, proportions, or relations. Form follows function—but it is *material*, not human, function. Many years ago *Progressive Architecture* magazine devoted a whole issue to the problem of scalelessness as "the New Scale of Today" and the danger that "scaleless space seems to be on the increase":

> *What does today's scale say about our age? Will future historians reveal that the 20th century, through its approach to scale, merely expressed the depressing inconsequentiality of the individual vis-a-vis the collective activity of society—merely the "scalelessness" of man himself within the vast megalopolitan complexes and the even vaster outer space?*

The answer is almost certainly: yes. Those who are shaping our buildings seem to care little for the humans who inhabit them.

––––––––––

But what would human scale actually mean in contemporary building, anyway? Is there any consistent measure by which a society could plan its buildings so as not only to eliminate the terrible dehumanizing effect of scalelessness but actually to enrich and humanize those who experience them?

I suggest there is, and moreover, that modern science gives us the way to determine it.

In the last twenty years or so there has grown up a group of schools devoted to measuring the human body and its actions, working in conscious opposition to the dominant industrial aesthetic. They take different names, depending more or less on the disciplines their adherents come from—ergonomics, anthropometries, sociometrics, human engineering, biomechanics, and the like—but what they have in common is the goal of scientifically discovering the way the human body actually functions and then designing tools, machines, appliances, furniture, living spaces, and workplaces to match.

Take the work of Alexander Kira, for example, a professor at Cornell University and one of the pioneers in ergonomic research. In 1966 he published a study called, forthrightly, *The Bathroom*, which was an exhaustive examination of the way people actually perform their human functions and the way most bathroom equipment is woefully mis-designed to serve them. For urination, for instance, he studied the role and workings of the kidneys, the distinctive features of the female and male anatomies, and the color, smell, and qualities of urine, and he then made empirical investigations of such things as stance, splash, noise, velocity of flow, target, and the like. He eventually concluded—as we all would expect—that the present Western toilet is totally inadequate, particularly for the male, in fact an outstanding example of an instrument in everyday use around the world designed entirely without sensible consideration of how people would actually use it. Kira then went on to design and build an improvement, a simple fold-down unit much like a restroom urinal, exactly 24 inches above the floor, with an 8-inch opening and an elongated funnel that fits into the regular toilet bowl below and can be flipped back out of sight when not in use; it allows a man to relieve himself comfortably, easily, without embarrassing noise or unsanitary splash. The solution wasn't difficult, once the problem had been properly posed, but it had just never been studied that way before, with the human function, the human form, coming first.

Another important ergonomic designer, Niels Diffrient, has limned the problem precisely: "There is not a comparable data bank for people in their man-made environment," he says, "as there is on the performance of mechanisms and their related systems." And yet, "without comparable data on people's feelings, physical and emotional, as there is for machines to meet quantitative performance, the result is bound to be a continuously degrading quality of life." Much of the problem, he feels, is that giantism has tended to eclipse humanism: "The macro-scale tendency in technology has seriously affected design. It has spawned large-scale planning efforts far beyond anyone's comprehension." And in buildings this has meant "a large segment of design activity in which architecture is not so much the creation of humane spaces as it is the production of architectonic sculpture."

It is extraordinary that such voices remain so few and so often ignored. After more than a decade now of solid work in these new schools and their absolutely incontrovertible findings about human functions, most of their research is shamefully neglected or at best made use of by a few industrial designers seeking better knobs for windshield wipers. Yet it is here that we can find invaluable scientific evidence of the kind of characteristics a successful human-scale structure might possess and the kind of architecture a rational society might promote.

We may begin with the human eye. The visual effect of a building is, after all, the first, and always the most indelible, whatever other sensory impressions may later accrue; the eye, if not precisely the window of the soul, may still be regarded as the gateway of the brain and the organ from which our most basic mental and emotional comprehension derives. Various scientific studies of the eye have been undertaken over the years, though remarkably the first complete ergonomic studies were not carried out until Henry Dreyfuss, a New York industrial designer, set his studio to the task in the early 1960s. Their studies, and later refinements by the Dreyfuss team, have been published as a series of detailed charts under the apt title of *Humanscale*, and have determined with some precision how the eye really functions:

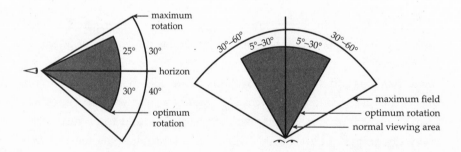

Now let us apply this to architecture. The best way to view a building is in its entirety, of course: as Aristotle among others has noted, it is always most satisfactory to see any object whole, at a single glance, so that its unity can be understood. If the maximum eye rotation above the horizon is 30 degrees, and the optimum is 25 degrees, as Dreyfuss's studies indicate, then the ideal vertical viewing angle should be something around 27 degrees. Now by a neat turn of trigonometry, this is exactly the angle established when you stand twice as far away from an object as it is tall, and the experience of centuries has confirmed that this is in fact a successful ratio for viewing both the details and the totality of any object. Thus to have a complete view of an ordinary two-story house at a single glance without moving your head, you would have to stand at a distance twice its height. Assuming 13 feet for each story and half of that for the pitch of the roof, it would then be necessary to stand some 52 feet away, thusly:

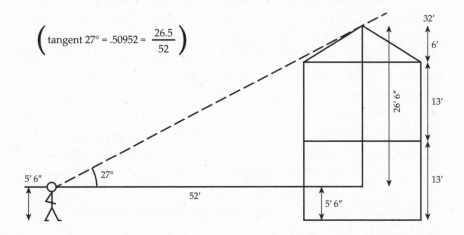

$$\left(\text{tangent } 27° = .50952 = \frac{26.5}{52} \right)$$

And that is why the most successful residential streets, those that satisfy in some indefinite way as you walk or drive along them, are those with houses set back from the street about 50 feet or so; farther than that and the buildings tend to get lost in the background, nearer than that and they give a sense of crowding, of looming.

And thus the human-scale module for any individual building.

In applying this scale to the design of cities, several further calculations based on the human form are necessary. Here we may be guided by a most extraordinary book that is fully as scientific as the modern ergonometric studies, but in fact was written a century ago, by a German architect we know only as H. Maertens. It says something about our mechanistic age that although his work has been influential for a number of later city planners—particularly Werner Hegemann and Elbert Peets in their 1922 study, *The American Vitruvius*, and Hans Blumenfeld in his brilliant *The Modern Metropolis*—the original remains virtually unknown and, as far as I can tell, seldom read and never translated.

Maertens began with the clever assumption that the maximum desirable vista for most urban life is that at which one person can recognize another. He then determined that the nasal bone was the smallest feature of the human face from which a person could be recognized, and he calculated the average nasal bone width to be about a quarter of an inch. From physiological optics he discovered that an object cannot be seen at a distance greater than 3,450 times its size—which is when the angle of vision is less than a minute—and he therefore concluded that a nasal bone could not be seen at any distance beyond 3,450 × ¼ inch = 862.5 inches = 71.875 feet. The basic module, then, for recognition and thus for any human-scale city would be roughly 72 feet; most particularly, that would be the maximum street width because that would be the maximum at which one person could recognize another across the street. In addition, Maertens determined that the maximum distance at which a facial expression could be easily read is about 48 feet (try it yourself; you'll see that it's about right) and therefore that would be the module for the ideal street width in those parts of a city, residential districts for example, where that kind of intimacy and community cohesion would be desirable.

Using the 27-degree formula along with Maertens's standards, we can then calculate the optimum heights for urban buildings. A street width of 72 feet provides a maximum building height of about 42 feet (tan. 27° × 72'= 36'8¼" + 5'6" = 42.2'), or somewhere around three stories; a street 48 feet wide would allow building heights of about 30 feet (tan. 27° × 48' = 24'5" + 5'6" = 30'), or somewhere between two and three stories tall. Interestingly, these are the heights that even now we recognize as being the "normal" size for urban dwellings and shops except in the most built-up parts of our city centers, the size that feels most natural and comfortable; just a couple of miles away from the enormous spires of Manhattan, this is in fact the size of most sections of the so-called outer boroughs. Interestingly, too, these are the heights that allow us to observe the tops of trees over the roofs, providing that touch of nature that always seems so satisfying in the middle of a city, so necessary even to the most cement-hardened urbanite.

Of course buildings of such heights seem unusually small when we compare them with the soaring achievements of contemporary skyscrapers. And yet, when we reflect on the genuinely most satisfactory parts of the cities we have seen, they tend to be those observing something like that scale. It would seem to be no accident that the traditionally most durable urban neighborhoods in virtually every city have been those with buildings at this general height: most of Greenwich Village and Brooklyn Heights in New York, the French Quarter in New Orleans, Society Hill in Philadelphia, Telegraph Hill in San Francisco, Georgetown in Washington, Chelsea in London, Montmartre in Paris, Trastevere in Rome, Gamla Stan in Stockholm. At this height, it seems, residents and visitors alike recognize something special about an area, they tend to feel it is containable, knowable, somehow embraceable, and they feel themselves an organic part of it. And in almost all of the successful medieval cities, the crucibles in which our very concepts of urbanity were formed, both business and residential buildings tended to be three or four stories tall—partly, of course, because they were built before the invention of the elevator, but also because they apparently were felt to work most harmoniously at this scale. That scale is observable still today in a number of European cities: Tubingen, whose market buildings date from the fifteenth century and are generally four, occasionally five, stories; Oxford, where both college and city buildings from the fourteenth century onward tend to be two or three stories, interspersed with a few frilly six- and eight-story Gothic towers; Amsterdam, where certain older parts of the city, like the sixteenth-century Beguines section, show an intimate neighborhood scale, with all buildings at two or three stories; most of those traditional English villages, like the Cotswold villages whose streets are still lined with two- and three-story homes and shops; and the wonderfully preserved Dutch city of Naarden, still today very much as it was in the late medieval period, which has almost no structures over three stories except the central cathedral and where you can walk down the streets and easily view the handsome, solid buildings and still see the leafy green tops of the trees beyond, the whole thing giving a feeling of such comeliness and serenity that it is astonishing to believe that you are in the twenty-first century.

One further dimension of the human-scale city can be obtained by extending Maertens's ideas and considering the distance at which it is possible to distinguish the general outlines, clothes, sex, age, and gait of a person, which experience shows to be somewhere around 450 feet; this is the distance, too, ergonomic studies show, at which the basic colors can be easily distinguished. Using that module, one might then derive the optimum lengths for city blocks, for open spaces, for parks and malls and plazas.

Again, it comes as no surprise to find that this measure has indeed been used throughout much of history for many of the most successful public spaces: the maximum visual distance of the Acropolis, measured as the eye takes it in from the Propylaea to the farthest corner of the Parthenon, is about 465 feet and the maximum width is about 430 feet; the marvelous oval in front of St. Peter's in Rome is 430 feet wide; the Place Vendome in Paris and Amalienborg Square in Copenhagen both have dimensions of 450 feet; the axis of the Imperial City in Peking, though it actually stretches for more than 8,300 feet, has no unbroken vista longer than 500 feet; and the maximum length of the Piazza San Marco, perhaps the most delightful plaza in a nation of extraordinary plazas, is 425 feet. New York City offers another telling example of public spaces: the blocks on the West Side of Manhattan, which as Jane Jacobs points out do not work well either aesthetically or socially, are about 800 feet long, while those on the East Side, which are far more effective and inviting, range from 400 to 420 feet in length. And one always gets a sense of vague discomfort in those urban spaces that exceed this optimum distance by much—as with the mall in Washington, DC, which stretches for more than 10,000 feet with only the slim Washington Monument to break it up; the Capitol, at the end of the mall, which is supposed to be a grand and important monument at its imposing height of 307 feet, tends to get lost in the surrounding background. Such similar excesses of space also destroy the vistas of the Arc de Triomphe in Paris, the Assembly building in Le Corbusier's Chandigarh, the main plaza of Brasilia, Independence Hall in Philadelphia, the Civic Center in San Francisco, almost all suburban shopping centers, and many of the newer downtown shopping malls. Hans Blumenfeld, who is both an architect and a city planner, and has designed buildings all over the world, has concluded: "There appears to be a definite upper limit to the size of a plaza, as to the length of a street, which can convey a strong spatial experience," beyond which "they can no longer be related to the human being: their scale is no longer 'superhuman' but colossal and inhuman." And he adds, "The measure of approximately 450 feet appears rather frequently in the most successful plazas."

Using this 450-foot module, by the way, suggests the optimum limit for the kinds of buildings that would ring such public spaces. To be taken in whole from the farthest side of a plaza of that length at an angle of 27 degrees, a building would have to be no higher than about 225 feet, or fifteen to twenty stories, a common and agreeable height for works meant as public monuments such as churches or civic centers; actually, following precepts common in public spaces since the Renaissance that the tallest buildings should be about a third of the longest dimension of a plaza, the optimum height might be closer to 150 feet, or ten to fifteen stories. In either case, one would avoid such urban design disasters as the Empire State Building, the World Trade Center, the Sears Tower in Chicago, the U.S. Steel Tower in Pittsburgh, the Transamerica pyramid in San Francisco—indeed, one could say almost all contemporary skyscrapers—which are built so far in excess of the spaces they are set in that, incredible as it may seem, it is actually impossible to find *any* point from which they can be viewed whole. (To view the World Trade Center in its entirety, for example, before it was destroyed in 2001, it would have been necessary to stand at a point roughly 2,700 feet—more than half a mile—away, and at that distance, unless you stood somewhere in the middle of the Hudson River, most of your visual field would be taken up with dozens of other intervening buildings.)

———

There is, however, something more to the human mode in architecture than just the height of buildings, as crucial—as fundamental—as that is. Those buildings that in some way or other relate to the human observer, that allow the person to feel a part of the building and to participate in its forms and spaces, also have other design elements.

It is extraordinary that, despite the years of talk in architectural circles about human scale, there is so very little written about these design elements and how they might operate, and only slightly less extraordinary that there is so little actual construction of them in the real world. Architecture still tends to be an abstract art, or at most a sculptural one, divorced in its inception as in its drafting from the people it will house. Professors Kent C. Bloomer and Charles W. Moore, in their cogent and most perceptive *Body, Memory, and Architecture*, put it this way: "The human body, which is our most fundamental three-dimensional possession, has not itself become a central concern in the understanding of architectural form." Yet obviously it is those elements that mirror or mimic or measure the human form that have been incorporated into all kinds of structures from the time that people started conscious building: doors and windows crafted to actual human dimensions, stairs reflecting the human foot and pace,* columns imitating the standing figure, domes and arches curved like the top of a head, doorknobs or latches formed to match the human hand, ceilings and walls easily measured at a glance, and so on. "These forms have been important to humankind," Bloomer and Moore argue, "because they accommodated the initial human act of constructing a dwelling, the first tangible boundary beyond the body, they accommodated the act of inhabiting, and they called attention to the sources of human energy and to our place between heaven and earth."

Such elements are not accidental and frivolous, gingerbread decorations out of some fevered Victorian mind. They are the vital parts of a building by which we know what *it* is and where, what *we* are and where. The whole business of seeing, after all, the very way in which we distinguish between two images in the eyeball, is the ordering of scale—that is, comparing known dimensions with those in our vision—so that although two trees appear on the retina at the same height we perceive *that* tree back there is so big and *this* tree up here is only so big. "Such a scale is psychological," James J. Gibson has written in his pioneering *The Perception of the Visual World*, "it is something we carry around with us and it is implicit in the very process of perception." Where there is nothing to order this scale, we are always disoriented and confused—as in those rooms in psychology labs with chairs twice as big as normal and windows exaggeratedly small, or with those optical illusions where the perspective lines are distorted and the bigger object appears smaller. Gibson, among others, believes in fact that this sense of scale, of what he calls the "basic-orienting system," is one of the five basic senses, along with sight, sound, taste, smell, and tactile ("haptic") perception. Current psychological research would seem to support him, particularly that which suggests that a relatively clear *psycho-physical* orientation, a sense of being "centered" in the world, is vital in creating a healthy sense of oneself, and hence of one's relations to others; the modern "body-image" school even suggests, with considerable

---

* It is from the Italian word for "stair"—*scala*—that we derive the very word *scale*.

anthropological as well as psychological evidence, that there may be an innate, unconscious human desire to locate oneself in three-dimensional space within defined and knowable boundaries.

If so, then contemporary buildings, at least the agglomerations of them in larger American cities, fail abysmally. "Our cities are stacked up in layers," Bloomer and Moore write, "which bear testimony to the skills of the surveyor and the engineer in manipulating precise Cartesian coordinates, but they exhibit no connection with the body-centered, value-charged sense of space we started with [from childhood]." And their colleague, West Coast architect Robert Yudell, adds:

> Why are we not moved by our neighborhood shopping mall or city center office tower? Take, for example, a typical curtain-wall skyscraper. Its potential for pulling us into a realm of a movement or sound game is almost nil. We can neither measure ourselves against it nor imagine a bodily participation. Our bodily response is reduced to little more than a craned head, wide eyes, or perhaps an open jaw in appreciation of some magnificent height.

There are no human-scale elements in such buildings, no sense whatsoever of how many of *us* it would take to make up one of *them*, no statement to us as to how we are to see, enter, or use it, nothing to convey a sense of intimacy, or invitation, or sociability, or humanity. The UN Secretariat—sad to say, given the humanitarian purpose it is supposed to symbolize—is a perfect example of such a scale-less structure: 505 geometrically abstract feet, cold and forbidding no matter what the time of day or year, windows and floors that might have begun to suggest human dimensions hidden behind a bland and uncalibrated glass wall on the long sides and unbroken slabs of marble on the ends. And looking at two such structures together, or whole canyons of them, makes one almost catatonic.

Try standing on New York's Sixth Avenue in the 50s or Wall Street off Broadway, or Peachtree Street in Atlanta, or in Embarcadero Center in San Francisco, or Century City in Los Angeles, or any other of those urban compression chambers across the land, and you can immediately experience a peculiar sense of dislocation. The eye is continually confused by changes in scale, and, what's worse, by the lack of scale altogether, so that it soon is forced to shun the towering facades and seek relief in whatever street-level doorways and arcades there may be to break up the geometry; and yet there persists a feeling of looming mass, an unshakable awareness of hovering gray colossi, gathered above like the overcast of some cloudy day. That way, it is not hard to feel, madness lies.

———————

Oddly enough, it is in the much-maligned—and usually quite undistinguished—single-family house that we normally have to look today for architectural homage to the human scale. As Hans Blumenfeld remarks, "The field of the 'normal human' and especially of the 'intimate human' scale has been the field of the home builder rather than that of the architect." Here, in the ordinary home, are the elements that are generally missing from the urban mass. The natural world is present: there are lawns and trees and gardens, a certain amount of open space and windows on every front, a prominent fireplace and a chimney visible from the outside, and in the most favored settings a pond or a stream or a fountain; in other words, echoic images of the four primal elements, earth, air, fire, and water. The human body is incorporated: in stairs and railings with normal scales, doorknobs that fit actual hands at comfortable heights for an extended arm, light switches at near-shoulder height, doorways built for people and not some race of giants, windows positioned at the level of normal visual fields, moldings or arches or newels or recesses or railings or vaults or columns imitative of bodily shapes. And the social dimension is recognized: by the central room with a fireplace and hearth, which is a slightly magic area for us as it was for our distant ancestors, around which we still place our icons and treasures, our best furniture and favorite paintings and cherished artifacts, and too by the usual spacious kitchen/ eating area like those in which people have gathered for food preparation and consumption from the time of the earliest hunting bands.

All of these things provide physical and psychological "centered-ness," order, scale, and some degree of stability and serenity. But we simply do not experience them during the course of most of our lives. As Bloomer and Moore conclude:

> *Offices, apartments, and stores are piled together in ways which owe more to filing-cabinet systems or the price of land than to a concern for human existence or experience. In this tangle the American*

116

single family house maintains a curious power over us in spite of its well-publicized inefficiencies of land use and energy consumption. Its power, surely, comes from its being the one piece of the world around us which still speaks directly of our bodies as the center and the measure of that world.

We shape our buildings and thereafter our buildings shape us.

12

The Search for Community

A nthropological evidence is somewhat sketchy, but it seems clear that the oldest human institution is not the family, as is popularly thought, but the community—the tribe, clan, troop, or village, the larger setting. The family is very old, of course, but as a permanent and conscious social unit it seems to have emerged slowly over tens of thousands of years, well after the early hominids had formed into tribal communities. Bernard Campbell of Cambridge University suggests that the family may have originated sometime in the period of the *Australopithecus* when small bands of hominids, perhaps a male and one or more females and their children, broke off from a larger community during periods when adverse weather caused food supplies to dwindle. Such small groups were probably able to travel easier and farther in search of food, and were able to exist more easily on limited resources, a pattern such as is found even today among certain baboon troops and among the Basarwa of the Kalahari. In time, or with successive hardship periods, such small groups might have eventually developed into deliberate families, lasting a generation and then for successive generations, though probably always within the confines of a larger social grouping.

In fact, it is reasonable to assume, as most anthropologists do nowadays, that it was some form of community living that made humans "human." In other words, it was not until some group of hominids meeting around some water hole began grunting and jabbering at each other in regular ways that speech developed, and those groups in which speech was most successful—where, for example, cries of warning or hunting directions were least ambiguous—were the ones that were more likely to survive. It was not until sufficient bands of people gathered for regular periods that fire, found in some tree trunk hit by lightning or dry grass sparked by a volcano, could be tended day in and day out, a task that was essential in those hundreds of thousands of years before our human ancestors had learned to create fire at will. It was not until individual hominids began operating as groups that they were capable of taking on the larger game animals and covering the kinds of geographic distances that would have been necessary for a regular supply of meat. It was not until groups began the regular sharing of food—a trait found in no other primate—that there were created the social ties and obligations, and eventually the kinship and mating systems, that distinguish humans from all other animals. It was not until early humans lived in settled groups that they developed art—such as the Lascaux cave paintings—and religion—symbolized by the Sapiens burials at Sungir, Russia, of 28,000 years ago—and manners and customs and traditions and codes and all that goes to make up a culture, however scanty and primitive. The very existence of the community brought about the development of so many of those traits that over countless millennia shaped the animal that is now known as "Modern Man."

Moreover, it can be said that the whole process of human success has depended precisely upon the ability of our species not only to live in small groups of twenty-five or so—for that is found in many other primates as well—but to create large communal institutions numbering into the several hundred, and to keep such gatherings intact by mutual aid and cooperation over years and decades and centuries. Amos H. Hawley, one of the pioneers in the study of human ecology, has argued that it has been this human capacity for living in community that has been the essential "adaptive mechanism" throughout human development. Human beings cannot adapt to their physical environment alone as individuals, he says; only by creating a "human aggregate," and thus practicing communal and cooperative efforts, are they able not only to survive but in many respects to prevail. One might even justifiably claim therefore that the instinct for community is as old and as vital and as powerful as the instinct for sex, since the former appears to be as necessary for survival as the latter is for procreation.

Indeed, there is every reason to believe that the human need and capacity for communality is genetically encoded in modern *Homo sapiens*. Rene Dubos, who was an eminent microbiologist at Rockefeller University in the mid-twentieth century, argued that "the social organization based on the hunter-gatherer way of life lasted so long—several hundred thousand years—that it has certainly left an indelible stamp on human behavior." He points out that 100 billion human beings have lived since the late

Paleolithic period, when the Cro-Magnons appeared, and "the immense majority of them have spent their entire life as members of very small groups . . . rarely . . . of more than a few hundred persons. The genetic determinants of behavior, and especially of social relationships, have thus evolved in small groups during several thousand generations." He concludes: "Modern man still has a biological need to be part of a group. [This] cannot possibly be altered in the foreseeable future, even if the world were to be completely urbanized and industrialized."

It seems safe to say, at the very least, that the organization of community is not simply *one* way of ordering human affairs but a *universal* way, found in all times and places, among all kinds of peoples. George Murdock, one of the giants of American anthropology, undertook an exhaustive ten-year "cross-cultural survey" for the Institute of Human Relations at Yale some years ago, during which he and his colleagues studied some 250 different human societies all over the earth, of varying periods, geographic settings, and stages of development. He concluded:

> *The community and the nuclear family are the only social groups that are genuinely universal. They occur in every known human society, and both are also found in germinal form on a subhuman level.*

As fundamental as the family is, however:

> *Nowhere on earth do people live regularly in isolated families. Everywhere territorial propinquity, supported by diverse other bonds, unites at least a few neighboring families into a larger social group all of whose members maintain face-to-face relationships with one another.*

Thus, though humankind has not shown itself to be adept at very many social relationships, it can be said that during the long eons of evolution it has probably had more experience with the small community than any other form, and has learned to live in groups of that size more successfully than any other.

Given that apparently incontrovertible fact, it would seem sensible for any rational society to attempt to protect and promote the institution of the community. And yet, for all the tossing about of words like *community center* and *community action*, we obviously are not doing so at present in this country or in very many parts of the industrialized world. Small towns everywhere are threatened, and rural populations dwindling; the newly burgeoning suburbs have shown themselves to be particularly weak in creating community cohesion and mutuality; and it is the rare section of the infrequent city in which any strong sense of communality is to be found any longer. It may be too strong to say, with Christopher Alexander, the urban planner at the University of California, that "Western industrial society is the first society in human history where man is being forced to live without" the intimate contacts of community, meaning that "the very roots of our society are threatened." Yet the increasing loss of communal life is undoubtedly at the heart of the malaise of modern urban culture, and its disappearance clearly cannot bode well for the future.

———

But is it not possible to envision the criteria for an optimum community in the modern world? Just as the human measure can guide us in the design of technology and the creation of buildings, can it not provide a guide in the development of communities?

The cardinal task here, it seems to me, is to discover the limits of a human-scale community, the size beyond which—as the Beanstalk Principle would suggest—it ought not to grow. And here, thanks to various anthropological and sociological records, we have a considerable body of interesting evidence.

The first set of numbers that come up here have been proposed by British anthropologist and evolutionary psychologist Robin Dunbar at Oxford University. He first observed the size limits of non-human primates and determined it was set largely by the size of their brains, specifically the neocortex: "The psychological demands of living in large groups meant that, in primates, species-typical brain size correlates rather closely to the species' group size." For humans he calculated that the normal size of a group "with whom one person can maintain stable relationships" was roughly 150 people.

He then found a number of other examples of what came to be called the "Dunbar number." The average size of English villages in the eleventh-century Domesday Book was 150. Eighteenth-century parish registers average 150. The average size for Hutterite and Amish villages before they are forced to split is 150 because they have found that beyond that number peer pressure gives way to some kind of policing. The basic unit of the British Army, the company, is from 120 to 180 soldiers. Gore-Tex set a maximum for its factory sizes at 150, after which a separate factory was formed. The average size of the group that Britons sent Christmas cards to (in an earlier age, it's true) was 150. But in a later age the number of people Dunbar found that most people on Facebook have close relationships with is around 120 to 130. And in a completely different study, Robert Carneiro of the American Museum of Natural History has observed that villages among the Amazonian people he studied in Brazil tended to split up at populations between 100 and 200.

As recurrent as this figure seems to be, I think what it best defines is what Dunbar calls a "social network," that is, the number of acquaintances an individual can have, suggesting rather close though not necessarily intimate relationship. But I would argue that for a unit that we would call "community," meaning a group with political (in the broad sense) as well as social cohesion, functioning in a more complex way than a simple network, a larger number is required. And the great body of evidence suggests that this is more than three times as large, or roughly 500.

John Pfeiffer, the anthropological writer who has perhaps as encyclopedic a vision as anyone in the field, goes so far as to call 500 a "magic number" because it recurs so often in human evolution as the limit of a community:

> The phenomenon becomes clear and meaningful only after taking census figures for a large number of tribes. Such studies reveal a central tendency to cluster at the 500 level, and this tendency is widespread. It holds for the Shoshoni Indians of the Great Plains, the Andaman Islanders in the Bay of Bengal, and other peoples as well as the Australian aborigines.

This number, Pfeiffer suggests, may have been determined by the nature of human communication and culture-sharing mechanisms: "There seems to be a basic limit to the number of persons who can know one another well enough to maintain a tribal identity at the hunter-gatherer level, who communicate by direct confrontation and who live under a diffuse and informal influence, perhaps a council of elders, rather than an active centralized political authority." That number may also have been determined by the optimum number of people for mate selection. Martin Wobst of the University of Massachusetts has made computer calculations of prehistoric societies and determined that for a male to have an adequate pool of mates in his age group in any society in which incest taboos prevailed, he would need a total population of approximately 475 people.

Supportive evidence comes from a number of sources. Accounts of those primates that have developed herds and clans in addition to small-group units often indicate a range from under 100 to more than 700, with an average around 400 or 500: the gelada baboons of Ethiopia, for example, have herds up to 400, while langur monkeys of India tend to split into several herds after more than 550 or so. Joseph Birdsell, an anthropologist at UCLA who has spent considerable time among the Australian Aborigines, has reported:

> *The Australian data show an amazing constancy of numbers for the dialectical tribe [i.e., speaking one dialect], statistically approximating 500 persons. This tendency is independent of regional density. Since the data cover mean annual rainfall variations from 4 inches to more than 160 inches, the size of the dialectical tribal unit is insensitive to regional variations in climatic . . . factors.*

Pierre Clastres, a French scholar, estimates that the traditional Tupi-Guarani villages of South America had "a mean population of six hundred to a thousand persons," based on various sixteenth-century documents, and an actual census in the seventeenth century showed about 450 per village among the Tupis. Various anthropologists in the United States have estimated that the "long houses" of the tribes of the Irokwa Confederacy—the meeting places for village gatherings—typically held no more than about 500 people. And archaeological research at sites throughout the Middle East—for example, the work in Mesopotamia of Robert Adams of the University of Chicago and his colleagues—provides evidence that the general size of the earliest village settlements, established in the two millennia after 5000 BC, varied from about fifty people to perhaps several thousand, but most often clustered somewhere around the 400–500 range.

We may leave it to Rene Dubos, once again, to sum it up: "The biology and psychology of modern Man has certainly been influenced by the fact

THE SEARCH FOR COMMUNITY

that, during the past 10,000 years, most people have lived in villages of some 500 inhabitants."

———————

There is another way of coming at the question of the human limits of a community: Hans Blumenfeld, the urban planner, suggests starting with the idea of the size at which "every person knows every other person by face, by voice, and by name" and adds, "I would say that it begins to fade out in villages with much more than 500 or 600 population." Constantine Doxiadis, after reducing thousands of data from various centuries, came to the conclusion that what he called the "small neighborhood" would hold approximately 250 people, a large neighborhood some 1,500, with an average around 800–900. Gordon Rattray Taylor, the British science writer, has estimated that there is a "natural social unit" for humans, defined by "the largest group in which every individual can form some personal estimate of the significance of a majority of the other individuals in the group, in relation to himself," and he holds that the maximum size of such a group, depending on geography and ease of contact, is about 1,200 people; he adds that business firms historically begin to face organizational problems at about this level. Terence Lee, a British sociologist who did a thorough survey of attitudes in Cambridge, England, reported in *Human Relations Journal* in 1968 that the people themselves thought of their "social acquaintance area" as containing from 0 to 400 houses (some people obviously were not too neighborly), or from 0 to 1,200 people, and the average was under 1,000. And examinations of successful communes over the last century indicate that for the most part they have tended toward an optimum size of 500—as Charles Erasmus, a University of California anthropology professor, has summarized the data, "Successful commune movements . . . have invariably been divided into communities averaging less than five hundred inhabitants." (He cites the upper limits of 600 for the Shakers, 500 for Amana groups, 300 for Oneida, 800 for Harmony, 500 for Zoar, and 150 for the Hutterites.)

Not many scientific studies have been done on what characteristics of the human brain may set these rough limitations on the size of successful face-to-face communities, but George Murdock has provided some evidence here. He asked his students and friends to list the people they regularly associated with and knew on a first-name basis; the results showed such a surprising unanimity, ranging from around 800 to around 1,200, that Murdock concluded that this represents the general "index of familiarity" for human groups. (Try it yourself sometime in a dull moment.) John Pfeiffer also notes that "there is an architect's rule of thumb to the effect that the capacity of an elementary school should not exceed 500 pupils if the principal expects to know all of them by name" (the average number of pupils in US elementary schools in 2000 was 467; in 2009, 475). He goes on to suggest that "the memory capacity of the human brain probably plays a fundamental role of some sort since that influences the number of persons one can know on sight."

It is possible, too, that the human visual capacity plays a role. Just as the optimal distance for determining the rough outlines of an individual has been determined to be around 450 feet, as we saw in the last chapter, the optimal distance for determining whether a distant object is human at all seems to be around 1,000 feet; this, too, is taken to be the normal optimum for the line of sight of an adult human. Now if we begin by taking this as the maximum space that an intimate community would occupy—the area in which the human form could be perceived from one end of the settlement to the other—the total space would then be 1 million square feet, or about 23 acres (1 acre = 43,560 square feet). Allowing a population density range of from, say, 15 to 40 people per acre (New York City, for comparison, averages 41 people per acre), that provides a community population of between 345 and 920 people. The eye, happily, seems to agree with the brain, again settling on approximately the same range around the "magic" 500 figure. Could that be a remarkable coincidence—or perhaps a reflection of the genetic coding that has effectively determined the limits of human social functions?

————

There is another number, or rather range of numbers, similarly "magic" perhaps, that recurs in the examination of community, suggesting another desirable, though somewhat larger, size for human groupings. Again, there is an interesting general agreement on the figures from a wide variety of sources.

Although it was the face-to-face village that was the primary communal unit, many societies, and particularly the more successful, often formed larger bands, or tribes, uniting these villages into a common culture. Anthropological evidence suggests that throughout prehistory the upper limit for such tribes—defined as those who speak the same dialect or language or who unite into an association of villages—was everywhere about 5,000 or 6,000. William Sanders and Paul Baker of Penn State University pointed out that tribal units sharing common customs, common language, and common territory might have grown as large as this limit, but at that point almost always split into new tribes or else imposed a limit on further growth by establishing a central authority capable of governing population. The University of Arizona's William Rathje, after using general systems theory to interpret Mayan culture, suggested that this 5,000 number may represent a level at which the social system, at least in early societies, had to limit itself to keep from overloading itself with complexities and burning itself out.

This was about the limit of the earliest cities, too, as near as we can reconstruct the sites—not only in the Middle East, an area that has been particularly well surveyed, but in India, China, North Africa, and Central America. A few might have grown to 20,000 and even 50,000 in their latest stages, shortly before collapse, but as a general rule the urban centers of the millennia before Christ seem to have stayed at between 5,000 and 10,000 people; in the words of Gideon Sjoberg, the urban sociologist, "It seems unlikely that, at least in the earlier periods, even the larger of these cities contained more than 5,000 to 10,000 people, including part-time farmers on the cities' outskirts." Architect and planner Constantine Doxiadis calculated that a population of about 5,000 and an area of about two square kilometers were typical of almost all early cities: "Very few of the cities known to have existed during these thousands of years did not have these characteristics." His explanation for this was that the human animal might have a "kinetic field" set by a ten-minute radius, thus establishing the limits of its normal daily activities, and thus the limits of the area the city could cover and the population it could hold.

This same figure emerges again when we come to the medieval period. Without doubt most places, at least in Europe, had fewer than 2,000 people, but the few trading centers that began to form after the twelfth and thirteenth centuries most commonly held up to 10,000 souls—as Chartres in the twelfth century (10,000), Ypres in 1412 (10,376), Basel in the fourteenth century (8,000). And when we look at the full-fledged cities, particularly those noted for their economic and cultural achievements, it is remarkable how often 5,000 is cited as the upper limit of the precincts, or quarters, out of which these new urban centers were created and into which they were divided. In fact, *quarter* originally meant literally a fourth part of a city (or thereabouts), and since we know from Lewis Mumford that the medieval city did not grow beyond about 40,000 people—that was the population of London in the fifteenth century—this would confirm an upper limit of approximately 10,000 people per precinct. There is a print showing the layout of the city of Aachen, in 1649, that might serve as a neat example: it shows a circular city bounded by heavily fortified walls, with a large cathedral at the very center and, at the points of the compass, four smaller churches—the church, of course, representing the heart, the "community center," of the medieval neighborhood. The population at the time was somewhere around 20,000, and the quarters then probably held about 5,000 each.

Coming down to the present, a range of 5,000 to 10,000 shows up with surprising frequency in the recommendations of architects and city planners for the preferred size of a community. Clarence Perry, the grandfather of contemporary planning and the man who redirected attention back to the idea of small-scale communities in the 1930s when they were first threatened by the onrush of the twentieth-century metropolis, is typical. After years of study he hit upon an ideal "neighborhood unit" of from 3,000 to 9,000 people, with an optimum size at 5,000. His theory was that a neighborhood had to be small enough so that everything important— schools, playgrounds, shops, public buildings—was within easy walking distance, and large enough to support an elementary school and a variety of local stores and services. Both conditions could be satisfied, he determined, with a population of about 1,000 to 1,500 families, or an average of about 5,000 people, distributed at roughly 15–20 people per acre, with the total unit then occupying about a half-mile square. Since Perry's formulation, a wide variety of other city planners, of different decades, philosophies, styles, and interests, has also arrived at about the same figure.

Perry's "walking distance" principle in particular has become standard among almost all urban planners who give any thought at all to community. Walter Gropius, the architect, has explained the rationale this way:

> The size of the townships should be limited by the pedestrian range
> to keep them within a human scale. . . . The human being himself, so
> much neglected during the early machine age, must become the focus
> of all reconstruction to come. Our stride determines and measures

our space- and time-conception and pegs out our local living space.
Organic planning has to reckon with the human scale, the "foot,"
when shaping any physical structure. Violation of the human scale
will cause further degeneration of life in cities.

Like Perry, Gropius observed that the maximum distance a person would walk comfortably for ordinary community affairs was about half a mile, and thus he too came up with an optimum "township" size of roughly a half-mile square. Now if we assume that half the space within that area would be given over to public buildings, shops, pathways, and parkland, and if we assume for the remaining 160 acres residential densities somewhere around the models of Gropius and the "garden city" planners, we come up with a range of population—no surprise—around 5,000–8,000 people.

One final piece of evidence on community size comes from Leopold Kohr, who has done more thinking about this from the perspective of the social sciences than anyone to date. Kohr argues that it would take about eighty to one hundred adults to provide the *convivial* society, that is to say, the number to "fulfill the companionship function to the fullest" and "to ensure both variety of contacts and constancy of relationships"; but, he says, it would take more than that for an effective *economic* society. In a society with basic specialization—a shoemaker, say, and a baker and a builder and so on—there need to be enough people to consume the goods and services during the course of a year, and eighty to one hundred adults is too small a pool; "economic optimum social size," he estimates, requires "a full membership of 4,000 to 5,000 inhabitants." At this level, he argues, "society seems capable of furnishing its members not only with most of the commodities we associate with a high standard of living, but also of surrounding each person with the margin of leisure without which it could not properly perform its original convivial function." And for the optimum *political* society only a few thousand people need be added—"a full population of between 7,000 and 12,000"—to provide a sufficient number who can be spared from basic economic routines to perform legislative, legal, political, and security tasks. This is the size, actually, of various real-world states that survive quite nicely, including the independent state of Nauru in the South Pacific, and such self-administered dependencies as Anguilla, the Cayman Islands, Montserrat, Falkland Islands, Saint Helena, and Tuvalu.

—————

What we have here, then, with our two ranges of "magic" numbers, is a rough measure of the two basic kinds of community that humans have apparently found the most useful and successful over their many millennia as social creatures. One is the face-to-face association group, with somewhere between 400 and 1,000 people and an optimum of perhaps 500—what we might call the common *neighborhood*, a small area usually of a few blocks where most of the people know one another at least by sight and in some cases can band together to form small-scale associations. The other is the extended association, a wider alliance of some 5,000 to 10,000 people, usually hovering around the lower figure, that, following Constantine Doxiadis, I would call the polis, the Greek word for a small close-knit city with shared customs. These numbers are only suggestive, of course, but if humankind in all races and cultures has chosen to live in these aggregates, the neighborhood and the polis, throughout its evolution, right down to the current era, and if to some degree at least it has solved the problems of collective living at these levels, then the levels deserve our consideration in a most essential way when we contemplate the design and reconstruction of our social settings.

A town of less than 10,000 is, in modern terms, small, of course—some might say hopelessly small. But, as Gropius says, "It is particularly the small size of the township with its human scale which would favorably influence the growth of distinct characteristics of the community," including regular associations between people, easy access to public officers, mutual aid among neighbors, and open and trusting social relations. Smallness is simply essential to preserve the values of community as they have been historically observed—intimacy, trust, honesty, mutuality, cooperation, democracy, congeniality. The record on this point is both ample and consistent and does not need to be rehearsed here: it is shown by the school of historical scholarship beginning with Sir Henry Maine and Georg von Maurer (among many others) in the nineteenth century, coming down to Lewis Mumford and Murray Bookchin (among many others) in the twentieth century, and then to Andres Duany and the New Urbanists as well as scholars and activists connected with the Institute for Local Self-Reliance in the twenty-first century.

Recent scholarship following Robert Putnam's *Bowling Alone* in 2000 has suggested that perhaps we have finally arrived at a place where community is in such decline that it barely exists. Putnam's point, well made and nicely supported, was that in recent decades participation in voting at all levels has declined, attendance has declined at public meetings, civic organizations from the Elks to Parent Teacher Associations have lost members, and the number of bowling leagues has declined so much that people are now bowling alone. After the jihadi suicide attacks in September 2001, and later after the Paris jihadi murders in November 2015, popular participation in general has declined as many became cautious about mixing in numbers in public places.

If that is true, it indicates a serious problem with this society and its dwindling "social capital." But all the soundings I have taken suggest that this has not diminished the felt *need* for community, an inherent longing for what was a deep, perhaps biologically imprinted, wish for the kind of support only a community can satisfy. It is still something taken into consideration by city planners, especially those of the New Urbanism that emphasizes neighborhoods of about a half-mile diameter with everything within a 5-mile walk, narrow tree-lined streets, and public spaces that make up a coherent community. The fact that since the 1980s such neighborhoods have been built in many places coast to coast by the New Urbanists and their followers, some of them commanding steeper house prices than their originators planned for, indicates that there is still a market for the inextinguishable need for community.

———

In 1898 a British army officer named H. Fielding Hall, who had spent a decade in Burma after the British conquest of that country, wrote a book, *The Soul of a People*, describing in some detail the workings of Burmese society, from all accounts an accurate picture of the land of that time—though a far cry from what the country, now Myanmar, has become. Hall was particularly struck by the way in which Burma was a land of villages and villagers, without large cities or even many sizable trading towns and, with the exception of a king and tiny royal family, without hierarchies or a fixed nobility or ecclesiastic powers or any notable division into classes or castes. He wrote:

Each village was to a very great extent a self-governing community composed of men free in every way. The whole country was divided into villages, sometimes containing one or two hamlets at a little distance from each other—offshoots from the parent stem. The towns, too, were divided into quarters, and each quarter had its headman. These men held their appointment-orders from the king as a matter of form, but they were chosen by their fellow-villagers as a matter of fact. Partly this headship was hereditary, not from father to son, but it might be from brother to brother, and so on. It was not usually a very coveted appointment, for the responsibility and trouble was considerable, and the pay small. It was 10 per cent on the tax collections. And with this official as their head, the villagers managed nearly all their affairs.

Their taxes, for instance, they assessed and collected themselves. The governor merely informed the headman that he was to produce ten rupees per house from his village. The villagers then appointed assessors from among themselves, and decided how much each household should pay. Thus a coolie might pay but four rupees, and a rice-merchant as much as fifty or sixty. The assessment was levied according to the means of the villagers. So well was this done, that complaints against the decisions of the assessors were almost unknown—I might, I think, safely say were absolutely unknown. The assessment was made publicly, and each man was heard in his own defence before being assessed. Then the money was collected. If by any chance, such as death, any family could not pay, the deficiency was made good by the other villagers in proportion. When the money was got in it was paid to the governor.

Crime such as gang-robbery, murder, and so on, had to be reported to the governor. All lesser crime was dealt with in the village itself, not only dealt with when it occurred but to a great extent prevented from occurring. You see, in a village anyone knows everyone, and detection is usually easy. If a man became a nuisance to a village, he was expelled. . . .

All villages were not alike, of course, in their enforcement of good manners and good morals, but, still, in every village they were enforced more or less. The opinion of the people was very decided, and made itself felt. . . . So each village managed its own affairs, untroubled by squire or priest, very little troubled by the state. That within their little means they did it well, no one can doubt. They taxed themselves without friction, they built their own monastery schools by voluntary effort, they maintained a very high, a very simple, code of morals, entirely of their own initiative.

And then Hall adds a particularly interesting comment on the Burman:

And so I do not think his will ever make what we call a great nation. He will never try to be a conqueror of other peoples, either with the sword, with trade, or with religion. He will never care to have a great voice in the management of the world. He does not care to interfere with other people: he never believes interference can do other than harm to both sides.

He will never be very rich, very powerful, very advanced in science, perhaps not even in art, though I am not sure about that. It may be he will be very great in literature and art. But, however that may be, in his own idea his will be always the greatest nation in the world, because it is the happiest.

13

The Optimum City

I t is quite remarkable that in the several thousand years people have been given to musing about that odd arrangement of society known to us as the city, they have continually come up with approximately the same idea of how big it ought to be. In general, it was agreed, a city had to be bigger than a village, even a small town, because a certain number of people were necessary to obtain what were regarded as the advantages of urban life: anonymity, diversity, complexity, opportunity, tolerance, specialization, innovation, self-expression, stimulation. And, it was also agreed, it had to be smaller than an entire nation, tribe, or empire, because with too many people these advantages became submerged under accumulating disadvantages: crime, filth, pollution, congestion, overcrowding, inhumanity, loneliness, political ineffectuality, social disintegration. A community of 5,000, or even 10,000, successful as it might be in providing cordiality, economic self-sufficiency, and democratic government, would still be too small, at least in post-classical experience, to provide the urban values: one virtue of the community, after all, is that it does *not* encourage anonymity. But similarly, an agglomeration of 10 or 20 million, though presumably capable of offering considerable variety and opportunity, would probably have more of those disadvantages than any one person could tolerate and so many other assorted ills that living there wouldn't be worth the effort.

Plato, one of the first people in the West to confront the subject of city sizes, was quite specific: a city, he said, should contain 5,040 citizens—i.e., male heads of households—which along with families, slaves, and metics, in the usual Greek fashion, would make a total population of perhaps 35,000 to 40,000 people. Aristotle, though not so precise, cautioned that "a great city is not to be confounded with a populous one" and suggested a limit of "the largest number which suffices for the purposes of life, and can be taken in at a single view," which scholars have generally agreed to be in the area of 30,000 to 50,000 people. Leonardo da Vinci posited an ideal city of 30,000. Thomas More's Utopia had cities of 6,000 families, or about 20,000 people. Montesquieu offered no numbers but favored small city-states on the order of his own Bordeaux—certainly under 60,000—and asserted: "It is in the nature of a republic that it should have a small territory." Rousseau similarly talked in terms of an ideal city comparable to his own town of Geneva, then with about 25,000 citizens, and at one point suggested 10,000 as a democratic optimum. Ebenezer Howard envisioned "garden cities" of roughly 30,000, surrounded by agricultural belts containing another 2,000 or so.

Most scholars in the mid-twentieth-century years were inclined to push the ranges upward just a bit—probably because modern technology is capable of increasing communication and efficiency somewhat—but the scholars still favored cities of about this size. The Ruth Commission in Great Britain, which was charged with studying these matters in the 1950s, concluded that cities of about 30,000 to 50,000 would be ideal, while the later Royal Commission on Local Government in the 1960s raised the limit to 100,000–250,000. The enterprising American investigator Otis Dudley Duncan once showed that cities between 50,000 and 150,000 had all the urban facilities any city would need, and a more recent counterpart, Werner Z. Hirsch, suggested that the most democratic and efficient cities were "medium-sized communities of 50,000 to 100,000 residents." Gordon Rattray Taylor suggested an upper limit of 100,000, and his countryman E. F. Schumacher—though as we know biased in favor of smaller forms—argued that there should be "ideally no major town more than a couple of hundred thousand or thereabouts." Ralph Borsodi, among his exhaustive researches into the human condition, wrote: "It is very probable that every need of a high culture with a high standard of living could be provided with cities of around 25,000 population and without any cities of over 100,000." And Robert Dahl of Yale, long one of the leading American political scientists, argued that for the most workable kind of modern city there might be "an optimum size in the broad range from about 50,000 to about 200,000."

In more recent years, there has been little work on optimum city sizes, the idea having mostly fallen out of scholarly favor, but some work has tended to argue that "city rankings correlate negatively with city size," while other work, chiefly by David Albouy, maintains that "neither population size nor density appear to negatively impact American QOL [quality of life]." A great deal of attention has been paid to studying how to make cities "sustainable" and walkable and eco-friendly, and economically and racially diversified, but the idea of optimum sizes, or of planning for size limits, has not been given much attention in this century.

Scholarly opinion aside, the small city was the model that the practical planners of the world, both East and West, favored in the first decades after World War II. The small cities that have been built, I hasten to add, have not all been unalloyed successes, but their deficiencies have nowhere been blamed on their sizes and the fact that they have all been designed around a specific population range is a revealing indication of an apparently cross-cultural perception of urban optimality. The New Towns that were planned in America in the late 1960s ranged from 30,000 to 120,000, with an average at about 73,000; the two most successful were Columbia, Maryland, with 43,000 (today about that, but the 2010 census included surrounding villages for nearly 100,000), and Reston, Virginia, with 35,000 (58,400 in 2010). The British New Town program, the most extensive in the world, created 27 cities with populations ranging between 35,000 and 135,000, with an average of about 60,000. Around the same time, the Chinese designed regional centers in the 50,000–80,000 range; the Soviet Union built model cities of 50,000–200,000 (with the "ideal communist city" said to be 100,000); the Dutch new towns had original targets of 100,000; Sweden's "primary centers" were planned for 50,000–100,000; and Israel has planned new cities for about 40,000.

This new-town movement had such a checkered success that in the twenty-first century little attention was paid to it until the world woke up to the fact that in 2007, 50 percent of the world's population was now in cities—and cities with multiple and multiplying problems. An International New Towns Institute was established in the new town of Almere, the Netherlands, in 2008, and has worked to study and encourage what it is calling "new new towns" all over the world. Its agenda calls for towns that are "socially inclusive," "ecologically sustainable," and "economically fair," but has nothing to say about sizes and indeed is headquartered in a "new town" begun in 1976 that now has 200,000 people and is planning to grow to 350,000 by 2030, a clear demonstration that the wisdom of the original movement has been lost today.

As for the reason there was such a striking degree of harmony on size in that original movement, I think it is probably to be found in one central fact: as near as we can tell, for most of human history, no matter what the continent or climate, regardless of political or economic conditions, cities only very seldom actually grew beyond the 50,000–100,000 range.

During most of its celebrated life, Athens as a city seemed to have hovered around 50,000 people, though at periods of particular power the surrounding Attic state may have grown to perhaps 150,000 or 200,000. Italian cities that began and nurtured the Renaissance, as we have seen, did not grow to more than 80,000, and most of them had closer to 50,000 — the Rome of Michelangelo with perhaps 55,000, the Florence of Leonardo 40,000, and Venice, Padua, and Bologna at their height probably 50,000–80,000. New York and Philadelphia at the time of the American Revolution had fewer than 30,000 people, Boston — the cradle — no more than 15,000. In fact, it seems that only on very rare occasions did pre-industrial centers ever go much beyond 100,000, and then only temporarily, when serving as the bloated capitals of empires, as with Babylon, Syracuse, Rome, Alexandria, Constantinople, Edo, Hangchow, and Peking; even then, Rome at its height probably had no more than 300,000 or 400,000, Babylon 110,000, and Alexandria and Hangchow perhaps half a million. It has only been in the last two centuries, as we have seen, that giant conurbations have emerged and lasted — though even today there are only 538 cities over a million and a half people; the nearly four billion urban dwellers live in places of less than 500,000, and 15 percent under 100,000.

The conclusion of the protean Constantine Doxiadis, after a lifetime of categorizing such things, seems quite on the mark: "If we look back into history . . . we find that, throughout the long evolution of human settlements, people in all parts of the world have tended to create urban settlements which reached an optimum size of 50,000 people." Indeed, he argued, the fact that the few cities that grew to larger sizes did not survive for long suggests that humanity has solved the problems of living in cities of up to 50,000 or so, but obviously not in units much above that size.

Thus we seem to have arrived at another set of "magic" numbers, similarly inexact and somewhat elastic, but similarly suggestive, which may provide some indication of the nature and the extent of the human-scale city. Obviously we must think of the desirable city as a congeries of neighborhoods and communities, for these have to be the building blocks out of which any larger entity is built; they must continue to supply the rootedness, even as the wider society supplies its diversity. But within that context it is still possible to find enough evidence—sociological, economic, political, and demographic—to permit some reasonable conclusions as to the validity of these magic numbers and the limits of the optimal city.

By Sociological Standards

The sociological verdict is generally that the quality of life in the larger American cities is—I can think of no better summary—solitary, poor, nasty, brutish, and short. There are no doubt compensations for it all in the minds of many, but the studies suggest that, as a rule, as cities get bigger they increase in density, fragmentation, deviance, criminality, social stress, anomie, loneliness, selfishness, alcoholism, mental illness, and racial and ethnic segregation. These ills begin to gather, it seems, somewhere around the 100,000 level, and without doubt the biggest cities are the worst.

There is considerable debate just now about whether it is crowding or higher densities or sheer numbers or the amount of interaction that produces the individual and collective pathologies of big cities. Biological studies show almost uniformly that crowding and high densities in animal populations produce such things as hypertension, stress, aggression, violence, exhaustion, sadism, mental disorder, infertility, disease, suicide, and death. For the human animal, rather more adaptable to its surroundings, the evidence is not quite so unequivocal, but ever since the work of Georges Simmel at the turn of the twentieth century it has been fairly well recognized that accumulations of people create accumulations of social problems, and the more people the more problems.

Simple enough, really. With more people there are bound to be more contacts among them in any given day—the New York Regional Plan Association, alarmingly, determined at one point that there were 11,000 people within a ten-minute radius in Nassau County, 20,000 in Newark, and 220,000 in Manhattan—and so to prevent a psycho-social "overload" a city dweller must either have fewer contacts, spend less time on any single contact, or be less intense and involved during any contact. That's what produces the familiar patterns of big cities. People create fewer contacts by developing ethnic ties and consequent separation from "outside" groups, by having unlisted phone numbers, by not making eye contact with people on the street, and by ignoring lifelong neighbors. They spend less time per contact by cutting out traditional courtesies such as "sorry" and "please," by treating supermarket checkers and short-order waitresses as faceless and history-less, by refusing "to get involved" when some unwanted contact intrudes. And they reduce the intensity of each contact by limiting their "span of sympathy" (in sociological parlance) to the immediate family, by supporting governmental agencies that take over their personal commitments (welfare, for example), and by emphasizing their privacy through personal-space "cocoons" in an elevator or at a lunch counter.

A goodly number of scholarly studies have compared the civility of people in large cities with those in smaller places, and with rare uniformity they show big-city dwellers to be, as the stereotypes would indicate, far more selfish, hostile to strangers, unhelpful, and unfriendly. In one study a group of researchers dialed phone numbers at random in various-sized cities and, concocting a plausible story about an emergency, asked the people who answered to look up and call a number for them and leave a vital message; people in the smaller cities were overwhelmingly more responsive. In another study, stamped envelopes were casually left around at restaurant tables, countertops, and the like in different-sized cities, and the ones from the smaller places were mailed back far more often. Students at the City University of New York compared the responses of people in Manhattan with those in small cities in upstate Rockland County when asked by strangers if they could come in and use the phone; an average of 27 percent of the New Yorkers allowed people in, compared with 72 percent of the others. And one researcher placed abandoned cars in middle-class neighborhoods, first near New York University in a city of 7 million and then near Stanford University in a city of nearly 20,000, and discovered that the car in New York was quite rapidly stripped and gutted while the one in Stanford was actually guarded by passersby against attempts to damage it. What is interesting in all these cases is that the very qualities of civility that the urban setting has traditionally been supposed to foster—the word *civility*, after all, comes from the Latin for "city"—are least in evidence there.

Aside from sheer civility and friendliness, smaller cities outperform larger ones in any number of social variables, and it is those in the 50,000–100,000 range that most often perform the best.

Crime is a particularly good index, not because the individual statistics are always so reliable but because they are plentiful and, year after year, for example, show a very sharp jump when a city population goes past 100,000. Using FBI statistics, one researcher found that in 2014, for example, the violent crime rate for cities of 10,000–100,000 people was 286 per 100,000 people, the murder rate 3; for cities of 100,000 to 250,000 the rates were 444 and 5.6; and for cities over 500,000 a jump to 706 and 9.3. Significant figures, significant differences.

Health statistics point to a similar, if somewhat less dramatic, pattern. Though big cities show a slightly better record than any others in terms of infant mortality, after that the data consistently favor small cities: there are fewer pollution- and stress-related diseases, lower death rates for cancer, heart disease, and diabetes, markedly lower incidences of bronchitis, ulcers, high blood pressure, alcoholism, and drug addiction. In general, there are proportionately fewer serious illnesses and fewer people laid up during the course of a year in small-city metropolitan areas than in either rural sections or bigger cities. As to *mental health,* the commonsense suspicion that big-city living increases nervousness and tension, with resulting high levels of irritation, overfatigue, and social friction, is borne out by the majority of studies. Schizophrenia is significantly more common in bigger cities, suicide rates are somewhat higher, and the risk of schizophrenia is twice as high in more crowded areas. Studies of mental illness in cities were reported on by Mazda Adli, executive director of the World Health Summit, in 2010, with the conclusion that "living in an urban environment is long known to be a risk factor for psychiatric diseases such as major depression or schizophrenia," with social stress being "the most important factor for the increased risk of mental disorders in urban areas." He drew this important conclusion: "Our brains do not seem to be optimally designed for living under our generation's urban conditions, in the large, densely-populated metropolises of our world."

Recreation facilities in small cities have been shown to be usually better than those in large cities and easier to get to. Cities in the 50,000–250,000 range have more park space per capita than cities of any other size, and their parks serve a clientele that is more mixed economically. Small cities in general spend just as much per capita to build and maintain their parks, and they have a higher percentage of people employed in recreation and entertainment than cities of any other size.

Finally, *education* statistics—these are from the 1970s but suggest what is still true—confirm the social desirability of the small city. One pioneering study using data from the United States and three other industrial countries determined that there were usually more people employed in education, for each million dollars of regional income, in cities in the 40,000–50,000 category than in either smaller or larger cities. Another recent survey found that employment in education and health is proportionately higher in metropolitan areas from 50,000–200,000 than in either rural areas or larger cities. And the Committee for Economic Development, part of the pro-business Conference Board, once determined that, in economic terms, when a school system has more than 2,000 pupils, "advantages continue to accrue until a school system reaches perhaps 25,000 students"—which in this country means cities with a maximum of 70,000–90,000 people.

The one area of social activity in which the small city has been most often faulted is that of high culture: symphony orchestras, opera companies, ballet and theater troupes, art museums. It is true that, particularly in the United States—though, interestingly, not in such countries as Italy, Germany, and Sweden—high culture has tended to be a product of the very biggest cities, principally those of the Northeast. But it does not follow that big cities are *necessary* for these cultural institutions. Small cities between 50,000 and 150,000 in this country as a rule sustain both libraries and museums of considerable quality, and attendance figures show that at this level they are used more per capita in smaller cities than in larger ones, suggesting that this might be the right population size for peak efficiency and usefulness. Small cities can and do sustain symphony orchestras—in a March 2015 report the League of American Orchestras counted 1,372 orchestras in the United States that gave 26,819 concerts—and regional theaters—a study in 2005 found more than 1,200 nonprofit companies doing 13,000 productions a year, and the League of Resident Theaters in 2015 reported 71 member theaters across the country from Portland, Maine to Portland, Oregon.

Small cities also have as a rule a far higher rate of *participation* in cultural matters, far greater contributions from all age, race, education, and economic sectors. Small cities have equal access to what is today the primary source of cultural dispersion—the internet, radio, and television—all capable of delivering superior performances. And small cities offer their cultural amenities without the prices, dangers, and distractions of big cities: the citizen of Albany who goes to hear the local orchestra on a moment's notice, with easy traveling, free parking, modest prices, cheap babysitters, and no fear of street crime, can hardly be said to be worse off than the New Yorker who goes to Lincoln Center for a $100-a-seat concert punctuated by subway rumbles and is mugged on the way home.

By Economic Standards

It has been traditional for economists to justify large cities with the doctrine of what they rather inelegantly call "agglomeration effects." This holds that big cities are most efficient and are necessary for a healthy economy because they lump everything together in one place: a large and varied labor pool, a large and easy-to-reach market, a wide variety of specialized goods and services, and so on. In the words of William Alonso, a pioneer in urban economics and a former professor of regional planning at the University of California, "Bigger cities are more efficient engines of production."

The only trouble with this doctrine is that, in at least three crucial respects, it is no longer true.

In the first place, in big cities today the effects of agglomeration are most likely to be disadvantageous for businesses. There are higher transportation and distribution costs because of traffic congestion; higher business costs because of a decrease in the number of hours worked per worker; higher maintenance and cleaning costs because of air pollution; higher energy costs because of the "heat island" effect over cities in the summer and the shading of dense buildings in the winter; higher security costs and higher property-loss rates because of crime and vandalism; higher costs in training new workers because of inferior schools; higher land costs and greater building-construction expenses; and higher insurance rates, higher wages, higher costs of living, and higher taxes. Many of these costs can be pushed onto the cities themselves—traditionally cities have been economical for businesses *only* because the citizenry at large paid for the streets, police and fire protection, water, garbage collection, snow removal, and the like—but at some point these service costs begin to push taxes higher for everyone, including the businesses.

Second, manufacturing in general is no longer located in big cities— the classic Detroit pattern no longer holds even in this country, and the majority of manufacturing plants are not even in this country. Ever since the 1920s, in fact, and particularly since the 1950s, even those larger businesses that have not sent manufacturing overseas have been moving *out* of cities, to smaller places where the costs are cheaper and social control over the workforce easier, where there is more space for assembly lines, where their executives prefer to live, and where an increasing percentage of its market is also moving. Transportation has changed, favoring road systems in the countryside over decaying rail and water systems; manufacturing itself has changed, with a trend to robotism and high technology and to finished goods rather than assembly operations.

Finally, there is the simple fact that big cities have not had any better economic record than smaller cities, as you would expect them to if agglomeration worked as the economists say. Studies show that they do not have greater economic stability; they are not better able to weather economic crises; they do not have any better record on unemployment rates; and they do not have a higher percentage of their population employed. In fact, they do not have any measurable superiority in economic diversity in the broad categories of employment that they offer. A study by two urban economists from Columbia University in 1952 (and still likely to be true today) found that small metropolitan areas, with major cities between 25,000 and 100,000 in size, had just as great a range of economic functions as the giant cities of a million or more—*and* a considerably higher proportion of people in agriculture and construction, appreciably higher in retail trade, domestic work, medicine, and education, and slightly higher in utilities. A comprehensive report issued in September 2011 examined the total productivity of economic areas across the country, and only one very large city was in the top 50 (that was San Francisco at 50th); more than half of them (28) were "micropolitan" areas under 50,000 people.

And that brings up another crucial economic fact: smaller cities, it seems, are more efficient in supplying municipal services than any other form of government. Urban economists are agreed that there is, in their terms, a "U-curve" for city efficiency that works as follows. From 2,000 people to about 30,000, cities are required to spend a lot of money to supply a large number of urban services, but at that level there are not so many economies of scale, start-up costs for each new service are considerable, and the tax base is still too limited to recompense the municipality sufficiently. Over that limit, and on to about 100,000 people, cities have a large enough tax base to fund new services, can buy supplies and build plants with economies of scale, and are still limited enough geographically so that they can supply services efficiently. Above 100,000 or so, all costs tend to rise slowly but inexorably as the city gets bigger, while its ability to get the services to the citizens just as slowly and inexorably declines. The optimum point in this U-curve comes somewhere between a 50,000 to 100,000 population for most city services, with some studies pointing to 200,000 or 300,000 population for a few municipal obligations, but most falling in a range that I have calculated averages out to 63,000 people. Percival Goodman, the architect and city planner, put it succinctly: "It requires no stretch of credulity to believe that from the viewpoint of conservation economics the future belongs to compact cities in the 50,000 to 150,000 population range."

Werner Hirsch, former professor of economics and director of the Institute of Government at UCLA, was probably the most diligent examiner of municipal performance in the late twentieth century. A few geographically diffuse services, he said, such as public health and electricity and water supply, may best be handled "on a district or countywide basis," but most municipal services can be operated best by small cities: "Local urban governments, particularly if they serve 50,000–100,000 citizens, can effectively provide education, library service, public housing, public welfare services, fire and police protection, refuse collection, parks and recreation, urban renewal, and street maintenance programs."

And if that academic opinion seems too esoteric, there is the practical opinion from a former city manager of Boca Raton, Florida, who spent several years studying city governments around the country while fighting through the courts for the right to limit the size of his city. "We estimate," he told the *New York Times*, "that the cost of providing municipal services increases sharply over 100,000. That's the breaking point when everything starts to cost a lot more."

By Political Standards

For several thousands of years there has been considerable agreement among students of political theory that a truly democratic community, a polis in the Greek sense, must have a relatively small scale. British historian H. D. F. Kitto tells a nice story to this point. Imagine, he says, a citizen of Periclean Athens transported to modern London, talking to a member of the posh Athenian club and being chided for the petty quality of political life in his ancient city compared with the marvelous grandeur of London:

The Greek replies, "How many clubs are there in London?" The member, at a guess, says about five hundred. The Greek then says,

"Now if all these combined, what a splendid premises they would build. They could have a clubhouse as big as Hyde Park." "But," says the member, "that would no longer be a club." "Precisely," says the Greek, "and a polis as big as yours is no longer a polis."

Yet it is precisely in this no-longer-a-polis world that most of us live today. Our major cities cannot lay any serious claims to being governed democratically. Citizen participation is limited almost entirely to quadrennial elections for mayor and city council, the candidates offered having been selected usually by one or another form of clubhouse politics. And even those elected officials are the first to admit that they are mostly in the grip of unelected forces—the bankers, the business elite, the city bureaucracy, and the municipal unions—thus making the citizens' connection to the actual governing of their city very tenuous indeed. It is this that accounts for the common findings among residents of large American cities of political apathy, cynicism, alienation, lethargy, and non-participation, all of which apparently increase as city size increases.

Indeed, Dougles Yates, when a political scientist at the School of Organization and Management at Yale, summarized the state of affairs in the title of his book *The Ungovernable City*. He was obviously not happy about it, but his analysis led him to the grim conclusion that "the city problem is a problem of government, that the large American city is increasingly ungovernable," and that this cannot be cured by weeding out corruption or improving the lot of the poor or any other palliative, since it is "a product of the city's basic political and social organization." His verdict on the big city was uncompromising: "Given its present political organization and decision-making processes, the city is fundamentally ungovernable . . . incapable of producing coherent decisions, developing effective policies, or implementing state or federal programs."

And here again, the smaller city apparently has a decisive edge. Political scientist Robert Dahl after considerable study formulated it into a kind of law: "The larger the place, the less likely is the citizen to be involved as an active participant in local political life." And the corollary: "The smaller the unit, the greater the opportunity for citizens to participate in the decisions of their government." Such studies as have been made on political participation generally support this commonsense view. One found that people with a high school education or better felt "more influential" and "significantly more confident" in cities under 100,000, and it concluded, "Persons living in small towns were significantly more likely than those in large cities to feel that they could influence political decisions." Another determined that "democratic participation" was enhanced in cities from 50,000 to 100,000, particularly in influencing decisions about city services. Still another determined that "the larger a city generally the less involvement in and 'attachment' to community affairs."

Of course there is no great mystery about this. To begin with, the sheer scale of events and organizations in the smaller city invites participation and creates the feeling that individuals have, or at least can have, some control over the events that affect their lives. Smaller cities also can be more efficient and responsive in meeting citizen needs, since there is likely to be more two-way communication, more and better message-sending to the people in charge, and easier access to their offices. And smaller governing systems are far more adaptable to any crisis, have far better information to rely on, and can depend on greater cooperation from the citizens. One measure of this effectiveness is found by one survey that shows the kinds of cities that are able to be governed by city managers—that is, those that are most amenable to efficient management or can escape the pull of political divisiveness, or both. In 2013, our most recent figures, 65 percent of cities of 10–25,000 had city-manager systems, 69 percent with 25–50,000, 74 percent with 50–100,000, and 77 percent with 100–200,000, after which it drops down sharply with only one city over a million.

Could it be that, given human frailty, a modest limit on political effectiveness is inevitable?

Dahl certainly seemed to come to this conclusion. After worrying it over in several books and a number of articles, spending more time on this than any of his academic colleagues, he finally decided: "I think that the optimal unit is, or rather could be, the city of intermediate size, bigger than neighborhood, smaller than megalopolis. . . . The appropriate size looks to me to be a city between about fifty thousand and several hundred thousand inhabitants."

———

Certainly there are very few who can any longer champion the big cities as they are, as they have been, increasingly, for several decades. Some may defend them because they themselves are still able to enjoy the benefits and cushion themselves from the ills—they can afford the tickets to the show, the dinner at the exclusive restaurant, and the taxis to and from work, and have air-conditioning, summer homes, and vacations in the Bahamas. But they are a lucky, and a dwindling, few. Some may also believe that, in time, the big cities will arrive at miraculous solutions—Jane Jacobs, for example, who loved cities and apparently loved them at any size and density, no matter what anyone says, argues that attempts to limit their size are "profoundly reactionary" because cities can always solve their problems by "progress" and "new technology." But this seems unduly optimistic—on the record, the cities' successes at solving such problems as traffic congestion, pollution, crime, and social decay after several centuries of trying does not inspire a lot of confidence in future techno-fix solutions.

The trend of the future, rather, seems clearly entropic. The big city, it is not too much to say, with very few exceptions has probably outlived whatever usefulness it may have had (as, for example, a center of political control or of industrial technology). The traditional reasons for the exis-tence of the big city—defense of the citizen, abundant employment, easy commerce, class and ethnic mixture, creative innovation—clearly no lon-ger pertain generally. Indeed, it is no longer a city at all, in the traditional sense, a coherent, visible, determinable place. Los Angeles, for example, could not be called anything more than a political fiction, certainly not a city, a place of defined spirit and cohesion, a place with a center, an agora or a market or a square, a place with *city-ness*. Murray Bookchin, whose critique of the city is one of the most penetrating we have, put it this way:

> If the word "city" traditionally conveyed a clearly definable urban
> entity, New York, Chicago, Los Angeles—or Paris, London,
> Rome—are cities in name only. In reality they are immense urban
> agglomerations that are steadily losing any distinctive form and qual-
> ity. Indeed, what groups these cities together under a common rubric
> is no longer the cultural and social amenities that once distinguished
> the city from the countryside, but the common problems that betoken
> their cultural dissolution and social breakdown.

And that is why demographers have been forced to give new names to these things—metropolis, conurbation, megalopolis, necropolis. For they are, alas, no longer cities.

14

Human-Scale Services

How would a human-scale society go about the business of providing the services that a modern community would probably deem necessary and desirable, from energy to education, and including food-growing, garbage disposal, transportation, and health care? And can it be done with appropriate limits and optimal scales at which they could satisfy all the needs of a modern society without the dangers and expense of the larger and more fragile systems we have with us now? Luckily at this stage the answers to both are relatively simple to discover, since all of the theoretical underpinnings and most of the practical technology is already known and proven. Let us take a look.

Energy

There is only one real solution to the energy problem, one obvious, renewable, non-polluting, free, and benign energy source: the sun. But not only is solar energy the solution to the energy problem; it is also an explicitly *human-scale* solution. Here's why.

Solar energy is ecological. It does not pollute; it is silent, odorless, and safe; it does not use irreplaceable materials; and it is completely natural.

Solar energy is conservational. Not only does it save fossil fuels for other restricted uses, but it forces people to make daily connections between the switch on the wall and the resources behind it and to consider the long-term consequences of their use of nature.

Solar energy is inherently democratic. The sun's rays fall in roughly equal proportion, given polar and equatorial variations, on every man, woman, and child around the globe and are available to any person, any family, any neighborhood, any community. Sunshine falls at an average of 17 thermal watts per square foot all over the United States—varying only by a factor of two between sunny Arizona and cloudy Washington—and enough of it descends in just half a day to supply, were it fully captured, the entire energy needs of the nation for an entire year.

Solar energy is localized, and adaptable to different geographies and settlements. In the United States, it would take different optimum forms in different regions: direct sunlight in the Southwest and Southeast, wind power on ocean and lake coastlines and in higher altitudes, water and wood power particularly in the Northeast and Northwest, methane production in rural areas of the South and the Plains States. In the rest of the world, it is particularly beneficial in direct form for the poorer nations, which tend to be in the hotter climates.

Solar energy is decentralized. Since the whole operation is controlled by those who use it—who thereby become active producers of energy instead of passive consumers of it—it can be specifically adjusted to what engineers call "end-use needs," i.e., the requirements of the individual family or community. It cannot be dominated or monopolized by large corporations or central governments, cannot be bought and sold, cannot be jacked up in price from year to year. (It is conceivable that a company or government could try to monopolize the *equipment* used for collecting and storing solar power, and there's every indication that this is in the minds of certain energy companies right now. But most of the hardware is so easy to produce from common materials, in any location, and there are so many different kinds of systems that can be built, that this attempt does seem problematical. The solar industry has expanded by 60 percent annually in the last decade and now numbers more than 8,000 businesses.)

Solar energy is flexible, adaptable to a great range of social and political conditions, foreseen and unforeseen, unlike present more rigid systems. An entire solar unit can be constructed, even for a fairly large building, within a matter of days and it can be enlarged or modified anytime, as needs suggest. A nuclear plant, by contrast, takes many decades to finance, build, and, eventually, decommission.

Solar energy is efficient. Very little of the original energy is lost through *conversion*—as when it changes from heat to hot water—and even less through *transmission*, since any solar unit is relatively self-contained. This is in contrast with a normal electric utility, which loses *50 to 65 percent* of its primary energy in conversion and transmission.

Solar energy is free for all, and though the means of collecting and dispersing it of course are not, most of that hardware is inexpensive or will soon be competitive with existing systems. Once in place, solar gear requires only the most minimal of maintenance costs and of course no fuel costs at all. What equipment expenses there are can be decentral- ized, absorbed by the respective buildings or communities, and therefore there need be no large, ongoing financial burdens on the nation as a whole, as at present.

Solar energy is economical in its scale. It does not require large predic- tion and planning studies, complex delivery systems, enormous storage capacities, elaborate backup mechanisms, expensive bureaucracies, and such overhead costs as advertising budgets, security systems, and labor. That's not to say there aren't massive solar installations where these concerns arise; but going solar does not demand going massive.

Solar energy is especially adaptable to alternative technologies. It is simple to understand—anyone who has ever gotten into a closed car on a hot day knows how it works—and simple to build, maintain, and repair, using standard common skills known to any do-it-your- selfer. Much of the technology—for windmills and stoves, for example—is very old and well tested, and most of the newer ele- ments are simple, cheap, and amenable to backyard innovations.

Solar energy is safe. It has, true enough, been used before as a weapon— Archimedes is said to have set fire to the Roman fleet using a mirror to reflect the sun's rays in 212 BC—and there is the story of that woman in California who surrounded herself with aluminum on a sundeck and got baked to death, like a potato. But those seem to be the limits of solar danger, and probably containable.

Solar energy is adaptable to any sort of thermodynamic job—uniquely so among energy sources, because it operates from low temperatures to higher instead of the other way around. It is gathered on the surface of the earth at about 70 degrees (the temperature needed for space heating) and then if necessary can be transformed by cells and concentrators up to 150 degrees (for hot water), 200 degrees (for heat-driven air-conditioning), 1,000 degrees (for electricity generation), or even 2,500 degrees (for steel and metal manufacturing). Oil, by contrast, has to be burned at about 500 degrees in a furnace before it can be used at all, uranium becomes useful only when it reaches 2,400 degrees, and then all that heat just has to be drained away to make it useful in heating a house to 70 degrees, a process of unimaginable inefficiency: it is, as the ecologists have been saying for some years, "the thermodynamic equivalent of cutting butter with a chain saw."

Finally, and most pertinent of all, solar is communitarian. There is no difficulty in imagining efficient solar-energy systems on an individual-building level, but if those buildings are linked in a fairly small system then a whole variety of problems can be eased and definite efficiencies and economies obtained. Amory Lovins, founder and guru of the Rock Mountain Institute energy think tank, has said:

> *There are often good reasons to share even simple energy systems among, say $10'-10^3$ people. For example, neighborhood solar heating systems (for individual or cluster housing) can clearly offer substantial economies over single-house systems through freer collector siting and configuration, reduced craft-work, reduced surface-to-volume ratio in storage tanks, more favorable ratio of variable to fixed costs, and perhaps even a bit of user diversity (different people using, say, hot water at different times, though this would be a very small term).*

Communal storage is particularly valuable in a solar operation. Since maximum storage systems, be they water or rock or salts, must be fairly large for long-term heat storage, it can be cheaper for a number of users to get together to create one large neighborhood storage chamber. This would be particularly desirable for annual (or "trans-seasonal") units that can store enough surplus heat in summer to provide complete heating needs all winter; according to the magazine *People and Energy,* "Annual storage systems are most economical for multi-family dwellings and small (in area) communities."

152

Electricity production, too, can usually be more efficient at this level. There are economies of scale in power plants up to the point at which there is more heat lost in transmission than actually gets through to the users, but that begins to happen after only a few square miles. A number of studies have shown that small plants (ideally photovoltaic and photo-thermal) serving about 5,000 people—the "magic" number, again—are most cost-efficient. A Spectrolab Corporation report to the Project Independence solar-energy team, for example, concluded: "Smaller plants, located close to an end-user, may compete with power worth up to three times the central power station costs due to the savings in distribution costs and the higher fuel costs of conventional 'intermediate load' plants"; it suggested an optimal plant of 4 to 10 megawatts of electricity, suitable to supply a community of 800 to 2,000 homes (3,000–6,000 people).

Communitywide systems, even more than individual systems, are especially suited to a mix of energy sources. Such "total-energy systems" typically capture the considerable quantities of "waste" heat (up to 70 percent of the original energy) that is expelled by a power plant and use it for space heating and air-conditioning of nearby buildings. A small total-energy unit of that kind could supply the full power needs of an area of more than a million square feet—a small urban neighborhood, a shopping center, an apartment complex—for 40 percent of the costs of separate units; in fact, these have become increasingly common in factories in certain high-energy industries like chemical and paper production. Larger units operating up to two square miles are possible before transmission wastage occurs, and even larger units, such as the "district heating" systems that supply up to several hundred thousand people in parts of Sweden and West Germany, are possible before conventional power systems are seriously competitive.

There is something to be said, too, for the sheer communitarian values of a locally based power system, approachable, guidable, and controllable by local citizens. As long ago as 1978, there was extraordinary support for such a system. When the Department of Energy held ten public hearings on energy policy that year, the Institute for Local Self-Reliance, contracted to monitor the hearings, reported:

> *The dominant theme of every hearing was strong support for the decentralizing and self-reliant characteristics of solar energy. Decentralization was emphasized not only because of cost advantages, but*

because it leads to a different relationship between the consumer and the energy he or she uses.

Many people saw solar as a way to build community. One speaker said, "Solar creates jobs in the local community and keeps the money there, rather than sending it to companies . . . and institutions miles away." Speakers repeatedly urged the government to decentralize its funding programs and emphasize small businesses, individuals, and small research organizations.

Community power control has, in fact, come of age. As of 2010, community-owned and independent power producers—not public or private utilities—generated some 85 percent of the electric megawatts in the United States. Many were in low-population areas—the typical system served only 15,000 customers, as against an average of 250,000 for the private utilities—and operation at that scale provided them special efficiencies, particularly because of moderate service limits and citizen cooperation. This, combined with the fact that they didn't have to pay any dividends to private shareholders, and to a lesser extent their exemption from income taxes, meant they operated 30 percent more economically than private utilities.

Rufus Miles, author of *Awakening from the American Dream: The Social and Political Limits to Growth*, is one of those who has perceived the liberatory effects of such community-based energy systems, concluding that "individual and community control over energy use and policies . . . would in fact help us to preserve and enhance democratic values." If small-scale solar plants did nothing more than that, they would be invaluable. The fact that they can do that *and* conserve energy, save money, and protect the environment makes them perfect instruments of a human-scale society.

Food

The case for the human-scale farm over large industrial agribusiness is so strong that the wonder is that it hasn't taken over all the farmland in America. As Peter Rosset, who was executive director of a California think tank known as Food First, said in 2000, "For every country for which data is available, small farms are anywhere from 200 to 1,000 percent more productive" per acre.

The research to support this is copious, and it points to one inescapable conclusion: the most technically efficient and optimum-sized farm—the human-scale farm—is a small unit of a few hundred acres run by a family or one or two people. The US Department of Agriculture has issued a number of studies over the last fifty years, all in general agreement with the position of the 1973 report:

> We are so conditioned to equate bigness with efficiency that nearly everyone assumes that large-scale undertakings are inherently more efficient than smaller ones. In fact, the claim of efficiency is commonly used to justify bigness. But when we examine the realities we find that most of the economies associated with size are achieved by the one-man fully mechanized farm. . . .
>
> The fully mechanized one-man farm, producing the maximum acreage of crops of which the man and his machines are capable, is generally a technically efficient farm. From the standpoint of costs per unit of production, this size farm captures most of the economies associated with size.

A 1967 study showed that the "modern and fully mechanized one-man and two-man operation," not the giant industrial farm, is optimal for economies of scale; a 1972 study showed that, in California, where the average corporate farm was 3,206 acres, the ideal size in terms of efficient production was actually only 440 acres; another indicated that although the optimum farm varies according to the crop being grown, the ideal vegetable farm would be only 200 acres and only a wheat-and-barley spread in Montana need be more than 800 acres. According to Michael Perelman, a professor of economics at California State, Chico, "small farms have higher yields than large farms" and "in any state the value of the crops grown on the average acre tends to be larger when the average farm is small." Finally, despite the beliefs of most bankers, it turns out that small farms are actually more stable and better credit risks than large farms, as a government official acknowledges: "We know from our studies in the Department of Agriculture that the rates of foreclosure and delinquency are greater on big-farm loans, for the large-scale farm units, than for smaller loans on family farms."

And just for good measure, evidence from international studies confirms the connection between output and size. Early research in Britain, Ceylon, Thailand, the Philippines, Brazil, and Guatemala found time and again that the smaller the farm generally the higher the yield per acre, in some cases 60 percent higher. It was on the basis of these studies, in fact, that the World Bank began in the 1970s to support small-farm development rather than pour all its grants into Third World agribusinesses trying to look like America's. The British publication *The Economist*, in commenting upon this shift, wrote tellingly:

> *This is not the romanticism of seeking out the noble peasant. It is a hard-headed calculation that small farmers, working for goals and returns they understand, on land where they have security of tenure and with enough co-operative credit and services to enrich their labour, produce the world's highest returns per worker and often per acre. And basically it is upon this strategy of backing the small men . . . that the hopes of feeding most of mankind in the long term depend.*

It stands to reason, actually. Large farms have administrative costs and bureaucratic inefficiencies that small farms don't, they depend upon hired labor and often on distant decision makers, they are forced to be highly mechanized in order to operate such acreage (and a tomato-harvesting machine costs up to $450,000), they have significantly higher labor costs, including overseers and corporate officers, and they have rental costs, overhead costs, equipment costs, and transportation costs that the smaller operations do not have. Whatever savings they make in cheaper bank loans, bulk buying, or market domination do not make up for those diseconomies. And no one realizes this more than the giant agribusiness firms themselves: as a Ralston Purina official once admitted, "The individual farmer or family corporation can meet, and many times surpass, the efficiency of the large corporations that operate with hired management." Even the Department of Agriculture's insistence on "mechanized" ought not to be taken too rigorously, for smaller farms are able to operate without most of the high-cost machinery that big spreads demand: you can go out and hand-spray an organic pesticide on an acre or two, and you don't *need* an expensive crop-dusting plane. Economist Perelman's work indicates that, "all other things being equal, mechanization tends to decrease yields." The Amish, for example, are a perfect case study in non-mechanized efficiency. They make use of contemporary scientific information about breeding and biological pest control, but they use no internal-combustion machinery whatsoever, relying wholly on animal and human labor and simple tools. Yet they consistently produce more per acre than their neighbors, various studies have shown, and of course, judged in terms of energy, harvest far more per unit of energy invested.

The experience of organic farmers, too, over the last 35 years—the number of certified organic farms in this country has grown from about 1,500 in 1979 to 3,587 in 1992 to 14,093 in 2014—has shown that it is possible not only to operate without chemicals and their attendant machines but to match crop yields at the same time, improve quality, and eliminate expenses. An early study from Washington University's Center for the Biology of Natural Systems that examined fourteen organic and fourteen conventional farms in the Corn Belt indicated that although crop production was the same for organic farms and conventional farms, which is significant in itself, the organic farms' cost per acre was $19 cheaper—and they use only about a third as much energy. The debate over whether organic agriculture could feed the world persisted for decades, though, as large chemical companies fought to maintain their hold on modern agriculture. That lingering question prompted UC Berkeley researchers to analyze the results of more than one hundred studies and in 2014 they concluded that organic methods could indeed generate crop yields sufficient to feed the world—and, of course, benefit soils, water, and biodiversity in the process.

All of which is not to say that optimum farms have to go back to the horse-drawn plow—far from it. With appropriate use of alternative technologies, it is possible for any smallholding to reduce the backbreaking part of farm labor without the budget-breaking enslavement to a fossil-fuel economy. On a small scale—and on a small scale only—it is possible to find the fitting balance between the mechanical and the human.

———

Smaller farms possess other virtues, too. They are able to switch to and use solar energy more easily, and without much difficulty become energy self-sufficient if they wish to. A series of tests by the Small Farm Energy Project in Nebraska has shown that retro-fitting and insulation, wind and biogas systems, and solar heat and hot-water collectors can be installed cheaply in single-family farms and that the savings they produce are almost immediate. More than 230 farms in the United States already turn the manure of their own animals into methane capable of powering about 70,000 homes, and biogas analysts suggest thousands more could, ultimately powering 1.1 million homes. There are at least 60,000 windmills in use on US farms to pump water or provide power. Smaller farms can more easily switch to and maintain such methods as organic, hydroponic, and biodynamic farming; hydroponics, using liquid fertilizers instead of soils, and biodynamic methods, using a compact-bed system practiced for years in France, have both been shown to increase crop yields from two to eight times normal. Smaller farms, because they can be located closer to cities, can also supply food directly to local markets, eliminating the extremely costly and energy-wasting practice of refrigerating and shipping vegetables from coast to coast—and providing far fresher and better food as well.

Smaller farms are especially valuable because they are uniquely suited for communitywide cooperation—and indeed the history of agriculture in this country for the most part was exactly the history of rural cooperation. The largest farms have little interest in cooperation, since they normally have all their own equipment and can throw their weight around in the marketplace, and the corporate farms of agribusiness of course operate completely vertically, back and forth to the corporate hierarchy, rather than horizontally, with the other farms in the area. But small farms have always felt the need to band together, whether for a barn-raising in the eighteenth century or to establish marketing co-ops in the 1870s or to buy bulk fuel in the 1920s.

Ultimately it is not hard to imagine this extraordinary communal tradition, providing it can survive the increasing hold of corporate agribusiness, evolving into a network of truly self-sufficient food communities. Indeed, there is not one region of the country that could not eventually become self-sufficient in food, with only the smallest dietary changes. Self-sufficiency is not as chimerical as agribusiness would have us think. We do not *need* to depend on complex intercontinental—and international—distribution systems. We import snails from France, for example, with great fanfare and considerable cost, but the fact is that the exact same animal, *Helix aspera*, is found naturally almost everyplace in this country; we get tomatoes from Florida even during the summer months because distributors and supermarkets are locked into marketing contracts, but the fact is that from May to September tomatoes can be grown anyplace in the entire country, and in greenhouses they can be grown locally the year around.

Above all, smaller farms are simply better for the social texture of rural America, for people. Two unusually comprehensive studies done in the premier agribusiness state, California, offer interesting confirmation of this.

The first was undertaken by a task force of the Small Farm Viability Project and presented to the state government in November 1977. It engaged a team of sociologists from the University of California at Davis to examine 130 towns in the San Joaquin Valley and compare the quality of life in those places with small-parcel holdings (under 160 acres) as against those with large cropping patterns (640 acres or more). Invariably, they found, the small-farm communities generated more local businesses, higher levels and diversity of employment, and better civic services and had more lawyers, dentists, doctors and medical specialists, elementary schools, movies, hospitals, pharmacies, farm-equipment stores, police, firefighters, and post office workers. They concluded:

> *Many have argued that large businesses are a financial boon to an area. Whether this assumption is valid or not, the suggestion here is that large-scale farming may have a less positive effect on the local community than small-scale farming. Large-scale agriculture offers the local communities no substantial advantage. The smaller scale farming areas clearly tend to offer more to the local communities than their counterparts.*

And they provided as additional evidence a finding by Berkeley economist George Goldman that converting a region from farms averaging 1,280 acres to ones averaging just 320 acres actually *improves* the economy of the area—generating 540 new jobs, increasing retail sales by $16 million a year, and raising personal income by $6.2 million—because more of the money stays in the locality and through its "multiplier effect" enriches the whole population.

The second study is a sociological classic that was originally conducted by Walter R. Goldschmidt of UCLA in 1945–46 and then updated and validated by two further investigations in 1970 and 1977. It compared two California towns of approximately the same size—Dinuba, with 7,404 people, and Arvin, with 6,236—but with totally different farm

159

communities, one of the traditional smallholding style and the other changed by agribusiness. Dinuba had 635 farms, averaging 45 acres, most of them family-owned, and only a third of its population was hired labor (down to 14 percent in the 1970s); Arvin had only 137 farms, averaging 297 acres, and many large operations, some of them absentee-owned and almost all dependent on hired workers, who made up two-thirds of the population (down to 38 percent in the 1970s). The difference between them was like corn and cattle.

Dinuba had a significantly higher standard of living, with more than half the population in farming or in white-collar occupations compared with one-fifth in Arvin, and 15 percent in skilled trades and professions compared with 6 percent. On a "level-of-living" index (measuring the number of homes with electricity, appliances, automobiles, et cetera), Dinuba had 38 percent of its residents in the top quarter, Arvin only 18 percent. Sales of home supplies and building materials were three times higher in the small-farm community, and it had almost twice as many small businesses and 61 percent higher retail sales (by 1976 that had grown to 70 percent). The Dinuba population had a higher percentage of high school graduates —38 percent to 19 percent—and supported four elementary schools and one high school, against a single elementary school for Arvin; Dinuba had two newspapers, each larger than the single paper in Arvin. Dinuba had twice as many church, civic, and social organizations, with higher levels of participation. And it had "more institutions for democratic decision-making and much broader citizen participation in such activities," one result of which was that it had "far better" public facilities, including sidewalks, roads, sewerage, garbage service, playgrounds, and parks.

Naturally these kinds of studies were anathema to the big-farm bureaucrats and companies, so there was a pushback in the 1980s, with one academic study arguing that the two towns were not really comparable and that Arvin had deficiencies beyond the influence of big farms. But two subsequent reports, one by Linda Labao of Ohio State University in 1990 of 3,000 US counties and another by Curtis Stofferahn of the University of North Dakota in 2006 confirmed the original Goldschmidt findings; as Stofferahn put it, large-scale industrialized agriculture "disrupts the social fabric of communities . . . poses environmental threats where livestock production is concentrated; and is likely to create a new pattern of 'haves' and 'have-not.'"

It was the continuing demonstration that factory farming had serious drawbacks that finally led the US Department of Agriculture to wonder if maybe its get-big-or-get-out policies should be revisited. It established a National Commission on Small Farms in July 1997 that issued a subsequent report leading the department to adopt a philosophy of support for small and moderate farms, especially as a way to keep the younger generation in farming and as a way to halt the decline in farms and the desiccation of rural villages. Concurrently a National Small Farm Conference began meeting in 1996, and it has met every three or four years since then, its latest meeting in 2016. At the same time state agriculture colleges and departments began what were called Small Farm Viability projects to study and promote farming, and these have now spread to practically every state.

So small farms have proven themselves and gained new champions. It is a little sad, then, to report that today—2016—both Arvin and Denuba have succumbed to large farms, now mostly citrus and dairy, and the populations are no longer diverse (heavily Hispanic), with few of the community institutions left.

Garbage

Reduce, reuse, recycle—that catchphrase, which perfectly captures the process of a human-scale treatment of waste, is more honored in the breach than the observance, despite the campaigns that have gone on now for forty years or more and efforts at all levels of government. Of the 35,000 municipalities in the United States, only some 9,800 had curbside collection recycling systems as of 2010. And not all of them included all types of waste: compostable, paper, glass, plastic, cans, and metals. The result is that in 2013 Americans generated about 254 million tons of trash but recycled and composted only 87 million tons of this material, equivalent to a 34.3 percent recycling rate—far better than our rate of 10 percent in 1980, but not much better than the 28.5 percent in 2000. On average, we generated 4.40 pounds of waste per person per day and recycled and composted just 1.51 pounds of it.

Part of the problem, as it always is, is size. In the larger cities that generate most of the waste, the participation rate, despite incentives and penalties, has been woefully low. With the exception of a few places like San Francisco (80 percent in 2011) and Portland, Oregon (59.3 percent), most cities are well below the national average and some, like Houston (10 percent) and Oklahoma City (3 percent), don't seriously try. Smaller cities usually are able to get more citizens to participate, in part because they can get the word out more easily and in part because their smaller landfills are likely to be full more quickly, making recycling imperative. In Oregon, one of the most successful recycling states, an experienced hand at the Office of Recycling Information, Bill Bree, has said that experience has shown that "easier communications, and more established patterns of social cohesion, make smaller towns easier to work within setting up recycling operations."

The Institute for Local Self-Reliance, mostly under the direction of its co-founder, Neil Seldman, has been a leader for forty years in show-ing communities how they can work out small-scale composting and resource-recovery operations. As their 2015 annual report put it, "A unique advantage of composting is its ability to be small-scale and local. We believe community-based composting is the foundation for the munic-ipal-wide programs that are also clearly needed," and they have taken this into all kinds of cities, big and small—but where big, always on a community-based decentralized basis.

Small-scale recycling operations in the future can be made even more efficient, by the application of both communitywide support and alterna-tive technologies. Studies have shown that the optimum efficiency for a recycling program is reached when every household in a community of 5,000 participates—at that level, a once-a-week collection can produce a large enough quantity of various materials to make a 15–20 percent profit on resale, and it will still not cover so much territory that it loses money in collection and transportation costs, which account for 70–80 percent of the overhead of an ordinary system. Collection could be even more economically done with small electric carts or trailers or ultimately with a simple network of underground, solar-powered conveyor belts that, in small areas, could be operated as efficiently as such belts are in any large factory today. *That* would be the most efficient and equitable separation and recycling operation of all.

A small-scale system would be most economical, too, if the community were to reuse everything within its own borders as raw material for its own products. Small-scale aluminum and de-tinning facilities can now be constructed for less than $10,000—10 percent of the capital needed for a primary production plant—and, using ordinary cans, could turn out metal for local production of bicycles, wheelbarrows, machine and auto parts, and the like. Paper-processing plants could easily convert wastes into newsprint or reusable paper or even into cellulose-fiber insulation. Bottling centers could either recap and reuse the bottles as they come in or crush them to use in road or building construction or, with currently available machinery, remold them into canning jars for neighborhood use. A somewhat more complex, but still small-scale, process can be used to convert plastic wastes into building materials, furniture, auto-body parts, or fish tanks. Human and food wastes could be fed to community livestock—pigs, as everyone knows, are marvelous waste-eaters and process even human excrement to a valuable manure—or composted collectively for community gardens; "graywater" (household water used for washing or bathing) could be piped from each house and, after a simple filtering, used for irrigation.

There seems to be a scale, that is to say, at which even such a process as garbage recovery can make economic and ecological sense. It is small, and human.

Transportation

About the existence of the transportation mess there is no question.

It begins with the motor vehicle. A study in 2015 for the National Highway Traffic Safety Administration using 2010 data found that vehicle crashes in America killed 33,000 people—someone has called it the most lethal device since the invention of the machine gun—caused 3.9 million injuries, damaged 24 million vehicles, and had a total economic cost of $242 billion, counting repairs, replacement, work time lost, air pollution, energy, and the like. The social cost, including lost quality of life, pain and suffering, loss of income, and aggravation, was figured to be $836 billion.

And that's just crashes. Figure also the cost of building and maintaining American streets and highways, for snow removal, highway patrols, and traffic courts, for traffic lights, bridges, and rush-hour police, for the costs of congestion, for the losses to a city of having half its land off the tax rolls—if all these costs were added on to the price of fuel at the gas pump instead of hidden and absorbed by the society at large, the average gallon of gasoline, it has been estimated, would cost $21.60 more in 2015.

And individuals bear significant costs. A 2015 calculation found that the annual ownership costs for Americans averaged $8,698 for gas, repairs, insurance, and other everyday expenses. Which may not seem much, but figured for 200 million drivers it comes to $17 billion a year, a serious burden for a society to bear.

In one sense, of course, America's auto-mania is "reasonable." For, given the spatial arrangements of America created by the preponderant use of the car—a radial society, distending the social fabric, pulling families and generations apart, spreading out neighbor from neighbor—the car is the most sensible instrument to use to get around them. Since the presence of the car in modern life has created suburbs and scattered-site housing and low-density cities, it is just about the only way to travel in and between them. Houston and Los Angeles and Phoenix don't have a lot of cars just because people *like* them—such cities were built precisely because of cars, to and for cars, and people *need* them.

A human-scale solution to the problem of the car, then, begins not with transportation but with settlements. The first and most essential way to deal with urban traffic, in other words, is urban design.

Now, traditionally, traffic experts have operated with one objective: to move people into and around cities as rapidly and efficiently as possible. Even some of the clearest thinkers—Doxiadis, Fuller, Soleri, Goodman— have sought to create elaborate mechanisms to whisk people from point to point. Speed becomes uppermost, and the fact that it is never obtained, no matter what contrivances the engineers make, never seems to deter them in their pursuit of it. Seeking the swift and unimpeded movement of people and machines, they do away with plazas and squares, remove traffic lights and put in beltways, eliminate intersections and construct cloverleafs. It sometimes seems that they may not rest until the most monumental traffic obstacle of all—the city and its impedimental buildings and people—is removed.

But of course that is no solution—in fact it's all backward. The thing to do is not to move people through cities but to stop them there. Isn't that why cities are built in the first place? Isn't that why cities are traditionally located where they are, the endpoints of traffic, both land and water? New York is built where a harbor offers shelter from an Atlantic voyage, where river traffic down the Hudson comes to an end, where land journeys from the southern slopes of the Adirondacks and the Catskills come to an end. New Orleans is built at the midpoint of the gulf that is the southern gateway to North America, and at the end of the Mississippi River and its enormous valley system. San Francisco is built upon the harbor that ends the voyage across the Pacific, at the terminus of both the Sacramento and San Joaquin valley systems, where movement from the Sierra Nevada's western slopes reaches its focus.

Cities are meant to stop traffic. That is their point. That is why they are there. That is why traders put outposts there, merchants put shops there, hoteliers erect inns there. That is why factories locate there, why warehouses, assembly plants, and distribution centers are established there. That is why people settle and cultural institutions grow there. No one wants to operate in a place that people are just passing through; everyone wants to settle where people will stop, and rest, and look around, and talk, and buy, and share.

Cities, in short, should be an end, not a means. Rationally one wants to have traffic *stop* there, not go *through*, one wants movement within it to be *slow*, not *fast*. Therefore, in thinking about urban design in connection with transportation, one might cleave to such concepts as these.

> *Cities should not try to move people to facilities but provide facilities where the people are.* Or as Barbara Ward has put it succinctly, the goal is "access not mobility." In a city built of roughly self-sufficient communities, each one should be able to provide all the important daily services within walking distance, thus eliminating the need for any but the thinnest ribbon of streets and freeing most space for pedestrian (or bicycle) paths or parklands. For the elderly and infirm, golf carts (miniature electric cars, actually) and multi-passenger electric tricycles would be a simple expedient.
>
> *Cities should be small enough so that inter-community trips, when necessary, could be managed either on foot, by bike, or with some simple subway or trolley system.* Obviously some cities today are so spatially unmanageable that getting around them by bike would be folly: these demonstrate the dangers of concentrating too many functions in a single center. What is wanted, instead of one large city glutted with all the attractions, is a series of smaller cities each with its own glitter and charm. This is the carnival principle: you don't put all the cotton-candy stands in one place and have everybody jam up there; you spread them through the grounds so that people will be dispersed.

*Cities should attempt to slow down the flow of traffic, particularly with
plenty of squares and plazas and parks, places where wheeled vehicles
are forced to halt, endpoints that invite stopping and resting.* It is not
for nothing that medieval cities had squares wherever one would
go and that the most charming cities of the world even now—
Salzburg, London, San Juan, Savannah—are those with repeated
interruptions of streets. Of course squares are not good for traffic,
and that's why most cities have removed them (New York City
even tried to do away with historic Washington Square Park a few
years ago), but they are good for people and for trade. It is around
the square that people will stop and shop and sit and drink and
learn the flow and pace of their community.

Cities should try to bring home and workplace back together—a point so
vital that it needs a little amplification.

———————

For most of urban history, it was assumed that people would work near
where they lived. Tradespeople lived above their stores, craftsmen and
their apprentices lived in the same building as their workshops, inn-
keepers lived in their taverns, professionals hung shingles outside their
residences. Not until the Industrial Revolution at the end of the eighteenth
century did this pattern slowly begin to change, and even then, even when
factories employing hundreds of people drew laborers from all over, the
workers normally lived within a short distance of the mill; the urban pattern for most of the nineteenth century was to have the workers' residential
district chock-a-block with the industrial district. It was around the end of
the nineteenth century that the real distention began. Trolley lines pushed
the city and its industries outward, and factories that began depending
on road transportation moved away from the congested centers. At the
same time workers' districts in the heart of town were taken over by retail
trade or by houses for the well-to-do, and workers were forced to resettle
in isolated pockets in undesirable spots around the city and in new towns
around the periphery, now usually many miles from their workplaces.
(Such resettlement also had the desirable effect, from the point of view
of the capitalists in charge, of reducing the workers' opportunity for
common action, lessening the chances that workers from the same factory
would live near each other, and thus dampening the labor militancy that

had been so virulent at the end of the nineteenth century.) The divisions in the city thus created were solidified by zoning legislation, created at about this time, which assured that the residential sections would be kept far from the industrial and commercial ones.

But now that the workers were over *here* and the work was over *there*, urban transportation became a serious problem, and so mass transportation and urban highway systems had to be built to get them together. But then it was not long before the availability of the private car encouraged people to move even farther from their places of work, out deeper and deeper into the suburbs, extending urban sprawl in all directions by the period after World War II. In effect, America decided to turn each of its cities into *two* cities, one large one for daytime use when everyone would congregate, the other a web of small ones for nighttime use when everyone would disperse; each would be left more or less vacant while the other was used, each would have to create its own lighting, sewage, road, telephone, police, education, medical, and political systems. And that meant again that the workers who were now way out *there* had to get to the jobs that were either still in *here* (particularly service jobs in commercial centers) or else all the way over on the *other side* of the city—hence the ever-growing networks of freeways and beltways and superhighways. Hence the madness of American transportation.

This story leads, I think, to only one conclusion: no solution of the transportation puzzle is possible until work and home are put back together (it is, after all, the comfortable condition of the nation's president) or at least within walking distance of each other.

It is obviously not impossible. Many towns operate that way in America today—in fact, according to the Census Bureau in 2009, 30 million people work at home at least once a week, 5.9 million "telework" from home full-time, nearly 4 million walk to work, and 766,000 use bicycles—that comes to over 3 million *more* than use all of public transit in the nation. That is the stated goal of the New Urbanism movement, and its high-density mixed-use neighborhoods, combined with bike- and walk-friendly streets, perfectly demonstrate how to solve the transportation problem.

Another aspect of a human-scale solution has to do with the transportation itself.

Obviously one desirable means of transportation would be something efficient, non-polluting, simple to manufacture and repair, energy-conserving, cheap, and harmless. It just so happens that such a means is available, indeed widely available, and has been for more than a century: the bicycle. S. S. Wilson of the Department of Engineering Science at Oxford puts the case neatly:

> The contrast between the bicycle and the motor car is a very good illustration of technology of human scale. The bicycle is a supreme example of ergonomics—the optimum adaptation of a machine to the human body, so that it uses this power efficiently. Hence the world-wide success of the bicycle and its derivations in meeting the real needs of the people in both rich and poor countries, with a minimum demand for energy and raw materials or ill effect on the environment. The motor car, on the other hand, is a machine of inhuman scale as regards its size, its weight, its power (from 100 to 1,000 times that of the driver himself) or its speed.

In terms of translating energy into transportation, there is *nothing*, neither animal nor mechanical, that is superior to a human being on a bicycle; as the chart comparing pedal power to even the wing power of fruit flies or jet planes makes clear. Pity the poor mouse watching us ride by on our bikes.

And the possible developments of the bike—long overlooked in this country until quite recently because the Model T came along only a few years after bicycles became popular and quickly displaced them—seem to be almost endless. Victor Papanek, the designer, once set a team of students in Sweden to work on the various potentials of the bike, and among the other models they came up with was an ingenious three-wheeled machine with a seat in the back that could be used for hauling heavy loads, had a gear system so that it could be pushed uphill with ease even when loaded, could carry stretchers or planks, and could be connected in tandem to make a short train.

Moreover, bicycles can be readily equipped with little "booster motors" for traveling over difficult terrain or uphill, or for the elderly and infirm. The one- and two-horsepower gasoline engines that are now found on mopeds represent one kind, and they don't use enough gas or cause enough pollution to be much of an ecological threat. Even better, however, are electric bikes, which can get up to 40 miles an hour with no more than a twelve-volt battery attached, use no fossil fuels, and create no pollution. Such machines

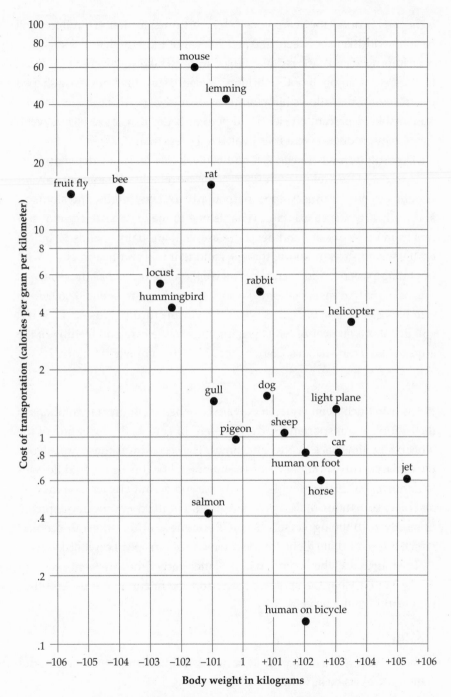

ENERGY EFFICIENCY OF
DIFFERENT MEANS OF TRANSPORT

have been around for years—one research firm said that 466 million will be sold worldwide between 2010 and 2016—but recently their designs have been improved and costs reduced. The Campbell bike, for example, invented by Dr. Peter Campbell of Cambridge, England, runs on a new disc-shaped electric motor that allows high torque even at low speeds and operates at a remarkable 75 percent efficiency, 20 percent better than most electric vehicles; the in-production cost is estimated to be less than $200.

Bicycling burns between 250 and 600 calories an hour, depending on the speed and the weight of the cyclist. It is extremely valuable not only for weight loss but for muscle tone, particularly for legs, thighs, and stomach, and for heart-muscle exercise. What is one to make of a society that suffers from gross obesity and heart disease, that annually spends $2 billion on the weight-loss industry, that jogs and tennises and health-clubs with unending passion, and then turns its back on the bicycle as the principal means of daily transportation? If a society is willing to spend $2,699 for a Life Fitness exercise bike, or $5,499 for an even sturdier Nustep TRS, and still devotes a quarter of all its waking time to the care and feeding of the automobile—can such a society be regarded as completely rational?

It was Ivan Illich's contention that there have been four great revolutions in the history of transportation. The first was, of course, the invention of the wheel, sometime back in Neolithic times. The second was the simultaneous use of the stirrup, shoulder harness, and horseshoe during the Middle Ages to improve the efficiency of the plow-horse and permit greater crop rotation and more cultivation of European farmland. The third was the development of sturdy oceangoing vessels by the Portuguese in the fifteenth century, which opened up the globe for the extension of European capitalism.

The fourth was the invention in the latter part of the nineteenth century of the ball bearing, the spoked wheel, and the pneumatic tire—and thus the creation of the bicycle.

Health

A health system in a human-scale society would ask that at least four associated processes be at work.

Nutrition. The very first priority would be to assure beneficial nutrition, since we know that much of the reduction in disease morbidity and mortality in our time is due to improved food habits. Imagine how much further our health could be improved if some sort of agricultural self-sufficiency were common and people had access to locally grown food that would not need to be processed or refrigerated and would arrive fresh on the dinner table at its nutritional peak. Or if our food were free of all the 3,000 unnecessary additives—some of them highly suspect as causes of disease, and the majority not even tested—now injected into it. Or if people had as equal and automatic access to nutritional foods as to junk foods, at equal prices, and with equal information. The staff of life itself may be symbolic here. At present most bread is made from white flour, from which 90 percent of the nutrients (including all the vitamin E, most B vitamins, most of the protein, and many minerals) have been processed away, and to which is added a great variety of substances (softeners, whiteners, preservatives) and enough vitamins to replace only about a tenth of the nutrient value that has been lost. (Dr. Roger J. Williams of the University of Texas once kept one batch of experimental rats on a diet of white bread and another on white bread plus vitamins and minerals. All of the supplement-diet rats were alive and growing after ninety days; one-third of the bread-only rats were stunted, two-thirds of them had dropped dead.) It would be far staffier, and do more for life, were it simply baked locally from local whole-grain flour—a process not so difficult that our grandparents couldn't manage it.

Living patterns. The second step would be restyling a few of the basic patterns of life to prevent most of the general, non-microbial causes of disease. Probably no single change would be more beneficial, particularly against heart and respiratory disorders, than strenuous exercise, through the increased use of bikes, encouragement of hands-on labor, regular opportunities in the community gardens, and emphasis on participatory instead of spectator sports. Relocation into optimal-sized cities and into rural areas would significantly reduce the stress of life as given to us by the big cities, which creates by itself various heart and nervous-system ailments and which leads on to those debilitating companions of stress, alcohol and tobacco. One could also imagine real protections being taken against job-related sicknesses—black-lung disease in coal mining, brown lung in textile production, cancer in asbestos plants, and so on—if workers themselves were to set the policies of the workplace and communities had some say in economic priorities. And similar worker and community decision making could lead to serious controls over industrial and municipal poisoning of air and water, which by itself would probably reduce the incidence of cancer in time by 70–80 percent.

Above all, smaller and less crowded settlements could simply *avoid* a good many diseases because, it turns out, most disease microorganisms need a large population in order to sustain themselves—as in the case of measles, which needs nearly half a million people in which it can operate before it can perpetuate itself. Interestingly, anthropological studies examined in some detail in William McNeill's *Plagues and Peoples* suggest that Paleolithic hunter-gatherers, operating in bands of fewer than a thousand, were apparently completely free from infectious diseases, or at any rate from those caused by microorganisms developed specifically to live off humans; it was not until agriculture made lives sedentary and then cities grew up that regular infectious chains were established.

Self-help. A third element to a rational system would be a reduction in the dependency on both doctors and drugs.

The extent to which quite ordinary people with quite limited training can tend to most everyday medical problems and often to even sophisticated and complex medical tasks must not be underestimated. The North Vietnamese, it is reliably reported, were able to teach laypeople to perform complicated eye operations even in the middle of an unstabilizing war. The Chinese system of "barefoot doctors" seems to be agreed upon—whatever one may think about the Maoist superstructure above it—as highly successful, and the job these minimally trained people did in setting up community clinics, teaching preventive techniques, and guiding campaigns to rid the country of such diseases as schistosomiasis as something close to a human miracle. China abolished the doctors in 1981, but two-thirds of the doctors working there today came through the barefoot-doctor system. Even in this country, similar lay operatives have shown themselves to be medically adept: paramedics, for example, with less than a year's training, have been used with considerable success in all but eight states of the union to provide front-line medical care (there were some 241,000 paramedics serving in 2014); and nurses and "physicians' assistants" with no more than two years of medical teaching now serve as doctors, with 95,583 P.A.'s at work in 2014.

Beyond that, the value of the simple and most elemental medical treatment—self-help—has been proven incontrovertibly. The remarkable growth of the women's health movement in the last generation, for

172

example—symbolized by the sales of the do-it-yourself book, *Our Bodies, Ourselves,* published in 1970 and reissued every four years since, now with more than 4 million copies sold—has shown that women the country over are capable of taking care of many of their own health problems without professional intervention. The so-called holistic health movement similarly has shown that people who work at controlling the health of their own bodies—eating natural foods, in limited amounts, fasting from time to time, exercising rigorously, meditating daily or through times of stress, using vitamin therapies, and the like—are unquestionably freer of disease than the general population. As a matter of fact, even the most quotidian kind of self-help that most people practice when they get sick—take two aspirin and don't call anybody in the morning—turns out to be probably the best treatment in the great majority of illnesses; studies in both Great Britain and Denmark have shown that the largest percentage of people begin to treat their ailments correctly even before they visit a doctor, and in most cases the doctors merely continue that treatment. There are literally millions of self-help groups across America—including 35 12-step programs—and there's a self-help "industry," including books, videos, seminars, and coaching, that was said to be worth $11 billion in 2013.

As to needing the medical establishment for drugs, this has obviously been blown far out of necessity and in general has proved more injurious than helpful. In fact there are many voices that argue that most prescribed drugs could simply be eliminated from the pharmacopoeia and, where necessary, substituted for by natural, or "herbal," elements— since, after all, that's what most of the laboratory drugs were based on in the first place.* In addition, there is a great variety of non-drug therapies

---

* It is well enough known that digitalis, used nowadays to regulate heart rhythms, is derived from the purple foxglove, an ancient Welsh medicine, and that rauwolfia, used to control high blood pressure, comes from a kind of snakeroot used for centuries as a sedative in India. It is less well known that there are effective herbal contraceptives, like the Chinese concoction from pine-tree sprouts, good for three years, and the South American Indian mixture reported by Nicole Maxwell, in *Witch Doctor's Apprentice,* that lasts for seven years unless a contra-acting fertility potion is taken. You can understand why Western drug companies have shown little interest in such long-acting agents to replace daily-pill dependency.

around, ranging from acupuncture and homeopathy, both proven for many decades but resisted by the medical establishment, to yoga and other Eastern psychosomatic techniques, whose results are sometimes impressive even if their workings still lie beyond the understanding of Western medicine.

Facilities. Lastly, after such steps as these, then and only then might one turn to consideration of medical facilities themselves. The number of hospitals has been shrinking since 1975, and the occupancy rate has declined from 77 percent then to 60 percent in 2013; the American Hospital Association now counts only 5,627 (2014). Increasingly health care is being done in ambulatory-care centers, clinics, and at home (including internet consultations), and in the near future it is held that at a community level, a small clinic with a nurse or a paramedic would easily suffice—experience under the present system has shown that a population of 5,000–10,000 can support a small facility, with patient visits averaging between ten and twenty a day.

For larger populations larger facilities would naturally be required, but as might be expected there is a point here too where the Beanstalk Principle operates. Studies of optimal-sized hospitals are for some reason notoriously unreliable—one of the ablest investigators, Sylvester Berki, has simply thrown his hands up and declared the whole matter intractable—but there are a few established facts, and they tend to favor hospitals of 100–200 beds (considered to be the upper range of the "small" hospital). Economies of scale in purchasing and supplies begin to operate over 100 beds and decline somewhere after 600 beds; but hospitals of more than 300–400 beds begin to show the strains brought on by problems of staff administration, recruitment, and communications; they suffer from all of the bureaucratic deficiencies any large organization experiences; and because they inevitably demand greater travel time they are consequently used by a decreasing percentage of the population. Moreover, hospitals of 100–200 beds in the United States today would seem to be as close to the optimum as we can get in practice with current standards: they have more admissions than any other sized facility, smaller or larger, see more out-patients and attend more births than any but the giant 500-plus-bed medical centers, and yet they are more efficient in terms of expenditure per patient than all other larger units, twice as efficient as the largest centers. And on the less quantifiable side of things, it appears that the smaller hospital has certain intangible advantages—in the words of the trade journal *Hospitals*, the smaller hospital has "this talent . . . to make its patients feel at home, cared for by friendly, attentive staff," and practically all reports agree that is of major significance in restoring most people to health.

And the population necessary to sustain a hospital of 100–200 beds? Both in Europe and in America such facilities have been shown to be most efficiently used and sustained in cities of 30,000–60,000 people. Extensive findings based on the comprehensive Chicago Regional Hospital Study in the 1960s indicate that, taking in a wide variety of variables—including economies of scale, travel time, degrees of care—the optimum patient population for any given center is somewhere between 20,000 and 40,000. And the Rutgers Community Health Plan has shown that health-main- tenance centers—HMOs—seem to operate with an optimum enrollment of 32,000. Not to overdo "magic" numbers—but the small city comes through once again.

Above this optimum level for everyday facilities, it may be desirable to have certain highly specialized medical services, not large in them- selves—in fact normally fewer than 50 beds—but which could serve large populations of 500,000–1.5 million or more through some sort of regional cooperative arrangement among a group of communities and cities. Crude forms of such an arrangement operate in a good many places today but in general each city tends to set up its own high-priced clinic with its own high-technology machinery even if it is consistently used way below its capacity. It would take not millions of dollars, nor millions of people gathered in a city, but only the simplest kind of cooperation and a very elementary form of ambulance transportation to create and maintain regional medical facilities that genuinely and rationally served a region.

Serious questions must intrude here, however, as to whether a society at one with its health would necessarily wish to invest huge resources in such things as burn centers and dialysis machines and CAT scanners and the rest, high-technology machines that artificially sustain life; or whether a society in ecological equilibrium could justify the construction and operation of such machines at great waste of resources and energy for the prolongation of a comparatively very few lives. Ivan Illich would answer—as he does in his *Medical Nemesis*—that such machinery is never morally justified and that an adjustment to the inevitable process of dying and death is one sign of a healthy society. Yet it might also be said that, insofar as such technology can be kept within certain community-established restraints—ecological, economic, ethical—there is no better purpose it could serve than the saving of human lives and limbs. Ultimately this would seem to be a decision that any given settlement or region might decide on its own terms and depending on its own priorities.

———

Those are the obvious steps to a rational and human-scale approach to health, and though they may seem in some regards utopian, they are all really very easy and well within the bounds of our capabilities. Just as is the utopian vision offered by Ernest Callenbach in his enlightening little novel, *Ecotopia*.

Callenbach imagines a time in the not-too-distant future after a new nation carved out of the Pacific Northwest from Santa Barbara to Canada secedes from the United States and establishes a decentralized, humanistic, and ecologically minded government. William Weston, a New York journalist, is invited to Ecotopia to report on its strange customs, and among the dispatches he sends back is this one on health care:

> *The greatest difference between Ecotopian hospitals and ours is in scale. Though the medical care I have received seems to be at the highest level of sophistication, from the atmosphere here I might be in a tiny country hospital. There are only about 30 patients all together, and we are practically outnumbered by the nursing staff (who, by the way, work much longer hours than ours, but in compensation spend as much time on vacation as they do on the job). . . .*
>
> *In one respect the Ecotopians have taken a profoundly different direction than our modern hospitals. They do not employ electronic observation to enable a central nurses' station to observe many patients at once. The theory, as I have gathered it, is that the personal presence and care of the nurse is what is essential; and the only electronic gadget used is a small radio call set that can retrieve your nurse from anywhere on the hospital premises without bothering anybody else. . . .*
>
> *The clinics and hospitals are responsible to the communities— normally to the minicity units of about 10,000 people. Thus the power of the physician to set his own fees has evaporated, though a doctor*

can always bargain between the salary offers of one community and another, and in fact doctors are reputed to have among the highest incomes despite the fact that they are much more numerous than with us. Doctors perform many duties that nurses or technicians perform in our more specialized system; on the other hand, nurses and technicians also perform a good many of the services that our doctors reserve for themselves.

Intensive-care units are also not developed as highly as in our hospitals. This clearly involves a certain hard-heartedness toward terminally ill or very critically ill patients, who cannot be kept alive by the incredibly ingenious technology American hospitals have. This may be partly an economic necessity, but also Ecotopians have a curiously fatalistic attitude toward death . . . when they feel their time has come, they let it come, comforting themselves with their ecological religion: they too will now be recycled.

On the other hand, the Ecotopian medical system has a strong emphasis on preventive care. The many neighborhood clinics provide regular check-ups for all citizens, and are within easy reach for minor problems that might develop into major ones. No Ecotopian avoids getting medical care because of the expense or the inaccessibility of health facilities.

On second thought, that's not so utopian at all.

Education

It is the classic theory advanced fifty years ago by Roger G. Barker, professor of psychology at the University of Kansas and director of the Midwest Psychological Field Station, a research center there, that it is possible to gauge the effects of size in any given institution by examining what he somewhat gracelessly calls its "behavior settings." If there are a lot of people in any one setting, he says—a meeting, for example, or a classroom—then each person has less influence on it, less chance to participate in it, less sense of responsibility for what goes on within it. If there are only a few, the chances are that each person involved will participate more, influence the events more, and have more intense reactions to what goes on.

Barker and his colleagues tested this theory in a great variety of situations over the years—in small towns, churches, factories, even jails—and it has been borne out with striking regularity. The setting with fewer people, they have found, because it is "undermanned," calls forth a much greater response in the participants. They work harder toward the desired goal, are less judgmental of their fellows and more cooperative with them, and end up with a greater sense of individual importance and self-worth. And although there usually have to be somewhat lower standards in settings with only a few people — a small high school orchestra, for instance — and hence lower levels of performance within them, the chances of the group ultimately succeeding at what they are doing are greater. There is, in sum, what Barker calls "a negative relationship between institutional size and individual participation."

Probably the most striking work that Barker and his colleagues undertook was their research on educational settings. In the late 1950s they spent three years studying thirteen high schools in eastern Kansas, some small, with only about forty students, some quite large, with two thousand and more pupils. They drew up lists of "behavior settings" for each institution — athletic contests, for example, classes, the school play, school elections — and then through careful observation and by subsequent surveys and interviews measured the amount of student participation in, and satisfaction with, each of them. Their findings, published with Paul Gump in 1964 as *Big School, Small School* — by now a classic in American psychology, though largely ignored by American education — were consistent and unqualified:

> *The large school has authority: its grand exterior dimensions, its long halls and myriad rooms, and its tides of students all carry an implication of power and rightness. The small school lacks such certainty: its modest building, its short halls and few rooms, and its students, who move more in trickles than in tides, give an impression of a casual or not quite decisive educational environment.*
>
> *These are outside views. They are illusions. Inside views reveal forces at work stimulating and compelling students to more active and responsible contributions to the enterprises of small than of large schools.*

For school activities, particularly in music, drama, journalism, and student government, "participation reached a peak in high schools with enrollments between 61 and 150," and was anywhere from three to twenty times as great as in the largest school. Although the large schools offered slightly more extracurricular settings—chess club *and* yearbook, volleyball *and* tennis—"the small school students participated in the same number" of activities as the students of the large school, and they were more likely to hold "positions of importance and responsibility" in those activities. The small school students reported that they were more aware of the attractions and obligations of non-class activities, and also felt "more satisfactions relating to the development of competence, to being challenged, to engaging in important actions, to being involved in group activities, and to achieving moral and cultural values."

As to classroom work—though, interestingly, this was found to account for only about 20 percent of the school's behavior settings—the findings are similar. Although big schools, as one might expect, did offer more kinds of subjects, "the large school students participated in fewer classes and varieties of classes than the small school students." In the case of music classes, studied in detail, it was found that the big schools produced more specialists—since individual students didn't have to learn several genres and could concentrate on a single instrument—but that "musical education and experience were more widely distributed among the small school than among the large school students."

The size of the town in which the school was located, the Barker team discovered, also turned out to be educationally important, for in the smaller places the students participated more in non-school affairs and the community members participated more in school affairs. Comparing the settings of the smallest schools—communities of 1,000–2,000—with those of the largest—a city of 101,000—Barker found "a wider participation by the adolescents in the business, organizational, religious, and educational settings of the towns than of the city." Like the small schools themselves, the small communities "provided positions of functional importance for adolescents more frequently," the cities less frequently. Moreover, although the urban environments presumably offered museums and theaters and other resources that the small towns lacked, this did not seem to make up for the "relatively meager" use made of them by the big school students.

In sum, the Barker study gave significant support to the idea that, the myths of most modern educators to the contrary, the small school actually best nurtures the values that educators have long sought to foster. How small a school? Well, Barker's group, being academics, naturally shied away from naming any particular optimum numbers, but it was emphatic that "a school should be sufficiently small that all of its students are needed for all of its enterprises" — and that condition, its fieldwork shows, pertains generally at enrollments of roughly one or two hundred students.

Just about, in fact, what common sense would suggest.

A human-scale education, thus, would obviously begin with the small school.

In addition to Roger Barker's pioneering work, there have been a host of later studies underscoring the virtues of small size. Allan Wicker, for example, reported that the "cognitive complexity" of students in smaller high schools — with junior classes of twenty to fifty members — was "significantly higher" than those where junior classes numbered four hundred or so. Leonard Baird, in an unusually wide sample of 21,371 high school students, found that "high school size has a considerable effect on achievement," with smaller sizes being particularly advantageous for both academic and non-academic success in writing and dramatics, of some advantage for music, and without much effect on science and art. Another pair of researchers was able to conclude simply: "Higher achievement results correlated with smaller schools at both elementary and senior high school levels."

All this continues to be reinforced by academic studies. A summary of the literature in 1997 concluded, "decades of research shows that student achievement in small schools is at least equal — and often superior — to achievement in large schools. Moreover, although it is often assumed that large schools are cheaper to operate and provide richer curricula than small schools, studies show that neither of these things is necessarily true. In addition, a large body of research in the affective and social realms overwhelmingly affirms the superiority of small schools." Lastly, one of the high points of this research, a study in 2003 by Thomas Toch of the Georgetown University McCourt School of Public Policy, who has been writing on education policy since the 1980s, was called simply *High Schools on a Human Scale*.

One additional aspect of this is the unequivocal finding that emerged from the famous report by James Coleman and his colleagues in 1966

(*Equality of Educational Opportunity*), based on a US Department of Education survey of 645,000 pupils, one of the most extensive educational studies ever conducted. They concluded that the major determinants of classroom success had very little to do with the actual content of courses or the amount of educational equipment or even the competence of the teachers, but rather with "the attitudes of student interest in school, self-concept, and sense of environmental control"—in other words, with the student's sense of being at one with the school. Moreover, the factor "which appears to have a stronger relationship to achievement than do all the 'school' factors together is the extent to which an individual feels that he has some control over his own destiny." It is exactly that control, that sense of oneness, which the small school has always been able to foster, simply by virtue of its size in relation to the individual student; it is exactly that which has been lost in the urban blackboard jungle.

That sheer *size* should play such a significant part should not be all that surprising. We all know that a young child going into a new school almost always feels nervous, and we know that when the school is large and the staff distant and the surroundings impersonal the nervousness can develop into real terror and dread, feelings that some children never get over even when they learn to get through the day. There is probably a biologically set level to which a child can adapt, beyond which a feeling of stress begins to accumulate and mental stability falters, and the younger the child the smaller are those levels: first the family, then the playgroup, next the intimate nursery class, much later the large classroom and the larger school, and only with full development the community at large. The World Health Organization once observed:

> So many wise books and reports have appeared in recent years on the principles which should be followed in organizing institutions for children that little discussion is called for here. All are agreed that institutions should be small—certainly not greater than the 100 children suggested by the Curtis Report—in order to avoid the rules and regulations which cannot be avoided in large establishments. Informal and individual discipline based on personal relations, instead of impersonal rules, is possible only in these circumstances. . . .
>
> There is no difference of opinion regarding the size of the group [within the institution]; all agree that it must be kept small.

The extent to which the small school interacts with its community is another crucial point in its favor. The large big-city school rarely establishes any contacts with its immediate neighborhood on any level above that of recurrent complaints; it will almost never make an effort to use the community elders as a resource; its teachers most probably live many miles away. The small school, by contrast, normally serves as a genuine community center, where townspeople gather for adult meetings and rallies as well as for the children's school plays and Christmas sings; the teachers are likely to know everybody in town and be able to call upon them to contribute their time and skills; and the children view their teachers not as some kind of foreign beings but as community fixtures, whom the parents have known for years and who are invited home for dinner at least once a year. The small school's board is most likely to be intimately tied to both community and school, knowing the bulk of the children and known to the bulk of the parents.

One particularly thorny problem that emerges whenever the idea of genuinely community-based school arises is what to do about segregation, should it happen that preferred residential patterns result in there being a lily-white school in one community and a coal-black school in another. It has been an article of faith that denying community cohesion and mixing up the schools—usually by closing the neighborhood black schools and busing the children to consolidated ones—is the fairest and most egalitarian way to further education and redress the past. But in fact there is no real evidence to show that black children do significantly better in integrated schools after about the third or fourth grade, and the reason for improvement up until then does not have anything to do with classroom integration but with the quality of the white school and its teachers. And there is indeed some research that indicates African, West Indian, and Afro-American children actually tend to develop at a slightly faster pace than white children, have more advanced motor skills, demand a "more active" environment, and therefore throughout their schooling need more open and active classrooms—in other words, their own schools. As Harry Morgan, professor of education at Syracuse University, points out, when they are put in the "formal and didactic" classrooms that have been created for white school children, "black children fall behind":

> *In the upper grades they work very hard at loosening up the classroom to make it more supportive of their style of learning. Too often,*

though, their release of energy and the school's reaction constitute a miniature battleground.

Often the result is that black children are given drugs or disciplined or suspended, at about four times the rate for white children—and more often than not the black children are the ones to drop out of school the soonest with the least education. Obviously nothing about the much-vaunted integration of schools is very valuable for *them*, and clearly having such children beside them cannot be helping the other children very much either. When this is compounded by the disintegrative effect on the community brought about by the absence of the school as an educational and social centerpiece, and still further by the remoteness parents begin to feel from the children's learning experience, it is hard to see that the children of any race are being well served by heedless integrative policies.

It is a sad fact that school boards and administrators, despite the clear evidence, continue to argue for larger school sizes—average pupil enroll-ment in 2000 was 440, up from 300 in 1959, and by 2015 it was 508. If you were looking for a reason for the miserable state of public education in this country, you could not do better than that.

———

The idea of education without schools is no longer such a heretical one, thanks to the work of a number of astute education critics—John Holt, Paul Goodman, George Dennison, and particularly Ivan Illich, whose *Deschooling Society* is a ringing denunciation of formal school systems in the West. In 2012 nearly 1.8 million American children—that's 3.4 percent of all school-aged children—were homeschooled, an increase of more than 60 percent since 2002.The appeal of this notion is obvious: if schools aren't educating, we can hardly do worse by eliminating them and probably do better by establishing creative alternatives. After all, we long ago gave up the practice of making church attendance compulsory—why do we still make school attendance compulsory? Aren't there hundreds of other ways that children can learn, particularly since we now know that only a minimum of learning takes place in the school anyway? And aren't there some odious side effects of compulsory attendance and regimented activ-ities and enforced obedience and rote learning that do not jibe well with our notions of a free society? If it didn't serve to keep most youths off the streets and out of the grown-ups' world; if it didn't keep them out of the labor force for an extra ten or fifteen years; if it didn't allow both parents to go off to work; if it didn't provide employment to so many otherwise economically marginal people and sustain such a significant part of the economy; if—in other words—it didn't play such a primary economic role in our nation, would we bother with school at all?

After all, where do people really learn? Most of us grasp the fundamentals—language, sociation, motor skills, and so on—in the home as children, pick up our everyday styles and worldly knowledge in the streets as kids, learn our craft or discipline on the job after graduating from school, and for the rest of our lives continue to gain such knowledge as we have through books, television, acquaintances, travel, and work. Schools generally play only a minor part. Ask yourself where you have learned the most in the course of your life, and the chances are that it is *not* in a school or college, even less likely in a formal classroom. For my own part, I think I can say unequivocally that I have learned far more in the 42nd Street Library of New York City than I ever did in sixteen years of schooling.

Thus it is possible to imagine children in a human-scale society taking advantage of a wide variety of other educational settings in addition to the school—or mix-and-matching them as their temperaments and interests dictate until they choose one adult niche or another. Some might choose to spend their time in a library, serendipitously led from stack to stack and shelf to shelf. Some might choose to use the community itself as a resource, poking into this or that enterprise, investigating this or that office, traveling to various sections of the area to see how the place really runs. Some children might welcome a return to a system of apprenticeship—say from the age of 13, the traditional point of adulthood, as the bar mitzvah reminds us—in which they could train in jobs consistent with their physical and mental ability, protection from abuse lying in the watchful eye of the community itself. Some older children might be encouraged to set up their own self-sufficient units, complete with farms and energy stations and handcrafts, and learn about life by living life. And some might simply choose to hang around a community center, horsing around, playing sports, watching films, reading magazines, talking with elders, doing odd jobs, waiting for the right moment in their lives to lead on to something else and learning unconsciously all the while.

The possibilities are almost limitless, once we remember what it is that we really want of our children. As William Godwin put it long ago: "Let us not, in the eagerness of our haste to educate, forget all the ends of education."

PART FOUR

ECONOMY ON A HUMAN SCALE

The conditions of a right organization of industry are, therefore, permanent, unchanging, and elementary. . . . The first is that it should be subordinated to the community in such a way as to render the best service technically possible. . . . The second is that its directions and government should be in the hands of persons who are responsible to those who are directed and governed.

—R. H. TAWNEY, The Acquisitive Society, 1948

Human institutions should not be allowed to grow beyond the human scale in size and complexity. Otherwise, the economic machine becomes too heavy a burden on the shoulders of the citizen, who must continually grind and re-grind himself to fit the imperatives of the overall system, and who becomes ever more vulnerable to the failure of other interdependent pieces that are beyond his control and even beyond his awareness. Lack of control by the individual over institutions and technologies that not only affect his life but determine his livelihood is hardly democratic and is, in fact, an excellent training in the acceptance of totalitarianism.

—HERMAN E. DALY, Steady State Economics, 1977

Plainly people want jobs and beauty, they should not in a just and human society be forced to choose between the two, and in a decentralized society of small communities, where industries are small enough to be responsive to each community's needs there will be no reason for them to do so.

—THE ECOLOGIST, A BLUEPRINT FOR SURVIVAL, 1972

15

Economy of Global Reach

E conomist E. F. Schumacher liked to tell a story that he felt explained
not only what he had in mind with his term *appropriate* technology
but the nature of the economic world in which that technology would
operate. One day, he said, a philosopher out walking in the wood came
face-to-face with a figure in a radiant beam of light, none other than God
Himself. Awed only temporarily—he had spent a lifetime, after all, pon-
dering His existence—the philosopher came directly to the point.

"You are the Lord, I presume."

"Yes," said God, "I am."

"Well then, my Lord, I wonder if you would be good enough to answer
for me a few simple questions that have been troubling me for some time."

"Certainly, my son."

"Is it true, Almighty, that what is for us a million years here on earth is
for you nothing but the merest moment?"

"Yes, my son, quite true."

"And is it also true," the philosopher went on, "that a million dollars
here on earth is for you nothing but a paltry penny?"

"Also quite true."

The philosopher paused only a moment. "Then I wonder," he said,
anxiousness showing, "if it would be possible for you, if it is not too much
trouble, to give me a penny?"

"Why certainly, my son," said God. "I'll be back in just a moment."

Different worlds inevitably operate at different scales, and it would seem
to be best all around if the human—no matter how great the temptation
—is not confused with the celestial. And yet it is something very like just
that confusion, it takes only a moment's thought to see, that in fact has
come to mark our present world economy, the economy of global reach,
of multinational systems and organizations, of interlocking worldwide

production, distribution, and consumption. For it is an economy, whatever else may be said for it, that is simply beyond the competence of any one person, or group, or nation, beyond the very real but very limited capacity of humans in any form, to plan, manage, control, or repair, and no amount of computer-ware techno-fixing, no scheme of trade agreements or common markets, can change that fact. Were it operating efficiently, providing healthy and productive lives for all the world's citizens without ecological or social disruption, its fragility and complexity might still be a cause for some concern. Operating as it does, however—as it has for decades and gives every sign of continuing to do—producing chaotic and devastating mixtures of inflation and stagnation, boom-and-bust, dividing the world into apparently unbridgeable camps of rich and poor, desecrating the resources of the global south to indulge and pollute the rest, in which no nation can be said to be truly prosperous and most exist in abject poverty, its uncontrollable enormousness—its very non-human scale—becomes a matter for justifiable alarm.

Our experience in all these decades past with operating a celestial economy has, for the greatest part, been a failure: we tried playing God, and it didn't work.

The question then becomes: is there a realistic alternative, some sort of economy built closer to the human measure, with institutions designed more for human control? For even if it is accepted that a reduction to the human scale might lead us to better health, more efficient transportation, better schools, nutritious food, recycled wastes, and all of that, is it realistic to think that such small units as these could work economically? Even if we were to agree that a human-scale *society* might be possible, with its reduced cities and ecological balance and alternative technologies, is there any reason to believe that a human-scale *economy* could actually survive? And if it did, could it provide the equal of our present standard of living without plunging us into the economic chaos of the dark and dismal past?

The answer is, in every case, yes.

What the human-scale economy means, as we shall see, is perfectly simple. It opposes to the present system of American industrialism and its oversized units—corporations that can be shown to be too complex for innovation or efficiency, factories that we can demonstrate are too large for optimum profitability or economy—a world of smaller, more manageable, more human enterprises that can provide us with all our needs and most of our wants without sacrificing anything substantive in our true material standards. It is founded on the all-important concept, once deemed fit for economists to explore, of the "steady-state" economy, one of stability rather than growth, preservation rather than production, that we will explore.

––––––––––

It is worth observing that the central reason for this immediate period of crisis—roughly since World War II—is the operation of the Law of Government Size.

As the American government in particular—though much the same is true enough of other industrialized governments as well—has expanded its role, its influence, its economic power, and its personnel, it has inevitably produced economic and social misery in ever-increasing degrees, sometimes in the high rates of inflation that serve to sap buying power from the general run of citizens, sometimes in the high rates of unemployment that leave more than a quarter of the productive citizens idle and impoverished. The way it works is this.

As the government takes unto itself more and more of the tasks of serving the citizens in their every waking moment, and not a few of their sleeping ones as well, it runs up an inevitable debt. Some of the value produced by all these government services is returned to the government through taxes, and ever-increasing taxes at that, but a great deal is siphoned off by private businesses in the form of their own profits—as, for example, when Washington builds a superhighway system and the trucking industry reaps the profits from it, or when the Atomic Energy Commission develops and promotes nuclear power for electricity at the cost of many billions and private utilities then use it for corporate gain. Some of these profits can be recovered by the government through corporate taxation, but proportionately very little, particularly since the tax system is deliberately designed to help corporations prosper, since both legal and illegal means exist by which corporations can hold on to their gains, and since out-and-out tax breaks of some hundreds of billions a year are handed out to businesses in a general policy of what's-good-for-General-Motors-ism. Thus, merely to keep itself going year to year—servicing its debts, meeting the costs of inflation, and all the while expanding its operations—the government has to increase its expenditures and hence its debt, at $19 trillion in 2016 and ever-growing.

At the same time, government expenditures foster corporate bigness and encourage monopolies in a wide range of industries, creating an economic segment that is in many ways immune to normal market forces. Large corporations are in the happy position of being able to expand profits by using government subsidies and tax write-offs without having to spend very much on enlarging their plants or increasing their wages, and passing on to the consumers such increases as inflation may create. Nor do large corporations do much to lessen unemployment, since they are the ones that can most afford automation, that benefit most by globalization, that can generally do without unskilled workers, and that can accomplish growth when necessary by merger rather than expansion.

But dire as the current economic crisis is, it represents only one side of the malady from which American capitalism is now suffering. The other is worse, because it is inherent and fundamental.

It is in the *nature* of capitalism, of course, to be unstable—boom-or-bust it's called, and Keynesian or central-bank fiddling doesn't seem to change it a lot—and that is bad enough, particularly when both boom and bust happen at the same time, as over this past decade when the rich have gotten the boom and the poor the bust, a trend that has been escalating to the current crescendo for decades. But, one is forced to say, it is also in the *nature* of capitalism to produce certain other ills, the accumulation of which in recent years has become serious enough to put the advanced industrial societies into the realm of what can only be called peril. Chief among them:

Exploitation of resources. There are no special penalties attached in capitalism to the profligate use of natural resources, and indeed the principle is that if you can do that cheaply enough you can even increase your profits: the more exploitation, the scarcer the resources, the greater the demand, and the higher the price. However, in the last decade we have come to realize not only that these resources are finite and irreplaceable but that our rapacious use of them—the United States uses up about 25 tons of raw materials per person per year—has serious economic and social effects. Petroleum is the familiar example—it used to be you could stick a pipe into any part of Texas to get oil, but now we have to spend $650 billion a year (2013) to find and produce it, much from the ocean floor—and though no one can say how much reserve is had, no one disputes that it is running out. Iron ore, too, has been rapidly exhausted in this country, our annual output down 20 million large tons since 1950, the number of producing mines reduced from 321 to 9 in the same period, and the high-grade Masabi range in Minnesota virtually depleted. Water is even more serious: North America now uses up *twice as much* water as is replenished by rainfall, and water tables all across the nation are dropping, particularly in the Southwestern states, where it is calculated that some aquifers may not fill up again for a thousand years and some may never. Forests have been consistently depleted, especially in the West, where the cutting of old trees well surpasses the planting of new, and in the South, where softwoods have replaced hard. All in all, the National Commission on Material Policy concluded way back in 1973, the United States is in the throes of "serious" shortages. Nothing has changed—or at least not for the better. In 2011 the Department of Energy said there were severe shortages in "16 critical materials" for energy production, and the American Enterprise Institute in 2012 pointed out that the United States is now dependent in all sectors (including cell phones, computers, and televisions) on imports of materials, mostly from China, for 81 percent of its cobalt and titanium and 44 percent of the iconic silicon. Industry sources predict even more acute shortages—and at the least, higher prices—in *two-thirds* of the basic raw materials upon which the American industrial machine depends. That's what happens with globalization.

Waste. Similarly, capitalism encourages waste, there being no special benefits attached to creating durable or recyclable goods and considerable advantage to getting people to throw away their old products and buy your new ones. (Indeed, there are positive values in making waste, inasmuch as the solid waste industry in 2000 had revenues of $43.3 billion and more than 27,000 businesses.) Large contemporary industries like the plastic and petro-chemical industry complex have been particularly culpable here, because their plants demand so much capital to build and so much energy to operate that they are forced to turn out their products in the largest possible numbers to make a profit; thus many plastic goods now appear everywhere in all kinds of guises not because there was any particular demand for them or because society made any rational decision that it wanted them but simply because the out-of-scale realities of the industry made them "necessary."

Ecocide. Not only is ecological damage an inevitable consequence of exploitation and waste, it is also built into the capitalist imperative of maximum profit: in economic terms it *makes sense* to pollute the atmosphere if it reduces production costs, to pour toxins in the rivers if safe disposal costs too much, to use fuels that produce carbon dioxide if there is a market that seems to want them. Probably most businesspeople are aware, as individuals, that the environment is being stretched to its regenerative limits by the industrial assaults upon it and will visit the dangerous consequences upon their grandchildren if not upon themselves, but as corporate officers they continue to put up the most toe-grabbing resistance to even the kinds of mild controls the government has enacted in the clean water and clean air acts.

Social burden. Say what you will about capitalism and its achievements, it has always exacted a certain social price, and that has become particularly high in recent years. Just the normal quotidian processes of American business create serious distending pressures for every American family bound up in it; they force couples to move a continent away and children to relocate school districts at a whim; they insinuate anxiety into every employee, from the marginal laborers right up to the scrambling executives; they tend to make all but the very topmost feel powerless and sometimes worthless, reducing their human needs simply to a weekly paycheck. If the environmental pollution of the industrial economy is severe, the behavioral pollution may be even worse, and in ways that we have yet to discover. Anthropologist Lionel Tiger once suggested: "The industrial system we take so much for granted is only several hundred years old. We are beginning, I think, to realize that it is an extremely demanding economic system under which to live." Perhaps the citizens are willing to pay the price for such trappings of modernity as we may boast, discounting the disintegrative effects; perhaps, however, we may be having second thoughts about the trade-offs as the possibilities of impending social chaos become ever clearer.

Social irresponsibility. The corporation in a capitalist system, existing essentially for profit rather than product, has no particular incentive toward well-made, durable, safe, or aesthetic goods; the corporation, being responsible to its managers and stockholders rather than its public, has no especial inclination toward healthy, safe, clean, or balanced environments. In this context, inferior products may generate more profits

194

because they must be continually replaced, unsafe products because they are cheaper to produce. It is *rational* to put poisons into food if they increase its shelf-life, to design cars with gas tanks that explode if they can be made cheaper, to offer drugs that maim or stupefy if they can be convincingly peddled. The corporation, with only tremulous limitations provided by law, acts pretty much as it wants to, regardless of broader social considerations: it may produce what it wants rather than what the society may need (another "air freshener" or $22 billion worth of pet food in 2015, twice as much as in 2000, while families starve); it may invest as it wants rather than as society might prefer ($70 million to develop and market potato chips in tennis-ball cans or $5 trillion, in 2015, invested overseas while our infrastructure deteriorates and unemployment festers); it may locate and relocate as it wants rather than as society might find rational (setting up a factory in an already congested area or abandoning a town after exhausting its resources). The only question is how long any society can, or should, suffer the consequences.

Overgrowth. Growth is the very wellspring of capitalism, the force that makes it succeed where it does, but the inevitable result of growth, as economists have long since discovered, will at some point be increasing concentration and eventual monopoly. In the United States growth has now reached the point, as we know, where no more than 500 corporations control about 40 percent of all private production and, in most major industries, two-thirds of the market is in the hands of four companies or fewer. The first effect of this is to develop increasingly overextended and overloaded systems both within and among corporations, so that, as economist Hazel Henderson pointed out, "when complexity and interdependence have reached such unmanageable proportions . . . the system generates transaction costs faster than it does production." In other words, the system costs more just to keep going than society can ever make from it—and the society goes broke. The second effect is to put these large corporations beyond the influence of *both* the traditional supply-and-demand market *and* the regulatory government: they can manipulate the market by virtue of their advertising, distribution, borrowing, and marketing power (in John Kenneth Galbraith's blunt words, "the big corporation eliminates or subdues market forces"); and they can circumvent government control by lobbying, tax breaks, bureaucratic interlocks, overseas plants, simple noncompliance, and the threat of loss of jobs. The society must therefore pay for the burdens of corporate complexity as well as the travails of corporate whim.

Instability. Inherent in the capitalist system anyway, this is exacerbated by the size and intricacy of the corporations and their national and transnational systems. In a small world, instability may have made little difference, but in a connected world it begins to affect everything. We find that a *managed* worldwide economy is simply impossible, clearly beyond the World Bank or the world government given the logistical and political complexities; we also find that an *unmanaged* worldwide economy is simply chaotic, unable to make rational decisions about resources or markets or employment or anything else, as the collapse of the housing bubble in 2008 made clear. It seems an inevitable working out of the Beanstalk Principle that the world economy in recent years has experienced, among other disasters, runaway inflation then a global housing crisis, unabating population growth, severe starvation in Africa and Asia, overconsumption of such scarcities as petroleum and copper, and the effective destabilization of the international monetary system.

All of that—exploitation, waste, ecological and social disarray, instability—does not by any means exhaust the characteristics of capitalism that, even if benign enough in the past, are now of such proportions that they pose a serious threat to a sustainable future; but it does suggest the most pertinent ones. I wish to stress that I do not mean to seem to be talking about them in moral terms, as being good or evil—I am not describing what *ought* to be but rather what is. It is important to appreciate that capitalism behaves as it does not because it is evil, and the corporations as they do not because they are immoral—that is the *nature* of the system; that is what, by the rules, is *supposed* to happen. At the same time, it is well to recognize that there may be limits to where such a system can lead us, limits to which in recent times it seems we may have come.

———

So the capitalist crisis, then, is really made up of two facts: first, that the industrial system is not working, even on its own terms; second, that it is.

Of course none of this is really news. Many have realized the quite catastrophic nature of what we have come to, not only as it impinges on the present but, even more, as it threatens the future. It was this that led some rather more farseeing capitalists to establish the famous Club of Rome, whose reports on growth that I cited earlier made clear the serious nature of the long-term crisis, presumably to allow rational businesspeople and politicians to devise some remedies before it is too late. It is this that has led the United Nations at various times over the last decade to sponsor a number of sober and comprehensive conferences on such matters as pollution, climate control, law of the seas, income disparity, food, and population.

Some who have seen the crisis have argued that everything will eventually shake itself out, technology will come to the rescue, and there's no real need to make substantive changes. This is the attitude of the standard American business sector and of mainstream free-market economists. Others who also take a somber but less optimistic view of the crisis have argued that it does indeed require thoroughgoing changes in economic and political systems, particularly in the direction of planning, especially governmental and intergovernmental planning. This is the standard socialist response. But business as usual or business by government does not seem to be much of an answer for anyone who has been paying attention to the world for the last century.

There is, however, a third response possible, and it is one to which a number of people, bidden and unbidden, knowingly and not, have been turning in recent decades. In place of optimistic drift and pessimistic planning, this response points rather to the reduction of all economic systems and organizations to the point where they can be controlled by those who are immediately affected by them. It emphasizes, for the individual, self-definition of the job, self-scheduling of time, work in small groups based on consensus and cooperation. It encourages the development of family-farm agriculture, the decentralization of industry, worker ownership and self-management of firms and factories, and alternative technologies and all that they imply. It seeks self-sufficiency and self-reliance for neighborhoods and communities, community control of industries, and regional cooperation where necessary. And overall, it favors an ecologically minded, people-oriented, small-scale, steady-state society.

British writer Gordon Rattray Taylor stands out among those who have studied and advocated this third response. He says simply:

> *The present system is biased in favour of goods as against other desirables; it neglects bads; it provides motives for anti-social and*

inhumane behaviour because it is mechanical and inhumane itself. The way to correct it is not to substitute vast monolithic publicly owned boards and corporations, which are equally open to inhumanity and distorted valuations. It is to substitute decisions made by that marvellous instrument the human brain, which alone can weigh all the factors, ponderable and imponderable, in a situation. And a 'personalized' economics can only be built from small-scale, face-to-face contacts: a 'polylithic' instead of a monolithic system.

16

Steady–State Economy

It was in 1848, that notably fruitful year, that the idea of the steady-state economy was first put forth, by the political economist John Stuart Mill, in his pathbreaking *Principles of Economics*.* Growth, as he saw, was inherent in capitalism, particularly the industrial capitalism then beginning to stamp itself upon his nation, the United Kingdom, and yet it was by definition a finite process: "the increase of wealth is not boundless." Capital will eventually cease to produce any sensible return for the capitalist, he posited, when the costs of extraction, manufacture, and disposal become great enough and when the redistributive tax systems of the state become extensive enough. At that point there will no longer be any point in being a capitalist: the breed will vanish. In place of the "progressive state," he envisioned the "stationary state":

> *I am inclined to believe that it would be, on the whole, a very considerable improvement on our present condition. I confess I am not charmed with the ideal of life held out by these who think that the normal state of human beings is that of struggling to get on; that the trampling, crushing, elbowing, and treading on each other's heels, which form the existing type of social life, are the most desirable lot of human kind, or anything but the disagreeable symptoms of one of the phases of industrial progress. . . .*

---

* Others before him had of course debated the idea of *growth*, especially economic growth, most notably the French physiocrats in the eighteenth century (they were mostly against it) and such Greeks as Aristotle (likewise). But Mill was the first to put the case of the "stationary" economy in positive, concrete terms.

*The best state for human nature is that in which, while no one
is poor, no one desires to be richer, nor has any reason to fear being
thrust back by the efforts of others to push themselves forward. . . .*

*It is scarcely necessary to remark that a stationary condition of
capital and population implies no stationary state of human improvement. There would be as much scope as ever for all kinds of mental,
cultural, and moral and social progress; as much room for improving
the Art of Living, and much more likelihood of its being improved,
when minds ceased to be engrossed by the art of getting on.*

Like many ideas, the measure of its worth varied indirectly with the
time it took to become recognized by others: for more than a hundred
years it was virtually ignored, and the few who noticed it—professionals,
mostly—understood it little. With the revival of interest in ecology in the
1960s, however, and then with the energy crisis of the 1970s, a number of
modern economists began to re-examine the notion of a stationary economy and reshape it for modern conditions.

Economist Kenneth Boulding in 1966 introduced the idea of
"spaceship earth," by which he meant to suggest that we live within
a basically closed system that must ultimately, like the spaceship,
depend on its use of recycled materials and renewable energy. British
economist Ezra Mishan in 1967 offered the idea of "growthmania" in
his elegant and influential *Costs of Economic Growth* and suggested the
rejection of "economic growth as a prior aim of policy in favor of a
policy seeking to apply more selective criteria of welfare . . . to direct
our national resources and our ingenuity to recreating an environment
that will gratify and inspire men." In 1971 Rumanian émigré Nicholas
Georgescu-Roegen, working out of the University of Tennessee, came
forth with the principle of increasing material "entropy," an idea borrowed from the Second Law of Thermodynamics, to suggest that the
excessive production and consumption of contemporary society was
exhausting the finite material and energy resources of the earth to
the point where soon the human species itself would be threatened.
And the next year, as we have seen, Jay Forrester, Donella and Dennis
Meadows, and others at MIT hit the headlines with their pioneering
computer models that became the basis of the Club of Rome's initial
admonitory book, *The Limits to Growth.*

After that, a continual drumroll. Herman Daly's explorations, *Essays Toward a Steady-State Economy*, became available in 1972, E. F. Schumacher's pathbreaking and deservedly popular *Small Is Beautiful* appeared early in 1973 as did Leopold Kohr's *Development Without Aid*, and the influential scholarly quarterly *Daedalus* came out with a full issue on "The No-Growth Society" in the fall of 1973. Other important writers joined in: Hazel Henderson, Rufus Miles, Rene Dubos, Barbara Ward, Robert Theobald, Howard Odum, William Ophuls. And by the end of the 1970s the notion of the no-growth, stationary, steady-state economy was sufficiently well established to be creating ripples throughout the circles of both academic and governmental economists.

Largely through the influence of Herman Daly, a Center for the Advancement of Steady State Economics was established in Arlington, Virginia, and it is now in 2017 a thriving institution with a staff of nine, led by economist Brian Czech (steadystate.org). And a Society of Sustainability Professionals was begun in 2006 and is still thriving.

Other movements challenging growth as an imperative have also sprung up over the past decades. Some, looking at our dramatic need to shift away from fossil fuels, focus not just on reaching a steady-state economy, but on actual de-growth to bring economic activity back within sustainable bounds. Still others simply opt to go with the more flexible ideals of post-growth, choosing neither steady state nor de-growth as a one-size-fits-all solution.

Though the visions of the steady-state or post-growth economy inevitably vary according to the particular proponent, they all agree on certain basic points. A growth economy uses up scarce resources, emphasizes consumption over conservation, creates pollution and waste in the process of production, and engenders inter- and intra-national competition for dwindling supplies. A steady-state or post-growth economy minimizes resource use, sets production on small and self-controlled scales, emphasizes conservation and recycling, limits pollution and waste, and accepts the finite limits of a single world and of a single ultimate source of energy.

Herman Daly puts it this way: "If the world is a finite complex system that has evolved with reference to a fixed rate of flow of solar energy, then any economy that seeks indefinite expansion of its stocks and the associated material and energy-maintenance flows will sooner or later hit limits." Nothing can expand forever. By contrast, the steady-state economy is one "with constant stocks of people and artifacts, maintained at some desired, sufficient levels by low rates of maintenance 'throughput,' that is, by the lowest feasible flows of matter and energy." Or as Boulding says it more elegantly: "The essential measure of the success of the [steady-state] economy is not production and consumption at all, but the nature, extent, quality, and complexity of the total capital stock, including in this the state of human bodies and minds included in the system."

It is the art of living, not the art of getting on.

Perhaps the best way to envision the steady-state economy is in terms of ecological harmony. For in a real sense a steady-state economy takes the stable ecosystem as a *model*, since a properly balanced environment is in fact essentially stationary. Growth occurs in fluctuations from season to season and species to species, but overall any given system may be basically unchanged for eons; and however fierce may be the competition between some species, however preoccupied each may be with its own survival, none of the elements within it (except, in self-delusion, the human) has found any particular advantage in the growth of the system as a whole.

———————

Obviously there is plenty of room for objection to the stationary economy, even after all the usual resistance of the myth-prisoners is disposed of.

The steady-state economy, say some, *is simply not necessary, it is a needless deprivation—for continued growth will provide the solutions to the admittedly severe but tractable problems we have now.* The idea that growth will provide technical breakthroughs is the old techno-fix response, and it amounts to recommending more arsenic for the patient dying of arsenic poisoning. The variant that it will create money we can use for, in economist Henry Wallich's phrase, "The Great Cleanup," is something like the assurance of the miser who asks us to let him hoard more money so that, someday, he may give even more of it to charity. And the idea that it will force people to pay more for scarce goods and thus eventually limit plunder by price is akin to allowing the rich kid to buy up all the candy on the block in the name of conservation and letting him sell it back at any price he chooses. You will recognize the tone of the growth-at-all-costs argument, of course, for it is the standard American business response become familiar now through years of ExxonMobil ads. That source does not necessarily discredit it, perhaps, despite its oil spills, but it does not lend it much credence either—especially since it is precisely American business that has gotten us into the fix we're in. Fat men don't cure obesity by eating.

But the steady-state economy, say others, *would mean a permanent under-class of the poor because where there is no growth there is no way out of poverty.* Of course growth *hasn't* eliminated poverty in all the centuries it's been tried, not even come close, and there's not much reason to expect that it somehow miraculously will. The reason is simple: except for a few exceptional cases of up-from-poverty, the wealth of capitalism tends to go largely to the same old wealthy families and entrepreneurs who have always had it. The advantage of the stationary economy here is that—especially if confined to a particular community or region—it puts its primary value on the *limitation* of accumulation and consumption; it does not have to operate within the profit matrix, which always forces prices up, and therefore it has more wealth to distribute generally; it explicitly values the human component in a balanced ecosystem, wherein the wastage of human potential would be considered as anti-social as the wastage of any other raw material. This is not to say that there might not be gradations of wealth within a steady-state economy—depending, of course, on the community's particular political and social ideals—but that these are not inherent as they are in a growth system, nor are they necessary or desirable, nor do the mechanics of the economy work to support them.

But such an economy, say still others, *would lead to greater unemployment and labor unrest, maybe even social conflict, because without growth there are insufficient jobs.* Aside from the fact that the growth economy, even in the United States, does not seem to have eliminated unemployment and labor unrest, it also has one insuperable built-in deficiency here. Because it depends on continual technical "progress," it always displaces the less educated and less skilled parts of the labor force with automated machinery and the skilled workers who understand it, leaving the former forever unemployed; and then it tends to restrict the chances for the necessary education and skills to the upper levels that already have them, the colleges remaining essentially the province of the upper-middle echelons. A stationary system, by contrast, with no careening interest in "progress," would welcome only those technical changes that remained consistent with its ecological values; it would also be labor-intensive rather than fuel-intensive, just out of simple conservation, and this would emphasize the employment of all able-bodied citizens; and especially if it were enmeshed in the small community, it would continually be generating countless occupations, from babysitter to health counselor, for the less able-bodied, the aged, and the young.

Even so, a final set of critics says, *the steady-state economy, supposing it were achieved and running smoothly, would soon lead to exploitation and chaos, on the one hand, or excessive government control, on the other.* For if you deny people the opportunity to exploit nature the way the Western world has been doing these past five centuries, they are likely to seek their advantage by exploiting their fellow humans; yet any system that was strong enough to prevent that and at the same time to assure that minerals were not exhausted or waterways polluted would have to be excessively autocratic. Several ready answers to this come to mind: this posits an unacceptably crude and greedy view of human nature to begin with; it does not recognize that exploitation may not be a necessity in economic systems other than capitalism; and it does not, alas, describe a world very much different from the one we have right now, which has plenty of both chaos and autocracy. But there is a more substantial point here, and it has to do with the very nature of a steady-state economy. To arrive at, much less to sustain, such an economy, the citizens as a whole would have to be able to see that it is in their collective self-interest, and of course in the interests of their children, to live within limits. They would have to experience in their daily lives the benefits of limits—such as, say, the absence of advertising and rush hours. Such a perception can come about, it is fair to say, only within a fairly small geographic compass, where people still can see the effect of each of these limits on the environment and on their fellows, where there is not an adversarial but a communitarian perception of government and society. But where it does take root, neither exploitation nor autocracy would be much of a possibility, for that would be at such odds with the general perception of the common good that it would seem as foreign as an endotoxin to a healthy cell, and be as quickly discarded.

The spirit of getting on, in other words, would be replaced by the spirit of living within. The steady-state economy means stewardship instead of exploitation, enough-ness instead of too-much-ness, living instead of making a living.

204

Many years ago Garrett Hardin, a professor of biology at the University of California, shocked the academic world with a parable he called "The Tragedy of the Commons." As he posited it, contemporary society is very much like the ancient commons ground upon which the village shepherds would graze their animals. At a certain point, inevitably, that commons will be unable to support any more sheep—there is just enough grass for each animal, and the addition of a single new animal will mean the overgrazing of the land and, eventually, as more sheep are added, the loss of all its ground cover, the erosion of its soils, and ultimately its effective destruction. And yet it is in the self-interest of each shepherd to add one more sheep to his flock because the added gain to him and his family, in terms of milk produced and meat to be sold, is considerably greater than any immediate loss from the eventual destruction of the commons. Thus each shepherd grazing sheep there, operating out of real and apparent self-interest, will continue to add more animals to his flock until the ultimate tragedy happens and there is no more commons for anyone.

This, Hardin suggests, is our present condition. The oceans continue to be overfished, particularly by Russian and Japanese fleets—despite international treaties—because it is in the immediate self-interest of each nation to take as much as it can from the sea, particularly if there is a threat of eventual depletion, even though every nation knows that at some near time there will be no more fish at all for any to catch. American coal-fired plants continue to resist measures to limit the poisonous emissions they pour into the air each day, because it is in the interest of each company to avoid the expense of pollution controls and redesigned furnaces for as long as possible, although all the executives know that they and their families and workers and townsfolk (or counterparts elsewhere) have to breathe the resultant polluted air and that this is very likely to cause severe illness and early death. The American West is becoming desertified, losing perhaps 10 million acres of grassland a year, for the simple reason that the ranchers of the area, acting out Hardin's scenario, continue to overgraze their herds in this sparse territory despite a decade-long policy of the Bureau of Land Management to curtail them; as reporter Molly Ivins in the *New York Times* once noted, these are lands where, "the early explorers wrote, the grasses brushed the bellies of their horses. Nowadays, the sorry weeds would be doing well to brush a trundling armadillo." The examples, alas, may be multiplied.

No doubt this parable does suggest an important, and unquestionably tragic, truth. But it contains something else as well: an indictment of the getting-on economy and an appreciation of the steady-state one. True, those who are operating out of *self-interest*, who do not see and cannot feel a *communal-interest*, will almost inevitably proceed to their self-aggrandizement and the destruction of their surroundings, moderated only by the feeble constraints of church or government. But if there were a stationary economy it would have to be grounded precisely in the perception of communal-interest, quite unable to exist without a realization of the unity of the ecosystem and the simple centrality of ecological balance. The shepherd would know the limits of the commons and its importance to his family, to his children and their children, to his neighbors, to the past and future of his community, and that overriding communal-interest would easily outweigh the possible personal gain of putting another animal out to feed.

This, in turn, is more or less a function of size, both populational and geographic. There can be no "communal-interest" among 325 million people, or 20 million, or even 2 million, because there is no way for the human brain with all its limitations to perceive the interconnectedness of all those lives and their relevance to its single life; we cheat on our income tax and drive over speed limits and ignore beggars on the street because we perceive no *community* at the scale at which we live. Nor can there be communal-interest over distances of 3,000 square miles, or 300 square miles, or even 30 square miles, because there is no way for the human mind in all its frailty to conceive the complexity of an ecosystem so large and its single place within it; we use plastic bags in the supermarket and wash clothes with phosphate detergents and drive un-tuned cars because we cannot understand ecology at the scale at which we function. Only when the shepherd knows his world and the people in it and feels their importance to his own well-being, only when he realizes that his self-interest *is* indeed the communal-interest, will he voluntarily limit his flock.

Only then will the looming tragedy of the commons be avoided.

———

In the midst of his arguments for a steady-state economy, Herman Daly tells the story of the village idiot who would be stopped every day by the townspeople and asked to pick between a nickel and a dime. The

idiot always chose the nickel and the residents always went away saying, "There, you see what an idiot he is." Except that the idiot in later life
explained: "After all, if I kept picking the dime they would have stopped
offering it to me pretty quickly. This way I kept getting nickels every day."

And just so with the stationary economy. Its riches might not be so
great at first, and we might seem to be idiotic for settling for them; but
over time they would be sure to accumulate. Eventually they would far
surpass those we know now.

17

The Logic of Size

T he size of hunting bands in early Paleolithic societies, as we have
seen, normally seems to have been no more than five, that number
apparently being found over the eons to be most harmonious for a human
group around the campfire and on the trails and still efficient enough to
bring down even the largest prey. From surviving Stone Age cultures,
particularly in Africa and Australia, it appears that most of the early lan-
guages did not even have a word for any number over five.

It was part of the customs of the early Greek maritime cities that ship
crews could have no more than five individuals, any number above that
being considered sufficient to engage in piracy.

In 1305 Philip the Fair of France, engaged in a protracted struggle with
the papacy, forbade unauthorized groups of more than five people to
congregate anywhere within his realm, on the assumption that a gathering greater than that was probably a Romanist clique bent on conspiracy
against the crown.

After he came to the English throne following the Cromwellian Protec-
torate, Charles II re-established the episcopacy, and his Parliament, in the
English Conventional Act, decreed that all home assemblies for religious
reasons of more than five people would be considered suspicious and
punishable by law.

Twentieth-century researchers, particularly the psychologists who
have carried out extensive experiments with small groups, have determined, according to the English management expert Charles Handy, "for
best participation, for highest all-round involvement, a size between five
and seven seems to be optimum."

C. Northcote Parkinson believes that most committees start with five
members—before that there is not enough sense of cohesion for the group
to consider itself a committee at all—and after a time, when they grow and

become unwieldy with new members, they tend to revert to the original size by establishing an "executive committee" or "board of directors," or some-such, of the five most powerful members.

One contribution to the basic *Handbook of Small Group Research* suggests that the optimal committee size is five, since below that number people tend to feel that getting together is "not worth it" and "won't prove anything," whereas much above that people start to participate less and eventually stop paying attention. This number, too, is good for decision making, because of course it is odd and because it is large enough so that no one feels isolated when taking a stand (divisions are most often three–two) and small enough so that participants can shift roles and points of view without onus.

A. Paul Hare, editor of the classic *Small Groups*, introduces a variety of laboratory studies showing that groups between four and seven are most successful at solving problems, and that as groups increase in size they tend to take more time to come up with solutions, make less accurate judgments, produce fewer ideas, achieve less communication, and stand less chance of reaching an agreement.

One leading sociologist, John James, determined several years ago that "action-taking groups" average out to 6.5 people and groups that get to be as big as ten and fifteen people are "non-action-taking." He also took the practical route of surveying the subcommittees of various legislatures—the places where the real work of any body gets done—and found an average of 5.4 people on US Senate subcommittees, 7.8 in the US House of Representatives, 4.7 in the Oregon state legislature, and 5.3 in the Eugene, Oregon, city government.

A study done in 2011 found that work groups of three to eight were "significantly more productive" than groups of nine or more, and of three to six both more productive and "more developmentally advanced" than groups of seven or more—and even that of three to four were superior than any others—"work-group size is a crucial factor," it concluded.

And Frederick Thayer, whose exclamatory *An End to Hierarchy! An End to Competition!* is a careful look at organizational forms, sums up: "While common sense would seem to dictate that there can be no 'magic' number, five appears so often in so many environmental situations as to carry persuasion with it."

Now I am, of course, fond of "magic" numbers, and it does seem obvious that through the ages people have decided that groups of about this size have an unusual power and competence about them. This is of some importance in considering a steady-state economy, because in such a system, where efficiency is inevitably of greater importance than it is in our profligate capitalist arrangements, and where happiness and worker morale are more vital than in the getting-on world of making a profit, it would be important to determine the optimum size for effective and congenial work units, workplaces, and work organizations.

Luckily there are innumerable studies here that can serve as useful guides.

As to the basic work unit, the small group, hovering somewhere right around the magic number of five, has proven time and again to be most effective in the workplace, easily outperforming both the isolated individual and the assembly line. There are literally hundreds of studies confirming that (particularly in small settings, but also in the larger factories) small groups tend to have higher morale, lower absence and turnover rates, fewer accidents and labor disputes, and—bottom line— greater productivity. Part of the reason for this seems to be that working without hierarchy, without managers and bosses wielding power, a work group sets its own tasks and pace most efficiently. Part has to do with the fact, borne out in innumerable cases, that the more you let workers run their own affairs, the better they will perform. And part is due simply to a group loyalty that tends in time to give individuals a cause, a sense of identity, a meaning—however limited—that inspires greater enthusiasm and productivity; research into wartime behavior similarly shows that it is the loyalty to the group—not to country or motherhood or democracy or the general—that produces the most successful soldiers and accounts for the exceptional feats of bravery and courage.

The classic case in point here is the "Relay Assembly" study made at the Hawthorne, Illinois, Western Electric plant in the late 1920s. Researchers from the Harvard Business School took a group of six women workers out of a department of a hundred and put them into a special test room, then variously altered their conditions of work—lighting, breaks, hours, lunchtimes, piece rates, and so on—to see how it affected productivity. Quite to the researchers' bewilderment, the women increased their output at *each* stage of the experiment, no matter which benefit was added or subtracted, ultimately with an 80 percent decrease in absenteeism, a 40 percent increase in hourly output, a clearly observable increase in morale on the job, and a new friendliness and cohesiveness after work. But the most extraordinary result was that the women's productivity increased even when, after many months, they were returned to the original conditions of work without any benefits at all. Consternation. The researchers were in a turmoil: what could explain it? Eventually, with academic ingenuity, the Harvardians determined it was something they called the "Hawthorne effect" — that is, simply taking people out of their ordinary routine and making them feel special will increase their productivity—and this became the standard business school line over the succeeding fifty years.

Clever, but it does seem something of a reach, doesn't it? What the researchers were observing, though they couldn't realize it, was simply and obviously the effect of two essential factors: the women were isolated in a small and coherent group with shared tasks and rewards, *and* within this group they were allowed an unusual degree of independence in setting the conditions of their work: they *saw* themselves as a small group, they *worked* as a small group, they felt themselves to *be* a small group. And small groups, particularly autonomous small groups, feel better and work better.

One might wonder why, after so many years of proof, corporate executives throughout America have not reorganized offices and plants into small work groups. In Europe this has been done in many industries in many countries—Saab and Volvo in Sweden, Daimler-Benz and Bosch in Germany, Fiat and Olivetti in Italy, overlarge companies but with right-sized teams—with the predictable beneficial results. The Singer sewing-machine plant in Karlsruhe, Germany, switched its 1,200 workers in most operations from assembly-line to small-group operation in 1977 because, according to General Manager Hans W. Gilbert, the line moved only at the pace of the slowest worker and if people made mistakes they "blamed the next man down." Since then "workers get greater job satisfaction, while their output is improved and increased," and the savings to the company were put at some $370,000 in the first year of the change. American firms, though testing small-group productivity in some instances, traditionally tended to resist any wholesale shift, and most places that tried it in the past chose to abandon it within a year or so.

Apparently managers are fearful of the kind of solidarity that develops within these groups, they worry about their jobs if it proves that supervision isn't necessary, and they basically distrust change of any kind. But that has changed significantly since the digital revolution, and Silicon Valley has found—and taught elsewhere—that what Amazon CEO Jeff Bezos has called the "Two-Pizza Rule" works best: "If a team couldn't be fed with two pizzas, it was too big."

Similar data about small offices and plants show that those places with a limited number of people, where workers and managers know each other personally, where bonds of conviviality and cooperation are forged, are much more satisfying and productive than larger, more impersonal workplaces.

Take any measure you like. Studies of worker morale show uniformly that unhappiness increases as plants get larger. One researcher who studied sixty-six manufacturing and twenty-seven nonmanufacturing businesses, with anywhere from 10 to 1,800 employees, found that "the overall level of satisfaction [with both the job and coworkers] decreased with size"; a study by the Acton Society in England found that as organizations become bigger the workers show less interest in the welfare of the business, know less about the administrators, are more inclined to accept rumors about the plant, have less devotion to "the work ethic," and display less cooperation with both managers and fellow workers. Absenteeism has also been found to be more prevalent in larger businesses; studies of airlines, metal manufacturers, engineering firms, coal mines, chemical plants, and package-delivery businesses all indicate that workers skip more days, come in more erratically, and take more sick days in the larger organizations. Labor disputes are less common in smaller firms, the rate of job turnover is lower, and the number of complaints about defective goods and inadequate service smaller.

And it is not only working stiffs. Even the managers, it turns out, are happier in small businesses. A five-year study of Stanford Business School graduates, who may be presumed to have settled into fairly cushy jobs and pretty much where they wanted to be, indicates that the "men in smaller firms were more satisfied with their work . . . had higher compensation and were able to participate more broadly in management"—better jobs and, surprisingly, more money. Two other surveys, one of 1,900 administrators and the second of 3,000, found that in both authoritarian and collegial managements executives in smaller organizations were significantly more satisfied both with their lives and with their jobs—though, as might be expected, those in the least authoritarian organizations were the most pleased.

In short, as sociologist Emile Durkheim discovered many years ago, "Small-scale industry . . . displays a relative harmony between worker and employer. It is only in large-scale industry that these relations are in a sickly state."

Fittingly, the logic of a steady-state society points exactly toward the "small-scale industry" and its harmony. For it would seem that any true steady-state enterprise would inevitably approach optimum smallness because such principles as minimal ecological intrusion, control over resource use, community involvement, and individual participation *necessarily* put limits on the extent to which any enterprise can grow. For example, a steady-state factory would not need a large sales and promotion staff, say, or an advertising department; it would not need to manufacture so many products, since it needn't create model changes or arbitrary differentiations, and would build for permanence rather than obsolescence; it would not want or need to compete against another firm simply to try to dominate a given market; it would have to keep production within the limits of finite resources and modest energy use; it would confine its output according to the declared needs of the community rather than trying to manipulate those demands; it would depend on alternative technologies that would not demand ever-larger machines; and, particularly where there was maximum participation by the workers in the firm's affairs, it would experience no need to expand operations beyond what was comfortable for the workers. The steady-state enterprise, in short, would have no *reason* to be big, every incentive to stay small.

———

Is it just a haphazard happenstance that the stationary system leads to inherent limitations on sizes, having to do with the number of contacts a person can make within different-sized committees? Or might there not be an underlying logic in all human behavior, allowed to play freely in such a stable economy as it is not now permitted in our exploitative one, that inevitably provides that small economic groups function better than large ones?

Mancur Olson, Jr., thought there was. He was a professor of economics at the University of Maryland—a quite conventional, even conservative, professor of economics, I should add—and his book exploring this precise question, *The Logic of Collective Action,* has become a classic in the field because it demonstrates this reason so convincingly. Olson challenged the standard notion that a normal group in an economy will just naturally act in its own self-interest—that works for small groups, he showed, but larger groups cannot function with that same self-interest and are thereby less efficient and effective. Olson bluntly summarized it thusly:

> *Unless the number of individuals in a group is quite small, or unless there is coercion or some other special device to make individuals act in their common interest, rational, self-interested individuals will not act to achieve their common or group interests. . . . If the members of a large group rationally seek to maximize their personal welfare, they will* not *act to advance their common or group objectives unless there is coercion to force them to do so.*

This seems a bit mysterious at first, since we all know of large organizations apparently operating in their own interests—unions, say, and professional societies. But Olson illustrated both theoretically and with real-world examples why *any* large organization cannot function optimally:

- In the small organization, any individual's share of the common good that the group can obtain is larger, since there are fewer people and only with a small group can the rewards exceed the effort or money put into it. Conversely, *"the larger the number in the group, other things equal, the smaller the* [gains for the individual] *will be, the more individuals in the group, the more serious the suboptimality will be. Clearly then groups with larger numbers of members will generally perform less efficiently than groups with smaller numbers of members."*
- In a small organization, because the rewards are clearer, there is a greater likelihood of one person, or a small subset, absorbing

extra costs or making some sort of a sacrifice so that the organization will continue. Conversely, "the rational individual in the large group in a socio-political context will not be willing to make any sacrifices to achieve the objectives he shares with others." Thus a Typical American Family faced with inflation will not cut spending by itself, even though it realizes that if every family did, inflation would be halted, because it knows its *own* spending won't have an appreciable effect on the nation as a whole and because if there is any ultimate lessening of inflation the family will automatically get the benefits without any sacrifice.

- Similarly, in a small organization each individual realizes that if any one member fails to contribute, "the costs will rise noticeably for each of the others in the group" who may then "refuse to continue making their contributions" and threaten the continuation of the organization, thus eliminating all of the common benefits. "By contrast, in a large group in which no single individual's contribution makes a perceptible difference to the group as a whole, . . . it is certain that a collective good will *not* be provided unless there is coercion or some outside inducements that will lead the members of the large group to act in their common interest."

- In a small group, the costs both of reaching an agreement and of carrying it out—communicating, bargaining, meeting, staffing, monitoring—are much smaller, sometimes quite negligible. But "the larger the number of members in a group the greater the organization costs, and thus the higher the hurdle that must be jumped before any of the collective good at all can be obtained."

- In small organizations, social and peer pressures can operate to encourage participation, and face-to-face association assures that individuals are known and snubbed for misbehavior. "In any large group everyone cannot possibly know everyone else, and the group will ipso facto not be a friendship group; so a person will ordinarily not be affected socially if he fails to make sacrifices on behalf of his group's goals."

There. Simple, really—and inexorably logical.

The point I am sure need not be labored unduly, but Olson offers a number of interesting illustrations:

A *partnership*, for example. This works when small and the rewards are clear, but "when a partnership has many members, the individual partner observes that his own effort or contribution will not greatly affect the performance of the enterprise, and expects that he will get his prearranged share of the earnings whether or not he contributes as much as he could have done."

Or a publicly held *corporation*. Stockholders as a rule almost never act to get rid of a particular management, even when it is performing disastrously, because "any effort the typical stockholder makes to oust the management will probably be unsuccessful; and even if the stockholder should be successful, most of the returns in the form of higher dividends and stock prices will go to the rest of the stockholders," particularly those who hold greater amounts. (Occasionally, of course, there are serious proxy fights, but this happens when one or two stockholders with large blocks of shares have an immediate self-interest in replacing the present management with one of their own.)

Or a *union*. In most large labor unions—as opposed to small, single shops—the value of the large organization is either so negligible that the individual worker has no incentive to join or so pervasive that the worker gets the benefit regardless of joining. Thus it has been necessary ever since the creation of large labor organizations in the nineteenth century for the union to operate by outright coercion—compulsory membership, a "union shop" or a closed shop, wage checkoffs, job control—and even then it gets the month-to-month participation of only a tiny fraction of its members.

Or a *professional association*. These now exist in all sorts of occupations, but the most potent ones are surely the state bar associations, which by law have been given absolute power over who can practice law and who cannot, and on exactly what terms. It is extremely doubtful that lawyers would choose voluntarily to be a member of a state bar association, since again the rule applies: if there is any common good created by these organizations, all lawyers will benefit, whether they contribute or not, so there is no incentive for anyone to join voluntarily; that is why membership is obligatory.

In short, Olson demonstrates conclusively that the difference between the small group and the large one is not simply one of numbers. There is a *qualitative* as well as a *quantitative* distinction, and the benefits come out so clearly on the side of the smaller organization that it appears larger ones *would not even exist* in a country with true economic freedom and would not be able to survive without some continuing form of compulsion.

That is an extraordinary thing to say about a country that prides itself on being a "democracy." And it opens up what may be the most important element of all in a human-scale economy: democracy—real, felt, active democracy—in the workplace.

————

Every student of economics knows the Law of Declining Productivity. Its unrelenting message: the increase in any economic variable (land, labor, capital, et cetera) while others remain fixed will reach a limit beyond which further increase diminishes productivity.

It is simple. If two people can turn out one table a day, it may be possible that four can turn out three, and five can turn out five, allowing for greater efficiency with shared tasks and specialization of added workers. If the quality of work remains fixed, however, and the space and the time, the addition of other workers is likely to make only a marginal difference, with seven people able to put out only six tables a day and a complement of nine so complex that it can manage only five. At some early point, because the workers begin to crowd into each other and the communication becomes more difficult and no one is quite sure what anyone else is doing and planning and coordination break down, productivity—and productivity per worker—inevitably declines.

The law has been around, on at least the textbooks, for a long time. That it has been broken often does not change its eternal validity. It embodies the logic of size.

18

Workplace Democracy

O ver the entrance to virtually every workplace in America, it has been said, is an invisible sign saying, "ABANDON FREEDOM ALL WHO ENTER HERE."

It seems strange that a nation conceived in liberty, inspired by independence, and devoted to democracy should condemn the majority of its working citizens, for the greater part of the day, to conditions of unrivaled autocracy far more stringent than anything practiced by George III. Yet in fact, during the hours that most of us are employed, we forgo most of our basic democratic rights:

- We do not vote on nor have any say whatsoever in what the company we work for will do or make, how it will raise money or invest its profits, or for the most part how it will operate the offices and plants in which we work.
- We do not have the rights of free speech, free assembly, or free press; we have no protection against personal or property searches or invasion of privacy; and we do not have the right to trial and due process within the workplace.
- We normally cannot modify or challenge the decisions that are made for us by a handful of distant people whom we do not elect to, and cannot remove from, office.
- We have no representation in the financial processes (excepting only as a union may intervene) and normally must accept the salaries, cuts, and raises offered by those over whom we have no control.
- And if we should displease this hierarchy for any reason we may be dismissed or disciplined at the whim of any superior (again except only as union power may intervene) and be out on the street without job or reference or—what's worse—recourse.

219

It seems somewhat stark when put like that, but no one really disputes that this condition—what Justice Louis Brandeis many years ago criticized as "industrial absolutism"—is the norm in American life. As one who should know, General Robert E. Wood, for many years the chairman of the board of Sears, Roebuck and Company, has said: "We complain about government and business, and we stress the advantages of the free enterprise system, we complain about the totalitarian state, but in our individual organizations . . . we have created more or less of a totalitarian system in industry, particularly in larger industry." And T. K. Quinn, a former General Electric executive, has described American business thusly: "The directors were in every case elected by the officers. We had then, in effect, a huge economic state governed by nonelected, self-perpetuating officers and directors—the direct opposite of the democratic method."

If a human-scale economy means anything, it means the elimination of such conditions of totalitarianism and the creation of workplaces where individual humans can have a full and constant voice in the matters that affect all aspects of their working life. It means, in short, democracy in the workplace.

Workplace democracy can be—given all the books and pamphlets, *has been*—defined in countless different ways, but all working definitions embody in some degree three essential characteristics: *ownership* of the enterprise by the workers involved in it, preferably operating cooperatively; *control* of the enterprise by the workers involved, through participatory machinery; and responsibility of the enterprise to the *community* in which it is located and in which its workers live.

There can be other ingredients and various mixtures, but these are the three indispensable characteristics, and the ones we will examine next.

Ownership

Nothing difficult about the idea of worker ownership: it simply means that the shares of an enterprise are bought and owned by the people who work in it, and when people cease working there they cease to be owners. Nobody on the outside, not brokerage firms or capitalists or little old ladies on pensions, can buy into it. In effect, this is like having labor "hire" capital, instead of the other way around as we normally do it, and it effectively reduces capital to a secondary element in the operation, behind the work itself. It also means that the workers have an equal share in any profits—and, similarly, losses—made by the company, and a "stake" in the firm's success proportional to the number of shares they own.

Thinking of janitors and lathe operators and secretaries as *owners* of the places they work in is startling, even frightening, for traditional types; as one consultant to a group of workers put it, "When we went to the big lenders, their first reaction was, 'Jesus Christ, the monkeys are going to run the zoo!'" But the fact is, today, according to the National Center for Employee Ownership in Oakland, California, there are 6,718 of them (usually with federally approved Employee Stock Ownership Plans) going strong and covering perhaps 25 million workers (2015)—and that's not counting the small producers' co-ops, food co-ops, and health-food restaurants, auto-repair shops, and bookstores found in most college towns and many large cities. The top 100 worker-owned businesses, employing 626,000 people in 2015, include Publix Super Markets based in Florida and range from an engineering firm in California to a construction company in Texas and a tree service in Ohio—in fact, the whole range of American enterprise.

Not only do they exist—they work, and work well. A 1976 study by Washington's Federal Economic Development Administration indicated that employee-owned companies have above-average profitability compared with regular firms operating in the same market. The University of Michigan's Institute for Social Research, in a study of thirty worker-owned firms, found that all "show a higher level of profitability than do similar conventional firms in their industry" and the "single most important correlate of profitability" is the percentage of the company's equity owned by the workers, especially the rank and file. Other research shows the same—perfectly obvious—thing: where workers feel that they have a real stake in what they are doing, they work with infinitely more care, concern, and commitment. Product and profit figures show the results.

The conventionalists can't believe that the people who actually do the jobs are more capable at running firms than the distant conglomerates, but in any number of instances it's been shown that worker-owners actually do know what they're up to.

Take, for example, the Saratoga Knitting Mill in Saratoga Springs, New York. Owned by the Van Raalte Corporation until 1968, it was taken over by the Cluett-Peabody conglomerate at a time when it was doing some $72 million worth of business a year. But Cluett-Peabody, with the infinite wisdom of the conglomerate, decided to eliminate the factory's sales force and take care of selling with its own existing staff—they knew the market better—and then found that its own people knew nothing about the Saratoga product line and couldn't get it into the stores; by 1974 it managed to reduce the annual sales to $20 million, on which it lost $11 million. Naturally its instinctive reaction was to get rid of a loser, shut down the plant, and protect the bottom line, and the 140 workers would take the hindmost. By 1976, though, the workers had managed to raise some capital from a few local banks and a number of their own mattresses, and they offered to buy Cluett-Peabody out. They did, with dispatch, immediately restored the sales force, improved production methods throughout the plant, and by the very next year the mill had not only pulled itself out of the red but showed a profit of $300,000. The fact that it was bought up by a North Carolina company in 1984 does not mean that worker-ownership was a failure, only that the workers decided to take advantage of a good deal.

Or take the Byers Transport company in western Canada. A successful trucking firm operating throughout the American Northwest, it was taken over by a hungry conglomerate, Pacific Western Airlines, in 1973. It immediately started to lose money. After four years and a loss of $600,000, PWA wanted out and offered it to the employees, who finally managed to get the capital to buy it out. In the very next year it made a profit of $200,000. Again, the fact that it was later bought out by Canadian Freightways in 2010 is more a testament to its success than any sign of weakness.

Or take Publix Super Markets, the largest employee-owned company in the United States. It was started as a small grocery by George Jenkins in 1930 in the face of the Great Depression and was employee-owned from the start, though it was a rarity at the time. That scheme worked so well that he opened his first full-fledged supermarket in 1940 and had a dozen stores in Florida by the 1950s, spread to Georgia in 1991, then South Carolina, Alabama, Tennessee, and North Carolina in 2014. Employee ownership—the basic plan provides associates with 7 to 10 percent of their salaries in free stock, giving them strong incentives to accomplish—has proved so successful that the company now has 180,000 employees in more than 1,100 stores, was the most profitable supermarket chain in the country, and was ranked number eight on the *Forbes* list of America's private companies in 2015 and 87th on the *Fortune* 500 list in 2016.

The monkeys, it turns out, actually know a lot about running the zoo.

Without doubt the most unlikely country in all the world is the setting for the most extraordinarily successful model of worker ownership in all the world. The country is Spain, a nation that during the Franco era had been about as hospitable to workers' democracy as to democracy of any kind or shape; the model began in 1956 as the complex of more than seventy interlocking producer cooperatives based in the small Basque city of Mondragón (population 22,000), which today comprises 257 different businesses with 74,335 employees (2015) with total revenues of $16 billion.

That this complex grew up in the shadow of the Franco dictatorship is probably due to the strong mutualist tradition of the Basque region and the leadership of one Jose Maria Arismendi, a Basque priest who happened to be assigned to Mondragon by the Catholic Church in 1941. That it has been so unusually successful, though, is due not to fortuitousness but to design—careful, slow, labored design.

The Mondragon idea began in a community-funded technical school that Arismendi helped to launch in 1943 to teach local youths both useful technical skills and the principles of worker participation. A number of graduates of the school, eager to put both into practice, decided to establish their own cooperative factory and by 1956 had managed to raise enough money from friends and families in the town to begin a plant, with twenty-three workers, producing stoves and cooking equipment. That cooperative, ULGOR, was a resounding success almost from the start, and upon its prosperity the rest of the complex was built, one firm at a time, two or three a year, first industrial, then agricultural, then financial, then educational, every one operating on the same principles of cooperative worker ownership in accordance with the rules of the International Co-operative Alliance.

Today the Mondragon complex has more than sixty industrial plants, six cooperative schools (with 3,500 students), five agricultural cooperatives, a consumer co-op, a research-and-development center, a welfare agency, and, knitting them altogether, a community bank—also a co-op— that develops, finances, advises, and regularly monitors each enterprise. They must be doing something right. Net profits have regularly averaged between 6 and 10 percent of annual sales and 18 percent as a return on capital, which is even above the average for manufacturing firms in the United States. Only one cooperative has had to be disbanded in these sixty years—and that failed largely because of ineptness by the Spanish government—and one went into bankruptcy (but was immediately bought out and restored), and not one has ever defaulted on a financial obligation. In all that time there has been no unemployment and no one let go for lack of work—even if there should be no job immediately available, a Mondragon worker is guaranteed 80 percent of regular pay at all times.

Hardly a wonder that two researchers from Cornell's Work and Participation Program were moved to conclude, "Nothing remotely like the Mondragon system has ever appeared before anywhere in the world." (True enough, but since then Mondragon has set up a unit to disperse its ideas throughout Europe and the Americas, and in fact several other places have begun successful Mondragon-style operations.)

The system of worker ownership is quite simple. Each worker puts up some membership capital—it has varied over the years but now ranges anywhere from $2,000–$6,000 depending on the enterprise—which can be paid in a lump sum or taken out of wages over the first two years; a quarter of that is automatically transferred to the collective for general operating funds, the rest remains as the worker's "capital account," on which annual interest is paid and to which the worker's share of the firm's annual profits is added. This account cannot be sold or transferred (and so in practice it usually remains available for the firm to use for reinvestment, thus creating new jobs), and it has to be withdrawn when the worker leaves, the full amount on retirement, around 80 percent if before retirement; in many years, for workers who have been with Mondragon for twenty years or more, this account on retirement has come to as much as $20,000 and $30,000—in addition to a retirement pension equal to 100 percent of the final salary. The individual's stake in the company is therefore obviously quite considerable, and all observers agree that this identity of interests is what creates the particular sense of motivation among the Mondragon workers.

When a new enterprise is begun, approximately 20 percent of its working capital is raised in this way from the people who will be working in it; at least 60 percent more is put up by the co-op bank, which has both the corporate accounts of the member firms and the private savings of most of the workers (and non-member citizens of the community) to draw on; and if needed, another 20 percent is available in long-term loans from the Spanish government under a program promoting cooperatives. The bank takes special care with its investments: it makes sure that any proposed project is studied for a full two years, that there are managers available who know how to run the plant, and that there is an ample market for the products when they come online; it also keeps a ninety-person "management service" (*empresarial*) department to keep an eye on managers and plant finances and offer advice when needed or asked.

Wages are established in each firm at a base level equal to the prevailing wage elsewhere in the province, and a differential of 3:1—here a remarkable feature of the Mondragon experiment—is fixed between the lowest salary and the highest. (You can get an idea of the sense of equality and solidarity this provides by comparing it with a large American firm where the differential between median employee and chief executive is more like 300:1.) Profits of course are redistributed to the worker-owners into their capital accounts at the end of the year, with the only stipulation being that at least 20 percent must be held back in the firm's collective reserve fund and at least 10 percent used for social services and projects in the community. (Losses similarly have to be borne by the workers, except in the first two years of a new enterprise, and are deducted from their capital accounts, up to 70 percent.)

Altogether it is a system of remarkable financial self-sufficiency, since almost all the capital needed to establish, operate, and expand the firms is available right there within the community, either from the workers' capital accounts or from the savings bank; no more than 20 percent ever comes in from the outside, and that infrequently.

Control over plant operations is nominally in the hands of the workers, as well, with the employees electing from their membership a board of directors (the *control board*) that meets once a month and sets broad policy for the firm, including the hiring and direction of top managers. In practice, control boards have tended to let their hired managers have a considerable degree of independence, so that frequently the enterprises operate just as if they were ordinary firms on the outside, with aspects of hierarchy, autocracy, routinization, and pay disputes. Still, managers are always aware that their jobs depend on keeping the allegiance of the very people they are overseeing, and they know that their decisions may be overridden by the control board or general membership at any time. In one instance, the managers turned down the request of the evening-shift workers for a 5 percent pay differential over the daytime workers, arguing that it would cost too much money; those workers called for a general assembly of the entire plant, put their case, and won over a majority; management had no recourse but to agree to the raise. In addition, most Mondragon firms have a "social council" made up of elected representatives from each shop to hash over grievances about working conditions and salaries and to present complaints to the management or the control board.

Mondragon is by no means a paradise; it has its problems, some general (too many routinized assembly-line jobs, a lack of democracy and solidarity in the larger firms), some particular to its own methods (workers voting against shutting down uneconomic branches, domination of the control boards by an active few). But it has shown beyond question that an economic system of worker ownership with a cooperative base is not only possible but profitable, that it can thrive in large and complex industrial plants as well as in small workshops and offices, and that it can survive and prosper for many years, even beyond the departure of the first generation. Beyond that it shows that economic enterprises that are immediately rooted in a community covering a small area, that explicitly have the community's interests at heart (as with the profit-sharing scheme), can rely on both the financial support and the popular enthusiasm of the citizens to a degree unparalleled elsewhere.

Could it happen elsewhere? Is it duplicable? The officers of the Mondragon bank certainly think so; they say that starting producer cooperatives is actually pretty simple, once you draw up the plans carefully and find (or train) the managers who can carry them out. There's nothing about Basque blood or the Spanish sun that makes such places unique to Mondragon, the bank president says, and adds that the only necessary conditions to imitate are an industrial tradition and sophisticated workers, both of which are found throughout the West.

Oddly enough, though, the only successful Mondragon model in the United States is not made up of sophisticated industrial workers but rather poor and generally unskilled workers in a Cleveland neighborhood called the Greater University Circle. There, in 2008, working with the local hospital and Case Western Reserve University, a group of inner-city citizens established three parts of the Evergreen Cooperative, made up of an Evergreen Cooperative Laundry, doing chiefly hospital linen, Evergreen Energy Solutions, working on solar power and LED-lighting systems, and Green City Growers, which uses a large greenhouse to grow gourmet food for local restaurants and grocers.

It has had some troubles, but today it has proved generally successful and established the worker-owned co-op as a workable economic system in this country—if anybody's paying attention.

Control

In countless cases, from small, cooperative health-food restaurants to large manufacturing plants, workers have found time and again that mere formal ownership doesn't necessarily have much to do with day-to-day authority. As Bertil Gardell, the leading Swedish expert on workplace democracy, has put it:

> With a few exceptions most experiments have very little to do with industrial democracy in a sense which includes forms for worker influence on larger economic and technological decisions. By and large these cases—important as they may be—represent only new ways to increased productivity through increased motivation to work. This means that this approach is not answering all the relevant problems involved—such as worker claims for a broader base in decisionmaking—and it also means that its potential is not fully realized.

It takes more than just worker ownership for the democratization of work—there's got to be some mechanism for worker *control* as well.

Control can come in a multitude of ways, and the range of experiments in employee democracy has included everything from meetings to decide how long the coffee break should be (at the McCaysville textile plant in northern Georgia) to weekly assemblies of entire factories to determine the following week's production quota (in a few self-managed plants in the former Yugoslavia). But certain features have proven to be basic:

- the regular and open *assembly* of all employees, empowered where necessary to elect (or, better, choose by consensus) whatever directors and officers seem necessary for the firm, with the right of immediate recall of any one of them;
- regular *decision making*, on all matters deemed to be important to the workers, by either the full assembly of the workers or some representative body;

- the easy acquisition and sharing of *information* about everything that goes on in the workplace, including who earns what and how much the raw materials cost and what the plans for long-range development are; and
- the regular and complete *rotation* of jobs, allowing every employee to sit anywhere from the metal punch to the treasurer's desk, with special encouragement for those who are reluctant.

Strongforce, a private group that operated in Washington in the 1970s and '80s, was a champion of worker self-management and proffered a checklist of the kinds of things over which any work group should be able to have a direct, informed, decisive, and regular say:

- Raising capital
- Allocating profits
- Determining investments in new plant and machinery
- Arranging job assignments, rotations, responsibilities
- Choosing the type of products or services, markets, and prices
- Organizing research and development
- Setting salaries, wages, and fringe benefits
- Hiring and training new workers
- Creating job security and layoff standards
- Setting work standards and work rates
- Establishing safety rules and practices
- Overseeing physical working conditions

In sum, the worker should control the workplace, not the other way around. Anything less and what you have is an operation devoted not to increased democracy but merely to increased productivity.

In recent years, beginning in 2004, a United States Federation of Worker Cooperatives has been established, and it hosts a weekly "webinar" on "Steps to Starting a Workers Cooperative" that has pretty much the same guidelines as those above.

———

Ultimately, it's clear, what all this is leading to is the abolition of the stratum in most workplaces known as management, and at first blush that seems a mad and foolish thing. After all, even the Mondragon cooperatives retain hierarchy and management. True enough—but might it not be said that to that extent they are not truly democratic, that in fact they have not altered the basic conditions of old-style labor by all that much? Would not the removal of such managerial aristocracy—outsiders, the highest paid, separate in habits of thought and living—be the necessary and desirable consequence of worker control?

Well, yes—but is it possible?

Indeed, it is, and not so rare as all that, either. In some collective workplaces the manager's job is rotated among the workers, effectively demystifying the role while giving everyone an understanding of what it entails. In other worker-run shops managerial decisions are reached collectively, by either vote or consensus, with each employee expected to have the requisite information and expertise. And in a number of places a managerial committee is elected by the workers at large to take on basic administrative tasks for a year, subject to intervention by the workers at any time.

There are problems in such a system, no one denies. Most people in our industrial culture are not used to doing without leaders and taking responsibility into their own hands. There is a sort of dependency mentality that in subtle ways gets ingrained in most of us, creating an inevitable resistance to the thought of taking charge: I don't feel like getting involved; it's too much of a hassle; I don't have the time. Most people, particularly women and often the undereducated, have little experience with leadership, are usually afraid to assert themselves, and tend to clam up when made to sit on a serious committee. And yet experience has shown that in practically every instance where it's given a real try, enough time and enough practice with self-management will overcome these difficulties.

Examples of non-managerial successes are not all that hard to find. In the classic study here, Seymour Melman, when a professor of industrial engineering at Columbia University, laboriously compared twelve industrial enterprises in Israel, half of them run with traditional managements and half run cooperatively, without bosses. By every measure—productivity of labor, productivity of capital, efficiency of management, cost of administration—the cooperative plants performed at least as well as, and in most respects better than, the regular ones: cooperative sales per production worker were 26 percent higher, sales/asset ratios were 33 percent greater, profit/investment ratios were 67 percent greater, and profits per production worker were 115 percent higher. Melman concluded, in his careful academese, that "industrial enterprises of a modern technical sort" can indeed operate without "management decision making" and that "cooperative decision making is a workable method of production decision making in the operation of industrial enterprise." As to the reason, Melman suggests that "this capability is linked to the pervasive motivational and operational effects of cooperation in decision making and in production, pressing toward stability in operations, and thereby toward optimal use of industrial facilities." In other words, people work better when they care. Now it is only fair to point out that the collective enterprises Melman studied were on Israeli kibbutz settlements and therefore the workers were presumably conscious of the entire community that stood beyond, and depended upon, their work, a strong motivating condition that presumably did not apply to the standard enterprises. Nonetheless, the *fact* of their superiority is unquestioned.*

An even more unusual example of dispensing with traditional management comes from Norway and involves ten oceangoing commercial ships—places where authority and rigidity have always been thought to be indispensable. David Moberg, writing in *In These Times* in 1977, described how it worked:

> *On the good ship Balao, for example, the traditional hierarchy was replaced with work planning groups. The newly integrated work crews required increased education and mechanical training for many of the lower level sailors. They learned how to navigate as well as to repair the ship, so they could work in nearly all areas. The old bosun, or supervisor, was eliminated in favor of the new job category of ship mechanic.*
>
> *Safety hazards were continually discussed in work planning groups, with the ship's crew completely in charge of designing all*

---

* Cooperation, according to two psychologists in the basic *Handbook of Social Psychology* (Volume II, 1954), normally leads to "strong motivation to complete the common task and to the development of considerable friendliness among the members." In numerous clinical studies, "with respect to group productivity the cooperative groups were clearly superior."

operations to maintain safety. Everyone was put on a fixed annual wage and a flexible work schedule for staffing the ship was established.

The key to the whole experiment's success was "for those who do the things to have the initiative and control" [according to Einar Thorsrud, the man who began the whole project back in the 1960s], "to put back into the job coordination and control." Now the captain on the ship is frequently overruled. There is no uniform relationship of superiors to subordinates, but an adjustment of rules according to each task. The four separate eating areas have been combined into one, and no one even sits regularly in the same chair. This uprooting of bureaucracy has increased the satisfaction and power of the crew. The ship owners now find it easier to recruit and hold workers.

And if it can be done on a *ship*, could it not be done anywhere?

Another example, closer to home, is the experiment run at the Rushton coal mine in eastern Pennsylvania 1973–75, in which one section of the mine, with three shifts of nine workers each, established an autonomous work group, working without managerial supervision. Every worker in the section was paid top union salary, each one was trained in all aspects of the job, and when they met at the beginning of each shift they would decide among them what jobs they felt like doing that day, their only conditions being that they had to keep production up and not violate any mine safety rules. The foreman, who in other mines was typically a mini-dictator telling workers where to cut, where to lay power cables, when to eat lunch, was not allowed to interfere with the daily work process in any way, could not give orders to the group, and had to make any suggestions to the entire shift, which would meet and decide whether to honor them or not.

The results proved conclusively that self-management was successful, both at maintaining productivity and, far more important, at increasing worker satisfaction. The actual tonnage mined during this period was not increased—it stayed roughly the same—but, according to Gerald Susman of the College of Business Administration at Penn State, during the first year the time lost to accidents declined 500 percent, safety violations were reduced from eighteen to six, and equipment breakage was down over previous years. ("It used to be when a machine got busted," one miner confessed, "we'd just sit around, happy-like, until the foreman spotted it and called in a mechanic. But when a machine breaks down nowadays, whenever we can . . . we just fix it ourselves.") Cost figures of the autonomous experiment are somewhat confused, but one measure of the apparent economic gain is that after a year the management of the mine announced that they wanted to open up a whole new section under the same autonomous rules. But what was most noticeable about the project was that the workers liked it. Reporters from a dozen major papers and the business press who visited the mine all heard the same kinds of remarks: "Now it's like being in business for myself"; "It's like you feel you're somebody, like you feel you're a professional, like you got a profession you're proud of"; "I'm not as tired when I go home any more, and my wife . . . told me just the other day that I was a lot easier to get along with." The United Mine Workers reported that "over and over again, we heard miners say that they would continue to work autonomously even if the pay differential were taken away, and that they needed no incentive outside the additional satisfactions they received to continue working autonomously."

It is not really anticlimactic to add that, in August 1975, after twenty months of the project, the miners themselves voted, 79–75, to discontinue it. The reasons? The UMW itself was no longer much interested in the experiment, having concluded that the workers in the *other* shifts, the non-autonomous shifts, were plainly angered both with the high salaries and with the independence their fellow miners enjoyed, and their votes were sufficient to end it.

On a larger and more successful scale, an example of a Mondragon-model worker self-management that has lasted for two decades now is found in the San Francisco Bay area, neatly called the Network of Bay Area Cooperatives, or NoBAWC—pronounced "Noboss." Started in 1994, and a member of the US Federation of Workers Cooperatives since 2006, it is now a collection of thirty-six cooperative workplaces—including pizzerias, bakeries, bookstores, food co-ops, an art gallery, a press—with 1,000 workers and annual sales estimated at more than $80 million. As one reporter described it in 2005, "everyone makes the same amount of money and everyone is responsible for making the business work. Everyone does all the jobs. No one gets summarily fired. Decisions are made by consensus. At the end of the year, some money goes to charity and some is invested back into the business. The rest of the profits, instead of enriching one or two individuals, are returned to all the worker-owners—a rising tide lifting many boats." And everyone seems happy.

The literature on worker participation is copious, and throughout it runs a single and almost unequivocal conclusion: when workers are given an opportunity, they work just as well if not better without bosses. There are studies in garment factories, insurance companies, medical laboratories, shoe factories, newspaper offices, and auto-accessory plants, among men and women and mixed groups, with production-line workers and salespeople and office workers and scientists, and they all indicate that increased participation, increased autonomy, increased control, invariably means increased satisfaction and more often than not increased productivity and efficiency. In the words of sociologist Paul Blumberg, author of the pioneering work *Industrial Democracy*:

> There is hardly a study in the entire literature which fails to demonstrate that satisfaction in work is enhanced or that other generally acknowledged beneficial consequences accrue from a genuine increase in workers' decision-making power. Such consistency of findings, I submit, is rare in social research.

Now I am not suggesting—nor do the studies conclude—that there is no need for *structure*, for organization, planning, guidelines, quotas, goals, and systems of responsibility. The absence of managers does not mean, as some (mostly managers) contend, the absence of order. There has been enough experience in the last decades or so with groups trying to work with complete spontaneity and randomness ("without all that capitalist structure bullshit") to show that, at least when anything more complicated than deciding who-sleeps-where is involved, such disorder is not particularly useful or, in the end, very satisfying. But hierarchy is not the only form of order, any more than autocracy is the only form of decision making. Cooperative structures, cooperative responsibilities, can easily be established and have been in countless enterprises.

Nor am I saying that *decisions* do not have to be made, on occasion in a hurry and sometimes by a single individual. Obviously certain minor problems should not require a full-scale general assembly, like the magazine collective that debated for a half an hour if the shades should be

233

drawn and if so how far—that decision could probably have been taken care of by the one in whose eyes the sun was shining. And obviously certain major problems should have an immediate yes-or-no answer that one person may have to give, though with the understanding that the decision will be reviewed sometime hence by the rest of the group, and either confirmed or modified with new guidelines for future occasions; just such a procedure was followed during the extraordinary journey of the Quaker ship *Phoenix* to Vietnam in 1967, when despite harassment by South Vietnamese gunboats and American planes the ship's leader did not once use his authority to make unilateral decisions but instead hammered out every procedure with other project members, *by consensus*, before acting. It is surprising how many matters of substance and duration can be decided, easily and rationally, by a coherent group properly informed.

Finally, I am not saying that there is never any need for *experts* of one kind or another in a complex business—it well may be that trained people are necessary as accountants, engineers, sales managers, and the like. Two points, however, must follow.

First, experts do not need to be *bosses*. The people with the expertise have no special reason to have the monopoly of power; they are workers just like the rest and should have the same say in the products and procedures of the workplace. They may have some special knowledge that the other people do not, but it is precisely in sharing that, and explaining decisions based on it, that others come to learn new roles and the group as a whole comes to make rational choices. Just as an architect does not normally dictate the way a house is built but works with and adjusts to clients, contractors, suppliers, and inspectors, so the expert in a worker-controlled operation would be expected to consult and discuss with all the others in the group.

Second, experience shows that with almost all jobs, and most particularly those of the kind that upper- and middle-level management occupy in American businesses, on-the-job training and general corporate experience is many times more important than prior academic preparation, a fact that virtually every manager will acknowledge. That means that the ordinarily intelligent worker is probably capable, in time, of learning the necessary skills of any managerial position—and can be presumed in addition to bring to it a certain valuable up-from-under perspective that no one else could have. Experiments in full job rotation have been fairly limited, confined usually to the communes and collectives in the 1960s and '70s that were explicitly committed to destroying the usual patterns of expertise and specialization. But they suggest that generally, though both the expert and the neophyte usually begin with great trepidation, it does not take long for even the most arcane skills to be shared. In some cases, according to a networking group in Cambridge called Vocations for Social Change, which has had experience with a great many alternative organizations,

> *when the task involves a difficult skill, there is often a dual rotation system. Two people do it at a time, but one person rotates off and is replaced by a novice half-way through the time period. Thus everyone is in training half the time and is the "expert" for the other half.*

Sometimes, too, a committee of trained people is established to take the place of a single expert and meets regularly both for basic policy and day-to-day decisions.

In general, the tenor of our economy seems to be moving away from hierarchical control toward more collegial decision making, even in the stuffiest, most conventional firms, and the benefits are now routinely touted by management consultants and workplace psychologists. Scott Burns, the Boston economist, argues:

> *What is lacking in public consciousness—or even in the literature of management—is recognition that the decline of authority is a consequence of far larger events than faulty child rearing, permissive schools, the power of the local union, and the other popular hobgoblins of disorder. The larger fact is that the economic drive which justified (or at least sustained) the hierarchic structure of industrial society has matured. As a result, all that would support the continued existence of powerful hierarchies, from the organizations within the market economy itself, is disintegrating. The day of large organizations and small elites is at an end.*

That may be somewhat optimistic, but there is no gainsaying the trend to which he points. As the Vocations for Social Change people put it in the title of their book: *No Bosses Here.*

Now there are—it will come as no surprise—size limitations on worker control, as anyone who has worked in a plant or office will realize. The mechanics of economic democracy—general meetings, group decisions, information sharing, job rotation—demand a certain cohesion, a certain constriction. Just as it is not possible to know a million people or hold a million dollar bills (they would make a stack 364 feet high), it is not possible to have an effective system of democracy in a workplace with more than a limited number of people.

Stephen Sachs, an official of the Association for Self-Management and one of the leading American researchers in this field, has surveyed the literature and determined that self-management is "more extensive and more successful in relatively small, face-to-face organizations than in larger organizations, and in smaller units of large organizations than in the organization as a whole." His work in the former Yugoslavia, a nation that did more than any other in the last quarter of the twentieth century to foster worker control throughout the economy until its collapse in 1990, confirmed this, for there, after a decade of experimentation, the Yugoslav government concluded that self-management "had generally been found to work better in smaller firms than in large ones" and officially moved to reduce the size of factories and offices and to break up large companies into semi-autonomous work units operating by direct democracy. In general, the Yugoslavs have concluded that when a workplace gets much beyond a hundred people its self-governing difficulties start: there is a significant drop in participation by the workers and a tendency to let supervisors and senior managers make all the important decisions, with ultimately a decline in morale and productivity.

The Israeli kibbutzim—with more people in them, by the way, in 2012 than ever before—offer another good real-world example. There most of the service groups—the basic "branches" that do the agricultural work, run the kitchens, operate the laundry, and so on—are seldom more than eight or ten people, even in the larger settlements of five hundred or more. The industrial units tend to be larger, but half of them have fewer than twenty-five people, less than a third have more than fifty, and only a handful have more than a hundred. Arnold Tannebaum and a team of academic researchers who examined industrial organizations in five Western nations found that the small size of the Israeli factory was the

236

crucial element in its success; large organizations, they determined, are always more hierarchic and authoritarian, no matter what ideologies they fly under, and are simply not conducive to worker self-management.

There is also the Mondragon example, again. "The success of producer co-operatives in Mondragon," a British team reported, "has been limited to small and medium-sized enterprises"; more than half of them have fewer than a hundred workers, and these are the ones agreed to have the most harmonious conditions. The only factory over 1,000 is the huge refrigerator plant with 3,500 workers, and this is the one that was regularly plagued by disputes and mismanagement and finally went bankrupt in 2013.

In sum, it seems safe to conclude that a small workplace will have no particular difficulty in achieving worker control and that units of even forty or fifty can find ways to maintain the necessary communications and intimacy, though at that point the strains begin to show; up to a hundred is still apparently often manageable, but over that the troubles mount and control becomes more and more distant.

As has been so artfully said, small is beautiful.

Community

Robert Dahl, the political scientist, offers a proposition in his analysis of democracy, *After the Revolution?*, that he calls the Principle of Affected Interests. It holds: "Everyone who is affected by the decisions of a government should have the right to participate in that government." It is a principle that would seem to be absolutely basic to any democratic system, and one that is very much in the American grain, something on the order of, say, "no taxation without representation." It would seem to be, moreover, a precept central to any democratic economy, speaking to the interests of the general public beyond the workplace, "everyone who is affected by the decisions" of the workplace: not just the workers but the people next door and the taxpayers who provide the roads and the couple who runs the luncheonette down the street and the accounting firm that does the books and the people downwind who breathe the air and every client and customer at its door. In short, what we may call—using the term in its very broadest sense—the community.

Just as *true* workplace democracy cannot exist without worker ownership and worker control, so it cannot exist without some form of worker community. It is a triad: ownership represents its economic side, control its political side, and connections and communication with the community its social side.

————————

For the usual private business in the capitalist system, the community is essentially non-existent. No matter how public a firm's activities may be—and who could deny that the activities of General Motors, for example, have enormous public consequence?—it is protected by the fiction of being a private organization in the hands of private citizens. Yes, it might give to the Community Chest or outfit a local softball team or sponsor a public-service program; it might create a "public relations" division to mix into civic affairs while promoting company affairs; it might even, as a few "enlightened" businesses have done, put a woman or a black or a student or some other "community representative" in a token spot on the board of directors. It also presumably has to abide by certain regulations designed to ensure public safety and pay occasional income and property taxes to offset the public services it uses. But for the most part the private firm is regarded as private, left to consider outside citizens only as they make themselves known through the market. The executives, who normally don't even live in the same town their offices are in, have no obligation to the community that sustains them, and a great many move from firm to firm with such rapidity that there wouldn't be much way for them to know the needs of their fellow citizens if they had. And the multinational firms are the most distant of all, because of course they have *no* community, not even a single nation, to which they have any loyalty or duty, nor any way to know about or respond to the interests of such a vast and worldwide public.

Things are no better, I hasten to add, under the "socialist" systems. There the idea of community is substituted for by the role of the state, which makes the laws and assigns the quotas and controls the markets, all presumably so as to evidence the public will. No matter how foolish or corrupt or anti-social, the state-owned firm is protected by the fiction that whatever it does will automatically be in the community interest—by definition. No doubt to some extent the socialist firm *does* respond in some way to community interest, in the sense at least that it cannot (as its capitalist counterpart can) flout government directives or discontinue an officially decreed product line or lay off its workforce or set up a runaway shop in the south. But it cannot represent the true wishes of the larger public because no one has any good way of knowing what those are, being determined in practice by diktat from the commissars in the capital—and if the commissars choose to divert a staggering amount of the national budget to armaments instead of automobiles (as in the former Soviet Union), well, that is the public will no matter what the public wills. Nor does anyone regard it as important to serve the needs and appetites of the local communities where the plants and offices are located, for the system is relentlessly centralized and individual managers must listen not to what their neighbors but to what their commissars say. In those conditions even outfitting a local softball team might be hard to do.

It is a sorry comment that neither of these systems, as we know from long experience, really works to represent the community interest, and both are a pitifully long way from allowing "everyone who is affected" by economic decisions to participate in making them. But a worker-owned, worker-controlled system—is there any reason to think that it could achieve the Principle of Affected Interests and give the community a real voice in economic affairs?

On a theoretical level there certainly is. One would expect that workers, living closer to their workplaces and representing a broader spectrum of social strata than today's executives, would inevitably bring a far greater diversity and intensity of community viewpoints into a firm's decision process. Presumably also they would take their families' and their neighbors' concerns into the job with them, and since there are no distant shareholders or absentee directors to worry about, their processes and products would reflect those concerns. And it's reasonable to assume that the whole experience of self-management would spill over into the workers' private lives and inject itself into the homes and neighborhood organizations, developing democratic and participatory habits through-out the community. Finally, it would seem that a firm truly attuned to what the community desired would be in a very advantageous position to make rational and finely tuned decisions about what kinds of services to offer and how much of what kinds of products to manufacture.

But fortunately we needn't remain on a simply theoretical plane here. There is enough evidence from the real world to show how community-workplace ties are forged and strengthened when almost any kind of worker control is practiced.

On one end of the scale, take the limited experiment with an "open system" at the Procter & Gamble plant in Lima, Ohio, begun in the late 1960s. Workers were given considerable power in setting their conditions of work, with control over hiring and firing, establishing pay rates, working out job rotation, and keeping the books. Predictably, productivity increased, quality improved and equipment costs decreased, and both salaries and profits showed a steady rise; but what was most surprising was the finding of Neil McWhinney, a psychologist from the University of California who helped to plan the Lima experiment:

> One of the striking features in our "pure" open systems plant is that workers take on more activities outside the workplace. The most visible involvements had to do with community racial troubles. Following major disturbances in the small city where they lived, a number of workers organized the black community to deal directly with the leaders of the city and of industry. . . . Blue collar workers won elections to the school board majority office and other local positions. Nearly ten percent of the work force of our plant holds elective offices currently. . . . We have noted that open systems workers join more social clubs and political organizations.

At the other end of the scale, there was the extraordinary system of self-management in Yugoslavia between the 1950s and '80s, when the government attempted to establish an entire worker-run economy, with every single workplace—industrial, agricultural, service—organized on self-management principles. Imperfections there were in the Yugoslav arrangements—particularly in the heavy roles played by the state apparatus and the Communist Party—but after thirty years of practical day-in-day-out experience, the success of it was beyond question: in fact, during the 1960s the Yugoslav economy grew at a rate second only to Japan's and in the 1970s, despite some slackening, the economy remained among the world's highest. And during this time there was a real and measurable increase in the involvement of workers individually, and their firms as businesses, with the wider community.

Stephen Sachs, of Indiana University, who did research in Yugoslavia on exactly this point, reported that he found a "strong indication that the participation by workers in management and organizational income

does in fact increase the concern of the enterprise for community interests and problems"—and to a level that "seemed to exceed significantly
that of business and business executives in the United States." He found
in the region he studied that the workers' councils regularly voted
to give money to special village projects beyond their regular village
tax—in one case for a new drinking-water system, in another for new
road pavement—and normally sponsored concerts, soccer teams, chess
clubs, dance companies, and the like. Facilities and services that a business had set up for its own employees—a bus service, for example, or
a meeting hall—were automatically free and available to anyone else in
the community, and even on-the-premises space and equipment—in one
case an entire workshop—were open to students at nearby schools and
technical colleges. And permeating most operations was the fixed idea
that the purpose of the business was to benefit not simply the workers
but also their families, their friends, their neighbors, their towns. It isn't
all perfect harmony, to be sure—in all too many firms the workers have
given over real decision-making power to the upper management, often
less attuned to community needs, and in others the workers need to be
prodded by "regulation from truly representative public institutions" to
keep community interests uppermost. Still, in general, Sachs found, "the
institution of workplace democracy significantly increases the community
spiritness of an enterprise," and "maximum social responsibility of enterprises can probably only be achieved in a society in which firms are fully
self-managed."

Yes, Yugoslavia is gone, and this was some time ago. But it proves what
can work: human nature has not changed.

———————

There are a multitude of problems with worker-controlled enterprises,
of course, particularly among those who have little training for such a
responsibility. But when the community makes itself felt, and autonomous workers realize that there is a constituency beyond the office walls, a
body of people out there dependent in some measure on their efforts, that
generally proves to be a real and potent solution to most of the difficulties. Among countless cooperative and worker-run firms in this country,
and in case after case in similar enterprises elsewhere where community
ties are strongest, the businesses tend to perform better, stay in business

longer, hold their turnover rates lower, and work with fewer internal conflicts. This is particularly true of retail businesses, of course, and people in food and bookstore co-ops and record-shop collectives are the first to say that community feedback is essential for success and the first to establish the means—regular open meetings, suggestion blackboards, Sunday-afternoon forums, local representatives in their councils—to ensure it.

The most telling example of this kind of influence is the Israeli kibbutz, for there a sense of shared commitment to the kibbutz ideal is added to the powerful day-to-day input of a close-knit community. We have already seen that the businesses on the kibbutz settlements are more productive and efficient than other Israeli forms, and in explaining that Seymour Melman says revealingly:

> The people working in the kibbutz enterprise are motivated to feel needed and wanted within the context of the total community. Such feelings, among people who share common tasks, are powerful motivating forces for individuals to give their best in the performance of shared responsibility.

Since originally there were no wages for work, and since everyone got an equal real income—this has changed in several modern kibbutzim and there are outside "hired workers" in many—it is status and admiration that normally act as the incentives for the kibbutz worker, and both of those are by definition *social*, dependent upon the wider community. Another researcher, Haim Barkai, has noted:

> Respect and esteem for a good day's work and for the success in managerial and entrepreneurial functions is undoubtedly an important factor in the attitude of individuals towards work and responsibility in the kibbutz environment. And per contra, the disfavor with which shirking is viewed is, in the closely knit communities, which even the largest kibbutzim still are, a powerful sanction.

Moreover, the kibbutz enterprise, whether agricultural or industrial, has to depend in very real and practical ways on the community, for its resources are limited—particularly labor, which has always been in short supply, and land, which has to be wrested from the desert—and the

242

settlement as a whole has to determine how they should best be allocated. Hence it is the general assembly of the whole kibbutz that actually decides what kinds of crops and products are to be produced, how big the work-teams should be, how the annual productivity targets are to be set, and what the development and reinvestment plans for the future are to be. And though there are obviously wide differences among the 270 or so kibbutzim (2010), the fact that they have all been economically successful suggests that this communal role has been unusually advantageous.

But I think it would be a mistake to assume that worker control and community self-interest will always coincide, as if by some communal magic. Enough evidence has come from the Yugoslav experience, as well as from any number of well-intentioned collectives and Community Development Corporations (CDCs) in this country, to show that there will be times when workers are going to put their own (or their firm's) concerns ahead of the specific considerations of the outside populace: they want a raise, the community wants a playground; they want to take off an extra week of vacation, the customers want the services continued uninterrupted; they want to make cars, the people would rather have buses. For such times, it pays to have systematic arrangements that guarantee some sort of mutuality.

The spectrum of possibilities is broad, but in general it has this four-part configuration: community representation through contract; community representation on workplace boards; community ownership, worker usufruct; and community ownership and direction.

Community representation through contractual obligation. Under this sort of plan, about the simplest, every self-managed firm by contract agrees to give back to the community in one way or another some of the rewards it gains from doing business there: by turning over a certain percentage of the profits beyond local taxes, or agreeing to the annual upkeep of one or another neighborhood institution, or maintaining a public facility on its premises. Most often such an obligation is voluntary, produced by groups that explicitly wish to demonstrate communal values—the collective bookstore that sets up a library available to any community person free of charge, or the CDC that writes into its charter the percentage of profits to be used for day-care centers; but on occasion it has been written in as a proviso of loans from a local bank, trade union, progressive foundation, or cooperative credit union.

An extensive variant of such a plan is found in the Mondragon system, where the central savings bank, the institution that funds and monitors all projects, stipulates in advance that each venture must pay back at least 10 percent of its annual profits to the community, with a sliding scale by which the more money a firm makes the more it has to turn over. This is reinforced, too, by the Mondragon cooperative school system, which acts as both a programmer and a guide—and ultimately as a kind of con- science—to ensure that each worker separately, and the multitude of firms collectively, do not shirk their social obligations. Although the system has expanded worldwide now with 74,117 employees, in the Basque head- quarters town, with only 23,000 people (2013), there continues a strong tradition of mutual cooperation and social cohesion, where people have seen in their everyday lives the practical benefits of shared resources. In the words again of the British economic team:

> *It means on the one hand, that [the cooperatives] receive the support and backing (notably savings) of the local residents; on the other, it makes possible the integrated planning of industrial initiatives, housing, education, the training of skilled personnel, and community services (medication, and social services). In other words, the whole operation is run by the community in the interests of the community.*

Community representation on workplace boards. Somewhat more formal and complex, though still quite accessible, this has been tried out by a number of the smaller cooperatives in the last decade and by many of the CDCs (though the latter are not necessarily worker-controlled) explic- itly devoted to local, often inner-city, progress. Normally several of the established neighborhood civic and religious organizations are asked to name a representative or two to the firm's board or send delegates to the firm's general meetings, but in some cases mass meetings or even special elections are used to select representatives at large.

One form of this representative arrangement was concocted by the Washington, DC–based National Center for Economic Alternatives in pre- paring its proposal for community ownership of the Youngstown, Ohio, steel mill that the Lykes Corporation decided to shut down in 1977. Under that plan, one-third of the new plant's board of directors would be elected by a nonprofit "community corporation" composed of "recognized community leaders"; one-third by the employees themselves, through an Employee Stock Ownership Plan (ESOP) scheme that would give every worker full voting rights and a slice of the profits; and one-third by individual shareholders, both workers and residents in the Youngstown area. (Interestingly, when this proposal was actually put to the Youngstown workers they asked for two significant changes to enhance the community role: the community corporation should be elected from a broad range of political and civic organizations, not just "leaders," and it should have only a quarter of the voting stock, with a full half to go to individual shareholders.) With the Youngstown populace unable to raise the purchase money, however, this scheme has never been put into practice.

A more complex and far-reaching version of this idea was recommended by E. F. Schumacher in *Small Is Beautiful*, where he suggested that half the shares of any enterprise be allocated to a public board (a "Social Council") chosen by public democratic vote and half of the profits allocated to it (in lieu of income tax) at the end of the year. This Social Council would have no power to vote the shares or to intervene in basic company matters—with twenty years as economic advisor to the British National Coal Board, Schumacher was not full of optimism on the ability of the public hand to guide private enterprise—but it would act as a regular watchdog with a place on the enterprise's board of directors and could appeal to a special court to intervene in cases where it felt the public interest was not being properly safeguarded.

Community ownership, worker usufruct. The old Latin concept of usufruct—use and enjoyment, rather than ownership, of property and goods—can be used to modify the straight-out idea of worker ownership, as another method of guaranteeing community interests.

This sort of usufruct proposal that was put forward in this country by Henry George, one of our most extraordinary (and today most neglected) economists, as long ago as the 1880s. George argued then that people should not have ownership rights to a piece of land or extract rent from it if they didn't themselves *use* the property; rather the land would be owned by the society at large and each person, family, or firm could make use of it as they saw fit. The society's obligation would be to ensure that the fruits of everyone's labors would be secure, and in return it would receive an appropriate rent on its property—in effect, a tax on the value of the land, "the taking by the community, for the use of the community, of the value that is the creation of the community." George wrote:

> *It will be obvious to whoever will look around him that what is required for the improvement of land is not absolute ownership of the land, but security for the improvements.*
>
> *Nothing is more common than for land to be improved by those who do not own it. The greater part of the land of Great Britain is cultivated by tenants, the greater part of the buildings of London are built upon leased ground, and even in the United States the same system prevails everywhere to a greater or less extent. Thus it is a common matter for use to be separated from ownership. . . .*
>
> *It is not necessary to say to a man, "this land is yours," in order to induce him to cultivate or improve it. It is only necessary to say to him, "whatever your labour or capital produces on this land shall be yours." . . . It is for the sake of the reaping that men sow; it is for the sake of possessing houses that men build. The ownership of land has nothing to do with it.*

The Georgist principles provide a way for a community to secure its financial interests in a rational economy of usufruct, but to guarantee its social and environmental interests something more may be necessary. One method that has been developed and put into practice in recent years is the *community land trust*, an arrangement by which a group of people can form a corporation to buy and hold land in perpetuity and then use and develop that land as they choose, guided only by their original contracts and whatever trustees they may elect—and by their consciences. Started by activists Ralph Borsodi and Robert Swann in the 1960s, the community land trust movement was organized through an E. F. Schumacher Society in Great Barrington, Massachusetts (now the Schumacher Center for a New Economics), and now has some 250 trusts with 10,000 or so housing units, most of them small (with ten to fifteen families) and many agricultural. But the principle seems to work, and there is no reason a full-fledged town with industries, farms, shops, and services could not operate in the same way: individual interests are secured by people acting to improve their own lives in their own settings, individual rights through contractual leases guaranteeing people the use of a certain amount of property; community interests are secured by contractual agreements and the election of trustees to oversee the well-being of the community, community rights by careful land-use planning and environmental allocation of land and by adherence to these plans and contracts.

Community ownership and direction. At the extreme, a community might simply take control of the entire economy of its area, allocating resources and assigning jobs, creating and guiding all enterprises and services, setting workplace conditions and quotas, and even controlling the allocation and distribution of goods. A truly self-sufficient community could decide whether or not it wanted to stick to standard market arrangements—you make, I buy, I service, you pay—for the distribution of goods or, in a more cooperative way, distribute according to work, or need, or even absolute equality—a system feasible, however, only on relatively small scales. It could decide as well whether to do away with currency (except for outside transactions) and replace it with other systems available to smaller units, such as scrip or (as in various nineteenth-century communes) "labor notes" or family-allowance credits, or even with simple barter; capital, after all, is an invention to assure the mobility of a product, but if mobility were unnecessary and products could be easily exchanged in a small area then capital would be essentially unnecessary.

Various more-or-less utopian experiments along these lines have been tried over the last century and a half, some with extraordinarily long-lasting success: the Warrenite communes of Utopia and Modern Times both lasted for nearly two decades with systems modeled on Josiah Warren's ideas of labor-for-labor exchange, and the Amana communities survived for well over sixty years on the basis of simple family allowances, until modern enticements and currencies intruded during World War I. The Shakers, who lasted nearly two centuries in small villages throughout the Northeast, operated essentially without currency (except for outside dealings) and for the greater part of their existence were able to distribute more or less along lines of from-each-according-to-his-abilities, to-each-according-to-his-needs. More prosaically, a number of small cities in Germany and Austria during the Great Depression abandoned the worthless national currencies in favor of their own local currencies, which immediately became accepted legal tender and were used for salaries, purchases, and the like within their conscribed areas. The town of

Worgl, Austria, a community of about 6,000 people, moved from wide-spread unemployment to nearly full employment within three months by the use of its own currency, since local people could understand that it had the real value of a day's work behind it and were willing to accept it as a means of exchange; naturally when the practice began to spread and threaten central bank holdings the government moved against it, and ultimately the Austrian Supreme Court declared it illegal.

Community control of community economies is by no means a far-fetched idea: that is exactly how most Israeli kibbutzim have operated for a century. They make no pretense to being cut off from the wider Israeli (and European) economy, of course, and their exchange system and currency are meshed with the rest of the nation. But they are islands of collectivism in a capitalist sea. In the kibbutz system, all property is owned by the community, all productive assets are the property of the community, the land is distributed and the labor allotted by the community, what is to be produced, with what, by whom, by when, what is to be paid for raw materials, how much is to be expended in production, what is to be done with the proceeds—all that is determined by the community. And not just some economic czar, either, or a bureaucracy—the essential decisions that guide the economy of each kibbutz are made by the general assembly open to all the settlers meeting weekly. Of course the assembly is guided by the individual firm and the branch experts and the secretariat charged with coordinating the economy, but the fundamental responsibility and decision making is that of the assembly, and in most kibbutzim this is taken as a heavy and a serious burden, upon which the fate of the settlement may rest. The proof that it can work, that it can even flourish, in more than 200 quite differently populated and differently endowed communities—despite all the problems the kibbutzim have had and all the turmoil that Israel has gone through—is in the settlements' extraordinary economic record.

––––––––

These forms of community economic involvement, merely the representative wavelengths along a very broad spectrum, are all quite different but they all seem to work in varying ways in varying communities. The precise form is obviously a matter for the people in any given locality to determine, providing only that there are some regular democratic channels for that determination to be made and, if necessary, revised. Ultimately the exact form will not matter quite as much as the social climate that those forms have to operate in, the political goals and philosophical styles and psychological aspirations of the inhabitants—for if that climate is not right it is hard to see how any economic contrivances will work.

And from both theoretical and practical evidence, it seems that one crucial determinant of that climate is size.

The very concept of "community" suggests limits—it is not "nation" or "region" or "city," all words with other connotations—and whether or not we pick for it that "magic" range somewhere around 500 people in a neighborhood or 5,000–10,000, there is no doubt that it demands some sort of circumscription. It is simply not possible to forge an economic identity with 7 million other people so that plans of allocation or production or distribution can ever be determined, much less harmonized, by even the most sophisticated methods; nor, really, with 500,000 others, or even 100,000. Nor is it possible to achieve a coherent economy adjusted harmoniously to the ecosystem and the health of the people who live in it without some clear and perceived geographic limits.

The face-to-face unit, in which everyone is known in some degree to all the others, and in which the quality of other people's work can be readily judged, seems to provide at least one size range for effective community-worker cooperation. We have already noted the success of the kibbutzim, and not a single observer, academic or other, has failed to comment on the importance of their small scale. From the beginning of the movement there has been an explicit policy of *fission*, splitting and setting up new units when one kibbutz feels itself becoming too big for effective communal control, and in practice that has been somewhere around 400 people, the average size of the current settlements, though a few are as large as 600 and 700 and three are over 1,000. Other examples are to be found in the more than seventy "communities of work" that flourished in southeastern France in the decades just after World War II; Boimondau, the largest and most successful and the model for the movement, had 150 households, or roughly 600 people. This, then, points to an effective economic community roughly within our previous "magic" range of 500–1,000 that defined a neighborhood.

There is also evidence, though, that workplace democracy can operate in units of even larger sizes, corresponding to what we earlier typified as a polis. The most complete evidence here is from the early years of the Spanish Civil War, when all effective national government had collapsed and hundreds of small towns throughout Catalonia, Aragon, Levant, Andalusia, and Castile organized themselves into independent communities, operating both agricultural and small-scale industrial enterprises as worker collectives under community direction and control. Most of these towns seem to have numbered between 2,500 and 6,000 people, none was much over 10,000, and I would calculate the average to be somewhere around 4,000—too large, generally, to have any but infrequent general assemblies of all the townsfolk but small enough to be easily coordinated by a collective committee elected by, responsible to, and often recalled by the assembly. (There were apparently some abuses by collective committees exchanging aristocratic hauteur with syndicalist disdain and running as roughshod over the peasantry as those they had replaced—but for the most part a rough democratic process seems to have remained intact.) In most day-to-day matters the individual enterprises were largely autonomous—the collective farms decided when and where to irrigate, the local plant set its own work conditions—but in all matters spilling over into the town—determining how agricultural machinery was to be shared or how the crops were to be marketed, and in many places how food and goods would be distributed—it was the community, through the collective committee, that made the decisions.

All of this seems to have happened more or less spontaneously in widely separated sections of Spain, mostly places that had some dim mutualist tradition but well beyond those that had been consciously organized by the anarcho-communalists of the Spanish National Confederation of Trabajo (CNT), and often among people who were illiterate, apolitical, and certainly untutored in self-management. And all of it seems to have enjoyed surprising success: for nearly two years, until overrun by Franco's troops or invaded by hostile Communist brigades, these collective villages ran the economy of a significant part of rural Spain, and by most accounts increased production, introduced new machinery, diversified local industries, redistributed the land, established new schools, created new welfare systems, and in general brought a prosperity to the regions, even in a time of war, beyond anything known previously. It seems to me telling that in one Castilian town the aristocrat who came to reclaim his expropriated and collectivized lands a few days after the Civil War was so astounded by the improvements made by the "ignorant" peasants—new irrigation systems, new fields under cultivation, a mill and a school and dining halls and houses—that he immediately turned over some of this property to the villagers and arranged for the release from jail of the man who had helped them draw up the plans.

The contemporary journals of Gaston Leval—an unabashed CNT partisan, but a careful and straightforward reporter—tells the story of some of these remarkable experiments in workplace democracy. Take Graus, a town of small industries and a population of 3,000 in the northern part of Huesca province, on the French border:

> *There was no forced collectivization. Membership in the collectives was entirely voluntary, and groups could secede from the collective if they so desired. But even if isolation were possible, the obvious benefits of the collective were so great that the right to secede was seldom, if ever, invoked.*
>
> *Ninety percent of all production, including exchange and distribution, was collectively owned. (The remaining 10% was produced by petty peasant landholders.) . . . Each factory and workshop selected a delegate who maintained permanent relations with the Labor secretariat [of the collective] reporting back to and acting on the instructions of his constituents.*
>
> *Accounts and statistics for each trade and enterprise were compiled by the statistical and general accounting department, thus giving an accurate picture of the operations of each organization and the operations of the economy as a whole. The list that I saw included: drinking water, bottle making, carpentry, mattress making, wheelwrights, photography, silk mills, candy, pork butcher shops, distilleries, electricity, oil, bakeries, hairdressers and beauty parlors, soap makers, house painting, tinware, sewing machines, shops and repairs, printing, building supplies, hardware, tile shops, dairies, bicycle repairs, etc.*
>
> *Everything was coordinated both in production and in distribution. . . .*

Or take Binefar, a Huesca town of 5,000 or so, where the townspeople first harvested the fields of the departed big landowners and then sat down to work out their economy:

After the harvest, industry and eventually commerce were socialized. The following are the rules that the popular assembly of all the inhabitants approved:

1. Work shall be carried on in groups of ten. Each group shall elect its own delegate. . . . The delegates shall plan the work, preserve harmony among the producers, and if necessary apply the sanctions voted by the popular assembly.
2. The delegates shall furnish the Agricultural Commission a daily report of the work done.
3. A central committee, consisting of one delegate from each branch of production, shall be named by the general assembly of the Community. . . .
4. Directors of labor for the collective shall be elected by the general assembly of all the collectivists.
5. Each member shall be given a receipt for the goods he brings to the Collective.
6. Each member shall have the same rights and duties. . . . All that is required is that members accept the decisions of the Collective.
7. The capital of the Collective belongs to the Collective and cannot be divided up. Food shall be rationed, part of it to be stored away against a bad year.
8. The general assembly shall determine the organization of the Collective, and arrange periodic elections of the administrative commission.

It was a most extraordinary, and largely ignored, period of modern economic history, of which these accounts can give us only the barest bones. But they do suggest, even attenuated, the kinds of local triumphs economic democracy is capable of—at least in its collectivized version—and they do allow us to see some real-world evidence of the success of community-level populations in making it happen.

And if that is not the Principle of Affected Interests in action, I don't know what is.

19

Self-Sufficiency

O nce upon a time the greater part of the world's population lived in conditions that, as we view them from our contemporary perspective, could only be considered opulent. They spent their time—all of them, regardless of birth or beauty—in the closest thing to indolence, working only a few hours a day, sitting around and sleeping and making love for hours at a time, literally living off the fat of the land and gorging themselves when food came along with little thought of saving for the morrow. They surrounded themselves with beautiful objects, participated in elaborate useless rituals, devoted resources to nothing more substantial than jewelry and wall paintings. They ate well, with balanced diets, got plenty of regular exercise, were spared most serious diseases, and lived to relatively ripe old ages. They were for the most part free of poverty, privation, pollution, crime, and war.

They were, as you have no doubt guessed, the *Homo sapiens* hunter-gatherers of prehistory—the "cavemen."

It is difficult to generalize about a period that lasted maybe 60,000 years and was at such a remove from ours, but the diligent researches and diggings of the last hundred years, reinforced by studies of contemporary hunter-gatherer societies in Africa and the Pacific, have given us a pretty careful picture of what these Paleolithic societies must have been like. They knew a mastery over their technology that produced an intricate array of tools—more than sixty types of knives, awls, burins, axes, scrapers, spear points, cleavers—including the lovely "laurel-leaf" stone blades of the Solutrean period, some of them as thin as four-tenths of an inch, a feat said to be beyond even modern machines. They were accomplished in the arts—as the Lascaux caves alone may attest—and in the basic sciences. They were socially advanced to the level of community solidarity, altruism, communal industry, dance and food rituals, and the elaborate burial remains from 28,000 years ago found in Sungir, on the banks of a river in modern Russia—three buried figures decorated with more than 13,000 ivory beads—testify to their elegant ceremonialization of death. And they made do without kings and armies and politicians and lawyers.

However rough and simple may have been the people produced by these early societies, they were by no means savages, they did not live in hand-to-mouth indigence, they were not ignorant of the workings of the world around them, and their lives were in no sense solitary, poor, nasty, brutish, or particularly short. (Dying very young was common enough to bring the average life span down to 32.5 years, but those that made it through childhood had a life expectancy of 54 more years.) Especially not when compared with the peoples of modern Calcutta, say, or the Sahel or Manila or Tijuana, or even the South Bronx. In fact, anthropologist Marshall Sahlins, whose *Stone Age Economics* does much to correct our "Alley-Oop" stereotypes, calls the Paleolithic "the original affluent society": "one in which all the people's material wants are easily satisfied."

True, those wants were not very extensive—they did not go so far as brocaded cloth and brigantines and Burgundy and electric blankets—but they were real, and felt, and they did not go unfulfilled. In our affluent society, by contrast, where everyone's wants are great, or made to be great, they are almost never fulfilled, even by the wealthiest among us, and they are hopelessly out of reach for the great majority. Yes, the Paleolithic peoples had what economists today might want to call a low standard of living, measured as the accumulation of material objects. But *they* didn't know that: they no doubt thought of themselves as "unencumbered."

Given their objective, given what they sought out of life, these early people were more often than not able to satisfy it and many times able to exceed it, and with a minimum of hardship and labor. Sahlins quotes Lorna Marshall, an expert on the Basarwa of Botswana, whom she lived among, off and on, for two decades following 1950:

> *They all had what they needed or could make what they needed. . . .*
> *They lived in a kind of material plenty because they adapted the tools*
> *of their living to materials which lay in abundance around them and*
> *which were free for anyone to take. . . . They borrow what they do not*
> *own. With this ease, they have not hoarded, and the accumulation of*
> *objects has not become associated with status.*

These Basarwa, and their identical remote ancestors, led a life of *perceived satisfaction*: want not, lack not. Who would not call it affluence?

———

Of course it is not the Paleolithic state of affluence that I suggest we all return to, but there is something in the Paleolithic understanding of the limits of material amassment that does seem pertinent. For what made them affluent was, in truth, their self-sufficiency, their ability to satisfy all of their needs within their own means. (And if that meant they had to regard those things beyond their means—mammoth-roasts every Sunday —as being unneeded, and hence unwanted, that was not a limit on their self-sufficiency but rather an improvement in their happiness.) And that kind of affluence, I propose, is available to us today, modified by our own vastly greater knowledge and our own vastly improved technologies, would we but direct ourselves to some small part of that Paleolithic comprehension.

Affluence, you see, is always relative. It is not only that of the car and the house and washing machine and vacation; it has something too of security and harmony and quiet and friendship and freedom from pollution and from powerlessness. Compare the inhabitants of ancient Media, learned in astronomy and science and skillful in the arts of administration but knowing little in the way of riches, with the Iranian followers of Cyrus the Great, mighty warriors fat with the plunder of nomadic bands but totally untrained in either artistic or scientific accomplishments: one man's Mede, no doubt, is another man's Persian, but who would want to say that all the affluence rested with the latter. Might the trade-off of a small-scale economy of sufficiency-enjoyed-by-all against the intricate multinational economy of wealth-for-a-few-and-poverty-for-many be, in fact, no trade-off at all?

———

Self-sufficiency may perhaps seem a foolish anachronism in a world of interconnectedness, an economic cul-de-sac in an era of mutual dependence. And indeed it may not really be obtainable in its most absolute form, since almost any society, no matter how cut off, will normally have some sort of contact and trade with the outside world and may be enriched thereby. But as a goal and an ideal, and as something to

255

be achieved in even imperfect conditions, self-sufficiency has inestimable virtues.

It is a way for a community naturally to achieve a stationary society, in absolute harmony with the environment, assuring to itself a rational control over resources and productivity. It allows the free establishment of workplace democracy in all its manifestations, unimpeded by economic tugs and pulls from other unsympathetic—or hostile—forces. It makes a place expand instead of contract, create instead of borrow, use instead of discard: just as a man left on his own, thrust on his own devices, develops strengths and uncovers inner resources and becomes the fuller for it, so too a community. Above all, it establishes independence: a self-sufficient town cannot be the victim of corporate-directed plant closings or a truckers' strike or an Arab oil boycott or California droughts; it does not have to maintain lengthy and tenuous supply lines of any kind, nor pay the shippers and the jobbers and the middlemen who are clustered along them; it does not have to be the accidental victim of toxic fumes or industrial poisons or nuclear wastes produced by, or passing through, the town; it does not have to bow to (always rising) prices set by distant suppliers in disregard of what the local farmer is in fact growing and the local shop producing; and ultimately it does not have to sway in the winds of the hurricanes of boom and bust as regularly generated, as it were offshore, by distant and uncontrollable economic forces.

It is on breaking the terrible dependence upon imports and exports, and the economic vassalage that results, that self-sufficiency must depend. A community grows and becomes more textured, as Jane Jacobs has noted, when it "replaces" imports—that is, when it manages to do on its own what before it had to pay others to do. She offers the example of Tokyo, where innumerable little bike shops grew up to repair imported bicycles, then started manufacturing spare parts, and eventually turned out the whole product, doing away with imported bikes entirely.* Any

---

* Jacobs does assume that Tokyo then has to go on importing some *other* goods, and creating more businesses to make exports so as to pay for them—and that is a trap that she, Tokyo, and the capitalist world seem unable to escape, the trap of growthmania: cities and societies always must grow and develop and extend and consume. It certainly does not *need* to follow, as one of her own examples makes clear: England's Manchester, which grew to enormous size

nation that comes to depend on imports will find itself perpetually vulnerable, scrambling always to create the exports that will be sent off in return or else living in ever-deepening enthrallment. The United States, despite being the world's dominant economy, is the world's second largest importer of goods, at a cost of some $238 billion (2015), and runs a balance of trade deficit now around $45 billion a year. The other side of the coin is no better, either: an overdependence on exports is usually a sign of nothing more nor less than colonialism. Most of the Third World today—Liberia exporting rubber grown on land that could be raising food, Ghana depending on cocoa exports and importing chocolate bars, Cuba devoting half its agriculture to the sugar export crop—lives in such a condition.

This is not to say that a healthy economy might not *include* some imports and exports—that would seem only natural for any but the most isolated community—but only that it *depends* on such trade to its peril and trusts in it to its detriment. Obviously the percentages will shift from place to place, but when any city or community starts to use more than a small proportion of its jobs and its resources to create things that will never be used by its citizens it begins to get into trouble, as the history of Manchester or Mohenjo-Daro or Milwaukee suggests.

Apart from its economic virtues, self-sufficiency conveys social benefits as well. It is a way for a community to survive, and thrive, as a closely knit group, to create stability and balance and predictability, to learn its own reserves, and to become developed in the fullest sense. In a town dependent on its own resources, people necessarily come to know each other, to appreciate each other's strengths (and weaknesses), in a way they never get to do in an atomized city, or even in many atomized small towns. Children are given the opportunity to learn the complexity of reality—a multiplicity of small shops and offices and plants and farms provides an unexcelled laboratory of the real world—so that they do not grow up believing that tomatoes grow in supermarkets and electricity comes from

---

and prosperity by total dependence on imports of cotton and exports of cloth, was a one-industry town that collapsed in the twentieth century when other nations began to spin their own cotton; Birmingham, which had a multitude of little independent workshops, none with more than a dozen workers, produced for itself the bulk of the products it needed and has remained a thriving city right to today.

a switch on the wall. And when grown, those children are more likely to stay in a place with its own developed businesses and opportunities, there being then no particular reason to go off to seek their fortunes elsewhere. Other citizens, too, should find inevitable opportunities and if they are forced to be plumbers as well as librarians, poets as well as farmers, this can only be enriching for the person, as for the community. The feeling of competence, of pride, of selfhood, of independence, that might attend the citizen of a self-reliant town could be duplicated nowhere else.

Frank Fraser Darling, the ecologist, once studied some remote Scottish villages that were essentially untouched by the outside world. He found that far from being stagnant and lifeless backwaters they were in fact teeming and surprisingly active eddies, far more diverse in both social and economic activities and generally more "alive" than company or single-industry towns or places like bedroom suburbs tied inextricably to distant cities. Their necessary self-sufficiency actually operated as a positive force: people coped better with the vicissitudes of life, they were more neighborly, and they had a greater diversity of jobs and responsibilities. And they had a better understanding of the town's natural environment and its importance in their lives, and were far less likely to despoil it—or let some intrusive entrepreneur despoil it—for some short-term gain.

Finally, one would have to believe that a self-reliant community would inevitably be less violent, both within its borders and without. Schumacher put it this way:

> As physical resources are everywhere limited, people satisfying their needs by means of a modest use of resources are obviously less likely to be at each other's throats than people depending upon a high rate of use. Equally, people who live in highly self-sufficient local communities are less likely to get involved in large-scale violence than people whose existence depends on world-wide systems of trade.

How many wars in history have been the result of one people's threatening to deprive another of some theoretically valuable resource, of one nation seeking to protect or expand its far-flung export-import markets; how many waged by peoples entire to themselves, self-developed and self-content, how many by the self-sufficient cities of the Middle Ages, by the self-reliant Amish and the Mennonites, by Switzerland?

That a human-scale economy would work toward self-sufficiency seems only natural, since it is only on the smaller scale that the human can understand and work some control over the surroundings, can perceive and regulate the variants in an economy, can determine the artifacts and services useful for or detrimental to the community. The human brain, however elaborate an instrument the human may consider it to be, is limited, and even extended as it is by certain modern technologies it cannot truly comprehend the labyrinthine involutions of any very vast scale—as the bewildered machinations of the official government economists over just the last five years show all too pointedly. On the other hand, an economy on too limited a scale will not be able to provide the complexity and diversity that goes into creating a full material life, and trading an economy of chaotic complexity for one of hair-shirt simplicity would hardly seem to be much of a bargain.

The balance that is to be struck of course depends on what it is that a community needs, or thinks it needs (though the Paleolithic precaution is that probably many of our needs are not in fact needed). A village of, say, 500 people could probably grow its own food, operate its own energy systems, create its own handicrafts, perhaps carry on some manufactures, much as the Israeli kibbutzim do; but it would be hard-pressed to go in for much in the way of extensive manufacture or construction, would not likely have much variety in its wares, would have to keep its services quite simple, and would have to accept fairly limited opportunities of conviviality and culture. Even figuring a labor force of 250 in such a settlement, somewhat high by current American practice, there would probably be no more than 100 people or so available for manufacturing and recycling, the rest employed in agriculture, energy and transportation, services, and handicrafts. That would certainly be sufficient for a dozen small manufacturing plants, since we know from current American manufacturing statistics that 75 percent of all the plants in this country operate with fewer than twenty people (in fact fewer than 6 percent have over 100), and in those plants *the average number of employees is only 5.5*; and it would no doubt cover such basics as lumber.

If several such neighborhood-sized populations join together, however, the possibilities become far richer. A community of 5,000–10,000 takes on the stature necessary for real economic independence—as indeed, if we needed reassurance, the greater part of human history has demonstrated. At that size, as we have seen, agricultural self-sufficiency and community energy systems are most economical and efficient, and at that level the labor force available for the rest of the economy (if it approximated current American percentages) would amount to between 2,000 and 4,000, divided about evenly between manufacturing and services.

As populations increase over this level, self-sufficiency in one sense becomes easier, since there are more workers and so more kinds of products and services can be created. As we saw in examining city sizes, a small city of 50,000 typically has just about all the service and production enterprises of any size city, and these are places that do not even consciously seek self-sufficiency. But problems begin to accumulate at this level as well, along the lines of what I am tempted to call the Rule of Eternal Dependency: over a certain minimum size, the greater the population, the more complex the institutions, the more elaborate and advanced the technical needs, the more difficult it will be to satisfy them locally or in any single place. For example: as transportation and distribution become more diffuse and widespread, you need to start thinking of trains and rails or cars and roads and traffic lights, of bridges and tunnels, of planners and coordinators; as agricultural areas expand to support such a population, new kinds of field and irrigation equipment may be necessary, storage problems will require warehousing and probably refrigeration, harvesting and distribution will take additional labor and coordination; as waste disposal creates a burden the land can no longer easily absorb, new collection and processing machinery becomes necessary, sewage lines and treatment plants might be required, composting and recycling will demand additional complex machinery. On top of this, the whole process of establishing the city's needs, deciding which have priority, coordinating production and services to meet them, and making sure that they are met, and at the right time in the right way, becomes significantly more tangled and demands human and technical resources of its own.

It is not that self-sufficiency is not possible at this level—I am quite convinced that it is, given the additional people there to cope with it, because experience indicates that this has been a size at which cities have been able to survive, healthily, for many decades, and even in interdependent economies operate most efficiently. But it is clear that the city would quite consciously have to make trade-offs that the smaller community would not have to face.

Self-sufficiency has never occupied much of a place in modern economic thought—the closest that traditional economists come is in their "economic base" and "central place" theories—so there are very few theoretical models, and as a consequence even fewer real-life experiments, that would indicate how and at what sizes it might work.

We do know that during most of humankind's settled existence—say from 6000 BC right through the nineteenth century—most people in the world lived in small towns seldom holding more than a couple of thousand people that were self-sufficient because there was no other way to survive. The Greek villages of the seventh to fourth centuries BC, as Mumford notes, "were both small and self-contained, largely dependent upon the local countryside for food and building materials." Monasteries from the sixth century AD on were noted as enclaves where both physical and spiritual needs—the former probably more limited than the latter—were met entirely by the collective gathering of brothers, usually numbering less than a hundred souls. In medieval Europe before 1500, as Ferdinand Braudel tells us, "90% to 95% of the towns known in the West had fewer than 2000 inhabitants," yet normally enjoyed a full range of craftsmen and artisans and merchants and farmers; throughout medieval times, as the *Encyclopedia of Social Sciences* notes, "provincial, even local, self-sufficiency was the order of the day." Even in the eighteenth and nineteenth centuries, and in some places well into the twentieth century, the basically self-sufficient village was the norm in Europe: a typical English town of several thousand as late as 1880 or 1900 would have blacksmiths and shoemakers, plumbers and carpenters, bakers and butchers, brewers and millers, saddle-makers and harness-makers, tailors and seamstresses, dentists and midwives, a pub and a church and a reading room, an inn and a market and a row of shops, and the food it ate was the food it grew.

All of these places, and others like them, made it clear that, at least at quite simple levels of living, self-sufficiency was certainly possible in units as small as several hundred and fairly easy to sustain in units as big as several thousand.

For contemporary models, however, we have to hunt farther afield. There are the Bruderhof communities, villages of 200–300 people who hold all goods and property in common and, with the exception of a toy-making business (Community Playthings) that has adopted a Japanese-style production operation, tend to confine themselves to a self-sufficient, deeply religious, communal life.

And there are the Mennonite settlements in Pennsylvania, villages and towns of only a few thousand, based on completely self-sufficient agriculture and essentially self-sufficient energy, services, and manufacturing—without outside electricity or internal-combustion engines, cars or tractors, radios or television.

And though it is not quite the same thing, the Transition Towns movement that began in 2006 in England—and by 2010 enlisted more than 400 towns in Europe and North America—is aimed at reducing the impacts of peak oil and climate change by developing local alternatives, or as the movement puts it "by engaging their communities in home-grown, citizen-led education, action, and multi-stakeholder planning to increase local self-reliance and resilience."

Self-sufficiency is often scorned for being simplistic. Indeed, I find that I am often taken to task for wishing to oversimplify things: "Life is just not that simple."

But in fact I wish to *complexify*, not simplify. It is our modern economy that is simple: whole nations given over to a single crop, cities to a single industry, farms to single culture, factories to a single product, people to a single job, jobs to a single motion, motion to a single purpose. Diversity is the rule of human life, not simplicity: the human animal has succeeded precisely because it has been able to diversify, not specialize: to climb *and* swim, hunt *and* nurture, work alone *and* in packs. The same is true of human organizations: they are healthy and they survive when they are diverse and differentiated, capable of many responses; they become brittle and unadaptable and prey to any changing conditions when they are uniform and specialized. It is when an individual is able to take on many jobs, learn many skills, live many roles, that growth and fullness of character inhabit the soul; it is when a society complexifies and mixes, when it develops the multiplicity of ways of caring for itself, that it becomes textured and enriched.

Those, obviously, are the ultimate goals of self-sufficiency.

————

With only a few simple steps, I would assert, a community as small as 10,000 people can achieve that self-sufficiency and provide for virtually all material needs—I stress *needs*, excluding the frivolous and superlative—on a household or community level, *and* make the goods more affordable, more durable, more aesthetic, more reparable, and more harmless, too.

Thusly.

By sharing. With a regular system of sharing goods and the creation of accessible neighborhood centers where they could be found, an enormous number of the artifacts, machines, and tools that we now produce could be eliminated. Is it necessary for every sub-urban garage to have a lawn mower, which is used at most once a week, and only in the summertime? For every third or fourth basement to have a complete set of power tools, some in disuse for months on end? For every breakfront to have the set of silver and the punchbowl that's used only once a year?

Various adaptations to communal living might be useful here, too. A neighborhood social center, in addition to its other inesti-mable virtues, might be able with a single instrument to replace a multiplicity of television sets and pianos and phonographs. Shared travel would mean fewer cars and trains, shared laun-dering fewer machines, shared newspapers and books fewer trees lost.

By recycling and repairing. The more you recycle, obviously the less you have to manufacture or import, so in addition to lessening waste and conserving energy you are reducing the manufactur-ing load and heightening self-sufficiency. Neighborhood-level recycling centers, which already exist in many communities in the United States, could expand their operations with the kind of additional public cooperation self-sufficiency might engender and probably be geared ultimately to a 90-percent-return level on all recyclable goods. (After all, it's figured that some $11.4 billion in recyclables is put in landfills every year.) Such centers could easily be coupled with repair workshops where volunteers (the high school tinkerer, the retired watchmaker) could fix up the multitude of products needing only an expert's touch and a little bit of solder: how many appliances are sitting now in other closets, as in mine, no longer working right but still essentially functional except for a frammis or a widget, put away on a high shelf because they could not be repaired and it never seemed worth the trouble to mail them back to some far-off manufacturer with some long-lost proof of purchase? At only a slightly more elaborate level, it is possible to establish "remanufacturing" centers, where a variety of slightly larger items like diesel engines and refrigerators can be salvaged and reconditioned with a few new parts and a little rehabilitation of the old. This is the sort of process at an informal level that has been going on for years in the poorer nations not permitted the throwaway indulgence, where it was not possible to buy replacements and not feasible to wait for imported parts, and it is one well worth borrowing from them.

By depending upon handicrafts rather than manufactures. At the modest scale of the self-contained community, there are many products that would not need to be—or could not be economically—mass-produced, eliminating the need for many factories; but most of those could be supplied by individual artisans crafting everything from clothes and pottery to furniture and tools. The costs would presumably be higher, as they are reckoned in the short run, but the difference in quality and durability is likely to make up for it in the long, as our grandparents—who had opportunities for handcrafted goods far more than we—used to keep telling us. (In a contemporary handcrafted shirt, for example, which is always made out of natural fabrics, there are at least thirty stitches to the inch rather than the ten or twelve stitches found in factory-mades, and shell buttons instead of plastic.) And the difference in the way the products look and feel, in the attitudes of the people who style them on us, in the satisfaction we get from them is, though possibly intangible, no less real. (To take bespoke shirts again, the exactness of the fit is assured by at least eighteen different measurements, including wrists and shoulder slopes and neck length, whereas department store shirts now frequently run in such generalized sizes as "14–15-inch" necks and "32–34-inch" sleeves.)

By developing and using local products and raw materials instead of depending on imported ones. Glass is almost always a better material than plastic, easier to work, cheaper to make, safer for the environment, simpler to recycle, and it can be made to be even more resistant to shattering, heat, scratching, and aging; it is made from the one mineral, silica, which is available in abundance in each one of our fifty states. Wood, stone, and concrete are building materials as good as aluminum or steel, and they are ubiquitous. Earth may be the best material of all, and it can be used for construction employing only the simplest tools; it will keep interiors warm in winter, cool in summer, fireproof and soundproof; it is as durable as—well, the earth—and as cheap as—well, dirt—and it is available, without transportation charges, practically anywhere anyone might want to live.

And special regions should be able to develop special materials and resources. Even as unprepossessing a region as the American Southwest has two such: a giant desert shrub called the jojoba, largely ignored today, that produces an oil that can be used for cooking, machine lubrication, paint additives, and at least a dozen other known things, and that can be stored for years without turning rancid; and a plant called the guayule, similarly undeveloped, that produces a latex almost identical to the kind derived from rubber trees and that could supply all of the rubber needs for the whole region from Texas to Southern California. Both of these plants were in fact proved to be successful substitutes during America's most recent period of self-sufficiency—in World War II when the government consciously developed alternative resources for threatened supplies.

Local-generation, as we might call this, seems particularly applicable to food. Self-sufficiency would probably mean the loss of Iranian caviar and Polish hams and French *fraises-des-bois*, not to mention in most cases Idaho potatoes, Wisconsin cheeses, and Florida oranges, except insofar as any particular community would feel it necessary to establish trade relations for such things or itinerant traders would find a market for them. And yet there is no region of this nation that was not once self-sufficient in food, coping for decades without the necessity of Brazilian bananas and Ugandan coffee and Indian curry, no region that could not be again. And not to its detriment but to its enrichment: the bounty from its own acres is infinitely cheaper, incomparably fresher, far more nutritious, free of shelf-life additives, and plain better-tasting. Is not the basic "peasant" cooking of any country always its best, was not the French "nouvelle cuisine" based exclusively on ingredients Paul Bocuse could buy that morning from the local market? Does it make sense for me to have to depend upon the cows 5,000 miles away to supply me with delectable cheeses if I live in an area that once was, and could be again, one of the prime dairy regions of the nation? Must people in New York import apples from Washington State, as the local supermarkets begin to do in November, when it is the second most prolific apple-pro-ducing state in the country?

I am not suggesting that there need be any back-to-berries deprivation here—many tropical products that seemed particu-larly desirable could be grown in community greenhouses, not on a large scale but sufficient for any local market, and probably certain kinds of sharing-and-bartering systems would naturally arise among communities and cities within a given bioregion. And I can't help thinking about the meal that was made up solely of the most elemental mundane offerings of the year-end harvest of one of America's least bountiful regions—that is the bountiful feast that was the first Thanksgiving.

By local ingenuity. If necessity is the mother of invention, self-sufficiency is obviously the grandmother. Local ingenuity and back-against-the-wall creativity have always been nurtured in the American small town—it accounted for the extraordinary number of inventions from such intentionally isolated communities as the Shakers (brimstone matches, the washing machine, a pea-sheller, clothespins, and a thresher) and the Oneidans (another washing machine, a rag-mop assembly, and a string-bean slicer)—and there's every reason to suppose such inventiveness would not only continue but flourish in an atmosphere that made its prod-ucts welcome. It is said that the reason for the lack of American inventiveness these days has to do with the forbidding legalistic red tape and the slim chances of design ever seeing reality—both these barriers at least would be removed in a self-reliant community eager for new methods that would conserve its resources and replace its imports: the medieval monasteries were almost single-handedly responsible for the agricultural revolutions in productivity and technique from the tenth century on.

Hubert Ignatious Fernando, an unknown technician for the Department of Agriculture in Colombo, Sri Lanka, created a working model of a revolutionary new rice-milling machine in 1972. His model uses local machinery and resources instead of imported ones, it costs about one-tenth as much to build, it uses almost no fuels beyond the waste products from the very rice it processes, and it increases the amount of finished rice—rice-on-the-plate, as they say in Asia—by at least 15 percent. Fernando had the inventiveness and the Sri Lankan farmers' organization had the interest in getting the machine into production, but unfortunately Sri Lanka is not self-sufficient. The four nations that dominated such technology—the United States, Japan, Germany, and Taiwan—decided, for various reasons, not to grant the rice-miller a patent, thus effectively preventing it from ever going into production. The way things are, it may have to wait as long as Hero's steam engine.

By using general instead of specialized machines. For the mass-production thinker this often doesn't make economic sense, but for limited markets the installation of multipurpose tools and assemblies can be far more efficient and economical. Only a limited number of such devices are available at present, there being no particularly strong market in the present production system, but there are many prototypes and no one doubts that the technology is simplicity itself. A boring machine, for example, that can rout out a small wire or a copper tube can be used to form a drainpipe or a sewage line, if it is retooled with a simple increase in scale; a lathe that can form a nail or a screw can be used for bigger tools and machine parts. Murray Bookchin's analysis of the effect of just this simple application of technology concludes:

> *A small or moderate-sized community using multipurpose*
> *machines could satisfy many of its limited industrial needs*

> *without being burdened with underused industrial facilities. . . .*
> *The community's economy would be more compact and versatile,*
> *more rounded and self-contained, than anything we find in the*
> *communities of industrially advanced countries.*

By networking, where necessary, with other communities. With judicious
linkages with nearby towns—a sharing on a municipal level like
the sharing on a personal level—a community could enlarge its
economic possibilities and diminish its manufacturing requirements without necessarily sacrificing its self-sufficiency. Perhaps all
that would be wanted is a communications network, with a wire,
phone, or computer link that could connect a wide range of people
for daily communications or emergency consultations or regional
conferences or just general access to information. Or several communities might get together for a major public-works project—a
modest dam to control seasonal flooding (if, of course, more ecological solutions aren't available)—or a public health program or
even a theater or orchestra. Or maybe nearby towns would want
to establish some sort of marketing network, increasing the distribution range for one or two special products, or a slightly more
complex system of resource networking, trading one community's
coal for another's copper, say, or some extra aluminum scrap in one
town for some leftover bushels of tomatoes in another.

The dangers of such networks are obvious enough, since
dependence upon them will eventually cut into any community's ability to act for itself, but kept within the bounds of simple
mutuality, such systems can usefully expand productivity and
save labor time.

Finally, and simplest, by doing without what is not needed. Bombs. Cos-
metics. Moon exploration. Greeting cards. Food additives. Junk
mail. Packaging. Cigarettes. Electric dishwashers. Plastic bottles.
Costume jewelry. Microwave ovens. Artificial fertilizers. . . .

Here is the point about self-sufficiency.

The little town of Lucca, a Tuscan community that lasted for at least
eight centuries as an independent entity within the *tempesto* that was

Italian society during those years, may serve as our model. Emerging as a free commune sometime in the late eleventh century, it became one of the fiercely independent republics in the thirteenth century—with a population then of perhaps 10,000–12,000—and for the next 400 years, surviving ups and downs and feasts and famines, it was one of the most prosperous places on the entire Italian peninsula, not to mention the entire European continent. It enjoyed a rich and self-sufficient agriculture, with fruits, grains, wine, vegetables, chestnuts, and grazing fields; it was a major banking center from the fourteenth century on (still with no more than 15,000 people), was famous for its velvet and other textile manufacturing, was the home of recognized artists, musicians, and writers; and it expressed its prosperity, century after century, in a magnificent array of churches (one, the celebrated cathedral of San Martino), *palazzi*, castles, fortifications, and town houses that was extraordinary even for those extraordinary years. Curtailed by the dead Spanish hand that closed over most of northern Italy after the sixteenth century, Lucca nonetheless survived as an independent and thriving trading town for another 250 years, its glory diminished but by no means extinguished. Then came the Napoleonic armies under the man who thought of himself as the emperor and unifier of Europe, and Lucca became a French plaything for a dozen years. After the Restoration, in the sweep of "nationalism" that moved over Europe, it was forced into a merger with Parma and then became part of a Tuscan state; in 1860 it fell under the control of Sardinia, which eventually became the foundation of the Kingdom of Italy, and under that banner the peninsula was "united" into the modern nation we know today. Union with successively larger territories in successively grander economies served mostly to impoverish the once-resplendent republic, and today it is mostly a backwater of 80,000 people, heavily dependent on tourism (plus the production of olive oil in the surrounding valley), the inescapable recipient of all that happens to an Italian economy of compounded chaos and inflation.

You could make it into a rule: in general, territories will be richer when small and self-sufficient than when large and dependent.

PART FIVE

POLITICS ON
A HUMAN SCALE

The first test to be applied in judging an alleged democracy is the degree of self-governing attained by its local institutions. . . . Only local government can accustom men to responsibility and independence, and enable them to take part in the wider life of the state.

—IGNAZIO SILONE, School for Dictators, 1963

I am calling also for an end to giantism, for a return to the human scale—the scale that human beings can understand and cope with; the scale of the local fraternal lodge, the church congregation, the block club, the farm bureau. . . . In government, the human scale is the town council, the board of selectmen, and the precinct captain. It is this activity on a small, human scale that creates the fabric of community, a framework for the creation of abundance and liberty.

—RONALD REAGAN, speech to the
Executive Club of Chicago, 1975

A small commonwealth is the happiest government in the world within itself, because everything lies under the eye of the rulers.

—DAVID HUME, Essays, Moral,
Political and Literary, 1741–42

20

The Malaise of Citizenship

For at least a half century, and demonstrably and palpably since 1972 (and perhaps since November 22, 1963), the American public, first the fringes and then the majority, has become disillusioned with the national government and apathetic or cynical about its efficacy. The ascendency and triumph of Donald Trump in the 2016 election was only the most recent demonstration of the antipathy to government that runs deep in America beyond the reach of all the do-gooding boosters and the high-pressure media to alter or cure.

Voting, that most basic and simplest of civic tasks, has been ingrained into us since the first grade as the very essence of our system, and the regular recurrence of national political campaigns every two years is always accompanied by well-financed and well-publicized appeals for us to get out and do it, as if this one activity were more significant than any other possible public activity. And yet every year the percentage of voters in the United States remains small, the smallest in the industrial world, and only rarely goes much above 50 percent of eligible citizens—which in turn is only around 60 percent of the total population—and then only in presidential elections. Since 1972 turnout has never been above 57 percent in presidential elections and averages about 53 percent, and in off-year elections never above 37 percent and averages about 35.

Pathetic evidence of citizenship decay, a malaise eating into our politics.

When asked why they don't vote, people give a variety of reasons—too busy, vote doesn't count, dislike candidates, no difference between parties, and above all that the government's run by big interests, anyway. A column on the liberal truthout.org website put it in 2014, after the dismal turnout that year: "These people are not stupid. They *do* care. What they don't believe is that voting alone will fix the problem.

"Let's stop kidding ourselves that voting alone will somehow magically change a system that has been decades in the making. It must be dismantled and evolved into new configurations of civic participation and collective action." As if.

The failure of "citizens" even to vote reflects the unquestionable malaise that has pervaded the land for a half century or so. Barbara Tuchman, a wise and learned woman whom I had always thought an imperturbable type, analyzed it this way as far back as 1976, when it was just starting:

> In the United States we have a society pervaded from top to bottom by contempt for the law. Government—including the agencies of law enforcement—business, labor, students, the military, the poor no less than the rich, outdo each other in breaking the rules and violating the ethics that society has established for its protection. The average citizen, trying to hold a footing in standards of morality and conduct he once believed in, is daily knocked over by incoming waves of venality, vulgarity, irresponsibility, ignorance, ugliness, and trash in all senses of the word. Our government collaborates abroad with the worst enemies of humanity and liberty. It wastes our substance on useless proliferation of military hardware that can never buy security no matter how high the pile. It learns no lessons, employs no wisdom and corrupts all who succumb to Potomac fever.

But in truth the malaise goes deeper than this. The crucial fact—the never-spoken, ever-present truth—is that Americans have given up their citizenship.

Citizenship—the act, the right, of participating in public affairs, of making the decisions that affect one's life, of having a continual voice in civic matters, of exercising regular judgment on the daily business of the state—has been sacrificed, in return for the right, if not the fact, of voting, the right to let someone *else* participate and legislate, the right to reaffirm every other November the loss of participation in public life. In past times when it was the locality that controlled daily affairs, the American adult participated in politics, joined civic groups, stood for office, took battles to the city legislature and problems to the City Hall, met and thrashed things out in town meetings and ward assemblies from coast to coast. But that has changed. Today the locality is merely an appendage of some larger government, most major matters are decided for us in Washington, and there is virtually no way that our voices can be heard at that level in any sustained and percussive sense, no matter how many special-interest groups we may join or how often we email the people in Congress.

Citizenship has simply evaporated in American life, leaving a residue of felt powerlessness. A president can declare a war or violate the territorial rights of 111 maritime nations all by himself and take countless secret actions at home and abroad jeopardizing millions of lives—even murdering by drone an American citizen never accused or convicted of a crime—without any reference either to us or to our representatives. A Congress can decide to increase the Social Security burden by 300 percent or give a tax break to the oil companies or establish a new agency or pork-barrel a new dam, and most of us will not even hear about it until after it is done, much less have a chance to be consulted and give our opinion on it beforehand. State legislators can increase taxes or censor textbooks or raise utility rates without any participation from the people who are to be affected other than their pulling a lever in a polling booth two years before. Robert Paul Wolff, a professor of philosophy at Columbia University, analyzed it this way:

> Since World War II, governments have increasingly divorced themselves from anything which could be called the will of the people. The complexity of the issues, the necessity of technical knowledge, and most important, the secrecy of everything having to do with national security, have conspired to attenuate the representative function of elected officials until a point has been reached which might be called political stewardship, or, after Plato, "elective guardianship." . . .
>
> It suffices to note that the system of elective guardianship falls so far short of the ideal of autonomy and self-rule as not even to seem a distant deviation from it. Men cannot meaningfully be called free if their representatives vote independently of their wishes, or when laws are passed concerning issues which they are not able to understand. Nor can men be called free who are subject to secret decisions, based on secret data, having unannounced consequences for their well-being and their very lives.

The simple fact is that in a system as large as ours it is essential that the individual *not* have a regular voice in political affairs. To allow each of 325 million people, or even the 250 million over 18, to participate in politics in a serious way would simply be too unwieldy, too chaotic; not even the wildest of techno-fix schemes of telephone voting and computer tallying could solve the sheer logistical problems if every person were to behave as, for example the Greek citizen of Periclean Athens, demanding to know the issues of the day, judging them, debating them, determining which were capable of being effected and when and how and by whom.

But not being able to participate has its terrible price. No wonder we feel so apathetic about voting: we do not have authentic political *selves*, we do not act politically, we do not know what is happening in and cannot much change the affairs of the nation, so the meager act of voting hardly carries much weight. *We do not understand ourselves publicly*, as public beings, nor could we be permitted to; we do not have public duties and public rights and public responsibilities of any meaning; there is nothing in our extended system that binds us as individuals to the public weal as there is in truly democratic societies.

We have sacrificed our citizenship to bigness, slowly over the decades—more rapidly in the last half century but still slowly enough so that we have hardly been aware that it is gone—so it is not surprising that we do not have the interests, the attitudes, of citizens. Thus we do not vote. We do not pay taxes voluntarily—corporations shelter in tax havens $2.1 trillion a year; individuals evade an estimated $500 billion and some $2 trillion income goes unreported (IRS 2008 figures). We do not always support our government in time of war, and the most recent wars, largely opposed, did not register long on public consciousness and are now almost universally condemned. We do not obey its laws by habit but by force, and a great many of the most highly placed people both in government and business, including even our presidents and our representatives and the executives of the largest firms, are regularly and increasingly seen to be disobeying these laws.

I do not think that any nation has long survived under such conditions, almost certainly none nurtured on the political traditions of ancient Israel, of democratic Greece, of republican Rome, of the egalitarian Enlightenment.

Once people realize that it's the *system*, they see there's no point in voting since the permanent parties run things regardless of elections.

Many years ago—more than a hundred, in fact—a publication called *The Rebel*, put out in Boston, carried this editorial from one Arthur Arnould:

> *An individual eats some mushrooms and is poisoned by them. The doctor gives him an emetic and cures him. He goes to the cook and says to him:*
>
> *—"The mushrooms in white sauce made me ill yesterday! Tomorrow you must prepare them with brown sauce."*
>
> *Our individual eats the mushrooms in brown sauce. Second poisoning, second visit of the doctor, and second cure by the emetic.*
>
> *—"By Jove!" says he, to the cook, "I want no more mushrooms with brown or white sauce, to-morrow you must fry them."*
>
> *Third poisoning, with accompaniment of doctor and emetic.*
>
> *—"This time," cries our friend, "they shall not catch me again! . . . to-morrow you must preserve them in sugar."*
>
> *The preserved mushrooms poison him again.*
>
> *—But that man is an imbecile! you say. Why does he not throw away his mushrooms and stop eating them.*
>
> *Be less severe, I beg you, because that imbecile is yourself, it is ourselves, it is all humanity.*
>
> *Here are four to five thousand years that you try the State—that is to say Power, Authority, Government—in all kinds of sauces, that you make, unmake, cut, and pare down, constitutions of all patterns, and still the poisoning goes on. You have tried legitimate royalty, manufactured royalty, parliamentary royalty, republics unitary and centralized, and the only thing from which you suffer, the despotism, the dictature of the State, you have scrupulously respected and carefully preserved.*

I do not claim that Americans in any great numbers are yet prepared to do away with the state that has made them so ill. But I do not believe I am wrong in detecting the beginnings, the stirrings, the growth, of a true anti-mushroom sentiment in the land: people who, perhaps only dimly, have come to realize that, as people began saying long ago, "the government cannot solve the problem because the government *is* the problem." Inchoate, to be sure, unexpressed except by a few, this sentiment is nonetheless found today in a thousand guises.

It is this that may ultimately point the way to the human-scale polity. I do not think that it is around the corner or necessarily inevitable. But I do think it is possible that it can be sufficiently appreciated now so that if there is any opportunity for the people to realize it, perhaps in the wake of the coming collapse of our civilization, it can take shape. The national political malaise is not going to be corrected until there is a devolution of power from the state to the locality and a decentralization of institutions to the point where individuals may in fact control them. A return to the power and sovereignty of the community: this is politics on a human scale, to which next we turn.

21

The Decentralist Tradition

The impulse to local governance, to separatism and independence, to regional autonomy, seems an eternal one and well-nigh ineradicable. The long experience of nation-states—in Europe going back several centuries at least, in parts of Asia somewhat longer—has not destroyed that impulse, not in those countries, such as Britain, say, or the United States, where the state has grown to be most powerful and ubiquitous, not those places, such as Iran, where it has been most overreaching and oppressive. Indeed, what is remarkable during these long years is how this decentralist tradition remains so resilient—so resilient that every time the power of the nation-state is broken, as during wars or rebellions, immediately there spring up a variety of decentralized organizations—in the neighborhoods, in the factories and offices, in the barracks and universities—that reinstitute government in local, popular, and anti-authoritarian forms.

The historical evidence is unmistakable on this point. In Paris in 1871 the collapse of the empire gave birth to the Paris Commune and its popular assemblies, while every neighborhood began its own committees of governance and defense and most of the business of the capital went on as usual, only with the workers themselves in charge: in Hannah Arendt's words, "a swift disintegration of the old power, the sudden loss of control over the means of violence, and, at the same time, the amazing formation of a new power structure which owed its existence to nothing but the organizational impulses of the people themselves."*

---

* Karl Marx himself saw in this neighborhood government system "the political form of even the smallest village," which looked as if it might be "the political form, finally discovered, for the economic liberation of labor." He was right, of course, but he forgot it.

In Russia in 1905, and then again more sweepingly in 1917, industrial workers organized themselves into committees that took over factories and shops in practically every industry after the owners and bureaucrats had fled, and the real work of running most of the cities was done—until Bolshevik violence eventually put an end to them—by local *soviets*, popularly elected assemblies.

In Germany at the end of World War I, workers and soldiers in a number of cities organized themselves into local councils—*Rate*—in defiance of the Social Democratic regime in Berlin, demanding a new German constitution based on local autonomy through a nationwide *Ratesystem*, in Munich even establishing for a time a *Raterepublik* of Bavaria where, a sympathetic observer noted, "every individual found his own sphere of action and could behold, as it were, with his own eyes his own contribution to the events of the day."

In Spain in 1936–37 the collapse of the national government was followed by the emergence of independent collective governments in hundreds of smaller towns, as we have seen, as well as in a number of the larger cities—Barcelona and Alcoy, particularly—where entire industries were run by self-management, municipal services such as the electric works and streetcar systems were operated by independent collectives, and political and economic affairs were in the hands of "technical-administrative" committees elected within each industry.

In Hungary in 1956, the uprising that toppled the Communist regime led immediately, even in a country little used to popular government, to the formation of an extraordinary array of local councils, in neighborhoods and coffeehouses, offices and factories, among writers and soldiers, students and—*mirabile dictu*—civil servants, indeed everywhere in the society, gradually coalescing within days into a rough network capable at least for a time of running the entire country.

In Iran in 1979, after the fall of the totalitarian government of the shah, local institutions long suppressed suddenly appeared overnight, independent *ayatollahs* took control of their own provincial towns, neighborhood *komitehs* (even their name reminiscent of the Paris Commune) emerged to control their own territories in the cities, and at least four of the ancient minorities—the Baluchis in the southwest, the Kurds and Azerbaijanis in the northeast, and the Arabs of the Persian Gulf—asserted their independence with armed rebellions and demonstrations in the streets.

No, most of these did not last long, and the forces of the statists soon dominated, but the same deep human spirit can be found, too, in America after 1776, in France in 1789, in several European capitals in 1848, in many parts of Italy during the 1850s, in parts of occupied France and Italy in 1918–19, in Ireland throughout the civil war of the 1920s, in China in 1949, in Cuba in 1959, in Czechoslovakia in 1968, in Chile in 1970, in Portugal in 1974–75, in Chiapas, Mexico, from 1994 to today, in fact as near as I can tell wherever and whenever a central government loses its hold (and before some new centralizing force, as often as not proclaiming itself revolutionary, takes over). Hannah Arendt has studied this phenomenon, noting with some wonderment how local councils and societies "make their appearance in every genuine revolution throughout the nineteenth and twentieth centuries":

> *Each time they appeared, they sprang up as the spontaneous organs of the people, not only outside of all revolutionary parties but entirely unexpected by them and their leaders. They were utterly neglected by statesmen, historians, political theorists, and, most importantly by the revolutionary tradition itself. Even those historians whose sympathies were clearly on the side of revolution and who could not help writing the emergence of popular councils into the record of their story regarded them as nothing more than essentially temporary organs in the revolutionary struggle for liberation; that is to say, they failed to understand to what extent the council system confronted them with an entirely new form of government, with a new public space for freedom which was constituted and organized during the course of the revolution itself.*

Everywhere it seems to be the case that the absence of government does not lead to bewilderment and confusion and disorder, as might be imagined if all of government's claims for itself were true, but rather to a resurgence of locally based forms, most often democratically chosen and scrupulously responsive, that turn out to be quite capable of managing the complicated affairs of daily life for many months, occasionally years, until they are forcibly suppressed by some new centralist state less democratic and less responsive. They seem to be, as Arendt says, "spontaneous organs of the people," expressive of the natural human scale of politics and inheritors of the long tradition of decentralism.

———

It is striking to re-read history with eyes opened to the persistence of this tradition, because at once you begin to see the existence of the anti-authoritarian, independent, self-regulating, local community is every bit as basic to the human record as the existence of the centralized, imperial, hier-archical state, and far more ancient, more durable, and more widespread.

Obviously for the two million years that humans have been on earth they lived in small clans and groups, as we have noted before, and for the last 10,000 years that they were becoming "civilized," they lived in small communities and towns, needing none but the most limited kinds of governmental structures. Even throughout the era of oriental empires—Persian, Sumerian, Egyptian, Babylonian—the greater part of the world's people still lived in independent hamlets, ever-resistant to the imposition of outside authority, and even within the empires themselves local self-governing communes always persisted. Later, the Essenes, the people of the Dead Sea Scrolls who established an egalitarian community in opposition to Romanic Jerusalem in the second century before Christ, were only one of myriad tribes and sects that lived deliberately outside the Roman imperial influence. And still later the Christians themselves often lived in democratic and independent communities, sometimes in secret and sometimes openly but always apart from and hostile to whatever state might claim sovereignty.

The settlements of Greece were typical of such resistant localism: for many centuries they clung to a fierce independence, city upon city, valley after valley, no matter what putative conquerors might intrude, in time achieving that Hellenic civilization that is still a marvel of the world. As historian Rudolf Rocker has written of them:

> *Greece was politically the most dismembered country on earth. Every city took zealous care lest its political independence be assailed; for this the inhabitants of even the smallest of them were in no mind to surrender. Each of these little city-republics had its own constitution, its own social life with its own cultural peculiarities; and this it was that gave to Hellenic life as a whole its variegated wealth of genuine cultural values.*
>
> *It was this healthy decentralization, this internal separation of Greece into hundreds of little communities, tolerating no uniformity,*

which constantly aroused the mind to consideration of new matters.
Every larger political structure leads inevitably to a certain rigidity
of the cultural life and destroys that fruitful rivalry between sepa-
rate communities which is so characteristic of the whole life of the
Grecian cities.

Even to call it "Greece" is indeed to employ a modern fiction: the citizens of that ancient culture thought of themselves as Athenians and Spartans and Thebans, not Greeks, alike in language and civilization but not in political stamp or rule.

Traditional historians write of the European period from the fall of Rome to the Renaissance as if nothing much were going on outside of the consolidation of feudal families into the monarchies of the subsequent nation-states. But that is like talking of the night as the presence of stars or the ocean as if it were only waves. What was going on throughout the continent from the Atlantic to the Urals, what kept European civilization alive for better than ten centuries, was the maintenance and development of small, independent communities—here in the form of Teutonic and Russian and Saxon villages with their popular councils and judicial elders, there as the medieval city-states with their guilds and brotherhoods and folkmotes, and over there as the chartered towns spread by the hundreds over France and Belgium with their special instruments of sovereignty and self-jurisdiction. Characteristic of the look of the continent were the divided cantons of what became Switzerland, beginning with the first democratic commune in Uri in the 1230s, a form that spread through dozens of villages in the fourteenth and fifteenth centuries and lasted until dominance by Napoleon at the end of the eighteenth century; at its height a typical canton, the independent Swiss Republic of the Three Leagues, covering about the area of Dallas, consisted of three loosely federated leagues, twenty-six sub-jurisdictions, forty-nine jurisdictional communes, and 227 autonomous neighborhoods—and, as an eighteenth-century traveler put it, "each village . . . each parish and each neighbourhood already constituted a tiny republic."

That Europe did eventually evolve some families designating themselves royal, and that some of those conquered vast areas of land they liked to call nations, and that the whole became a system of border-drawn nation-states such as we know today, does not mean that this was the tide and trend of that long era. Indeed, as between the statist tradition and the decentralist, these thousand years were clearly the period of the latter, into the fifteenth century in western European territories, in some places into the nineteenth century in eastern. No one has understood this period better than the Russian scientist and anarchist Peter Kropotkin, whose careful researches into its long-neglected intricacies, built upon the absolute explosion of interest in village government by scholars everywhere in the nineteenth century, have given us a telling picture of those centuries:

> *Self-jurisdiction was the essential point [of the commune] and self-jurisdiction meant self-administration. . . . It had the right of war and peace, of federation and alliance with its neighbors. It was sovereign in its own affairs, and mixed with no others.*
>
> *In all its affairs the village commune was sovereign. Local custom was the law, and the plenary assembly of all the heads of family, men and women [!], was the judge, the only judge, in civil and criminal matters. . . .*
>
> *[In medieval towns] each street or parish had its popular assembly, its forum, its popular tribunal, its priest, its militia, its banner, and often its seal, the symbol of its sovereignty. Though federated with other streets it nevertheless maintained its independence.*

This was the rule, mind, not the exception; it was exactly this self-governing community, through pestilence and war, the vicissitudes of nature and of kings, that sustained the many tens of millions of people of Europe for a millennium and more.

Nor did the tradition end with the rise of the nation-state. In many places it persisted quite a time—France did not outlaw local folkmotes until 1789, and Russian communes continued to exist in countless places until finally gutted by Stalin as late as the 1930s—and even in the age of nationalism it is not difficult to find, just below the surface, the roughly independent peasant village, the headstrong town, the self-minding neighborhood, in almost any country of Europe.

————————

And in America. The decentralist tradition, manifested in a persistent anti-authoritarianism and a quite exuberant localism, is basic to the

American character. (I am thinking of the European element here, but of course before that was the culture of the original Americans, almost everywhere communal, non-hierarchic, anti-institutional, and carefully localized.)

The Plymouth settlers, after all, were a proud and independent people who made the journey precisely to escape the press of the authoritarian state, and their original village was egalitarian enough, at least in its first two years, to have communal farming, the equal distribution of clothes and food, and cooking and laundry done in common; it turned out to be not a great success and it was abandoned, but it was what they hoped in their souls they could achieve. And when that first village tried to assert its control over such free spirits as Anne Hutchinson and Roger Williams, they simply moved on and started their own independent colonies—the beginning of a long, regular, native pattern of settlement that marked this land for at least three hundred years, until the Pacific stopped the march.

Others, too, who came here were anti-authoritarian by temperament, or tempering—the Quakers and the Mennonites, escaping state persecution, the freed convicts and indentured workers, the entrepreneurs and political freethinkers seeking fresh territory. Even such modest governments as the colonies represented seemed to chafe such people, and their resistance climaxed in the "insurrections" of 1675–90, in response to which William and Mary granted new and more lenient colonial charters. That did not halt the movement toward independence, however, and even the kinds of concessions later offered by George III and his ministers—and they were generous—did not succeed in abating the strong separatist spirit. Resistance to unwanted laws and the flouting of colonial authority were common well before the Revolution itself, and riots and rebellions—the Regulator movement against the governments of the Carolinas in the 1760s, for example, and the Green Mountain Boys against the government of New York in the 1770s—were recurrent. These fledgling Americans wanted to be left alone, to sink their roots how and where they pleased.

The Revolution was precisely in this tradition, and the document that began it is permeated with the principles of the sanctity of community borrowed from the philosophers of the Scottish Enlightenment, of the primacy of the people over the state plucked from Rousseau, and of the inviolability of local governance that was largely ingrained in the

POLITICS ON A HUMAN SCALE

Americans themselves. No better confirmation of these principles was needed than the experience of the colonies in the early years after the Declaration, when most of the British institutions had collapsed and many of their leaders fled, and yet the citizens went right on administering their own affairs, and successfully too. Largely through town meetings, common from Massachusetts to Virginia, and not alone in New England, the settlements of the new country raised money and volunteers for the new army (in which, incidentally, the soldiers usually elected their own officers), organized militias for self-defense, and took care of the plowing and planting, the road-repairing and bridge-building, the schooling and policing. As Tom Paine was later to write:

> *For upwards of two years from the commencement of the American War, and for a longer period in several of the American states, there were no established forms of government. The old governments had been abolished and the country was too much occupied in defence to employ its attention in establishing new governments; yet during this interval order and harmony were preserved as inviolate as in any country of Europe.*

The government that eventually did take shape over these lands, under the Articles of Confederation, was little more than an extension, a federation, of these existing forms. The Articles, much maligned by statists and regularly misconstrued by textbooks written from the viewpoint of a later age, were "weak" enough, as conventional opinion has it, if by "weak" is meant that the affairs of the country would continue to be the stuff of the daily chaffer-mugger of the village square and the town meeting and not matters exclusively for professionals in some inaccessible capital; "weak" if by weak is meant that, in the words of the Articles' first and most basal provision, "each state retains sovereignty, freedom, and independence"; "weak" if popular government be weak, if local control be weak, if direct democracy be weak. Such matters will always be murky, but there is excellent evidence that the greatest part of the free population supported the Articles wholeheartedly and was little interested in the drive for a stronger government that such misguided people as Hamilton and Madison began pushing after the war. And even when the centralists and commercial interests pushed it through, the Constitution was approved only after the state legislators, "in order to prevent misconstruction or abuse of its powers," demanded that a Bill of Rights be added to it: the danger of the central government being uppermost even in the minds of those who were constructing it.

Certainly those citizens who quickly came to feel its pinch had reason enough to look with suspicion on the new government. We remember them now as authors of the series of revolts—such as Shays's Rebellion in Massachusetts and the Whiskey Rebellion in Pennsylvania—by local communities, mostly rural, that had just finished fighting for the right to run their affairs without the taxations and surcharges of an unrepresentative government and would, by God, do it again. Common to these revolts was the publicly stated desire to escape the hand of usurious banks, to establish local control over currency and taxation, and to select local officials (in the words of Shays's followers, to allow "each town to elect its own justices of the peace, each county its judges, and each military company its officers")—all demands that seemed reasonable enough in the light of the principles of the Revolution and the experience of the Articles. But such resistance was inevitably met with force and put down with considerable ferocity by federal troops and state militias, with jail terms for the leaders who survived.

———

Not that the youthful US government was a particularly autocratic one, not that at all. In fact, it was run by men who saw themselves as truly libertarian, in service to those principles of federalism and republicanism that did much to spread power out from the center to the state capitals and the counties and towns. But it did not take more than a few dozen years before the acute Thomas Jefferson, who had done so much to assure that the new government would be restrained, began to fear that even this much centralism, in the hands of such tyrannically tempered men as Alexander Hamilton, was beginning to rot the republic and remove the essential affairs of state from those who should of right be tangling with them. Around 1816, after having served his stint in the presidency, perhaps not wisely nor too well, he began to revive an idea that had long been part of his political creed: ward government. A system of small "elementary republics," he began to feel—units of perhaps a hundred men or two, populations of 500–1,000 in all—was essential to the salvation of the

American state, and a better alternative than his earlier notion of recurring revolutions ("a little rebellion, now and then"). What he urged on all who would hear him was "small republics" by which "every man in the State" could become "an acting member of the Common government, transacting in person a great portion of its rights and duties, subordinate indeed, yet important, and entirely within his competence." "Divide [government] among the many," he declared, so that each citizen may feel "that he is a participator in the government of affairs, not merely at an election one day in the year, but every day; when there shall not be a man in the State who will not be a member of some one of its councils, great or small, he will let the heart be torn out of his body sooner than his power wrested from him by a Caesar or a Bonaparte." Thus a nation of face-to-face democracy, of town meetings, of neighborhood government, where "the voice of the whole people would be fairly, fully, and peaceably expressed, discussed, and decided by the common reason" of every citizen, every day, everywhere.

The Jeffersonian formula was never tried, not even seriously debated in the land—Jefferson himself had effectively retired from public life and chose not to enter new lists at this late date, his passions not quite up to his convictions. And even as it was being voiced, the large shadow of the federal and state government was moving slowly out to dim and extinguish the small lights of self-government that existed: one after another the towns and cities of the mid-Atlantic region abandoned town meetings or made them ritualistic annual affairs; the corporate form of city government, with mayors and councils, was pushed by conservatives as a way to keep the peace and put decisions into "responsible" hands; and the township system was downgraded in favor of greater power to the state and, to a somewhat lesser degree, federal government. It was, as historian Merrill Jensen has put it in his authoritative *The New Nation*, "the counter-revolution."

But the Jeffersonian ideal remained, in one form or another, the philosophic pole at one end of American politics throughout at least the first half of the nineteenth century. It was the guide for Thoreau ("That government is best which governs not at all") and for Emerson ("The less government we have, the better—the fewer laws, and the less confided power"), for Calhoun and the Carolina Nullificationists, and for both white abolitionists and black insurrectionaries who repeatedly defied state and federal laws. At mid-century there were many who would say with Thoreau:

> *This government never of itself furthered any enterprise, but by the alacrity with which it got out of the way. It does not keep the country free. It does not settle the West. It does not educate. The character inherent in the American people has done all that has been accomplished; and it would have done somewhat more, if the government had not sometimes got in its way.*

The illegal war of 1861 and its centralizing aftermath—wars are always centralizing; that's why governments have them—brought a temporary halt to this Jeffersonian tradition and weakened the principle of states' rights forever. But a trace of it broke out again with real ferocity once more in the latter part of the century. Against the increasing monolithicity of government, industry, and political party, there sprang up a variety of movements diverse in cause but similar in resistance to the centralists: the Greenbacks, the Grangers, Oklahoma Socialists, Knights of Labor, Georgeists, feminists, anarchists, communists, Utopians, and above all the groups that fused to become, around 1880, the Populists. The Populists seemed almost to be that party Emerson had dreamed of—". . . fanatics in freedom: they hated tolls, taxes, turnpikes, banks, hierarchies, governors, yea, almost laws"—except that they added to this anti-authoritarianism a profound regard for communalism, cooperation, federation, networking, and localism, and actually developed an extraordinary variety of ventures to foster those. From Texas to the Carolinas, the Populists represented a major part of American politics, winning over whole towns in the South and West, achieving electoral victories in several states—in fact, gaining control of the North Carolina legislature in 1890 and passing laws for local self-government through county autonomy. It may in the end have proved a failure, but Populism was American to the grain, Jeffersonian at its core, built upon the small farmers and artisans of the still-frontier settlements, rooted in the values of the local community and those enterprises —grange, church, school, newspaper, local shops—that gave them expression, set against all those Eastern institutions—industrial trusts, railroads,

POLITICS ON A HUMAN SCALE

big-city machines, national banks—that in fact in time were to suffocate those enterprises.

With the first two decades of the twentieth century, the triumph of federal power was made manifest. The central government was acknowledged as supreme, its authority over its population's pockets (the Income Tax Amendment of 1913) and habits (the Prohibition Amendment of 1919) and even lives (the Selective Service Act of 1917) fully established. Those who resisted, on whatever grounds, were given a show of raw federal power: the Espionage Act of 1917, the Immigration Acts of 1917–18, the Sedition Act of 1918, the Red Raids of 1919, the Palmer Raids of 1920, and countless little sins of commission in between. What happened then in the 1930s and '40s, with the familiar events of New Deal consolidation, seemed only a natural extension of the past autocracy.

Even then, the decentralist spirit did not disappear. It found expression in the Agrarian movement of the 1920s and '30s against corporate giantism and the growing industrialization and urbanization of the South; in the cooperative movement, both agricultural and consumer, that set roots then that are still in place today; and in a variety of homegrown radicalisms—of Ralph Borsodi's homesteaders, Arthur Morgan's communitarians, the Catholic distributists, the Technocrats, the folk-schoolers, the Black Mountain anarchists, and so on. Many of these eventually joined to found the journal *Free America*, which for ten difficult years 1937–46 represented, as nothing in that century did, the voice of decentralism in America, summed up in its founding creed:

> Free America *stands for individual independence and believes that freedom can exist only in societies in which the great majority are the effective owners of tangible and productive property and in which group action is democratic. In order to achieve such a society, ownership, production, population, and government must be decentralized.* Free America *is therefore opposed to finance-capitalism, fascism, and communism.*

In the middle of the last century the decentralist tradition shook itself awake again after the deadening hand of the Cold War years, aroused first by the black and student insurrections of the 1960s, expressions of a generation that sought, as the *Port Huron Statement* of the Students for a Democratic Society put it, "a democracy of individual participation, governed by two central aims: that the individual share in those social decisions determining the quality and direction of his life; that society be organized to encourage independence in men and provide the media for their common participation." The convincing disillusionment with government power as symbolized by Vietnam and Watergate of course added to this spirit, and then evidence of FBI and CIA repression, congressional illegalities, bureaucratic failures, and, with Carter, government ineptitude added further, producing what ex-Congressman Michael Harrington in his farewell statement to the House in 1978 called "a tide of revulsion and rejection" that was "unique to our time, at least in its intensity." And on the other—its more positive—side, it has produced a quite extensive resurgence of localism and a lively renewal of the quest for the authentic community.

The decentralist tradition, no matter what, will not die, for it is as wide in the American soul as the country is wide, as deep in the American psyche as the riches are deep. One may well wonder, with historian C. Vann Woodward, why, given its steady opposition to centralization and authority, the American environment nonetheless "should have proved so hospitable to those same tendencies in government, military, and business. A huge federal bureaucracy," he taunts, "a great military establishment, and multinational corporations, not to mention big labor, seem to have successfully surmounted all the handicaps to centralization." But the answer is as easy as it is revealing. The centralizing tendency has always existed in this country alongside the decentralizing—for every Anne Hutchinson a Governor Winthrop, for every Jefferson a Hamilton, for every Calhoun a Webster, for every Thoreau a Longfellow, for every Davis a Lincoln, for every Debs a Wilson, for every Borsodi a Tugwell, for every Brandeis a Frankfurter, for every Mumford a Schlesinger, for every Schumacher a Galbraith. And obviously this century, not only in this country but around the world, has belonged to the centralists and all their totalitarian machinery. But the decentralist movement has not disappeared either, and it seems to have survived Woodward's decades of bureaucracies and multinationals quite intact. Indeed, one gets the sense that these next few decades may provide its chance again, and I would argue that the anti-establishment support that arose for Donald Trump in 2016 is a sign of that Jeffersonianism is still at work.

Our model is the pulse of the twentieth century into the twenty-first: the decentralism of the world. The five empires that existed in 1945—English, French, Spanish, Portuguese, and Soviet—have all collapsed, spinning off scores of smaller, independent states. The United Nations began with 51 nations in 1945; today it has 193, with 8 more outside, including the Vatican. Czechoslovakia has split in two, Yugoslavia in seven (counting Kosovo and Montenegro), the Soviet Union into fifteen. There are separatist movements everywhere. Global politics is living out the Yeatsian message: "Things fall apart, the center cannot hold."

22

Society Without the State

I n a healthy society of non-human primates, there are no nations, no extended organizations, no supra-territorial forms that might resemble a state. Troops of primates do have a social cohesion about them, creating various temporary leaders or hierarchies according to the function at hand—one for fighting, say, another for vigilance, a third for feeding—and establishing customs and ground rules of permissible behavior. But nowhere do these basically autonomous troops combine into larger associations, nowhere do members of the same species, though clearly knowing themselves to be essentially related, attempt to create large-scale units of social control. "Super-organizations, alliances made up of two or more troops," as anthropology expert John Pfeiffer notes, "have never been observed among baboons or any other nonhuman primates."

In a healthy brain, though there are many major processes operating at once, there is none, either physical or psychological, that is dominant. In the words of neurologist W. Grey Walter:

> *We find no boss in the brain, no oligarchic ganglion or glandular Big Brother. Within our heads our very lives depend on equality of opportunity, on specialisation with versatility, on free communication and just restraint, a freedom without interference. Here too, local minorities can and do control their own means of production and expression in free and equal intercourse with their neighbours.*

Only in the diseased and malfunctioning brain does one process ever become dominant.

In a healthy ecosystem, the various sets of animals, whether themselves organized as individuals, families, bands, or communal hives, get along with each other without the need of any system of authority or dominance—indeed, without structure or organization of any kind whatsoever. No one species rules, not one even makes an attempt; and the only assertion of power has to do with territoriality—the claim of one or another species to a particular area to be left alone in. Each community in the system has its own methods of organization, its own habits and styles and food supplies, and none attempts to impose these on any other, or to set itself up as the central source of power and sovereignty. Predation there will be within such an ecosystem, and some basic wariness by the fly of the frog and the frog of the snake and the snake of the hawk, but there is no *inter-species* warfare, no pseudo-Darwinian war of all against all; on the contrary, there is balance and adjustment, the broad cooperation of nature's communities with each other and with their particular environment. Independence, complexity, variety, flexibility—these are the characteristics of the healthy ecosystem, and, among all creatures, only the human has ever tried to transgress that principle.

———————

In a world in which the decentralist tradition was allowed to proceed to its logical endpoint, in which separatism and localism were permitted to run their courses, the importance of the centralized state would of course diminish rapidly. It is not even difficult to see, in time, the beginning of that process long held dear by philosophers both of the right and the left, the "withering away of the state." For as local units took unto themselves the regulation of internal harmony and democratic governance, the point and purpose of the traditional nation-state would rapidly decline, its functions absorbed by local populations with a more precise perception of the problems and a more realistic understanding of their solutions.

Examples of societies that have lived, and lived long and well, without the trappings of the state are surprisingly common, once one begins combing through the scientific literature. In fact they are so common, occurring right throughout the native societies of both North and South America, through much of North Africa and almost all of the great region from the Sudan to the Kalahari, and throughout the islands of the South Pacific from Sumatra all the way to Polynesia; occurring among patrilineal as well as matrilineal societies, settled and pastoral as well as hunting and nomadic, large and scattered as well as small and cohesive, isolated and ingrown as well as confederate and cooperative, occurring in such variety and profusion that it comes to seem from the anthropological evidence that this is indeed the basic natural organization of human societies. As British anthropologist Aidan Southall has said about the historical spectrum, "People with state organizations were exceptional."

This is the way most humans have organized their societies since the very earliest beginnings of anything that could be called human, so long ago that there is a sense in which its patterns may be encoded in our genes. This is the way even more developed societies must have formed themselves since the beginnings of settled bands and tribes some 15,000 years ago. This is the way the greater part of all humanity must have lived even after a few isolated peoples began forming fixed hierarchies and chieftaincies and states some 5,000 years ago.

Clearly any method of living that has been so widespread and so long-lasting must have something going for it, must be considered in some way successful, even if largely for "primitive" people in "prehistoric" times. Its success in almost every instance seems to be due to a very simple mechanism: the social control exerted by those who feel themselves part of a single, cohesive, multi-entangled social group such that the transgression of one is likely to threaten the well-being of all. It needs no parliament to decree that my act of theft or murder is going to be wrenchingly disruptive of a community, and that if I have even a minimal sense of self-preservation I had better not commit such acts. It needs no chief or ruler to tell me that I must at times tend my neighbor's cattle and help him in his harvest, for it is perfectly obvious that my own survival depends on his doing the same for me. It needs no policeman or soldier to prevent me, nor prison to scare me, from acts of social disruption, for the social well-being that I shatter, the social peace I destroy, is my own. There is nothing to keep me, strictly speaking, from mayhem; yet there is nothing to propel me either, and everything to restrain me.

As Southall puts it in his important entry in the *International Encyclopedia of Social Sciences*:

> *Fundamental responsibility for the maintenance of society itself is much more widely dispersed throughout its varied institutions and its whole population in stateless societies. . . . In stateless societies every man grows up with a practical and intuitive sense of his*

responsibility to maintain constantly throughout his life that part of
the fabric of society in which at any time he is involved.

Or, more bluntly, Peter Farb about the Basarwa:

They have an intuitive fear of violence because they know the social
disruption it can cause in a small group. And they know that because
of the poisoned arrows always at hand, an argument can quickly turn
into a homicide. This explains why the Bushmen attach no honor or
glory to fighting and aggression. Their culture is without tales of
bravery, praise of aggressive manhood, ordeals of strength, or com-
petitive sports.

What's missing from such societies, and what makes them seem so
strange to our eyes—as to the eyes of the first Europeans who encountered and usually misreported them—is the concept of *power*, and hence
of hierarchy, control, obedience, all the elements that are necessary to
contrive a state. No one here has power, no one wants it, no one even
thinks about it—or has a way to think about it. Competence, yes, ability,
skill, these are all desirable, even the talent to lead in battle or in dance or
in harvesting or in magic. But never does it imply power. French anthropologist Pierre Clastres has described the pathetic turn of Geronimo's
career, after that Apache warrior had been a successful leader of troops
in battle and tried to make himself into a chief with political power,
demanding that the Apaches join him in further wars against the Mex-
icans: "He attempted to turn the tribe into the instrument of his desire,
whereas before, by virtue of his competence as a warrior, he was the
tribe's instrument." Quite naturally, the Apaches would have nothing
to do with him, and he spent the next twenty years in silly, futile battles
with a handful of followers, becoming a chief, and heroic, only in the eyes
of the white myth-makers who never understood. Clastres's conclusion
for the Apache, as for the dozens of Central American cultures he has
studied: "One is confronted, then, by a vast constellation of societies in
which the holders of what elsewhere would be called power are actually
without power; where the political is determined as a domain beyond
coercion and violence, beyond hierarchical subordination; where, in a
word, no relationship of command-obedience is in force." Even those

tribes that create leaders of a kind, people we might call chiefs, do not invest them with power:

> *The chief has no authority at his disposal, no power of coercion, no means of giving an order. The chief is not a commander; the people of the tribe are under no obligation to obey.* The space of the chieftainship is not the locus of power, *and the "profile" of the primitive chief in no way foreshadows that of a future despot. . . .*
>
> *Mainly responsible for resolving the conflicts that can surface between individuals, families, lineages, and so forth, the chief has to rely on nothing more than the prestige accorded him by the society to restore order and harmony. But prestige does not signify power, certainly, and the means the chief possesses for performing his task of peacemaker are limited to the use of speech . . .* the chief's word carries no force of law.

Even the word *chief*, it should be noted, is European. Such cultures as these have neither the word nor the concept.

How does such a society work, how *can* it work? What is to prevent, as Hobbes envisioned life for such peoples, "continual fear and danger of violent death" and "a war as is of every man against every man"?

Let us take a look at one such society, the Dinka of the Southern Sudan. At the time of the most careful study of these people (by anthropologist Godfrey Lienhardt, between 1947 and 1951) they numbered about 900,000 — proving stateless societies can encompass very sizable populations — with a common language and common cultural traits but no sense of being in any way united, of being a "nation." They were divided into some twenty-five loose "tribal groups" averaging about 35,000 each (though ranging from 3,000–150,000), each with its own clear but fluctuating territory, but so far from there being any union among these groups, there simply wasn't any organized way for them to *relate* to each other, and if any two had a dispute they weren't even organized in such a way that they could *fight* each other. Within these tribal groups were identifiable tribes, with populations that averaged around 10,000 or so, and this was the basic unit both for defense — the limit of the people who would come to your aid if attacked from the outside—and for the mediation of disputes—the limit of those who could agree to a settlement by compromise and compensation.

But even these tribes had no political shape, no permanent bodies, no structured rules. It was in still smaller units, "subtribes" that would contain about 1,000 people living in the same village, swelling to 3,000 at the most, that anything representing a political office existed. Each subtribe would have a priest ("spearmaster"), who was the interpreter of local magic and tradition and the mediator in interfamilial disputes, and a warrior, who was expected to lead the village in the occasional fights against other subtribes (which were fought with clubs only, nothing more lethal). But though these positions were hereditary, attached to a particular lineage that was thought to supply the best of each officer, the process was fluid, and if someone in the job turned out to be an inept priest or a timid warrior they were simply bypassed, with no ceremony about it, in favor of someone who could measure up.

Loose as it was, this system seems to have worked with persistent success over many generations and going back who-knows-how-many centuries. (It has been considerably shattered since the civil wars in the Sudan in the last 30 years, and as many as half may have emigrated in that time, but there are still Dinka clans in the countryside.) Allegiance to family, village, tribe, was strong enough to establish a sense of community such that the disruption was so anguishing it was felt by all and avoided as much as possible. If disputes did arise between families—perhaps over cattle, for the Dinka were herders—and could not be settled by the family heads, they could be taken to the spearmaster to hear his opinion; and though that would only be a recommendation and not a judgment, it would often be followed as a simple face-saving device for all. Disputes between villages, the subtribes, were likely to be less frequent but more heated when they came, occasionally escalating to retributive theft and even murder; such feuds, seriously disrupting the valued harmony of the region, would normally occasion the gathering of the tribal elders—not any fixed officers or legislators or judges, merely the oldest males around, meeting informally—who would hear both sides, offer opinions, try to set compensation (normally payments of cattle), and do what they could to get everyone back to the tenor of their ways. They would have no body of laws to refer to, of course, merely the accumulated wisdom and accepted tradition of the tribe, and they had no method of enforcement other than the abiding morality of the community. (Plus, to be sure, the abiding custom that the aggrieved villagers would go and grab the recommended number of compensatory cattle from the neighboring village's fields.)

Thus government for the Dinka was self-government in the very best sense. Common rules and practices were observed because they were seen to be, in normal daily life, the most harmonious for the individual, the family, the village, the tribe; they did not have to be legislated and codified and policed because they had everyday meaning. Transgression was viewed as disrupting the safety, security, and harmony of the unit, leading to a threat to the life not only of any one individual, but potentially of the whole tribe. Such disputes as might arise could be handled through local machinery brought into temporary operation for that single occasion and then disbanded, and warfare was such a rarity—absolutely unheard-of between villages, for example—that to have kept a standing army would have been egregiously wasteful. Thus, in Dinka eyes, a state would be superfluous: with a system as neat as theirs, what earthly use could there be for lawmakers and kings and sheriffs and soldiers?

Obviously such a system must have a well-tuned sense of balance, of limits, in order to keep working, and that in turn was based on two other essential features of the stateless tribe: self-sufficiency and limited size.

In the Dinka economy there was no place for the individual accumulation of property or for the market system that extends from it. Aside from the most minimal personal possessions—a few clothes, some jewelry, maybe a piece of furniture—no Dinka ever had, or seemed to want, additional property: what, after all, could anyone *do* with such additional baggage, especially when moving around to find suitable watering holes in the dry season? Similarly, since there was no exchange of goods with any other society and each village wanted only enough cattle and food to guarantee security in lean years, why would anyone want to build up a surplus of goods, what could any village *do* with it? The economy was entirely local, entirely self-reliant, and thereby entirely free of the pressures that come into play with the purposeful and unending accumulation and exchange of properties. And more: a society (hardly what I would call "primitive") that does not amass personal property does not normally build up an economic hierarchy, one that does not accumulate surplus goods for trading and "becoming richer" does not so easily go to war, coveting other people's lands and goods and "riches." Self-sufficiency, as we noted before, inherently tends toward stability.

Similarly, in the Dinka system as in most stateless societies, there was the conscious and regular limitation of the size of the constituent units. Since order was to a large degree dependent on a sense of communality— one person being known to, and the concern of, all—there was an obvious need to hold the basic population below the point where that sense became diffuse and fragile. Basic to the Dinka polity, therefore, was the easy fragmentation and fission of villages and tribes, as Lienhardt notes:

> It is part of Dinka political theory that when a subtribe for some reason prospers and grows large, it tends to draw apart politically from the tribe of which it was a part and behave like a distinct tribe. The sections of a larger subtribe similarly are thought to grow politically more distant from each other as they grow larger, so that a large and prosperous section of a subtribe may break away from the other sections, with its own master of the fishing spear, its own separate wet-season camp, and eventually its own age-sets. In the Dinka view, the tendency is always for their political segments . . . to grow apart from each other in the course of time and through the increase in population which they suppose time to bring.

Or as the Dinka say with sophisticated simplicity when asked to explain why a village divides: "It became too big, so it separated." And this system pertained, mind, among quite large populations—the Dinka numbered 900,000, the Tiv, in Nigeria, at least 800,000, the Lugbara of Uganda perhaps 240,000.

Absolutely fundamental to the stateless tribe, in other words, is, in both demographic and economic terms, the human scale.

Nor should one think that it is only among such archaic peoples that forms of statelessness exist. One can encounter much the same sort of thing, sometimes with a few more touches of formality, often enough in the histories of peoples of acknowledged sophistication.

The Greeks, for example. From the eighth century BC on to as late as the fourth, the great majority of Hellenic villages and cities operated without kings, without ruling priesthoods, without fixed aristocracies, organizing their daily affairs through assemblies of citizens and popularly elected leaders. The Greek polis may have created more civic officers than the Dinka did, and it may have relied to a greater extent on codified law, but it had the same avoidance of authoritarian forms, the same distrust of chiefly powers, the same dependence upon popular assemblies for the settlement of disputes. Even Athens, probably more encumbered than most Greek cities because of its size and prominence, studiously avoided the governmental trappings of the riparian empires that had preceded it. It was governed not by imperial wizards and pharaohs but by a public assembly, the *ecclesia*, a regular gathering of all (male) citizens who wished to participate, which made all important decisions and set all guiding policies and then elected a rotating body of fellow-citizens, the Council of 500, and an assortment of citizen committees to carry them out. So far from having a permanent monarch, Athens until Periclean times generally selected a new "president"—in effect the mayor—every single day by lot from among the Council of 500, and his duties were totally symbolic and ceremonial. And none doubts the sophistication of *that* culture.

Similarly, the medieval cities were without anything that could be thought of as a state, certainly nothing recognized beyond their narrow borders. They did have their forms of governance, to be sure, somewhat more complicated than the Dinka, with town officers and magistrates and written charters. But they knew no authority beyond their fortified walls, no lord or nation or king (which is why even today the British monarch theoretically has to ask permission to enter the City of London). They were entirely self-administering, self-governing, self-adjudicating (in most places, until the fifteenth century, local priests and often local feudal lords were subject to the decisions of the city's folkmote or juries). They recognized only the authority of their own citywide folkmotes, open to all citizens, which in turn generally selected the military *defensor* and the judicial *magisters* for the town (and it is precisely because they did not have such folkmotes that certain cities—Paris and Moscow for sure, and possibly London and Lisbon as well—were chosen by certain feudal lords and bishops to be the capitals of their growing dominions). And they regarded themselves as completely sovereign, even granting their own citizenship (as Braudel points out, each city "was the classic type of the closed town, a self-sufficient unit, an exclusive Lilliputian native land").

Even then, the average independent city hardly resembled what we would think of as a "state," so decentralized were the effective functions of municipal life. Especially in northern and western Europe, each neighborhood or parish normally had its own forms of governance for most day-to-day affairs, its own assembly meeting once a month or more, its own tribunal, priest, militia, and emblems. In addition, each trade had its own guild to see to the welfare, protection, and health of its members, with its own assembly, its own courts and punishments, and its own military force armed with its own bows or guns. It was only disputes between the neighborhoods or disagreements among the guilds that went up to the consideration of city officers, and most of these were settled by schemes of local custom and adjudication as honored and respected as those among the Dinka.

There are many other examples of stateless societies to be found in more contemporary history. In sixteenth-century Ireland, we are told, there was "no legislature, no bailiffs, no police, no public enforcement of justice . . . no trace of State administered justice." The Swiss Confederation in the eighteenth and nineteenth centuries was so formless that it had no central government at all but rather an obedient secretariat of two regular officials and a few aides that moved around the country from canton to canton (the entire apparatus of the "state" was once stuck in the snow in a single railway coach near Mellingen), and even though those cantons enjoyed almost total internal autonomy, most matters of substance in them were in fact decided by "sovereign villages." Such religious communities as the Quakers, Dukhobors, Mennonites, and Hutterites have lasted for centuries without any trappings of the state—nor do most of them formally recognize the civil states around them—and with their own law and governance as established by religion, custom, community, and popular democratic assemblies.

But it is probably among the classic New England towns of the eighteenth century that the best modern example of the essentially stateless society is to be found.

———————

Although in strictly legal terms the towns of the province of Massachusetts were part of a considerable state, consisting of a governor and legislature in Boston and a king and parliament in London, in any practical sense the provincial charter of 1691 established a territory without a state, without effective central authority of any kind. Such governance as there was—and it did not intrude much into citizens' lives—was grounded in the towns, the small, scattered settlements, very few with more than a thousand people in all, that stretched from the Atlantic to the Berkshires. As Michael Zuckerman describes it in his excellent *Peaceable Kingdoms* (an awkward misnomer that, for they had nothing to do with kings), these towns "were free enough of both Boston and London to enjoy an autonomy which, if never total, was always genuine," enabling them to establish "local custom and usage as guides for the management of most facets" of their politics; and they were even able to "set the law aside, without ever a word that went beyond the town boundaries, when the law proved inconvenient for local purposes," so that "effective law in the provincial community was ultimately only what each particular place would abide by."

> *Their operative ideas of appropriate authority and meet relations among men were those they drew from daily conduct in the communities. . . . The town became the only governmental agency with more than a sporadic impact on the lives of its residents, and as it came to provide most of them with the only essential experience of public authority they would ever know, it encroached ineluctably upon the traditional prerogatives of the central government. As the Revolution eventually revealed, the very maintenance of order in the province had come to depend, in the eighteenth century, upon the towns.*

Talk about the decentralist tradition.

Not only did these towns manage their own affairs for upward of a century, they did so with extraordinary peace and harmony. The local church, the local market, the town schools, the town meeting, all taught concord and control, all emphasized harmony and homogeneity. And with such success that Zuckerman figures on average only one town out of the 200 in any given year had a quarrel serious enough to take to the legislature in Boston to settle for it.

And of course there was no need for official agencies of public control and public order. There was, to be sure, a constable for each community, but he was a person elected annually, seldom in office more than a year at a time, almost always serving with great reluctance, and having no enforcement powers whatsoever beyond those sanctioned by the town as a whole: "Constables . . . could command compliance only when almost everyone was prepared to give it anyway." There were in certain centers courts of law, but they were seldom used (it is said that there were probably no more than a dozen lawyers in the whole province in 1750, and most of those in Boston), and they were without any real powers of enforcement; most parties in dispute preferred to establish their own arbitration committees, call together the church elders, or even ask in impartial men from neighboring communities. What kept the peace, what maintained order, were the communal bonds and religious ties, and behind it all, the town meeting.

The town meeting, despite its look of formality, was an instrument hardly more statist than the council of elders of the Dinka. It was nothing more—though nothing less—than the regular occasion for the expression of community solidarity through popular decision making, about everything that affected the town, from the upkeep of the roads and the tax rates to the amount of firewood to be cut for the minister. All decisions were normally unanimous—what, after all, would be the point of a victory by a majority that left unhappy a minority of neighbors and friends?—and since "the recalcitrant could not be compelled to adhere to the common course of action," as Zuckerman notes, "the common course of action had to be shaped so as to leave none recalcitrant, and that was the vital function of the New England town meeting." Even more than in the Greek or medieval city, this was "government by consent of the governed"—always remembering that women were regrettably, except in their lobbying function, excluded—for this depended on the open consent—active, perceived consent—by all, not merely a majoritarian segment of, the governed. One can read over and over again in the records of town meetings throughout Massachusetts, and similarly throughout the rest of New England, recurrent variations on this theme: votes "by the free and united consent of the whole," "by all the voters present," or this especially felicitous one from Weston, "By a full and Unanimous Vote that they are Easie and Satisfied With What they have Done." It was this unit, this expression of the real general will, that was the essential political embodiment of the New England people for generations on end.

Here at the very beginnings of American society, here at the fount of the American soul, we find the most developed, the most settled, the most reasonable demonstration of the worth and happiness of life without the state.

We do have to go back for some time in history—except for those few remaining examples of the archaic state particularly in Africa and Australia —to find examples of societies without the state, that being the particular burden of the contemporary world. And yet when we do, through anthropologists and archaeologists and historians, we almost never fail to find an extraordinary record of stability and equilibrium that suggests, and goes a long way to proving, that the human animal, without the patterns of the state and the pillars of authority, tends to peace not war, to self-regulation not chaos, to cooperation not dissension, to harmony not violence, to order not disarray. Indeed, looking at the long human record, it is hard not to find an increase in all of the *latter* characteristics *with* the development of the state.

It took me many years to understand it, but I do now—the remark of Proudhon that liberty is not the daughter of order, but the mother.

23

The "Necessity" of the State

B ut "let us put away our infantile fantasies, the yearning to return to an infancy of the species that never was, where mankind existed in small and totally autonomous units like tribes or villages and practiced primary democracy and knew peace and harmony. It may be that if most inhabitants and the technical know-how already existing on humanity's fragile and crowded spaceship are consumed in a thermonuclear Judgment Day, the survivors might be able to exist, for a time, in tiny, fully sovereign, widely separated units. Only a madman would think that a solution. No, because the species *is* interdependent, giant political systems are a necessity."

So scolds Robert Dahl, and he is such an eminent political scientist that it behooves us, I suppose, to listen. Of course, as we have just seen, it's not true that a small village of peace and harmony "never was," nor is there any reason to believe that the world's population would have to be reduced to a handful to accommodate separate sovereign units. And it is not easy to see in what way this "interdependence" works—the Manchurian peasant and the Chilean barber? the Ghanaian professor and the Alaskan fisherman?—or why it should necessitate "giant systems" even if it did pertain.

Still, let us put these quibbles aside, for Dahl is a learned man and he may indeed be expressing those resistant feelings any American might experience on being told that it is possible to live without a state:

> As for making all large political systems vanish into thin air, when
> the silk scarf is pulled away there in full sight are matters that cannot
> be handled by completely autonomous communes, neighborhoods, or
> villages: matters of trade, tariffs, unemployment, health, pollution,
> nuclear energy, discrimination, civil liberties, freedom of movement,
> not to say the whole tragic range of historically given problems
> like the threat of war and aggression, the presence of great military

establishments around the world, the danger of annihilation. These problems inexorably impel us to larger and more inclusive units of government, not to small and totally autonomous units.

Again, we must take the man seriously, though again I do sense some confusion. Aren't the problems of war and aggression and nuclear energy and tariff barriers *caused* rather than solved by big governments? (They certainly *haven't* solved them, in any case, have they?) Surely if there were no giant governments there would be no "great military establishments" around the world and a good deal less "danger of annihilation." And if we have in fact been impelled to "larger and more inclusive units of government" because in that way we would solve the problems of unemployment, pollution, and discrimination, it does not take any special genius to show that it seems to have been rather futile, or at the very best inadequate; if to provide us with high levels of health care and a profitable balance of trade, it does seem to have failed, or at the best proven highly erratic.

I would be readier to see the end of those "infantile fantasies," as Dahl calls them, if he did not put up against them so many adult ones of his own.

———————

But we should confront the philosophy that stands behind the Dahlian attack, because in truth the line of criticism is common enough and deserves examination. Historically there have been four general arguments for the necessity of the state (and, in modern terms, for the necessity of large governments):

- To provide defense in case of attack and to guarantee peace and security.
- To provide economic regulation and development.
- To provide public services beyond the competence of the community and the individual.
- To assure social justice and protect the rights of the individual.

These arguments have a persuasive feel to them. They should; they've been drummed into us for centuries. But it is fair to ask: do they stand up? are they sufficient justifications for the existence of the state? and do they refute the desirability of small-scale politics?

Defense

Traditionally the state's initial claim to necessity was that it prevented warfare by erecting firm barriers of defense. As we have seen, this is tommyrot: the Law of Government Size shows that the duration and severity of war has always increased with an increase in state power. Larger states, far from providing peace, merely provide larger wars, having more human and material resources to pour into them. War is the health of the state, as Randolph Bourne once said, precisely because it provides the excuse for increased state power and the means by which to achieve it. (Victory, by the same token, is incidental: many losing nations emerge from wars with more powerful governments.) In fact, what goes by the name of the defense of the citizens by the state may really be better thought of as the other way around.

Insofar as "defense" implies security, the state is the instrument least capable of providing this. Indeed, in the contemporary world of massed nuclear weapons, there simply *is* no defense of the citizens from a hostile aggressor—if Russia, for example, should unleash all of its missiles against this country, the only "defense" we would have would be to launch ours back again, guaranteeing the population nothing but nuclear holocaust. The very presence of the state and its huge pile of threatening weapons endangers rather than protects the populace, by inviting pre-emptive strikes; the fact that the United States is now sitting on something like 7,100 nuclear warheads, the equivalent of 500,000 Hiroshimas, cannot be said to provide the ordinary person with the sense of security and safety implied by the word *defense*.

Moreover, in the course of attempting to provide its defense the state exercises its own forms of coercion and violence. It entices some 2 million young people into its military and deploys them overseas as often as it likes; it forces the wider population to pay for warfare and its preparation through increased taxation, which has never in history been paid voluntarily; it sustains a military-industrial complex that is an important element of the US economy and does not diminish in peace or war. And such a state, preoccupied with defense, begins to justify all acts, however dangerous, in its name (as presidents justify all crimes with "national security"): when all you own is a hammer, as Mark Twain once said, all problems begin to look like nails.

I am not positing a polyanalysis of human nature that argues all warfare will disappear and all defense become unnecessary in a world of small societies. I am only suggesting there are a number of reasons to believe that the occurrence and severity of warfare would be diminished.

To begin with, it is likely that a small society, particularly if concerned with a steady-state equilibrium, would not amass the kinds of glittering riches that would attract some predatory outsider; the riches of the stable community are likely to be in its air, its range of foods, its quiet streets, its heightened participation, not the sorts of things inspiring envy and conquest. By the same token, a small society already enjoying stability and some prosperity might well be reluctant to sacrifice that for a war whose economic benefits would be so unclear; as the University of Chicago's famed economist Henry Simons once put it, "No large group anywhere can possibly gain enough from redistributing wealth to compensate for its predictable income losses from the consequent disorganization of production." Nor would such a society particularly want to divert from its economy the kind of human and material resources that would be necessary for it to amass a strong fighting force capable of successful aggression.

Yet all that supposes rationality, and since the history of warfare is marked just as much by madness as by calculation, we would have to expect that somewhere war is bound to erupt even when it seems most illogical. Still, the very nature of that warfare depends on the size of the society waging it: with limited populations and limited resources for weaponry, wars cannot have the sweep and severity they do when waged by powerful nation-states. Nuclear warfare would certainly be almost impossible, not only because of the expense of such weaponry would be beyond any stable economy but, at bottom, because no small society could think of sacrificing millions of people and still surviving in the way current superpowers can.

Historical evidence is abundant to show that even the wars that do take place in small societies tend to be—well, if not pacific, at least constrained. A typical account in the anthropological literature is the one by Australian scientists C. W. M. Hart and A. R. Pilling, in *The Tiwi of North Australia*, describing how two bands declared war, amassed their armies, met around a clearing at dawn, and then began throwing spears at each other—but with the *oldest* men throwing the spears, none too accurately, the oldest women careening around trading insults, and as a result "not infrequently the person hit was some innocent noncombatant or one of the screaming old women who weaved through the fighting men, yelling obscenities at everybody, and whose reflexes for dodging spears were not as fast as those of the men." Stateless or not, such small bands and tribes rarely engaged in warfare for plunder or conquest, and territorial aggression and enslavement is practically unknown. Similarly, we have evidence from early Greece that at least some towns and cities worked out ways to make wars more like athletic events than battles-to-the-death, fighting to "maintain honor" or display manliness with games and contests; as early as the seventh century a "war" between Khalkhis and Eretria was fought out as a kind of wrestling contest, apparently quite vicious and serious but managed without spears, arrows, or slings and with the only stakes being honor, pride, and boasting rights.

And even the small regimes of the late medieval period, though undeniably and elaborately "stated," fought their wars at scales much smaller than our Hollywood conceptions would have led us to believe. Three or four knights and several dozen crossbowmen would make up a standing army, battles would commonly rage for no more than an hour or two before everyone was exhausted, and whole wars would be over in a month, the casualties rarely more than 1 or 2 percent of the fighting force. The Duke of Tyrol, it is said, declared war on the Margrave of Bavaria over some real or pretended slight, their war went on for two weeks, one man was killed, one village overrun, one tavern emptied of its wine, and in the end the Margrave paid a hundred thalers in reparations. And however many minor feuds and wars there may have been in a middle Europe of duchies and principalities and republics and palatinates, that was as nothing compared with the wars wrought when they were all united into the *reichs* of Germany.

In a world of small societies, in fact, size itself would likely act as some kind of deterrent to aggression. Who could picture an American continent composed of even fifty different nations deciding to pool its resources to fight a little nation around the world in the jungles of Southeast Asia? Would Texas, say, or Ohio, be sufficiently rapacious—or, let's say, heroic—to want to mobilize its forces and send them across the Pacific to save Saigon from Communism? It is hard to see how the citizens of, for example, Bavaria, no matter how bellicose they might be, could have such a grievance against the citizens of Brittany that they would want to travel half a continent away to fight about it—though as we know when those citizens are combined into the larger states of Germany and France they had no trouble going at each other's throats with some regularity. There is something in the very size of the modern nation-state that leads it not into tranquility but into temptation, and even when it builds up power that is supposed to be purely defensive it always seems to have a way of turning it offensive without much trouble. The Germans have a saying that fits: *Gelegenheit macht Diebe*—opportunity makes thieves.

Yet suppose that somehow a single large superpower should appear (or remain) in a world of smaller communities. What is to be done with the legitimate fear that, in Robert Dahl's words, "in a world of microstates, let there arise only one large and aggressive state and the micro-republics are doomed"?

Historically the response of small states to the threat of such large-scale aggression has been temporary confederation and mutual defense, and indeed the simple threat of such unity, in the form of defense treaties and leagues and alliances, has sometimes been a sufficient deterrent. The record of medieval Europe in fact, during a period when small territories were confronted by rising states, is absolutely teeming with leagues and federations and compacts and associations among towns and cities that joined together to establish peace and to resist the martial incursions from the outside. The Lombardian and Tuscan Leagues in Italy, the Westphalian, Rhenish, Swabian, and Hanseatic in Germany, the Lyonnais and the Marseillaise in France, the Flemish, the Swiss, the Dutch, everywhere small towns came together with independent cities, the cities united with each other throughout a region, and though experiences naturally differed, the rule was of long periods, several generations, of unperturbed calm that were broken seldom, if ever, by the federated small communities themselves.

Moreover, the difficulties for any large power trying to subdue a host of smaller societies are truly formidable and would be additionally so if those societies, in a human-scale world, were efficiently governed, harmonious and homogeneous, and concertedly self-protective. The problems that Nazi Germany had controlling a Europe of large nation-states were bad enough, but they would have been infinitely greater if each little community had been independent, without connections to centralized systems of administration and control, with effective traditions of local autonomy and defense. The material game of conquering—and controlling—a small society that offered a great deal in the way of resistance and very little in the way of exploitable riches would hardly seem worth the military candle.

As recent history, indeed, suggests. Despite the existence of a num-ber of enormous states, the events of the contemporary world give little support to the idea that Gargantuas are out there dying to subdue all the Lilliputs. But in general the pattern has been one of the division and independence of states, an increasing number of smaller states, not of conquest and subjugation by the superpowers. Scores of quite tiny states exist, most under the economic pull of one large state or another, but politically autonomous and without much fear of being taken over. And some of the smallest states in the world—Andorra, San Marino, Liech-tenstein, Switzerland—have existed for many centuries quite untouched and unthreatened.

In sum, the long human record suggests that the problem of defense and warfare is exacerbated, not solved, by the large state, and that smaller societies, especially those without governmental apparatus, tend to engage in fighting less and with less violent consequences. Indicating that a world of human-scale polities would not be a world without its conflicts and disputations, but would likely be a world of comparative stability.

Economic Development

The justification for the state in classical economic theory is that it is sup-posed to stabilize economies over wide geographic areas, standardize currencies and measurements, establish protective tariff barriers and regu-late international trade, prime the productive pumps for sustained growth and steady employment, and ultimately promote economic development and stability. To which we may add a contemporary responsibility, the regulation of businesses on behalf of the public so that it is not recklessly overcharged and endangered, fleeced and fummeled.

Of course the easy response is that if *this* is what the state is so vital for, it does not seem to have proved its worth. What has characterized all large national governments, particularly in the last hundred years, is their clear *inability* to provide economic stability, security, or employment, to secure people against the dangers of depression and inflation, in either capitalist or "socialist" worlds. A nation like the United States, assumed to be the most powerful of all, though it has a truly mighty Gross National Product (GNP) and has recently enjoyed a period of high imperial prosperity, has not been able to forestall regular depressions, prevent inflation, maintain the dollar, regulate tariffs to the benefit of national industries, provide either jobs or income security, create a stable retirement system, or manage any but the most meager protections against the corporate contaminations of food, air, water, waste, or soil.

Still, it is perfectly true that national governments do issue and protect a standard currency—the only trouble is that this is of itself one of the major causes of inflation, and always has been, and the advantages of it could be as equally well enjoyed by a congeries of cooperating communities accepting certain common tokens—much as the cities of Europe agreed to accept the coins of Florence (hence the florentine) in the thirteenth and fourteenth centuries. Nor do these governments ever manage to keep their currencies stable for very long, as theory would dictate—as the worth of the dollar would testify.

Well, then, what about tariffs—are not nations necessary to maintain them? Right enough—only the reason that tariffs exist in the first place is to protect the state, enable it to develop while new industries grow within its boundaries, for its own aggrandizement; the advantages to the consumer are negligible, if existent. Like armies, tariffs are there to safeguard the state, not vice versa.

International trade? Nothing that *couldn't* be done without the state, as is amply demonstrated by the history of Europe between 1000 and 1500, a period of the most extensive and elaborate sort of trade relations, fundamental to the development of capitalism, quite separate from any national machineries. In fact, it *is* being done without the state—for the operations of the current multinational corporations, as any number of studies have shown, are essentially beyond the control of any serious governmental regulation of any kind. Moreover, though certain numbers are in dispute, the various components of the current international trade system have proven seriously damaging for American manufacturing industries and for the white middle class whose incomes have suffered over the past two decades (and who made up much of Trump's armies).

Pump-priming? Governments have become better at this since the advent of Keynes, but there is not one of them, including those that Keynes advised, that has succeeded in creating unabated growth without regular severe downturns, not one of them, indeed, that has succeeded in directing the flow of those pumps out of the front yards of the rich and toward the backyards of the poor. And might a process efficient at sustaining growth—even if the nation-state could achieve it—be out-moded in a world where it is not growth but stability we wish to sustain, where growth has in fact become a threat?

Shortages? The idea that big governments are good for monitoring and allocating precious resources—as with gasoline shortages, for example—so as to distribute them fairly to all has a nice socialist ring about it and is John Kenneth Galbraith's favorite idea ("more big government"). But those who remember the government's skill at monitoring and planning Vietnam (and Iraq and Libya, and so on) and swine-flu shots and public housing, the post office, the Veterans Administration, the Traffic Safety Administration, and—need I go on?—may not relish the prospect of its handling irreplaceable resources.

Regulation? Aside from added costs to consumer and taxpayer, the trouble with governmental regulation is that it is always a catch-up operation, fighting the problem at the wrong end *after* the damage has been done. If the only criteria in the economy are those that capitalism dictates, as they are, then of course there will be those problems that no amount of government law or supervision can correct. If the primary purpose of the government is to protect the smooth workings of the corporate system, as it is, then of course its attempt to restrain its excesses by patchwork presidential edicts is always doomed to failure. Thus the famous actions against cartels and monopolies have proved insignificant, as the existence and growth of conglomerates and oligopolies makes clear; the regulation of public utilities has been almost useless, as the existence of telephone gougers and electricity polluters, the awful failure of nuclear plants, makes obvious. But wouldn't the consumer be in even more trouble *without* government regulation, however expensive and inept? Perhaps so. But probably not if at the same time the myriad government supports favoring large (and therefore largely unresponsive) businesses were withdrawn and the small firms in the market had to offer—as they did in an earlier age—"good goods at a fair price" in order to compete successfully. (It is not competition but the *lack* of it that fosters abuses, not the neighborhood butchers but the large meat-packers that produced the fetid *Jungle*.) Certainly not if in each office and shop the full range of workers made self-managed policies, in each community the full range of citizens set democratic decisions, as to what products and services would be sold.

One needn't claim that economic relations among small and self-regarding communities are going to be untrammeled bliss to reject the notion that state supervision will solve more difficulties than it manufactures.

Yes, the kinds of cooperation within a community, the kinds of federations among communities, would, in the absence of a state, take skill and savvy. Yes, careful balances would have to be wrought between upriver towns and downriver cities (the word *rivalry*, after all, comes from the Latin *rivus*, for river); between the community that had surplus steel and the community with surplus grain; between the city with all the copper and the other with all the zinc. But it need not be all that complicated, nor need it entail some *deus ex civitas*. After all, the stamps of all 195 independent nations of the world are recognized by all the others and the mail goes around the world without any state to guarantee it; the railroad cars of thirty-one sovereign nations travel the same rails for 4 million square miles throughout Europe without any state, not even any central agency, to oversee them. International telephone and telegraph systems, worldwide maritime regulations, international airline agreements, global currency exchanges, and dozens of other forms of cooperative arrangements all prove to be successful without any universal state, or anything near it, to supervise them. Would the cooperation of a half a dozen small communities in a single limited bioregion be all that hard to effect?

Public Services

As Robert Dahl puts it, the state is ultimately necessary on grounds of the "criterion of competence": "Only the nation-state has the capacity to respond fully to collective preferences," only the state can supply public goods in the common interest, which individuals and communities won't do by themselves. Who but the state can control population growth, say, or feed the starving, secure public health, build highway systems, provide welfare, offer disaster relief, distribute scarce supplies? Who but the state—to pick the most commonly cited example—can control pollution?

This is the way Dahl poses the problem, given a polluted Lake Michigan:

> *Let us assume, without arguing the matter, that the capacity to reduce pollution in Lake Michigan is, up to some threshold, a function of size. A citizen who wants the lake cleaned up might well reason as follows: If the authority to deal with pollution is left to local governments, the*

job is unlikely to be accomplished even if a majority of people around the lake—not to say in the whole country—would like it cleaned up. For those favoring vigorous pollution control may be in a minority in some towns. Consequently, that town will probably continue to pollute the lake. Thus only a regional or perhaps even a federal agency, responsible to regional or national opinion, can be effective. Of course I am bound to have only negligible influence on the decisions of such an agency, whereas I might be highly influential in my own town. Nonetheless, on balance I prefer the agency to the present system of decentralized and uncoordinated units.

The hidden assumption here, of course, is that the federal government is in fact a solution. In real life it doesn't quite work out that way. The first problem is to get the government to take any action at all, to rouse the politicians or the bureaucrats somehow, to force the courts to intervene, and that may be an expensive and time-consuming task for any individual, especially since the object of the appeal is probably 600 miles away in Washington, DC. The next problem is to see to it that the action will be appropriate, that the decisions of all these people will be wise. Immediately following comes the problem of making sure that the wise decision can actually be carried out, that the competence to do the job is in human, or at least bureaucratic, hands in the first place; the inability of any government to keep the various oil spills from polluting Alaskan and Gulf beaches in recent years suggests that there are some matters as yet beyond our skills to solve. And making sure that it *is* carried out, and carried out properly, by government officials whose interest in the task may be minimal and whose budgets may be small, without any unintended side effects. And the final problem is keeping the government always around to make sure that the elegant solutions stay in place and the errant polluters don't backslide when no one is looking—since the solutions have been imposed on them by a higher authority rather than drawn from them by cooperation and negotiation. Oh—and paying for it all.

Still, even if we concede that the federal government *is* a solution, and a benevolent one, wouldn't it be more rational for Dahl's citizen to figure out why that pollution exists in the first place and trace the problem to its source? The cause may be an accident, or ignorance, in which case the polluter doesn't need the heavy hand of federal regulation but a little help, or information, or some money, any of which can be supplied far more easily and cheaply by the concerned majority around the lake than by federal intervention. If the pollution is found to be deliberate, it is most likely to come from some anti-social corporation—the battery company, the detergent manufacturer—passing its "external" costs on to the public, which it has been allowed to do by provisions of governmental law for a hundred years or more, and ignoring any but its own sheer profit considerations, which it is explicitly *protected* in doing by the same long line of laws. Or if the pollution is from a municipal agency, it is probably because of federal provisions that defy ecological balance—for example, Washington's funding complex sewage systems instead of septic tanks and composting toilets, or giving tax credits to utilities for expansion but not for conservation, or spending billions to develop nuclear rather than solar power. In other words, Dahl's citizen would find that the state may be the underlying *cause* of the pollution Dahl would ask it to *cure*.

To find the government as the root cause of such problems, of course, should not surprise us by now: it is in the nature of the state, we have repeatedly seen, to create the problems that it then steps in to correct and uses to justify its existence. But there is a further point to that process that is pertinent here; in the words of British philosopher Michael Taylor:

> The state . . . in order to expand domestic markets, facilitate common defence, and so on, encourages the weakening of local communities in favour of the national community. In doing so, it relieves individuals of the necessity to cooperate voluntarily amongst themselves on a local basis, making them more dependent upon the state. The result is that altruism and cooperative behaviour gradually decay. The state is thereby strengthened and made more effective in its work of weakening the local community.

This is important: it is exactly this that accounts for the inability of the Lake Michigan communities to regulate their pollution problems in the first place. Communities that were in control of their own affairs, whose citizens had an effective voice in the matters that touched their lives, would almost certainly choose not to pollute their own waters or to permit local industries to do so, out of sheer self-interest if not out of good sense—particularly if they were small, ecology-minded, economically stable, and democratically governed.

(And if by some chance a community or two did go on polluting, resistant to all appeals, their toxic effects would likely not overstrain the lake's ability to absorb them.) It is this process, moreover, that accounts for the failure of the concerned majority to have cleaned up the pollution once it existed. Individuals and communities conditioned to cooperative and federative behavior, particularly those whose interests are greatest (in this case fishing villages, towns with bathing beaches, beach clubs, marinas, lakefront hotels, boardwalk businesses), would almost certainly work out, and pay for, a way to restore the lake—especially if there were no federal or state governments to siphon off the locally generated money through taxation.

As with pollution, so with the other public services of the state. There is not a one of them, not one, that has not in the past been the province of the community or some agency within the community (family, church, guild) and that has been taken on by the state only because it first destroyed that province. There is not a one of them that could not be re-absorbed by a community in control of its own destiny and able to see what its natural humanitarian obligations, its humanitarian *opportunities*, would be. Invariably when the state has taken over the job of supplying blood for hospitals, there is a shortage, even when it offers money; the United States now gets much of its blood from overseas. Invariably when a community is asked to do it voluntarily, and when the community perceives that the blood is to be used for its own needs, there is a surplus. This is not magic altruism, the by-product of utopia; this is perceived *self-interest*, community-interest, made possible (capable of being perceived by the individual) only at the human scale.

Indeed, there is not one public service, not one, that could not be *better* supplied at the local level, where the problem is understood best and quickest, the solutions are most accessible, the refinements and adjustments are easiest to make, the monitoring is most convenient. If it be said that there is not sufficient expertise in a small community to tackle some of the complicated problems that come along, the answer is surely not a standing pool of federal talent but an appeal throughout neighboring communities and regions for a person or group who can come in to do the job. (This is in fact what the federal government itself most often does today, hence the great reliance on contract firms and $650-a-day consultants.) If it be said that some problems are too big for a small community to handle alone (an epidemic, a forest fire, or some widespread disaster),

319

the answer is clearly not the intervention of some outside force but the ready cooperation of the communities and regions involved, whose own self-interest, even survival, is after all at stake. And if it be said that there is not enough money in a small community to handle such problems—well, where do you suppose the government *got* its money in the first place, and how much more might there be in local pockets if $500 billion of it weren't spent by Washington, $200 billion by state capitals, every year?

I cannot imagine a world without problems and crises, without social and economic dislocations demanding some public response. I see no difficulty, however, in imagining a world where those are responded to at the immediate human level by those who perceive the immediate human effects and control their own immediate human destinies.

Social Justice

The final argument for the necessity of the state is that it alone can provide social justice for all its citizens and guarantee civil rights and liberties to every individual.

To be sure, it *doesn't*, not anywhere in the world. Even in this country, so concerned with these matters, the areas of social injustice and individual repression are wide, and certain people—Native Americans, poor blacks, prisoners, Hispanics, and, until recently, homosexuals among them—are particularly ill served by the state. Indeed, the case could easily be made that over the years as many inequities and injustices have been *caused* or fostered by the government with its left hand—let's mention only slavery, Native American genocide, union suppression, the Palmer Raids, Japanese prison camps, FBI and CIA illegalities, Watergate, illegal NSA intrusions, sky-high black incarceration—as are *prevented* by its right. Not that the United States should be singled out in this regard: over the world, states have been claiming to offer social justice and equality for five hundred years now without ever having achieved it, or an approximation of it, not even the most benevolent of them. And even the well-meaning attempts to do so, which have proved extremely costly and in many instances socially rebarbative, have very often been accompanied by iniquitous or punitive or violent ends, the state taking more power to itself in order to make its interference more successful—perhaps the long British campaign against slave-trading and Lincoln's war against the Confederacy and its aftermath may stand as sufficient examples of this.

320

But still, the state presumably *means* to protect its individuals, and presumably they would be worse off without state intervention. Didn't the American government abolish slavery, establish civil rights for blacks, outlaw segregated schools, and work to end racial discrimination in housing, hoteling, hiring? Hasn't it treated minorities—the Inuit in Alaska, the Hispanics in Texas—better than they would have been treated in racist local communities?

Perhaps. The record is by no means perfect even here on its more positive (right-hand) side, and many would say that alacrity was not among its notable features—but yes, the American government has effected certain reforms and has maintained certain freedoms. But who exactly would want to say that this is *because* of the state, that the government accomplished these goals by sighting a problem on its own, tackling it boldly, wresting a solution? I cannot think of a single victory in this area that has not been extracted by force from the government, has not been achieved by the affected parties themselves, pushing, cajoling, petitioning, suing, marching, demonstrating, usually quite on their own; and as often as not—as with the abolitionists of the 1840s, the labor organizers of the 1890s, the strikers of the 1930s, the McCarthy victims of the 1950s, the initial civil-rights demonstrators of the 1960s—they did so *against* the agents and stated policies of the national government. When we look at the great accomplishments here, what we find is the state against the victims of injustice—against Zenger, Thoreau, Nat Turner, Susan B. Anthony, Eugene Debs, Margaret Sanger, W. E. B. DuBois, Norman Thomas, Martin Luther King, the NAACP, the ACLU, the Communist Party, SDS, even (as in the Pentagon Papers) the *New York Times*.

What we generally have, in other words, is another example of the state, having taken power into its own hands, sitting on those hands until somebody shoves it off—at which point one of the hands goes to congratulate the shover and the other points grandly in a gesture of "Look-what-I've-done!" That minorities are protected as much as they are is due mostly to minorities; that individuals have the opportunities they have is due mostly to individuals; that the press has its freedoms is due mostly to the press. The Bill of Rights, we must not forget, was put there not as an instrument of the state for the citizens but as a means of protecting the citizens *from* the state.

It is also worth noting that even after all of these gains, it is fairly said that the freedom of the press is enjoyed only by the person who is rich enough to own one. Individuals still, as a rule, have very limited use of freedom of the press, very circumscribed access to free speech beyond their own shouting range, very restrained possibilities of free assembly that the police do not sanction; they still have very fragile real-world protection against searches, seizures, brutality, and cruel and unusual punishment by police agents of the state; and they still have only the most tenuous guarantees in practical terms of truly due processes of law, speedy trials, impartial (or any) juries, or freedom from cruel punishment in prison. And what is true for the ordinary, God-fearing, white, well-dressed, comfortable, and respectable individual is, sadly, even more true for the tinted, tattered, timid, tasteless, or tipsy one.

But is there an alternative: is it possible to think of a community achieving justice for individuals and minorities it did not find congenial?

Historically the community is noted for its failure in this regard: small towns, neighborhoods, even homogeneous cities, can be extraordinarily narrow-minded and cruel, inhospitable and downright vicious to people and opinions and customs they don't happen to like. But it is also true that they can be very receptive to minorities that they do not think of as threatening or that they regard as enriching, and they have a well-known capacity to tolerate a great variety of eccentric individuals—the town drunks, the Elwood P. Dowds, the Tom Edisons—who accept them in return. Should we posit communities in true harmony with their surroundings, with some democratic and cooperative operation of their economy, and some form of participatory governance, then it would be reasonable to suppose that much in the community would already operate to soften personal animosities, to accommodate differing minorities, to harmonize a wide range of opinions and beliefs. Without outside pressures, either legal or coercive, such a town could no doubt mute if not solve the essential problems of injustice and intolerance.

But even should this not be possible, there are the recourses known to centuries, indeed millennia, of human history: migration and division.

For the individual, the most successful relief from injustice, should the community be unresponsive, is not the appeal to the state, whose workings are always lengthy and uncertain, but migration and relocation.

This is not easy, especially for people burdened with families and homes and investments, but it is obviously the most immediate and effective solution; and in a nation where one out of five families change residences every year anyway, it cannot be all that difficult. If the individual cannot get along with the community, and the community cannot tolerate the individual, what real good will state intervention produce—wouldn't separation be, in any world, the rational, non-coercive, non-violent solution? Yes, it might be possible to contrive a state process that would force a Jewish community to accept the Nazi individual, or a racist white community the despised black, or a fundamentalist community the threatening atheist. But it needs only for the principle of free travel to be observed—to the advantage of both the leavers and the stayers—and the Nazi, the black, the atheist can all find congenial communities of their own. The virtue of a multi-communitied world would be precisely that there would be within its multitude of varieties a home for everyone.

And for the aggrieved minority, the obvious way to win relief is not to use the state to demand rights (which only inspires hostility in the majority) or to interpose restrictions (which ensures implacability in the majority), but to divide and resettle. As was true in the Dinka village and the New England town, and as we shall see in more detail in the next chapter, the eternal human solution to dissension has been division, the separation and sometimes relocation of the disgruntled minority. It is possible for a minority to use the machinery of the state over many years and, at the cost of considerable anguish and enmity, secure minority rights, but it is also possible for it to relocate with peace and goodwill and to create its own society on its own terms somewhere else. The commodious solution is not minority *rights*, but minority *settlements*.

Clearly I am not supposing a communitarian world without problems, even its instances of inadequacy and injustice. No one could expect that. I am only positing a world in which the community is empowered to seek the solutions right where the problems erupt, to deal within its bosom with the people it knows, and to seek migration and division when all else fails. Compared with the record of what the state in all its glory, all its centuries, has accomplished, this, for all its difficulties, seems simpler, safer, cheaper, surer.*

---

* It used to be argued that only national governments could achieve justice because they were free of the corruption of small towns—though anyone familiar with pre-Mao China or modern Africa or Asia might have doubted. Since Watergate, and NAFTA, and the NSA revelations, and the Panama Papers, we hear that less often.

In a hierarchy of necessities, the things provided by the family, the neighborhood, the community, the small city, would certainly come first: love, fraternity, security, cooperation, sex, comfort, order, esteem, above all *rootedness*. ("To be rooted," as Simone Weil has shrewdly noted, "is perhaps the most important and least recognized need of the human soul.") Those provided by the state—taxation, standing armies, police, regulations, bureaucracies, courts, politicians, nuclear power, corporate subsidies, moonshots—especially when taken in balance with its deficiencies, would no doubt come last. Looked at that way, they just may not even be necessities at all.

"Giant political systems are a necessity" in the mind of someone like Robert Dahl, and who is really to blame him? But in the light of what would seem to be the decentralist tenor of our times, of the documented and apparently unavoidable failures of the encrusted state, "a system incapable of action" as Jimmy Carter once put it, it is not irrational to disagree. Even such an arch-conservative as Herman Kahn has been forced to acknowledge that the institution of the state may be—though of course he probably would never use the term—"withering away." The nation-state, in his view, historically had two essential reasons-for-being: to wage war and to foster economies; it will shortly find, particularly in the developed world, that in a nuclear age the dangers of doing the first are too great to risk, and in a multinational age the second is unnecessary, so its role and importance will decline in the decades to come.

That does not seem so fantastic. If humans lived for the first three million years without a state, and most of them for the next 8,000 years without one, and the experiments with the nation-state as we know it are only a few hundred years old, there is clearly nothing eternal about it. It may have been a serviceable device for one small period of human history, but as we move out of that period it may begin to lose its value and its meaning in the daily life of the planet, even eventually disintegrating from disuse, to be remembered as we now remember the wooden plow or the sundial—a quaint tool, useful no doubt for its time, but of course no longer important, no longer . . . necessary.

24

The Importance of Size: Harmony

W e see it in the archaic villages, the Greek city-states, the medieval municipalities, the New England towns, the religious communities: the regulation of size. It is the instinctive, eternal application of the Beanstalk Principle to human affairs: for every harmonious, self-governing human unit there is a size beyond which it ought not to grow. And, one might add, a fairly conscribed size, too, as the long chronicle of human settlements, regardless of culture, complexity, or continent, amply shows.

In each of these societies, and in countless others, the regulation of size was most often achieved not through warfare or infanticide or starvation, though all were certainly known, but through *division*, whether the process be separation, segmentation, fission, resettlement, partition, or colonization.

When a village in the Dinka system became "too big" and split, a man who for some reason was bypassed in the village systems of power (the younger brother of the man to whom the office of spearmaster descended, for example) would be permitted to round up his family and a few followers in other families and start a new village nearby with its own grazing areas and water holes. Or families whose feuds with the rest of the village became so fierce that daily community life became tense would be encouraged to move elsewhere, perhaps with the parting gift of an extra cow or two.

In the eighteenth-century New England towns, the process of fission was so essential and regular that it made up the greatest part of the business that communities had to do with the colonial government in Boston, it being necessary to get state approval to establish a new town. Even separation into quite tiny settlements was preferred to continuing disputes or quarrels: "We acknowledge we are but small," ran a fairly typical petition from the town of Dunstable, "but we apprehend a small society well united may more easily go through such business of building a meeting house and settling a minister than a greater number when there is nothing but discord and disaffection."

In Switzerland, where regions have been dividing and subdividing for at least six centuries, the guiding principle has always been to provide minority territory rather than go through the endless struggles of minority rights. The canton of Appenzell, for example, while nations all around it were fighting bloody religious wars in the aftermath of the Reformation and would continue to persecute religious minorities for centuries more, peaceably agreed to divide itself: the new Lutheran minority cut itself off as the discrete community of Ausser Rhoden, the Catholics stayed in the new community of Inner Rhoden, and they lived in peace for the succeeding 400 years.

And so we find it elsewhere, too, practically everywhere that people are free to move and no coercive state insists on unity, the ancient and rational practice of *harmony through division*. The Beanstalk Principle at work.

And here we come to the last and perhaps the most fundamental reason proffered for the "necessity" of the state: that it provides social harmony and prevents criminal disruption. Ecological harmony and workplace democracy and all that are fine, so it is said, but given human nature we cannot assume that people will always be good or curb their impulses to destruction. It is therefore up to the state, and the state's apparatus of law and police and courts and jails, now as it has always been, to control criminal, deviant, and disruptive behavior.

The first answer, of course, is that, on the evidence, the state has *not* controlled or prevented crimes in any society where it has become powerful, particularly not in those modern nations where it has become most powerful of all. The United States, easily the mightiest in the Western world, has easily the highest crime rate and the greatest prison population. One project estimates that the FBI has spent $178.3 billion from 1962–2014, the Bureau of Prisons spent $151.6 billion in that time, about $28 billion a year was spent from 2013–17 in the war on drugs, and the Department of Justice is funded for about $30 billion a year; but despite a dip in the new century for most places, crime has not appreciably diminished, the public streets are not safer, and the populace does not feel itself significantly more secure. It might be regarded as perhaps too extreme to say that the state actually has less interest in *eliminating* crime than in justifying its existence and expanding its power by *allowing* crime to continue, but that at any rate is the effect of its performance, not only in the United States but around the world. The laws don't work, the police don't work, the courts don't work, the prisons don't work—this is not any contrivance of mine, this is the accepted judgment of criminologists of many stripes—and yet what we hear as the solutions, and what we are forced in fact to pay for, is more of the same. Can this be serving society's interests in any real way—or only the state's?

The second answer is that the state *cannot* control criminality—not at that size. For what we have to realize is that there is always and everywhere a connection between population size and social harmony, and the large state is beyond the point of effective stabilization.

———

Let's look at it from the standpoint of "human nature." There are no certainties here, and the issue continues to generate arguments among all kinds of scientists—ethologists, biologists, psychologists, anthropologists—and no doubt will for some time to come. But whether one wants to side with the aggressivists—Lorenz, Dart, Ardrey, et al., who argue that humans are naturally warlike and disputatious, bloodthirsty and competitive—or the pacifists—Montagu, Leakey, Dubos, et al., who find that humans are essentially cooperative and neighborly, peaceful and altruistic—there seems to be this common ground: humans have the capacity for great evil and great good, great aggressiveness and great generosity, and a given set of circumstances tends to promote one and discourage the other. Thus a human male defending his family might, like the baboon male in similar straits, become a raging, killing maniac, shorn of mercy or reason; or a human male enjoying a feast might, like the chimpanzee in similar circumstances, share his food with any fellow creatures who happen along, the very soul of generosity and brotherhood. A person surrounded by subways and blaring radios, beset on every side with clamor, confusion, filth, boredom, and hopelessness, might well strike out in rage when provoked; a person surrounded by calm, decorousness, purposefulness, and comfort is less likely to. Behavior basically depends on the setting—the time and place and society in which it happens. Obviously the desired effort is to find those settings in which the benevolent side of our human nature is encouraged and the malevolent side dampened: that will not *ensure* constant and unvarying harmony, it seems safe to say, but it certainly will go a long way to permitting it and fostering it.

And without question such settings, as our examination of stateless societies has shown, are those of the small community. In small places it is difficult to commit malevolent acts without being seen and identified, and therefore known and punished, and this sense of being in the public eye, whatever the unpleasant consequences, certainly discourages misbehavior. Moreover, if the result of being identified is the disapprobation of friends, or ostracism, or ultimately exile, this puts a heavy and very real social weight against disruption. Self-interest also enters in as a deterrent, since if your acts are likely to create serious turmoil in the community and prevent it from being able to protect itself or carry on its commerce or harvest its crops, that is going to adversely affect you, too.

In a more positive vein, living at a small scale generally creates a sense of friendship among neighbors, or at least of trust and honesty, and it becomes very difficult to violate that, even if individual self-interest didn't argue for its reciprocity. Likewise, can a sense of cooperation and mutuality arise among those who continually rub shoulders—it is difficult to think of "cooperation" among millions, but very easy to conceive of it among hundreds—that works against aberrant behavior both practically and psychologically? Psychological health, indeed, is essential for social harmony, and as we saw in discussing city sizes the evidence is strong that the small, cohesive community is by far the most beneficial unit because it provides a spirit of belonging, of place—what the Spanish call *querencia*, suggesting the inner well-being that comes with knowing a particular spot as your home. It also works psychologically in providing predictability and order, and thus cushioning against the dislocations of "future shock" that make city dwellers anxious, and in supplying the systems of support and friendship that encourage a sense of individual security and self-worth. (French philosopher Michel Foucault even argued that the concept, if not the very fact, of madness was born in the sixteenth century, after the decline of the stable and supportive small medieval community.)

The increased participation in all aspects of life that is fostered by the small community is also beneficial. In social terms this allows an individual to ventilate grievances and to make changes, escaping the pressures that tend to build up in people who feel powerless or useless or ignored. And in political terms participation allows people to see that the process of decision making, having included them, is fair, and that the decisions themselves, having been influenced by them, are fairly arrived at—the very two reasons, not so incidentally, that historically people have obeyed laws and honored social norms.

What we know about human nature, in short, suggests that its better side is more likely to emerge in smaller settings than in larger ones. And if we then suppose those settings to incorporate some of the human-scale features we have already noted, the likelihood of social harmony is even further increased. To the degree that a community can incorporate into its society a regard for the human being's natural and interlocking place in the biosphere, it will encourage people not to do unnecessary violence to any part of that world, their fellow creatures presumably included. To the extent that it can provide organizations and systems at sizes where individuals may feel some sense of control, it diminishes the kinds of psychological and social dislocations that arise when people face large, depersonalized, and violent ones. And to the degree that it can develop a community-controlled, self-sufficient, and participatory economy, it is likely to remove many of the causes of crime, because that should provide everyone with not only the general economic satisfactions but the fullest and most rewarding kinds of employment.

That all may discourage malevolent behavior, right enough, but even in such a world, I think we should be prepared to say, there will be deviates and "criminals," people who for reasons sane or insane may cause private harm or shatter public harmony. What is to be done with them?

Obviously any community may make its own rules and regulations—will have to make them, unless it wants half the people stopping on green lights, the other half on red—and can set its own patterns as to how its transgressors are to be judged and treated. And I'm afraid the record here is not unblemished: we know that "witches" were burned in small towns, popular justice can sometimes get inflamed into lynch-mobbery, and Shirley Jackson's "The Lottery" is not wholly far-fetched. But for the most part these were the aberrations, not the rule—as they would have to have been, if the town was not to lose half its population at the stakes and hanging trees, as we know from the accounts of myriad small societies around the world whose justice, however rough, did not often descend to this sort of irrationality. And for the contemporary self-governing community there are so many examples of other fair and reasonable means there is little reason to think that the bizarre ones would ever prevail.

The first thing the commodious community would do would be to put an end to executions: official violence always begets violence rather than deterring it, it creates severe psychological tensions in any close-knit population where it is sanctioned, and it ultimately puts a disastrous social weight at the wrong, the punitive, end of the process of justice. The practice of imprisonment would also seem to be counterproductive, since the whole bizarre notion of sending someone to jail to get rehabilitated is as sensible as sending someone into a rainstorm to cure a cold; and the financial costs of building and maintaining prisons—it now costs an unbelievable $30,620 a year to maintain a federal prisoner (2014), money that would be better spent if it was just given to the inmate, who would then be put on parole—clearly outweigh whatever they offer in temporary security. (Interestingly, the institution of the civil prison is unknown through most of history, becoming common only with the rise of the nation-state in the nineteenth century.) Even those individuals driven so mad that they need to be kept away from others lest they do more harm—and I must add that they are quite rare in the records of village life—do not have to be put into prisons to safeguard the populace—they can be treated therapeutically in hospitals or kept under the watch of family or therapists in controlled settings, at a neighborhood scale.

For the normal run of wrongdoing, a variety of non-violent options is open to a community conscious of the fact that it is dealing not with an unwanted monster but a friend and neighbor who is part of its daily life. Some sort of therapy, or "re-education," can be sanctioned in the worst instances, where there is some thought that misperceptions or ignorance are at work; or a system of reparation and restitution, requiring the transgressor to repay the injured party or the community at large through money, property, or labor; or community ostracism or humiliation, which can be particularly painful in small societies; or the withdrawal of mutual aid and of the normal forms of cooperation. Each of these has been used by self-regulating communities and all of them have been shown to be generally successful in deterring and in punishing, depending of course on the effective social cohesion and interdependence of the population. Compared with what these can achieve, the recourses of the state apparatus in being today seem crude indeed.

Essentially all that such a method of justice requires is a sense of *responsibility*: to the individual transgressor, to the customs and patterns of the community, to the collectivity as a whole. That is not a great deal to ask, nor in the self-governing community is it rare to find. It is only in the giant systems of the contemporary world that we see so little of it, for it is here, where the state takes over responsibility, that the individual is asked to shoulder none. An individual living in New York City cannot feel a responsibility to deter a crime or stop a robber running down the street or see that a suspect is properly processed or guarantee that justice will be meted out or assure that punishment will not be cruel: these are the things that the state is supposed to be responsible for and there is very little way one could (safely or effectively) have anything to do with them. Hardly surprising, in a system in which all power and responsibility lie with some remote government, that there is very little that black communities are able to do to diminish the high crime rates around them.

———

I have so far begged the question of *what* size it is that we might expect to find most desirable for achieving social harmony and stability. But it will be apparent from my use of the words *neighbor* and *community* that I think it is to be found in populations in the range we have used for community throughout.

Of the general connection between the size and social control there is no disagreement whatsoever: the larger the group, the more difficult it is to keep pace. Anthropologist William Rathje, who has studied a variety of ancient societies in the Americas, puts this as a general theory: as the size of a population *doubles*, its complexity—the amount of information exchanged and decisions required—*quadruples*, with a consequent increase in stress and dislocation and a consequent increase in the power and sweep of the mechanisms of social control. That seems perfectly plausible when we consider that in a group of 25 people there are theoretically 300 possible conflicts between two people at any given moment and in a group of 10,000 no fewer than 50 million possible conflicts.

Anthropology and history both suggest, as we have seen, that humans have been able to work out most of their differences at the population levels clustering around the "magic numbers" of 500–1,000 and 5,000–10,000.

For the first, John Pfeiffer notes that anthropological literature indicates that it is when a population reaches about 1,000 that "a village begins to need policing," and as we have seen, traditional Dinka villages (before the civil wars), like villages in most stateless societies, hold about 500 people on average and almost never more than 1,000. (Rough figures for village sizes in some other stateless societies: 100–1,000 for the Mandavi, 50–400 for the Amba, 300–500 for the Lugbara, 200–300 for the Konkomba, 400–500 for the Tupi.) Evidently in these face-to-face societies, where every person is known to every other—and presumably every idiosyncrasy, sore spot, boiling point, and final straw—it is comparatively easy to keep the peace and comparatively easy to restore it once broken. Confirmation comes from the New England towns, the great majority of which were under 1,000, where harmony was the regular rule and "concord and consensus" the norm; from the Chinese villages of all periods until the most recent, with rarely more than 500 people, where traditional law of many varying kinds operated independently of dynastic decrees; from Russia, where the traditional *mir*, with seldom more than 600–700 people, was the basic peacekeeping unit for more than a millennium, each with its own version of customary law and all without codification or judicial apparatus.

Even in the archaic societies, however, wider "tribal" units of several thousand people, though rarely more than 10,000, were common—this being apparently the level best suited for the settlement of those disputes that would break out among the villages, the level found effective for the combined defense of the villages against outside threats. Common customs would prevail among groupings of this size and common agreements could exist as to how disputes could be settled peaceably; beyond this level, where no formal agreements existed nor even any machinery for accommodation, disputes when they arose tended to escalate to violence. The reason is conjectural but reasonable: at such levels, up to about 10,000, it is not possible to be on a first-name basis with everyone, but there would be enough interaction at ceremonial occasions, on market days, during seasonal migrations, and in occasional wartime camaraderie so that the elders of any one of the dozen or so villages would be known to all the others and some rough assessment of their capabilities and temperaments made by all. This is, interestingly, the maximum level at which the basic Greek criterion for successful harmony would seem to operate—"that the citizens should be known to each other," as Plato put it, that "they must know each other's characters," as Aristotle said—for much beyond 5,000–8,000 and, even in a densely knit society, it is humanly impossible to recognize the faces, much less the characters, of most citizens.

There is also some evidence that tends to confirm the stability of small populations in many different settings. On the whole the more successful city-states of Greece, Italy, and Germany—peaceful, as a rule, in their internal affairs no matter how many defensive wars they were forced to fight—ranged from as small as 5,000 to nearly 20,000, though to be sure the smaller were the more peaceful. Some of the most pacific societies in the world—San Marino, the world's oldest republic, dating from the fourth century; Andorra, which has been a quiet and stable state since the thirteenth century; Liechtenstein, virtually without a police force for most of its 250 years and never once having an army—lived most of their lives with populations of 8,000–12,000, though today they are all closer to 25,000 (and beginning to display the resultant difficulties).

Or take the undeniably pacific nation of Switzerland. This land of small villages and small cantons has, by staying atomized, always offered stability; in the words of the sixteenth-century Venetian diplomat, Giovanni Battista Padavino: "Traveling in Switzerland is very secure; one can travel the roads day or night without any danger and can halt in woods or mountains, and every class and family enjoys its own profound peace and unbelievable security." Nothing much has changed to this day, and outside of the major cities, crime rates are among the lowest in Europe. All this with populations of only rarely more than 10,000; even as late as 2010, 88 percent of the communes were under 5,000 people per commune, 37 percent in the 1,0000–5,000 range, and only 4.3 percent were over 10,000.

Or take our own country. It is a universal truth, confirmed time and again by sociologists and criminologists, that in general the bigger the city the bigger the crime rate, in all categories. For example, during a period of relative quiet for crime, property crimes in 2015 decreased the most in cities under 10,000; a 12 percent drop in non-metropolitan areas compared with a 6 percent drop in metropolitan areas. A few years before a study found that there were 409.4 crimes per 100,000 people in metropolitan areas as against only 117 in non-metro areas.

In sum, I do not think it is a reach to conclude once again that humankind seems to have worked out another problem—the one of keeping the peace—in fairly small units, roughly corresponding to the neighborhood and the community, and moves beyond those limits not to its swift and immediate, but to its eventual and ultimate, detriment. Just as certain circumscriptions must be placed on population levels so as to achieve ecological balance and economic self-sufficiency, so—and in direct and overlapping ways—must they be placed for harmony and stability.

Gandhi once said it was foolish to dream of systems so perfect that people would no longer need to be good. That may be true, though I must say I despair at the thought of constructing systems where people *do* need to be good: that seems like a difficult goal, no matter what your view of human nature might be, and one that various saints have failed at time and again over many thousands of years. I would rather contemplate a system so simple that people would no longer need to be bad—that is to say, a system of support and sustenance, of rough equality and comfort, that would so guide and goad, chide and chivvy, prompt and protect, that the individuals in it would be inclined out of sheer self- and community-interest toward morality and harmony. The small community has provided such a system—not molded through any special design, nor guided by any millennial genius, nor organized by any party or sect, but simply by working out the rough, hard problems of existence as they have come along for many thousands of years. I see no reason to think that, left alone, it could not do so again. The mistake is probably to try to devise systems that revise human nature, reforming people and making them moral and upright; the better part of wisdom is to take people as they are and determine under what conditions they are by themselves more likely to perform the moral act than the immoral—to reform the conditions, not the people.

"You are a very bad man," Dorothy told the Wizard.

"No, my dear, I'm a very good man," the Wizard replied. "I'm just a very bad wizard."

As I see it, the idea of the human-scale community is that it can provide the opportunity for there to be very good men without the necessity of there being very bad wizards.

25

The Importance of Size: Democracy

We have already seen the myriad ways in which it is ludicrous for successive governments in Washington, DC, to declare themselves "democracies." We do not, as I have made clear, any longer have "representatives," people who *represent* our views or feelings or even interests or lifestyles; nor do we have the elemental qualities of citizenship that are essential in a democracy; nor do we even have that democracy itself. Whatever its patrons may find to say in favor of our present system of government, there is no pretense, except perhaps in some unrevised sixth-grade civics text, that it is designed to evince the popular will, or allow even a majority of the people to establish national policies, or let the public en masse behave as truly sovereign. It might be better to call our system—a system in which some of the people select between two candidates who are already beholden to other interests and are in no way bound to listen to these voters—an oligarchy of the elite, which we have had the good fortune to experience as essentially benign during most of its duration. But it is not a democracy.

I do not especially wish to debate the merits of democracy, since its merits have been amply proven by innumerable political philosophers over the last several thousand years and, one would think, should be axiomatic by now. Suffice it to say that, whatever else its problems, in its uncorrupted forms—and where the majority is kept severely in check—democracy provides more benevolence, stability, participation, responsibility, productivity, efficiency, diversity, justice, fairness, freedom, and happiness than any other known system of government.

Nor is there much point debating what democracy is. Democracy means the direct one-person-one-vote popular assembly of every citizen.

It does not mean the bill-of-rights freedoms, it does not mean republican government, it does not mean federalism or pluralism. Above all, it does not mean *representation*: representative government may be a desirable expedient in a government of great size, but as we have clearly seen it has nothing to do with citizen participation, popular decision making, or democracy. Rousseau may have been a great waffler on many questions, but about this he was Alpine clear:

> *Sovereignty . . . consists essentially in the general will, and the will cannot be represented. Either it is itself or it is something else; there is no middle ground. The deputies of the people, therefore, are not nor can they be its representatives; they are merely its agents. They cannot conclude anything definitively. Any law that the people in person has not ratified is null; it is not a law. . . .*
>
> *The instant a people chooses representatives, it is no longer free; it no longer exists.*

The only true democracy, therefore, is direct democracy.

———————

Many disparate types of theorists have analyzed the nature of democratic government, but virtually all are agreed on one point: a true democracy requires a small society. The human mind is limited, the human voice finite; the number of people who can be gathered together in one place is restricted, the time and attention they are capable of giving is bounded. From simply a human regard, there is a limit to the number of people who can be expected to know all of the civic issues, all of the contending opinions, all of the candidates for office.

The Greeks in general, whether partisans of democracy or not, agreed with Aristotle that the well-run polis had to be small: "If citizens of a state are to judge and to distribute offices according to merit, then they must know each other's characters; where they do not possess this knowledge, both the election to offices and the decisions of lawsuits will go wrong." European thinkers, likewise, though not all of them democrats, assumed with Rousseau and Montesquieu and Hume that populations and territories had to be kept circumscribed. "A fundamental rule for every well-constituted and legitimately governed society," Rousseau said, "would be that all the members could be easily assembled every time this would be necessary," and therefore "it follows that the State ought to be limited to one town at the most"; and though he is never specific as to the size of its population —indeed, he argues sensibly that it depends on the geography and fertility of a region—he refers at one point to maximum freedom in a state of 10,000.

All subsequent democratic theory has proceeded from like assumptions. The triumph of the American and French Revolutions recast much of this theory into national molds, and there were those who tried to argue that large-scale representative or republican systems retained "the essence" of democracy, but Madison himself acknowledged that a "pure democracy" was "a society consisting of a small number of citizens, who assemble and administer the government in person." Even John Stuart Mill, who was dealing with an England of millions, agreed that "the only government which can fully satisfy all the exigencies of the social state is one in which the whole people participate," and that, he said, cannot take place "in a community exceeding a single small town." The twentieth century—and with undoubted good reason—has had occasion to reiterate that view in the face of mass parties, mass politics, and mass governments claiming to be democratic. John Dewey may have spoken for his generation—"Democracy must begin at home, and its home is the neighborly community"—as Lewis Mumford for his—"Democracy, in any active sense, begins and ends in communities small enough for their members to meet face to face." More recently, the eminent Robert Dahl: "Any argument that no political system is legitimate unless all the basic laws and decisions are made by the assembled people leads inexorably to the conclusion that the citizen body must be quite small in number." And Leopold Kohr puts it in this delightful perspective:

A citizen of the Principality of Liechtenstein, whose population numbers less than fourteen thousand, desirous to see His Serene Highness the Prince and Sovereign, Bearer of many exalted orders and Defender of many exalted things, can do so by ringing the bell at his castle gate. However serene His Highness may be, he is never an inaccessible stranger. A citizen of the massive American republic, on the other hand, encounters untold obstacles in a similar enterprise. Trying to see his fellow citizen President, whose function is to be his servant,

337

> *not his master, he may be sent to an insane asylum for observation*
> *or, if found sane, to a court on charges of disorderly conduct. Both*
> *happened in 1950. [And times subsequently.] . . . You will say that in*
> *a large power such as the United States informal relationships such*
> *as exist between government and citizen in small countries are tech-*
> *nically unfeasible. This is quite true. But this is exactly it. Democracy*
> *in its full meaning is impossible in a large state which, as Aristotle*
> *already observed, is "almost incapable of constitutional government."*

This *is* exactly it.

The actual experience of direct democracy over the ages seems to have confirmed these theoretical insights—was no doubt the source of many of them—and suggests the possible population sizes at which it may operate. The results will not surprise you.

The cradle of direct democracy, of course, was Greece, from about the seventh to the fourth centuries BC, and the hand that rocked the cradle was quite small indeed: the *Encyclopaedia Britannica* may even be a little generous in asserting that Hellenic democracy operated in areas that were "generally confined to a city and its rural surroundings, and seldom had more than 10,000 citizens." Athens itself may have outgrown those limits at several points in its career, and possibly a few other cities as well, but the Greek experience overall indicates that about 5,000 people would be the upper limit for regular and sustained participation in daily or weekly matters. The Athenian assembly at its best periods seems to have numbered around 5,000—one record suggests a quorum may have been 6,000, and Plato speaks of the ideal number of citizens as 5,040—and though that seems to us a large number for debate and decision, it seems to have worked. Obviously certain constraints have to apply at that number. Not everyone can speak on every issue, for example, because if they met for ten hours a day and each one talked for as little as ten minutes it would take them eighty-four days to debate a single issue.* Not all issues can be brought to the group for

---

* This is what Bertrand de Jouvenel has called "the Chairman's Problem"
(*American Political Science Review*, June 1961), and pertains in a group of any size.

discussion, because the maximum number of decisions that could be taken, even assuming a fairly rapid rate of one a day, would be no more than about three hundred a year. That in turn means that some degree of cohesion and agreement has to exist beforehand in the community at large; it needs the refinement of many issues to a limited number of viewpoints (this, of course, is what the *agora* and *gymnasia* were all about) and the acceptance of a limited number of spokespeople to put forth a particular cause; and it requires a willingness to let minor decisions be taken by functionaries (chosen by lot or election) operating outside the assembly. But given these restraints, and they seem to have come perfectly naturally to Greece, the Hellenic system was beyond question, despite its occasional flaws and lapses, one of the finest that humankind seems ever to have crafted.

Interestingly enough, the other extraordinarily successful experience of direct democracy took place in another mountainous country, and the record there is even longer. The Swiss mountain cantons, whether as completely independent entities in the earlier centuries, or as parts of various loose alliances and federations later on, used a system of regular popular assemblies, referendums, and initiatives from the thirteenth well into the nineteenth century. Even now, according to Cambridge University historian Jonathan Steinberg, "underlying the provisions of a Swiss constitution is the assumption that ultimately the ideal state is the direct democracy or the *Landsgemeinde*, the assembly of all free citizens in the historic ring," and he notes: "This, the pure form, not the clauses of a constitution or its preamble, is the truly venerable element in Swiss political life." The ancient "fundamental law" of Canton Schwyz gives some notion of what the *Landsgemeinde* must have meant:

> *The May* Landsgemeinde *is the greatest power and prince [in the old sense of that word, meaning principal body] of the land and may without condition do and undo, and whoever denies this and asserts that the* Landsgemeinde *be not the greatest power nor the prince of the land and that it may not do and undo without condition is proscribed. Let a price of one hundred ducats be set on his head.*

Even the punishment is typically Swiss.

Because each canton was a federation of districts, and each district was divided into communes, each commune was made up of sovereign villages, it is not possible to describe the "typical" democratic system in Switzerland. But in the main the *Landsgemeinde* covered a population averaging 2,000–3,000 people, of whom only the adult men were allowed to debate and vote (hence an assembly of around 500), and would meet roughly once a month or in some places once a year. The meetings were wide-open affairs, with plenty of horse-trading and even some vote-buying going on beforehand, and any number of factions would appear in the course of debate; but somehow after the decisions were taken, the divisions healed—they could hardly be allowed to fester in such small populations—and implementation was normally accepted and shared by all. In between meetings, for any particular matter of even the remotest seriousness, the *Landsgemeinde* officials would submit referendums to the citizens and accept as a matter of course the direction of the vote; at the same time the citizens whenever they wanted could force an initiative with a small number of signatures on a petition, and if the initiative passed it had the force of law. So well entrenched are both the referendum and initiative that they are active parts of the politics of a number of modern-day Swiss cantons, and of the federal system as well.

Modern Switzerland has found, though, that increasing popula-tions—and increasing pressures from the outside (especially corporate) world—have forced changes in their traditional democracies. There are only two cantons (out of twenty-six) that run their affairs through annual cantonal meetings of all the citizens, but the turnout tends to drop as the size increases, and the cantons average about 308,000 people now (2011), ranging from 1.4 million to 15,854 (2009). Town meetings show similar effects: the city of Grenchen, with 16,000 people and 9,000 voters, has found that only about 400 people show up for town meetings these days, whereas in nearby Wangen, with 1,900 people, 90 percent of the citizens may turn out for votes and assemblies. If there is a "tipping point" for Swiss democracy to work effectively, it would seem by my calculations to come at around 10,000, perhaps slightly fewer.

The last historical example of direct democracy in action is one we have already touched on: the New England town meeting. As a rule, the towns in which they took place traditionally held no more than about 1,000 people, meaning that the assembly itself would attract upward of about 200 peo-ple (originally, only property-owning males were theoretically eligible), depending on the issues to be discussed or officials to be elected. At first, in the seventeenth century, the meetings would be monthly affairs, some-times even weekly, but gradually by the eighteenth century the practice was to have them quarterly or annually and to let the elected officers of the town—typically there would be more than forty of them, from selectman to meeting-hall-sweeper—and the various designated committees—usually a dozen, from finance to roads—carry on the town business in the interim. These meetings, however infrequent, left little enough initiative to the town officers, though—they would declare on everything from whether the town should have a new bridge to which bushes marked the town boundaries, and the officials were entrusted merely with carrying out their wishes. And even when a town official made bold enough to propose a new course, he would not act on it until authorized by the town meeting, no matter how urgent, because he knew full well that it would never be carried out unless it had the meeting's sanction.

Town meetings still exist today in many parts of New England, though except in Vermont they are a dying institution as states intrude to take over more local functions and the federal purse looms behind practically any project of size. But they still decide the laws that are to govern the town, the budget to be followed, the local taxes to be paid, the policies to guide the town officers, and who those officers are to be, much as they did 300 years ago. It is no longer local control in any real sense, what with the press of outside polities, but it is still direct democracy and, as political scientist Jane Mansbridge has determined, there are "citizens still directly controlling important decisions that affected their lives." Her reaction, in one town of 500:

> I left the town meeting grinning. . . . These people had debated ener-getically the practical and the ideological sides of issues vital to their town. They had taken responsibility for the decisions that they would have to live with. Votes had been close. Farmers and workers had spoken out often and strong. The town had no obvious "power elite."

Most such towns that still have annual meetings are small, averaging perhaps 4,000 or so, though they include many places of 500 and quite a number with 7,000–8,000. Joseph Zimmerman, a professor of political science at the New York State University at Albany and one of the leading academic experts on the town meeting, believes that there are definite limits on how well they can operate before things get so large that only special-interest groups bother to turn out:

> *A lot of studies claim that the New England town meeting is undemocratic, because only special interest groups show up and only a small percentage of the voters come out, which is certainly true once a town gets up to 8,000 or 10,000 residents. But below that level it is a sort of informal representative government, where the people who don't go in effect elect the people who do go to act for them. If they don't like the results, they turn out in force the next time.*

Again, the upper limits of the community.

———

The most enterprising modern examination of the connection between population sizes and democratic government that I know of is a slim volume called *Size and Democracy*, by Robert Dahl (an absolutely indefatigable toiler in the theoretic vineyards, as we've seen) and Edward R. Tufte of Princeton University. As befits a scholarly study, it is barely able to offer itself of any firm conclusion, and it is evident that the authors are quite bewildered by their own evidence, which in the end they choose mostly to disregard. But the evidence is clear enough, and hardly surprising: in smaller units, people are more politically active, can understand the issues and personalities far more clearly, participate more in all aspects of government, and regard themselves as having some effective control over the decisions of their lives.

There have been any number of surveys of citizen behavior both in this country and around the world, and Dahl and Tufte have surveyed most of them. Their summary: "Citizens tend to believe that their local government is a more human-sized institution, that what it does is more understandable, that it handles questions they can more readily grasp, and thus is more rewarding, less costly, to deal with." As to power:

> *Citizens saw local units as more accessible, more subject to their control, more manageable. In the United States, only one citizen in ten thought he would stand much chance of success in changing a proposed national law he considered unjust; but more than one out of*

342

four thought they could succeed in changing a proposed local regulation they considered unjust.

As to participation:

In a number of countries, including the United States, levels of political participation other than voting are higher at local than at national levels. . . . Two to four times as many people said they had tried to influence their local government as said they had tried to influence their national government.

As to equality:

Only in smaller-scale politics can differences in power, knowledge, and directness of communication between citizens and top leaders be reduced to a minimum. . . . Larger-scale politics necessarily limits democracy in one respect: the larger the scale of politics, the less able is the average citizen to deal directly with his top political leaders.

In short:

The relative immediacy, accessibility, and comprehensibility of local politics may provide many citizens with a greater sense of competence and effectiveness than they feel in the remoter reaches of national politics. What defenders of local government have contended throughout an epoch of growing centralization and nationalization of political life may prove to be more, not less, valid in the future: the virtues of democratic citizenship are, at least for the ordinary citizen, best cultivated in the smaller, more familiar habitat of local governments.

As the centerpiece of their findings, Dahl and Tufte offer evidence from what they call "the largest and most careful study bearing on the relation of size to democracy" ever undertaken, a $1 million survey by the Local Government Research Group of Sweden and the departments of five Swedish universities, from 1966–70. In a close examination of the populations of thirty-six different-sized localities carefully selected to elicit the maximum information about citizen political participation and feelings of power, the group found that political awareness, political discussion, membership in political and voluntary organizations, and involvement in local government were far greater in units under 8,000 people than in any larger sizes. As Dahl and Tufte say, with some italicized astonishment: "The major finding of the study is that in Sweden the values of *participation and effectiveness are best achieved in densely populated communes with populations under 8,000.*"

Even a democracy at its optimum size can have its problems, however, and it seems pertinent to confront the two most common: that it tends to operate with either-or voting systems that do not represent accurately the true popular will, and that it thus tends to promote factionalism, especially of the majority against the minority. The criticisms are valid enough, and experience even in small communities has shown them to be all too likely. The problem lies, however, not with democracy, but in the method of decision making.

Majoritarian voting—win-lose, binary, or zero-sum, as the games theorists who have studied it like to say—is both imperfect and unrepresentative. The famous "voting paradox," first formulated by the Marquis de Condorcet in the eighteenth century, shows that majority-rule voting, despite our grade school teaching, in fact has no necessary relation to the actual preferences of the majority of the voters. In one form we see it in the presidential pairwise elections, as for example a case in which (as we would know from polls) Ford could beat Reagan, Reagan could beat Carter, and Carter could beat Ford, so the true attitude of the electorate is unknowable. In a more sophisticated form, we might imagine that Reagan was actually favored by 44 percent of the voters, Ford by 30, and Carter by only 26. The Reagan supporters, however, are split 22–22 among Republicans and Democrats, while the Ford people are 24–6 Republicans, so in a primary runoff Ford would win 24–22. In the general election, however, Ford goes up against Carter, but having alienated the Reagan people he pulls none of those Democrats and only half of those Republicans, 11 percent, for a total of 41 percent with his own supporters counted in; Carter, with some of the alienated Reaganites, perhaps 18 percent, and his own 26, gets a total of 44 percent. Thus the man actually preferred by a distinct minority of the public can win in a series of pairwise elections.

The same sort of thing is often seen, too, in legislation, where a bill will pass or fail depending solely on the order in which the amendments to it are considered; indeed, it is possible to arrive at any one of three different outcomes depending purely on what part is up for a vote at what time, which pretty much plays havoc with "will of the people." In schematic form, the paradox looks like this:

One-third of the legislators prefer A to B to C
One-third of the legislators prefer B to C to A
One-third of the legislators prefer C to A to B
Therefore, if A vs. C, C wins, then C vs. B, B wins
If B vs. C, B wins, then B vs. A, A wins
If A vs. B, A wins, then A vs. C, C wins

Therefore, *any outcome* is possible, theoretically representing the "majority will," depending merely upon the order of the vote.

Majoritarian voting also generally leads to confrontation of one sort or another and hence to divisiveness. Life is very seldom either-or, but voting is, and that tends to cause a great many in-between possibilities to get lost and makes people cluster unnaturally around one or another pole. Particularly on a larger scale, but also in face-to-face democracies, such factionalism can get formalized into parties, which represent the rigidification, one might almost say the ossification, of politics. Too many sociological studies show how even fairly small units can break into bitterly opposed camps over electoral matters, creating divisions that can move into social affairs as well.

An alternative that normally avoids both these deficiencies of majoritarianism, and one that has been studied extensively in recent years, is the process of consensus. (Not to be spelled *concensus* and confused with poll-taking; *consensus* comes from the Latin *con*, together, and *sentire*, to feel.) Despite the contemporary misuse of the word, it means the achievement of an agreement with which all the people present can feel comfortable and none disagree strongly enough to blackball—not total agreement, merely agreement not to obstruct—and clearly where it can work it obviates the problems of both voting and factionalism. And it also solves the difficulties surrounding what are perceived to be "immoral" or "unjust" majoritarian votes—to go to war, to enslave a person, to deny rights to homosexuals, to permit leg-hold animal traps—since such actions cannot be taken where there is even a single person morally opposed and willing to speak out. To be sure, that will tilt consensual communities toward conservatism, since a lack of consensus will mean inaction on any given measure; but it will by the same token make them more stable, more predictable and more "comfortable," and less prone to ill-considered decisions.

It can be argued that there are certain issues so pressing and demanding that they should be addressed by measures certain to provide a quick decision, avoiding democracy in any form, and certainly consensus. This has been heard recently, for example, on the question of climate change, by those who argue that unless action is taken quickly the atmosphere will become so overheated that life on earth will be threatened—no time to wait around for the deniers to be converted and the developing nations to give up their ideas of industrialization. The problem here is that even if we assume that the United Nations Secretary General becomes a dictator overnight, he will find that not everyone is agreed on just what kind of quick actions should be taken, by whom, and where. An arbitrary decision for this or that course might solve the problem, and might not, but the price, in either case, would be the trampling of whatever systems of government existed hitherto and a world of such massive, centralized autocracy that the rescued earth would hardly be worth living on. Besides, whatever decision was made could not be either swiftly or efficiently carried out since such an autocracy would be impossibly corrupt, bureaucratized, inept, and, like a monstrous cargo ship at sea, extremely difficult to maneuver. The game could not possibly be worth the candle.

I also want to emphasize that the *process* of consensus is nearly as important as its result. The emphasis is on a search for agreement rather than, as in majoritarian assemblies, the clarity of divisions—on compromise and cooperation, that is, rather than maneuvering and competition. In order to try to get a whole meeting over to your position, it will not help to score debating points or ignore opponents' criticisms, and if you want to get out before dawn it is best to work out some arrangement with the other points of view rather than simply to solidify your own. As often as not the compromise, because it is a synthesis of a number of positions, turns out to be stronger and more durable than any original position, as iron gains strength when manganese and tungsten and carbon are added in the process of making steel. And because it has the assent of all the people who will be affected by it, it stands a better chance of commanding obedience and being implemented the day after—whereas in towns with majoritarian voting it is not uncommon to hear of decisions that remain null after a vote because it would cause too much friction to carry them out or there aren't enough volunteers to do the job. (In big cities, of course, they are carried out by duly appointed officers whether anyone likes them the next day or not.)

When it works, consensus has some remarkable effects. Hallock Hoffman is here trying to sell the system and may not be completely objective, but he is describing the process as he experienced it during many decades of Quaker meetings, all of which are governed by consensus:

> *Although it may take longer for the meeting to act, when it acts it acts as a whole. No protection for minorities is necessary. There is no minority. Decisions need no refurbishing, as they often do under majority processes. Members develop the habit of questioning their own opinions—the individual conscience is uncoercively subjected to the examination and illumination of the group. In complement, the meeting questions itself and checks itself as a whole from suppressing the conscientious declaration of any member. Perhaps most important, when the meeting achieves its ideal, discussion is remarkably free and candid. The commitment is to truth, to light, and to divine inspiration. The love of all for each and for the meeting permits disagreement, inquiry into reasons for opinions, and mutual probing into matters elsewhere considered personal rather than public. In psychological terms, each member, secure in the affection of each other member, feels free from defensiveness and anxiety. The result is not victory for any part of the group. The only victory lies in the common achievement, without repression to anyone, of a decision satisfactory to all.*

It is, self-evidently, a process that is not without problems. It relies upon a certain common understanding, a shared commitment. It works only when the group begins with some points of unity, in religion, geography, purpose, or philosophy, and best with all of these. It demands more time than up-and-down voting, more time in give-and-take, than most people are used to spending. It may not work in emergencies—though the story of the Quaker ship's successful consensual decision making on a journey to war-torn Vietnam tends to belie that—and it may mean delaying actions for weeks until differences can be reconciled. It depends upon some minimal participation from everyone, even the wallflowers not used to unburdening themselves in public gatherings. It requires a certain forbearance on the part of the meeting toward the individual dissenter who refuses to go along, just as it does a certain temerity on the part of the dissenter before opposing the meeting. And ultimately it means that the perpetual dissenters must recognize that it is in the interests of everyone for them to leave the community with which they are at such odds and go and find a more congenial one somewhere else.

Impossible, you say? Too demanding for real life? Evidently, not so.

Quaker meetings, for at least the past 300 years, have operated by consensus, not only in local meetings of from a dozen to several hundred, but in state and regional meetings where as many as a thousand might gather. Some of the Northeast American Indian tribes, certain Chinese and Japanese communities, and the villages of pre-colonial Java used to use consensus; even in modern Japan, it is said, "there is still a deep feeling in many quarters that it is immoral and 'undemocratic' for a majority to govern, for decisions to be reached without compromise with the minority." Some nineteenth-century intentional communities, usually those with religious underpinnings, had consensual governments for many years, though commonly in groups of only a few dozen and rarely of more than a hundred. Consensus was, and is, the goal of the villages in India that a generation ago embraced Vinoba Bhave's *sarvodaya* movement—the movement that helped to push its own J. P. Narayan to the prime ministership in the 1970s—and at least a few thousand settlements, ranging in size from a few hundred to several thousand, have found it possible to live by consensual government for decades. The settlements of eighteenth-century New England would operate by a kind of informal consensus, not dictated by parliamentary rules but simply called forth by the need for small-town harmony; and this is not so far from the practice of town meetings today that, as Mansbridge has found, do have votes and divisions but "still . . . prefer to make decisions unanimously rather than by majority vote," and "when deeply held agreement seems impossible, they usually strive at least for absence of conflict."

348

Many twentieth-century "alternative" groups—communes, typically, intentional communities, co-ops, political organizations—also attempted consensus government, with greater or lesser success depending upon their prior degree of agreement. Lew Bowers, a skilled and sensitive "facilitator" of many hundreds of consensual meetings, believes that the process can easily be assimilated into any group with shared interests that numbers as many as thirty or even fifty, but is skeptical about unanimity over that number. Indeed, at certain numbers, say a community of 10,000, experience has shown that it is desirable to break into smaller groups, maybe 500 or so, which make their decisions by consensus and then select a delegate—not a "representative" with an independent vote but merely a "spoke" to convey this consensus—to a community coordinating body. This body, with a workable size of a dozen or so (above the ideal five, it is true, but with never more than twenty in a community of 10,000 divided into neighborhoods of 500 each), could then harmonize the various neighborhood positions, easily referring back to neighborhood assemblies or committees where necessary, and then act as a kind of secretariat in carrying out the agreed-upon actions. This is a process of some complexity, to be sure, and each community would need to develop its own styles, but what we know of political affairs suggests that most aspects of governance are simpler at these levels—communications are easier, information is more readily and reliably gathered, feedback is faster and more reliable, participation is greater, personalities and competences are known, and agreements are more easily reached. Perhaps best of all, there are no fixed hierarchies here, no presidents or legislators or parliaments, no grand windy institutions beyond the citizens' control, no roles of such complexity and specialization that they cannot be filled by practically any citizen; which is not to say that there could not be "leaders," people whose intelligence or experience gives them special stature within their neighborhood—indeed, one would expect, and welcome, such people—but only that there is no statutory sanction, no official power, given to such figures, and therefore no abuse of it.

The process with a city of 50,000 is obviously somewhat more complex, and here one might imagine standing committees or full-time officials (their power limited by rotation and recall) necessary to coordinate and carry out consensual policies. But it could still work at that level, even though attenuated—either through a two-level system of neighborhood assemblies and a citywide delegate body of fifty or so (that would be large—Dahl and Tufte show that countries of 20,000–50,000 have parliaments of eighteen to twenty-five people—but not impossible) or a three-tiered system with delegates from the community level to a citywide body, which would then be around five or ten (if five communities of 10,000 or ten of 5,000). At this level one could not expect shared principles and ideologies to any great degree, but on the other hand since most real matters of the day would be taken care of at the neighborhood and community level anyway, the numbers and kinds of decisions that need to be citywide would be minimal. All that need be borne in mind—engraved on city monuments, flown from city flagpoles—is the maxim that decisions should be reached at the level where people of ordinary middling competency can have control over them, and merely coordinated after that. *Vox populi, vox civitas.*

———

It is easy enough to prove that small size is a *necessary* condition for the proper functioning of a direct democracy—even more for a consensus one—but could it also be a *sufficient* condition?

In truth, I do not think it would really be obligatory in a harmonious world that every community be a democracy, if only it remained of human-scale proportions. I could imagine each community going for its own singular form of governance—some might choose a republic, others a monarchy, some might want an oligarchy to rule, others an elected triumvirate, some may prefer a socialist dictatorship, others a cooperative federation, and only a few of the finest and most harmonious opt for a consensual democracy—and as long as none of them tried to impose upon the others, the conditions for a stable, ecological world would be met; and as long as the citizens of each had a free right in the choice of government, and the free right to leave the community if that government palled, then the conditions of justice and freedom would be met. The essential underpinning of a sound and stable society, I am convinced, is the community that is built to the human scale in all its proportions and cleaves to the human scale in all its institutions, not necessarily one that is democratic.

And yet, to my reading, history and logic both argue that a small community will tend toward the democratic, whether or not it expresses it formally, simply by virtue of the fact that individuals are known to each other, interaction is common and regular, opinions are freely exchanged, and every ruler is also a neighbor. In a small society even the prince will probably be accessible—as in Liechtenstein—and every parliament familiar; where the government is inherently limited in scope and accumulation, it is extremely difficult for any individual or set of individuals to dominate and overpower the populace at large, and extremely unlikely that the citizens will permit them. As Leopold Kohr has put it:

> In a small state democracy will, as a rule, assert itself irrespective of whether it is organized as a monarchy or republic. . . . Even where government rests in the hands of an absolute prince, the citizen will have no difficulty in asserting his will, if the state is small. The gap between him and government is so narrow, and the political forces are in so fluctuating and mobile a balance, that he is always able either to span the gap with a determined leap, or to move through the governmental orbit himself.

Moreover, any small society that sought stability and permanence, efficiency and rational governance, would most likely tend toward democracy almost automatically, as it were. Governing by diktat may look easy, but it does not permit reliable information coming in from below in conception, it does not allow diverging opinions to be heard in deliberation, and it does not encourage smooth and willing cooperation in execution. A community that wanted to be sure it knew what all its people were thinking, what the gripes and problems were, that wanted to hammer out the best solutions to the difficulties as they arose, and wanted to be sure its suggestions were carried out and its regulations obeyed, would inevitably work toward some form of direct democracy. Likewise, a community that wanted to create the maximum participation in the political process so as to give outlet for grumbling and dissension, that wanted to develop feelings of self-worth and effectiveness for the citizens' own psychic health, that wanted to ensure loyalty and cooperation through common understanding of the political machinery rather than through coercion, would instinctively move toward some kind of participatory democracy. Healthy not only for the individuals in it but for the community itself, democracy would be likely to come to the fore in any rational community kept at a manageable size, no matter what its trappings may look like.

———

The great English biologist J. B. S. Haldane, the man who gave us our earlier analysis of the beanstalk giant, was once asked, in a group of distinguished theologians, what he could conclude about the nature of the Supreme Being out of his immense store of knowledge of the nature of the universe. The old man thought for just a moment, bent forward and replied, "An inordinate fondness for beetles."

And indeed the scientist's perception was accurate: of the perhaps eight million animal species known, perhaps 80 percent are insects, and of these insects maybe about 40 percent are beetles.

Whether or not the secret to God's plan is in fact the beetle, as I must confess myself reluctant to believe, two indisputable truths seem to be revealed in the natural world. The first has to do with diversity, an incredible diversity, that generates so many hundreds of thousands of insects, and something like 350,000 kinds of beetles, more different kinds than of any other known animal species—spotted and striped, checkered and solid, green, yellow, purple, and rose, some living in sand and garbage, some in trees and roses, some quite minuscule and almost invisible to the unaided eye and some at least a foot long, some unisexed and some multisexed, some in the tropics, some in the Arctic, some indeed everywhere in the world. The second has to do with size, for the great preponderance of the many billions of insects are smaller than a human finger, and yet there are many times more species of small animals than of large ones, by a ratio of at least ten to one.

Does nature by any chance have a political message for us?

PART SIX

CONCLUSION

In speaking about the definition of the ideal, we of course have in mind the definition of only four or five prominent features of this ideal. Everything else must inevitably be the realization of these fundamental theories in life.

—PETER KROPOTKIN, The Ideal of a
Future System, 1873

Once utopia becomes a goal, the long and difficult undertaking of defining the content for a new society can begin.

—RUDOLF MOOS and ROBERT BROWNSTEIN,
Environment and Utopia, 1977

There is a means of realizing various microsituations through the voluntary actions of persons in a free society. Whether people will choose to perform those actions is another matter. Yet, in a free system any large, popular, revolutionary movement should be able to bring about its ends by such a voluntary process. As more and more people see how it works, more and more will wish to participate in or support it.

—ROBERT NOZICK, Anarchy, State, and Utopia, 1974

26

Parthenogenesis

T he tenth chapter of Leopold Kohr's *The Breakdown of Nations* is an elegant summation of the arguments he has adduced in the previous 187 pages to show that, the large states of the present being unwieldy and disadvantageous, it would be possible to divide and reorder them, eliminating the great powers, liberating the small ones, matching future human politics exactly to those of small, democratic, humanitarian states. "The condition of a small-state world," he concludes, "could be established without force or violence," taking only "the abandonment of a few silly, though cherished, slogans," plus "a bit of diplomacy, and a bit of technique."

The eleventh chapter is the shortest in history. It is entitled: "BUT WILL IT BE DONE?" Its single word: "No!"

I have no easy answer to that hard question nor any sanguinity about the future. But obviously I would not have taken us all this far if I agreed with him. Not only do I believe, and I hope I have shown, that a human-scale world is *necessary* and *desirable*, I absolutely believe that it is *possible*. (And in moods when I am struck by its apparent improbability I recall what Polish philosopher Leszek Kolakowski has said: "It may well be that the impossible at a given moment can become possible only by being stated at a time when it is impossible.")

Not that a human-scaled world is in any sense inevitable; I have no illusions about that. We are, as I said at the beginning, in a crisis wrought by the excesses of an industrial civilization knowing no limits or proportions that seems certain, if there is no change in its current course, to bring that civilization to ruin: parthenothanatos. If anything can halt that process it would be the sort of awakening that I have called for in these pages, a swift recognition that our current paths and processes are unsustainable, and an immediate attempt to reorder our lives in their entirety, according the multiple postulates of human scale: parthenogenesis.

The possibility of such an awakening is hard to imagine, I would admit, but it is not thereby less probable. Thomas Schelling has sagely warned against "a tendency in our planning to confuse the unfamiliar with the improbable," thusly: "the contingency we have not considered looks strange; what looks strange is thought improbable; what is improbable need not be considered seriously." It is exactly that syllogism used by those who find themselves in control of the dominant organs of society, so that they may ridicule what they do not understand, as surely as they must have once mocked Columbus, and Copernicus, and Darwin. They mock in order to dismiss, that they will not have to consider. And if forced to consider they often cannot see—as the ancient Greeks were essentially insensitive to color and did not distinguish between green and blue—and so misinterpret, that they will not have to change. They can, they need, to find ultimate refuge in that nice old English saying, "It won't work and we know because we haven't tried it."

I hope that what I have tried to set out at such considerable detail in the preceding pages offers a way to begin thinking more coherently, more rationally, about this alternative possibility, even for those who may have come to mock. Out of these details, these theories, these visions, it is possible to construct a coherent idea of what a human-scale world, for ourselves particularly but also for the rest of the planet, might look like, how it might work through redesigned settings and institutions to remold and refurbish our lives. No utopias, no panaceas: rather the nuts and bolts of what is needed, what has been done, what might be done, how best the human animal can contrive a world of harmony and plenty, of dignity and freedom, and the scale at which that might be done.

I have no blueprint for how such a human-scale world is to come about, and obviously if I did it would be ripped asunder and trampled on by free individuals and communities deciding for themselves what they wanted to build and how they wanted to make it. I can suggest a goal, I can certainly urge the necessity and dangle the desirability of that goal, but I could not suggest the way to get there—and if I did suggest one way, one answer, then immediately it would not be a human-scale solution, diverse for diverse people and local conditions, rooted in people's own conditions, wrought by people's own communities. (Anyone who can lead you into paradise, Joe Hill used to say, can lead you out.) If there is to be any realization of the goal, it will come not as someone dictates a path but as people work out for themselves a great variety of ways of taking control over their lives, varying as times and peoples and necessities and settings differ. I do not, as a matter of fact, imagine that it is all that difficult to accomplish, should the need be perceived and the will exist, and I have a sense that in any case the process itself is essential for every group and community to go through in its own particular way.

By saying that, I do not mean to abdicate an authorial responsibility. It is not equivalent to sitting back and saying, in that old barroom phrase, Let's you and him fight it out. It is just that I am as certain as tomorrow that there is no mass party, no first or second or third party, no vanguard or elite, no leader or guru, no treatise or formula, that is going to bring about the human-scale future or could possibly set for us the way it has to come about. That is an animal, as the Germans say, which there is not any of, and it would be irresponsible, however comforting, to suggest otherwise. There is nothing more here than the clean, hard task of showing what the needed and preferable future is, and seeing that the complicated, exciting process of reaching it begins as soon as possible.

Nothing more—and nothing less.

———

We are at a turning point in world history. I know no better than you what is to come. But the choices are clear: destruction or decentralism.

We can go on as we are, heading toward greater political and economic chaos, a world increasingly roiled by war, famine, and pestilence, depending on ever-more-complex technologies and wreaking environmental disaster on an unprecedented global scale. Or, we can work to achieve systems and organizations of a size where we may regulate them, to reshape our landscapes to permit ecologically sound and locally rooted settlements, to create for ourselves a world in which our societies, our economies, our politics are in fact in the hands of those free individuals, those diverse communities and cities, that will be affected by them—a world, of course, at the human scale.

A world dying . . . or a world being born.

Acknowledgments

I wish to thank the following people for their aid and coopera-tion: Maurice Ackroyd, Gar Alperovitz, Ben Apfelbaum, P. Max Apfelbaum, Ernest Bader, Donald Barthelme, Philip Bereano, Peter Berg, Myrna Breitbart, Brian Carey, Don Carmahan, John Case, Robin Corey, Richard Cornuelle, Bob DaPrato, Rhoda Epstein, Jiirg Federspiel, Annie Fitzpatrick, F.X. Flinn, Gil Friend, David G. Gil, Bertrand Goldberg, Vince Graham, Phillip A. Greenberg, David Gurin, Chuck Hamilton, Cynthia Oudejans Harris, Neill Herring. Don Hollister, Lee Johnson, Marion Knox, Milton Kotler, Hal Lenke, Donald Livingston, Mildred Loomis, Dick and Pat Mackey, Jenny Mansbridge, Michael Marien, John Tepper Marlin. John McClaughry, Linda McDermott, Cynthia Merman, Griscom Morgan, Thomas Morgan, Lynn Nesbit, Robert Nichols, Constance Perrin, John Pfeiffer, John Ramsey, Ray Reece, Pam Roberts, Joyce Rothschild-Whitt, Norman Rush, Kalista Sale, Rebekah Sale, Michael Schaaf, Gertrude Schafer, Daniel Schneider, Ronald Schneider, Neil Seldman, Edward Sorel, Leo Srole, Barry Stein, Bruce Stokes, Bob Swann, Lee Swenson, William I. Thompson, Jaraslov Vanek, Charles Walters, Jr., Matthew Warwick, Bill Whitehead, Langdon Winner, Margaret Wolf, and the staffs of the libraries of Cold Spring, New York State, and New York City, and the US Military Academy.

A special debt within words is owed to my former editor, Joe Kanon, and to my present editor, Joni Praded.

A special debt beyond words is owed to my now-deceased wife, Faith Sale, and to my present partner, Shirley Branchini.

References

Abbreviations:

GPO = Government Printing Office; w.p. = Wikipedia; *NYT* = *New York Times*; SA = Statistical Abstract of the United States; *UP* = *University Press*.

Chapter 1: Parthenothanatos

Parthenon destruction: Acropolis of Athens, w.p.; *NYT*, 6/10/1975, 6/23/1978, p. A2; *Chemistry*, July 1975; *New Yorker*, 1/31/1977; *Time*, 1/31/1977; *Nation*, 6/9/1977; 1974–87 Director General Amadou-Mahtar M'Bow (Senegal), in 1977.

Restoration: Acropolis Restoration Service (website), http://www.ysma.gr/en, see restoration /history; www.ysma.gr/en/news (website), see June 3–5, 2014, 9/12/2014; 6th Annual Meeting for the Restoration of the Acropolis Monuments, October 4–5, 2013; *Archaeology* (magazine), 10/7/2015; Claire Soares, "Acropolis Now! A Museum for the Elgin Marbles," *Independent*, 6/20/2009, http://www.independent.co.uk/news/world/europe/acropolis-now -a-museum-for-the-elgin-marbles-1710787.html.

Parthenon scale: William Bell Dinsmoor, *The Architecture of Ancient Greece: An Account of Its Historic Development* (NY: Norton, 1975); Le Corbusier, *The Modulor: A Harmonious Measure to the Human Scale University Applicable to Architecture and Mechanics* (Cambridge, MA: Harvard UP, 1980); Kent C. Bloomer and Charles W. Moore, *Body, Memory, and Architecture* (New Haven, CT: Yale UP, 1977); Roger Ling, *The Greek World* (Oxford, UK: Elsevier-Phaidon, 1976).

Athens: Lewis Mumford, *The City in History: Its Origins, Its Transformations, and Its Prospects* (NY: Harcourt, Brace & World, 1961), p. 124 and chs. 5 and 6 generally.

Chapter 2: Crises of Civilization

Ecosystem: Science 308, no. 5718 (4/1/2005).

Social ecology: Tom W. Smith, "Trends in Confidence in Institutions," NORC/University of Chicago, August 2008, http://gss.norc.org/Documents/reports/social-change-reports/SC54 Trends in Confidence in Institutions.pdf.

Political deterioration: Wars in the World (website), http://www.warsintheworld.com; MintPress News (website), http://www.mintpressnews.com; "The 2014 Corruption Perceptions Index Measures the Perceived Levels of Public Sector Corruption in 175 Countries and Territories," Transparency International, 2014, https://www.transparency.org/cpi2014.

Exponential growth: Hubbert, *NYT*, 12/3/1976; M. King Hubbert, w.p.; Moore's Law, w.p.; Club of Rome, Donella H. Meadows, et al., *The Limits to Growth* (NY: Signet Books, 1972, 1975; 2nd ed., Chelsea Green Publishing, 2004); Matthew R. Simmons, "Revisiting *The Limits to Growth*: Could the Club of Rome Have Been Correct, After All?," October 2000, http:// greatchange.org/ov-simmons,club_of_rome_revisted.html; Graham Turner and Cathy Alexander, "Limits to Growth Was Right. New Research Shows We're Nearing Collapse," *The Guardian*, 9/1/2014, https://www.theguardian.com/commentisfree/2014/sep/02/limits -to-growth-was-right-new-research-shows-were-nearing-collapse.

Chapter 3: The Human-Scale Future

Papal encyclical: Word on Fire (website), https://laudatosi.com/watch.

Human scale: Le Corbusier, *The Modulor* and *Toward a New Architecture* (Praeger, 1974); Constantinos A. Doxiadis, *Ekistics: An Introduction to the Science of Human Settlements* (NY: Oxford UP, 1968); Paul D. Spreiregen, *Urban Design: The Architecture of Towns and Cities* (NY: McGraw-Hill, 1965); Edward T. Hall, *The Hidden Dimension: An Anthropologist Examines Man's Use of Space in Public and in Private* (NY: Doubleday, 1969), ch. 13; John Michell, "A Defence of Sacred Measures," *CoEvolution Quarterly*, Spring 1978.

Schumacher: E. F. Schumacher, *Small Is Beautiful: Economics as if People Mattered* (NY: Harper & Row, 1973; Hartley & Marks, 1999), and *Good Work* (NY: Harper & Row, 1979).

Chapter 4: The Beanstalk Principle

Size matters: J. B. S. Haldane, "On Being the Right Size," *Possible Worlds* (Harper, 1928); D'Arcy Wentworth Thompson, *On Growth and Form* (Cambridge UP, 1942); John Maynard Smith, *Mathematical Ideas in Biology* (London: Cambridge UP, 1968); Jean-Jacques Rousseau, *The Social Contract: And Discourses* (NY: E. P. Dutton, 1950), book 2, chs. 9 and 10; Galileo Galilei, *Dialogues Concerning Two New Sciences* (NY: Macmillan, 1914); St. Augustine, *City of God*, book 3.

American universities: US News and World Report, http://usnews.rankingsandreviews.com; Algo and Jean Glidden Henderson, *Higher Education in America: Problems, Priorities, and Prospects* (San Francisco: Jossey-Bass, 1974), ch. 11; Bernstein, "How Big Is Too Big," in Dyckman W. Vermilye (ed.), *Individualizing the System* (San Francisco: Jossey-Bass, 1976), pp. 18–28; Jonathan A. Gallant and John W. Prothero, "Weight-Watching at the University: The Consequences of Growth," *Science* 175, no. 4020 (1/28/1972), pp. 381–88.

Chapter 5: The Condition of Bigness

Radio City: Saul Maloff, "Literature Behind Bars," *Commonweal*, 4/28/1978.

Big cars: National Traffic Safety Administration, http://journalistsresource.org/?s=National +Traffic+Safety+Administration.

Texas: John Bainbridge, *The Super-Americans: A Picture of Life in the United States, as Brought into Focus, Bigger than Life, in the Land of the Millionaires—Texas* (NY: Doubleday, 1962), p. 19.

de Sales and German journalist: Ibid., p. 18.

Creation of the internet: Internet, w.p.

Nuclear industry: Union of Concerned Scientists, http://www.ucsusa.org.

Walter Adams: Ralph Nader and Mark J. Green, *Corporate Power in America* (NY: Grossman Publications, 1973), p. 14.

Defense: http://www.usgovernmentspending.com/search_gs.php?q=defense.

Bureaucracy: Cyril Northcote Parkinson, *Parkinson's Law and Other Studies in Administration* (Boston: Houghton-Mifflin, 1957); Chris Edwards, "Why the Federal Government Fails," *CATO Institute Policy Analysis*, no. 777 (7/27/2015), https://object.cato.org/sites/cato.org/files /pubs/pdf/pa777.pdf; Paul C. Light, "A Cascade of Failures: What Government Fails, and How to Stop It," Brookings Institution, 7/14/2014, https://www.brookings.edu/research /a-cascade-of-failures-why-government-fails-and-how-to-stop-it.

American corporations: Barry A. Stein, *Size, Efficiency, and Community Enterprise* (Cambridge, MA: Center for Community Economic Development, 1974), pp. 20, 13–14.

Mumford: The City in History, p. 239.

Chapter 6: Beanstalk Violations

Kohr: Leopold Kohr, *The Breakdown of Nations* (London: Routledge & Kegan Paul, 1957; American edition, NY: Dutton, 1978), pp. xvii–xix.

Government size: Office of Personnel Management, https://www.opm.gov; John J. Dilulio, Jr., "The Rise and Fall of the US Government," *Washington Monthly*, January–February 2015; Goodwin, *New Yorker*, 1/28/1974.

Chapter 7: Prytaneogenesis

Kohr: Leopold Kohr, *The Breakdown of Nations*, pp. 62–64.

Government regulations: James Hammerton, "The Hidden Cost of Regulation," *Freedom Works*, 6/10/2011, http://www.freedomworks.org/content/hidden-cost-regulation.

South Bronx: Jack Newfield and Paul Du Brul, *The Abuse of Power: The Permanent Government and the Fall of New York* (NY: Penguin Books, 1978); *Fortune*, November 1975; Women's City Club of New York, "With Love and Affection: A Study of Building Abandonment," 1977; w.p.

State power: Mumford, *The City in History*, p. 355; Peter Kropotkin, *Mutual Aid: A Factor of Evolution* (NY: New York UP, 1972); Sir Henry Sumner Maine, *Popular Government* (Indianapolis: Liberty Classics, 1976); Hilaire Belloc, *The Servile State* (London & Edinburgh: T. N. Foulis, 1912); Kohr, *The Breakdown of Nations*.

Mail service: John Haldi, *Postal Monopoly: An Assessment of the Private Express Statutes* (Washington, DC: American Enterprise Institute, 1974); Bob Black, *United States vs. Alternate Systems, Inc.* (Pittsburgh, KS: privately printed, 1976); Mathew J. Bowyer, *They Carried the Mail: A Survey of Postal History and Hobbies* (Washington, DC: Robert B. Luce, 1972); FedEx, w.p.; UPS, w.p.; *NYT* editorial, 1/5/1978.

Education: Lawrence A. Cremin, *Traditions of American Education* (NY: Basic Books, 1977); League of Women Voters, "The Role of the Federal Government in Public Education: Equity and Funding," 2011, http://lwv.org/content/role-federal-government-public -education-equity-and-funding; Stephen J. Caldas and Carl L. Bankston III, "Federal Involvement in Local School Districts," *Society* 42 (4), May 2005: *NYT*, 7/18/1977.

Chapter 8: The Law of Government Size

Warfare: Quincy Wright, *A Study of War* (Chicago: Chicago UP, 1965; *not* 1983 abridged reprint), esp. tables 22–54; Pitirim Sorokin, *Social and Cultural Dynamics: Fluctuation of Systems of Truth, Ethics, and Law*, vol. 2 (American Book Company, 1937); Lewis F. Richardson, *Statistics of Deadly Quarrels* (Chicago: Quadrangle Books, 1960).

Historical record: Arnold J. Toynbee, *A Study of History: Abridgement of Volumes I–VI* (NY: Oxford UP, 1947), pp. 244, 553; Mumford, *The City in History*, pp. 42–45, 197, 214, 239, 242.

British historian: Thomas Frederick Tout, in Mumford, *The City in History*, p. 353.

Price index: E. H. Phelps-Brown and Sheila Hopkins, *Forbes*, 3/1/1975, 11/15/1976.

Growth: Gerald D. Nash, *Perspectives on Administration* (Berkeley: California UP, 1969).

French Convention: Quoted by Kropotkin, "The State," e.g. in Martin A. Miller (ed.), *Selected Writings* (MIT, 1970).

Napoleon: Alexis de Tocqueville, *The Old Regime and the French Revolution* (NY: Anchor, 1955), p. 209, and *Democracy in America*, vol. 2 (NY: Knopf, 1951), p. 268.

Chapter 9: Ecological Hubris, Ecological Harmony

Malaria: NYT, 8/23/1977, p. 20, 11/9/1977, p. 2; *Newsweek*, 6/26/1978; UCSF, "Malaysia," Global Health Sciences: Global Research Projects, http://globalprojects.ucsf.edu/locations /malaysia; Christopher Oliver, "Global Malaria Mortality between 1980 and 2010: A Systematic Analysis," Journalist's Resource (website), 2/28/2012, http://journalistsresource .org/studies/international/development/global-malaria-mortality-1980-2010-systematic -analysis.

Estimates: Lee Raymond Dice, *Natural Communities* (Ann Arbor: Michigan UP, 1952), p. 7.

Exterminations: Center for Biological Diversity, http://biologicaldiversity.org.

Bioregionalism: Kirkpatrick Sale, *Dwellers in the Land: The Bioregional Vision* (San Francisco: Sierra Club Books, 1985; Georgia UP, 2000); A. E. [George William Russell], *Interpreters* (London: Macmillan, 1922).

Ecological hubris: Archibald MacLeish, "America Was Promises," 1939, from *New and Collected Poems, 1917–76* (Houghton Mifflin, 1983); Chauncey Starr, speech to Electric Power

Research Institute symposium, San Francisco, April 1979; Arthur E. Morgan, *Dams and Other Disasters: A Century of the Army Corps of Engineers in Civil Work* (Boston: Porter Sargent Publisher, 1971); Wesley Marx, *Acts of God, Acts of Man* (NY: Coward, McCann & Geoghegan, 1977), p. 43; Kirkpatrick Sale, *After Eden: The Evolution of Human Domination* (Durham: Duke UP, 2006); William Leiss, *The Domination of Nature* (NY: George Braziller, 1972); Barry Weisberg, *Beyond Repair: The Ecology of Capitalism* (Boston: Beacon Books, 1971).

Climate change: United Nations Intergovernmental Panel on Climate Change (UN IPCC), 2014, https://www.ipcc.ch/pdf/assessment-report/ar5/wg1/WG1AR5_SPM_FINAL.pdf; James Hansen et al., "Ice Melt, Sea Level Rise and Superstorms: Evidence from Paleoclimate Data, Climate Modeling, and Modern Observations That 2ºC Global Warming Could Be Dangerous," *Atmospheric Chemistry & Physics Journal*, July 2015; Word on Fire, https://laudatosi.com/watch; G. Evelyn Hutchinson, "The Biosphere," *Scientific American* 223, no. 3 (September 1970).

Groundnut scheme: Ritchie Calder, *After the Seventh Day: The World Man Created* (NY: Simon & Schuster, 1961), pp. 302–08; Lord William Malcolm Hailey, *An African Survey: A Study of Problems Arising in Africa South of the Sahara* (NY: Oxford UP, 1957), pp. 844–46, 906–07, 1296, 1559.

Chapter 10: Human-Scale Technology

Jacques Ellul: In Robert Hunter, *The Enemies of Anarchy: A Gestalt Approach to Change* (NY: Viking Press, 1970), pp. 155–56.

Hand-axe: Sale, *After Eden.*

Appropriate technology movement: Berry, in Kirkpatrick Sale, *Rebels Against the Future: The Luddites and Their War on the Industrial Revolution: Lessons for the Computer Age* (Reading, MA: Addison-Wesley Publishing, 1995, 1996), p. 263.

Alternative technology generally: David Dickson, *The Politics of Alternative Technology* (NY: Universe Books, 1975); Langdon Winner, *Autonomous Technology: Technics-out-of-Control as a Theme in Political Thought* (Cambridge, MA: MIT Press, 1978); P. D. Dunn, *Appropriate Technology: Technology with a Human Face* (NY: Schocken Books, 1979); Ivan Illich, *Tools for Conviviality* (NY: Harper & Row, 1973); Godfrey Boyle and Peter Harper, *Radical Technology: Food, Shelter, Tools, Materials, Energy, Communication, Autonomy, Community* (NY: Pantheon Books, 1976); *RAIN* editors, *RAINBOOK* (NY: Schocken Books, 1977); Lane De Moll, *Stepping Stones: Appropriate Technology and Beyond* (NY: Schocken Books, 1978); Nicolas Jéquier (ed.), *Appropriate Technology: Problems and Promises* (Paris: Organization for Economic Co-operation and Development, 1976); Lewis Mumford, *The Myth of the Machine: The Pentagon of Power* (NY: Harcourt, Brace & World, 1970); Murray Bookchin, *Post-Scarcity Anarchism* (Berkeley, CA: Ramparts Press, 1971); Schumacher, *Small Is Beautiful*; Volunteers in Technical Assistance, *Village Technology Handbook* (VITA Publications, 1970); Ken Darrow and Rick Pam, *Appropriate Technology Sourcebook* (Volunteers in Asia, 1976); Eugene Eccli, *Appropriate Technology in the United States: An Exploratory Study* (Integrative Design Associates, 1977); Paul T. Durbin and Carl Mitcham, *Research in Philosophy and Technology: An Annual Compilation of Research*, vol. 1 (Greenwich, CT: JAI Press, 1978).

Herbert Read: Sale, *Rebels Against the Future.*

Banks machine: Banks, *CoEvolution Quarterly*, Spring 1975; J. Baldwin, *Soft-Tech* (NY: Penguin Books, 1978), p. 35; w.p.

Chapter 11: We Shape Our Buildings

Churchill: Parliament.uk (website), "About Parliament," http://www.parliament.uk/about, "The Building and Its Collections," http://www.parliament.uk/building, and "Winston Churchill and Parliament," http://www.parliament.uk/about/living-heritage/transformingsociety/private-lives/yourcountry/collections/churchillexhibition.

Buildings effect: Amanjeet Singh et al., "Effects of Green Buildings on Employee Health and Productivity," *American Journal of Public Health* 100, no. 9 (September 2010), pp. 1665–68; Robert Gutman, *People and Buildings* (NY: Basic Books, 1972); William L. Yancey, "Architecture, Interaction, and Social Control," in John Helmer and Neil A. Eddington (eds.), *Urbanman: The Psychology of Urban Survival* (NY: Free Press, 1973); Oscar Newman, *Defensible Space: Crime Prevention through Urban Design* (NY: Macmillan Publishing, 1973); Oscar Newman, Defensible Space (website), last updated 1/2/2009, http://www.defensible space.com; Robert A. Nisbet, *Twilight of Authority* (Indianapolis: Liberty Fund, 2000), p. 36; C. M. Deasey, *Design for Human Affairs* (Schenkman-Wiley, 1974).

Architecture and human scale: Cyril Daryll Forde, *African Worlds: Studies in the Cosmological Ideas and Social Values of African Peoples* (London: Oxford UP, 1954); Heath Licklider, *Architectural Scale* (NY: Georges Braziller, 1965); Bruno Zevi, *Architecture as Space: How to Look at Architecture* (NY: Horizon Press, 1957, 1974); Andres Duany et al., *New Civic Art: Elements of Town Planning* (NY: Rizzoli, 2003); Andres Duany et al., *The Smart Growth Manual* (NY: McGraw-Hill, 2009); Alexander Tzonis, *Towards a Non-Oppressive Environment: An Essay* (Boston: i Press, 1972); Jonathan Lang et al. (eds.), *Designing for Human Behavior: Architecture and the Behavioral Sciences* (Stroudsburg, PA: Dowden, Hutchinson, and Ross, 1974); Rudolf H. Moos, *The Human Context: Environmental Determinants of Behavior* (John Wiley and Sons, 1976); Geoffrey Scott, *The Architecture of Humanism* (Gloucester, MA: Peter Smith, 1965); Georges Gromort, *Essai sur la Théorie de l'Architecture* (Paris: Vincent, Frère, 1946); Mumford, *The City in History*; Spreiregen, *Urban Design*.

Bruno Zevi: Architecture as Space, p. 76.

Progressive Architecture: Jan C. Rowan (ed.), *Progressive Architecture*, June 1965, http://www .ncmodernist.org/PA/PA-1965-06.pdf.

Ergonomics: Alexander Kira, *The Bathroom* (NY: Viking Press, 1976); Niels Diffrient et al., "Dimensions of Experience: Understanding and Measuring Human Experience in the Designed Environment," *Design Quarterly*, no. 96 (1975), pp. 1, 3–43; Niels Diffrient and Associates, *Humanscale: Manual* (Cambridge, MA: MIT Press, 1974); Henry Dreyfuss, *The Measure of Man: Human Factors in Design* (NY: Whitney Library of Design, 1966).

Design of cities: Hermann Maertens, *Der Optische Maassstab, oder die Theorie und Praxis des asthetischen Sehens in den bildenden Kiinsten* (Berlin: Kgl. Baurath, Wasmuth, 1884); Werner Hegemann and Elbert Peets, The American Vetruvius: *An Architect's Handbook of Civic Art* (NY: Wenzel and Krakow, 1922); Hans Blumenfeld, *The Modern Metropolis: Its Origins, Growth, Characteristics, and Planning* (Cambridge, MA: MIT Press, 1967), esp. ch. 23.

Building design elements: Kent C. Bloomer and Charles Willard Moore, *Body, Memory, and Architecture* (New Haven, CT: Yale UP, 1977), pp. ix, 77, and ch. 4; James J. Gibson, *The Perception of the Visual World* (Boston: Houghton Mifflin, 1950).

Robert Yudell: Bloomer and Moore, *Body, Memory, and Architecture*, p. 61.

Single-family house: Blumenfeld, *The Modern Metropolis*, ch. 23; Bloomer and Moore, *Body, Memory, and Architecture*, p. 4.

Chapter 12: The Search for Community

Early communities: Campbell, in John E. Pfeiffer, *The Emergence of Man* (NY: Harper & Row, 1972), p. 104; Amos H. Hawley, *Human Ecology: A Theory of Community Structure* (NY: Ronald Press, 1950); Dubos, in Constantine Doxiadis (ed.), *Anthropopolis: City for Human Development* (NY: Norton, 1974), pp. 259–60.

George Murdock: George Peter Murdock, *Social Structure* (NY: Macmillan, 1949), pp. 79–80.

Loss of community: Alexander, in Helmer and Eddington, eds., *Urbanman*, p. 246.

Community size: R. A. Hill and R. I. M. Dunbar, "Social Network Size in Humans," *Human Nature* 14, no. 1 (March 2002); Pfeiffer, *The Emergence of Man*, pp. 376–77; Michael Chance and Clifford Jolly, *Social Groups of Monkeys, Apes, and Men* (NY: Dutton, 1970); Birdsell, in Pfeiffer, *The*

Emergence of Man, pp. 376–77; Pierre Clastres, *Society Against the State: The Leader as Servant and the Humane Use of Power among the Indians of the Americas* (NY: Urizen Books, 1977), p. 72; Adams, in John E. Pfeiffer, *The Emergence of Society: A Pre-History of the Establishment* (NY: McGraw-Hill, 1977), pp. 155–56; Dubos, in Constantine Doxiadis (ed.), *Anthropopolis*, p. 259.

Neighborhood: Blumenfeld, *The Modern Metropolis*; Doxiadis, *Ekistics*; Gordon Rattray Taylor, *Rethink: A Paraprimitive Solution* (Penguin, 1962), pp. 151–52; Terence Lee, "Urban Neighbourhood as a Socio-Spatial Schema," *Human Relations*, 21, no. 3 (August 1968), pp. 241–67; Charles Erasmus, *In Search of the Common Good: Utopian Experiments Past and Future* (NY: Free Press, 1977), p. 130.

Brain characteristics: Murdoch, in Pfeiffer, *The Emergence of Man*, p. 377.

Tribal size: Sanders and Baker, and Rathje, in Pfeiffer, *The Emergence of Society*, pp. 467–69.

Early cities: Sjoberg, in Gerard Piel, *Cities: A Scientific American Book* (NY: Knopf, 1966), p. 28; Constantine Doxiadis, "Man's Movement and His City," *Science* 162, no. 3851 (10/18/1968), pp. 326–34, and Doxiadis, *Ekistics*.

Community size: Clarence Arthur Perry, *Neighborhood and Community Planning*, vol. 7, "The Neighborhood Unit," Regional Survey of New York and Its Environs, 1929; see Melville Campbell Branch, ed., *Urban Planning Theory* (Stroudsbourg, PA: Dowden, Hutchinson & Ross, 1975). *Architectural Forum* July 1943, August 1943; N. L. Englehart, *Architectural /Forum, July, 1943;* Constantin Pertzoff, *Architectural Forum*, April 1944; J. L. Sert, "The Human Scale in City Planning," in Paul Zucker, ed., *New Architecture and City Planning: A Symposium* (NY: Philosophical Library, 1944); Barbara Ward, *Home of Man* (NY: Norton, 1976), p. 131; Walter Gropius and Martin Wagner, "A Program for City Reconstruction," *Architectural Forum* 79 (July 1943), pp. 75–82; Leopold Kohr, *The Overdeveloped Nations: The Diseconomies of Scale* (NY: Schocken Books, 1977), pp. 14–19.

Decline of community: Robert D. Putnam, *Bowling Alone: The Collapse and Revival of American Community* (NY: Simon & Schuster, 2000).

Hall: H. Fielding, *The Soul of a People* (London: Macmillan, 1920).

Chapter 13: The Optimal City

Optimal city: Murray Bookchin, *The Limits of the City* (NY: Harper & Row, 1974; Montreal: Black Rose, 1996); John E. Gibson, *Designing the New City: A Systemic Approach* (NY: Wiley, 1977); Erwin Anton Gutkind, *The Expanding Environment: The End of Cities, the Rise of Communities* (London: Freedom Press, 1953); Malcolm Getz, "Optimum City Size: Fact or Fancy?," *Law and Contemporary Problems* 43, no. 2 (Spring 1979), pp. 197–210, http://scholarship.law.duke.edu/lcp/vol43/iss2/6.

Modern scholars: Duncan, in Paul K. Hatt and Albert J. Reiss (eds.), *Cities and Society: The Revised Reader in Urban Sociology* (Glencoe, IL: Free Press, 1951); Hirsch, in Harvey Perloff and Lowdon Wingo Jr. (eds.), *Issues in Urban Economics* (Baltimore: Johns Hopkins UP, 1975); Schumacher, *Small Is Beautiful*, p. 63; Borsodi, *Green Revolution*, May 1979; Robert A. Dahl, "The City in the Future of Democracy," *American Political Science Review* 61, no. 4 (December 1967), pp. 953–70; David Albouy, "Evaluating Efficiency and Equity," *Journal of Political Economy*, 96, 9, 2012; Dionysia Lambiri et al., "Quality of Life in the Economic and Urban Economic Literature," *Social Indicators Research* 84, no. 1 (October 2007); http://pavelpudolyak.blogspot.com/2014/11/optimum-city-population-size.html.

City sizes: UN, "World Urbanization Prospects: 2014 Revision" (2014), https://esa.un.org/unpd/wup/Publications/Files/WUP2014-Highlights.pdf.

Doxiadis: Ekistics.

Civility: Stanley Milgram, in Helmer and Eddington, *Urbanman*; Claude S. Fischer, "The Effect of Urban Life on Traditional Values," *Social Forces* 53, no. 3 (March 1975), pp. 420–32; Bruce Mayhew and Roger L. Levinger, "Size and the Density of Interaction in Human Aggregates," *American Journal of Sociology* 82, no. 1 (July 1976), pp. 86–110.

Crime: Irving Hoch, "City Size Effects, Trends, and Policies," *Science* 193, no. 4256 (9/3/1976), pp. 856–63; David Franke, *America's 50 Safest Cities* (New Rochelle, NY: Arlington House, 1974); Uniform Crime Reporting, "Crime in the United States 2012," https://ucr.fbi.gov /crime-in-the-u.s/2012/crime-in-the-u.s.-2012, and "Crime in the United States 2015," https:// ucr.fbi.gov/crime-in-the-u.s/2015/crime-in-the-u.s.-2015; Mason Johnson, "FBI's Violent Crime Statistics for Every City in America," *CBS Chicago*, 10/22/2015, http://chicago.cbslocal .com/2015/10/22/violent-crime-statistics-for-every-city-in-america; James J. Nolan III, "Establishing the Statistical Relationship between Population Size and UCR Crime Rate: Its Impact and Implications," *Journal of Criminal Justice* 32 (2004), pp. 547–55, http://theipti.org /wp-content/uploads/2012/02/covariance.pdf.

Health and mental health: C. W. Namey and R. W. Wilson, "Health Characteristics by Geographic Region, Large Metropolitan Areas, and Other Places of Residence, United States 1969–70," *Vital and Health Statistics* Series 10, no. 86 (January 1974), pp. 1–62; Duncan, in *Cities and Society*; Lennart Levi and Lars Andersson, *Psychosocial Stress: Population, Environment, and Quality of Life* (NY: Spectrum Publications, 1975); Lennart Levi, *Society, Stress and Disease* (Oxford University Press, 1971); R. C. Schmitt, "Density, Health, and Social Disorganization," *Journal of the American Institute of Planners* 32 (January 1966); Mazda Adli, "Urban Stress and Mental Health," *LSE Cities*, November 2011, https://lsecities .net/media/objects/articles/urban-stress-and-mental-health/en-gb; Leo Benedictus, "Sick Cities: Why Urban Living Can Be Bad for Your Mental Health," *Guardian*, 2/25/2014, https:// www.theguardian.com/cities/2014/feb/25/city-stress-mental-health-rural-kind; Helmer and Eddington, *Urbanman*, pp. 246ff.

Recreation: Duncan, in *Cities and Society*; Thomas M. Stanbach and Richard V. Knight, *The Metropolitan Economy: The Process of Employment Expansion* (NY: Columbia UP, 1970), table 4.3.

Education: Colin Clark, "The Economic Functions of a City in Relation to Its Size," *Econometrica* 13, no. 2 (April 1945), pp. 97–113; Betsy Levin et al., *The High Cost of Education in Cities: An Analysis of the Purchasing Power of the Educational Dollar* (Washington, DC: Urban Institute, 1973).

Culture: http://americanorchestras.org; League of Resident Theatres, http://www.lort.org; William Alonso, "Urban Zero Population Growth," *Daedalus* (Fall 1973), pp. 191–206.

Economics: Joel Garreau, *Edge City: Life on the New Frontier* (NY: Anchor Books, 1992); Arthur O'Sullivan, *Urban Economics* (NY: McGraw-Hill, 2003); Richard Arnott and David McMillen, *A Companion to Urban Economics* (Malden, MA: Blackwell Publishing, 2006); José Lobo et al., "The Economic Productivity of Urban Areas: Disentangling General Scale Effects from Local Exceptionality," Santa Fe Institute Paper, September 2011, http://santafe.edu/media /workingpapers/11-09-046.pdf; Alonso, "Urban Zero Population Growth"; generally, William Leroy Henderson and Larry C. Ledebur, *Urban Economics: Processes and Problems* (NY: Wiley, 1972); Brian J. L. Berry and Frank E. Horton (eds.), *Geographic Perspectives on Urban Systems with Integrated Readings* (Englewood Cliffs, NJ: Prentice-Hall, 1970); Perloff and Wingo, *Issues in Urban Economics*; Stanbach and Knight, *The Metropolitan Economy*.

Municipal services: Percival Goodman, *The Double E* (NY: Anchor Books, 1977), p. 26; Shirley Svorny, "The Economics and Politics of City Size," January 2003, http://www.csun.edu /~vcecn007/publications/Economics_City_Size_Svorny_2003_Unpublished.doc; Lobo, "The Economic Productivity of Urban Areas"; Hirsch, in Perloff and Wingo, *Issues in Urban Economics*.

Political standards: H. D. F. Kitto, *The Greeks* (Baltimore: Penguin Books, 1957), p. 79; Douglas Yates, *The Ungovernable City: The Politics of Urban Problems and Policy Making* (Cambridge, MA: MIT Press, 1977), p. 5; Dahl, "The City in the Future of Democracy"; Ada W. Finifter and Paul R. Abramson, "City Size and Feelings of Political Competence," *Public Opinion Quarterly* 39, no. 2 (Summer 1975); Claude S. Fischer and T. K. Hirsch, in Perloff and Wingo, *Issues in Urban Economics*; Robert A. Dahl and Edward R. Tufte, *Size and Democracy* (CA: Stanford UP, 1973); Alan Altusher, *Community Control* (Pegasus Books, 1970); "2013

Municipal Yearbook," International City/County Management Association (http://icma
.org/en/icma/home); Lawrence J. R. Herson and John M. Bolland, "The Urban Web:
Politics, Policy, and Theory" (2014), last updated 8/30/16, http://homepages.wmich.edu
/~shoffman/urbanweb.
Bookchin: The Limits of the City, p. 66.

Chapter 14: Human-Scale Services

Solar energy: Solar Energy Industries Association, http://www.seia.org; Amory Lovins, *Soft
Energy Paths: Toward a Durable Peace* (London: Penguin Books, 1977), *Reinventing Fire*
(Chelsea Green Publishing, 2011), and Rocky Mountain Institute, http://www.rmi.org;
Greg Pahl, *Power from the People: How to Organize, Finance, and Launch Local Energy Projects*
(Chelsea Green Publishing, 2012); *Energy Strategies*, US Senate Select Committee on Small
Business, 2 vols. (GPO, 12/9/1976); Barry Commoner, *The Poverty of Power: Energy and the
Economic Crisis* (NY: Knopf, 1976); Denis Hayes, *Rays of Hope: The Transition to a Post-
Petroleum World* (NY: Norton, 1977); Alan Okagaki et al. *Solar Energy: One Way to Citizen
Control* (Washington, DC: Center for Science in the Public Interest, 1979); w.p.
Lovins: Soft Energy Paths, p. 45.
Spectrolab: Okagaki, *Solar Energy*, pp. 81–92.
Community solar: Institute for Local Self-Reliance, *Self-Reliance*, September–October 1978;
Energy Sage (website), "Solar Calculator," https://www.energysage.com/solar/calculator;
Community Renewable Energy (website), http://communityrenewableenergynow.
com; Rufus E. Miles, *Awakening from the American Dream: The Social and Political Limits
to Growth* (NY: Universe Books, 1976), p. 135; Peter M. Rosset, "Small Farms Are More
Efficient & Sustainable," *Multinational Monitor* 21, nos. 7 & 8 (July–August 2000), https://
www.organicconsumers.org/old_articles/Organic/smallfarmsbetter.php; Warren R.
Bailey, *The One-Man Farm* (Washington, DC: Economic Research Service, US Department
of Agriculture, 1973); Perelman, and government official, in George Baker and Richard
Merrill, *Radical Agriculture* (NY: Harper & Row, 1976), ch. 6; *Economist*, quoted in *Resurgence*
(UK) 8, no. 5 (November–December 1977), p. 27; Wallace E. Huffman, "The Status of
Labor-Saving Mechanization in U.S. Fruit and Vegetable Harvesting," 4/24/2012, https://
migrationfiles.ucdavis.edu/uploads/cf/files/2012-may/huffman-fruit-feg-harvesters-042412a
.pdf; Ralston Purina, Joe Belden, *Toward a National Food Policy* (Exploratory Project for
Economic Alternatives, 1976); USDA National Agricultural Statistics Service (USDANASS;
https://www.nass.usda.gov), 2012 Census of Agriculture: Organic Survey (2014),
AC-12-SS-4, https://www.agcensus.usda.gov/Publications/2012/Online_Resources/Organics
/ORGANICS.pdf; Robert Klepper et al., "Economic Performance and Energy Intensiveness
in Organic and Conventional Farms in the Corn Belt: A Preliminary Comparison,"
American Journal of Agriculture Economics 59, no. 1 (February 1977), pp. 1–12; Sarah Yang,
"Can Organic Crops Compete with Industrial Agriculture?" *Berkeley News*, 12/9/2014,
http://news.berkeley.edu/2014/12/09/organic-conventional-farming-yield-gap; Small Farm
Viability Project, *The Family Farm in California: Report of the Small Farm Viability Project,
Submitted to the State of California, November, 1977* (State of California, 1977).
Food: Paul Gipe, *Wind Energy for the Rest of Us: A Comprehensive Guide to Wind Power and How to
Use It* (Wind-Works.org, 2016).
*Goldschmidt: Small Business and the Community: A Study in Central Valley of California on Effects of
Scale of Farm Operations*, US Senate report, Special Committee on Farm Problems, December
1946, in Peter Barnes (ed.), *The People's Land: A Reader on Land Reform in the United States*
(Emmaus, PA: Rodale Press, 1975);Walter Goldschmidt, *As You Sow* (Free Press, 1947);
update in Belden, *Toward a National Food Policy*; Michael N. Hayes, Alan J. Olmstead,
"Farm Size and Community Quality: Arvin and Dinuba Revisited," *American Journal
of Agricultural Economics* 66, no. 4 (November 1984); Heather Gray, "Land Reform and

American Agriculture," 5/24/2006, http://www.counterpunch.org/2006/05/24/land-reform
-and-american-agriculture.

Garbage: Seldman and Bree, in Niel S. Seldman, *New Directions in Solid Waste Planning*
(Washington, DC: Institute for Local Self-Reliance, 1977), https://ilsr.org.

Transportation: NHTS Administration, DOT #HS812013; *Your Driving Costs: How Much Are You
Really Paying to Drive?* (AAA, 2015), http://exchange.aaa.com/wp-content/uploads/2015/04
/Your-Driving-Costs-2015.pdf.

Cities: Barbara Ward, *The Home of Man* (London: Deutsch, 1976), p. 150.

Work at home: Census Bureau, https://www.census.gov/hhes/commuting/files/2012/Home
-based%20Workers%20in%20the%20United%20States%20Infographic.pdf; Kenneth
Rapoza, "One in Five Americans Work from Home, Numbers Seen Rising Over 60%,"
Forbes, 2/18/2013; Global Workplace Analytics, globalworkplaceanalytics.com.

Bicycle: Wilson, *RAIN,* October 1976, and *RAINBOOK,* p. 233; Victor J. Papanek, *Design for the
Real World: Human Ecology and Social Change* (Chicago: Academy Chicago, 1985), pp. 201–16;
Energy efficiency chart, by Vance E. Tucker, Duke University, from *Scientific American,*
March 1973; Campbell bike, *Doing It!,* no. 4 (December 1976), p. 19; Ivan Illich, *Energy and
Equity* (NY: Harper & Row, 1974), pp. 59–61.

Health: Williams, *New Times,* November 1978; William Hardy McNeill, *Plagues and Peoples*
(NY: Anchor Press, 1976); Bureau of Labor Statistics, US Department of Labor, "EMTs
and Paramedics," *Occupational Outlook Handbook, 2016–17 Edition,* http://www.bls.gov
/ooh/healthcare/emts-and-paramedics.htm; Self-help, w.p.; "Fast Facts on US Hospitals,"
American Hospital Association (AHA), last updated 1/2016, http://www.aha.org/research
/rc/stat-studies/fast-facts.shtml.

Optimal hospital size: Hospitals, 10/1/1974; Leonard Ullman, *Institution and Outcome: A Comparative
Study of Psychiatric Hospitals* (Oxford, UK: Pergamon Press, 1967); Lawrence Linn, "State
Hospital Environment and Rates of Patient Discharge," *Archives of General Psychiatry* 23,
no. 4 (1970), pp. 346–51; M. S. Feldstein, in Harry Greenfield (ed.), *Hospital Efficiency and
Public Policy* (NY: Praeger, 1973); Ruth Roemer, *Planning Urban Health Systems: From Jungle
to System* (NY: Springer Publications, 1992); Chicago Regional Hospital Study, *Misused and
Misplaced Hospitals and Doctors,* Association of American Geographers, Resource Paper No.
22 (1973); Rutgers, *NYT,* 5/21/1978, p. 47; 1969 survey, Greenfield, *Hospital Efficiency and Public
Policy;* Ivan Illich, *Medical Nemesis: The Expropriation of Health* (NY: Pantheon Books, 1976).

Ecotopia: Ernest Callenbach, *Ecotopia: The Notebooks and Reports of William Weston* (Berkeley, CA:
Banyan Tree Books, 1975), pp. 142–44; w.p.

Education: Roger Barker and Paul V. Gump, *Big School, Small School: High School Size and Student
Behavior* (CA: Stanford UP, 1964), esp. pp. 195–202; Allan Wicker, "Cognitive Complexity,
School Size, and Participation in School Behavior Settings: A Test of the Frequency of
Interaction Hypothesis," *Journal of Educational Psychology* 60, no. 3 (June 1969), pp. 200–03;
see also Anita A. Summers and Barbara Wolfe, "Which School Resources Help Learning?
Efficiency and Equity in Philadelphia Public Schools," *Business Review,* February 1975;
Herbert J. Walberg, "Class Size and the Social Environment of Learning," *Human Relations* 22,
no. 5 (October 1969), pp. 465–75; Stanton Leggett et al., "The Case for a Small High School,"
Nation's Schools 76 (September 1970), pp. 45–52; Edwin P. Willems, "Sense of Obligation
to High School Activities as Related to School Size and Marginality of Student," *Child
Development* 38, no. 4 (1967), pp. 1247–60; A. W. Wicker, "Undermanning, Performances, and
Students' Subjective Experiences in Behavior Settings of Large and Small High Schools,"
Journal of Personality and Social Psychology 10 (1968), pp. 255–61, and "Size of Church
Membership and Members' Support of Church Behavior Settings," *Journal of Personality
and Social Psychology* 13 (1969), pp. 278–88; Thomas Toch, *High Schools on a Human Scale:
How Small Schools Can Transform American Education* (Boston: Beacon Press, 2003); Thu Song
Thi Nguyen, "High Schools: Size Does Matter," *Study of High School Restructuring* 1, no. 1

(March 2004); Valerie E. Lee and Julia B. Smith, "High School Size: Which Works Best and for Whom?," *Education Evaluation and Policy Analysis* 19, no. 3 (Fall 1997); Kathleen Cotton, "Affective and Social Benefits of Small-Scale Schooling," *ERIC Digest* (ERIC Clearinghouse on Rural Education), ED 401088 (December 1996); Coleman Report, files.eric.ed.gov/fulltest /EDO12275.pdf; World Health Organization (WHO), in Arthur Morgan, *Community Comments* (Yellow Springs, OH, 1970); Harry Morgan, op ed, *NYT*, 11/29/1978; Pupil enrollment, National Center for Education Statistics, https://nces.ed.gov/fastfacts/display.asp?id=98.

Chapter 15: Economy of Global Reach

Exploitation: US Energy Information Administration (USEIA), http://www.eia.gov; American Enterprise Institute (AEI), https://www.aei.org, accessed 4/5/2012; Ugo Bardi, *Extracted: How the Quest for Mineral Wealth Is Plundering the Planet* (Chelsea Green Publishing, 2013).

Waste: Penton, Waste 360 (website), http://www.waste360.com.

Tiger: Lionel Tiger, "My Turn: A Very Old Animal Called Man," *Newsweek*, 9/4/1978.

Overgrowth: Hazel Henderson, "The Entropy State," *Planning Review* 2, no. 3 (April–May 1974), and see Hazel Henderson, *Creating Alternative Futures: The End of Economics* (NY: Berkley Publications, 1978); John Kenneth Galbraith, "A Hard Case," *New York Review of Books*, 4/20/1978 (review of Irving Kristol, *Two Cheers for Capitalism*, NY: Basic Books, 1978).

Taylor: Rethink, p. 258.

Chapter 16: Steady-State Economy

Mill: John Stuart Mill, *Collected Works of John Stuart Mill*, vol. 5: *Essays on Economics and Society*, part 2, ch. 5, http://oll.libertyfund.org/titles/mill-collected-works-of-john-stuart-mill -in-33-vols.

Modern sources: Boulding, e.g., in Herman E. Daly, *Essays Toward a Steady-State Economy* (Cuernavaca: Centro Intercultural de Documentación, 1971); E. J. Mishan, *The Costs of Economic Growth* (NY: Praeger, 1967); Nicholas Georgescu-Roegen, *The Entropy Law and the Economic Process* (Cambridge, MA: Harvard UP, 1971); Donella H. Meadows, *The Limits to Growth: A Report for the Club of Rome's Project on the Predicament of Mankind* (NY: Universe Books, 1972); Schumacher, *Small Is Beautiful*; Leopold Kohr, *Development without Aid: The Translucent Society* (Wales: Christopher Davies, 1973); Steady-State Economy, w.p. and references; Center for the Advancement of the Steady State Economy, http://steadystate .org; Herman Daly, *Steady-State Economics: The Economics of Biophysical Equilibrium and Moral Growth* (San Francisco: W. H. Freeman, 1977), p. 47.

Tragedy of the Commons: Garrett Hardin, "The Tragedy of the Commons," *Science* 162, no. 3859 (12/13/1968), pp. 1243–48, and *Exploring New Ethics for Survival: The Voyage of the Spaceship Beagle* (NY: Viking Press, 1972).

Ivins: NYT, 7/29/1979, p. 1.

Chapter 17: The Logic of Size

Five: A. Paul Hare, *Handbook of Small Group Research* (NY: Macmillan, 1972 and 1976), pp. 221ff.; Charles B. Handy, *Understanding Organizations* (London: Penguin Books, 1976), p. 152; Parkinson, *Parkinson's Law, and Other Studies in Administration*, ch. 4; Edgar F. Bogatta et al., *Small Groups* (NY: Knopf, 1967); John James, "A Preliminary Study of the Size Determinant in Small Group Interaction," *American Sociological Review* 16, no. 4 (August 1951), pp. 474–77; Susan Whelen, *Social Group Research* 40, no. 2, 2009; Hamid Tohidi, "Review the Benefits of Using Value Engineering in Information Technology Project Management," *Procedia Computer Science* 3 (2011); Thayer, *New Viewpoints* (Franklin Watts, 1973), pp. 8, 199–200.

Small-group studies: Moos, *The Human Context*; Barker and Gump, *Big School, Small School*, part 2, chs. 11 and 3; D. W. Johnson and Frank P. Johnson, *Joining Together: Group Theory and Group Skills* (Englewood Cliffs, NJ: Prentice-Hall, 1975); Elton T. Reeves, *The Dynamics of Group Behavior* (NY: American Management Association, 1970); Bernard P. Indik,

"Organization Size and Member Participation," *Human Relations* 18, no. 4 (November 1965), pp. 339–50; Lyman Porter and Edward Lawler III, "Properties of Organization Structure in Relation to Job Attitudes and Job Behavior," *Psychological Bulletin* 64, no. 1 (1965), pp. 23–51.

Hawthorne: Elton Mayo, *The Human Problems of an Industrial Civilisation* (NY: Macmillan, 1933); and for crucial reanalysis, Paul Blumberg, *Industrial Democracy: The Sociology of Participation* (NY: Schocken Books, 1973); Gilbert, *NYT*, 3/18/1978, p. 29; Jeff Bezos, "Jeff Bezos Invests in Business Insider [Full Internal Memo]," *Business Insider*, 4/5/2013, http://www.business insider.com/jeff-bezos-invests-in-business-insider-2013-4.

Small offices: Sergio Talacchi, "Organization Size, Individual Attitudes and Behavior: An Empirical Study," *Administrative Science Quarterly* 5, no. 3 (December 1960), pp. 398–420; Moos, *The Human Context*, esp. pp. 257ff., 336ff., and 410; Stanford Business School, in Moos, *The Human Context*.

Underlying logic: Mancur Olson, *The Logic of Collective Action: Public Goods and the Theory of Groups* (NY: Schocken Books, 1971), quotes from pp. 2, 28, 34–35, 44, 48, 54–55, 62, and 166.

Productivity: Kohr, *The Breakdown of Nations*, pp. 157ff.

Chapter 18: Workplace Democracy

Totalitarian industry: Louis Dembitz Brandeis, *The Curse of Bigness: Miscellaneous Papers of Louis D. Brandeis* (NY: Viking Press, 1935); Wood, quoted in *Nation*, 11/27/1976, p. 564; Quinn, *Nation*, 3/7/1953.

Workplace democracy: See generally Jaroslav Vanek (ed.), *Self-Management: Economic Liberation of Man: Selected Readings* (London: Penguin Books, 1975), *The General Theory of Labor-Managed Economies* (Ithaca, NY: Cornell UP, 1970), and *The Labor-Managed Economy: Essays* (Ithaca, NY: Cornell UP, 1977); Gerry Hunnius et al. (eds.), *Workers' Control: A Reader on Labor and Social Change* (NY: Vintage Books, 1973); C. George Benello and Dimitrios I. Roussopoulos, *The Case for Participatory Democracy: Some Prospects for a Radical Society* (NY: Grossman Publishers, 1971); G. David Garson, *On Democratic Administration and Socialist Self-Management: A Comparative Survey Emphasizing the Yugoslav Experience* (Beverly Hills, CA: Sage Publications, 1974); *Journal of Social Issues* 32, no. 2 (June 1976); *Annals of American Academy of Political and Social Science* 431, no. 1 (May 1977).

Ownership: "An Introduction to the World of Employee Ownership," National Center for Employee Ownership, https://www.nceo.org/employee-ownership/id/12; Michigan's Institute for Social Research (ISR), in D. Zwerdling, "Employee Ownership—How Well Is It Working?" *Working Papers for a New Society*, May–June 1979, http://home.isr.umich.edu; w.p.; Warren Cassell, "6 Successful Companies That Are Employee-Owned," *Investopedia*, 5/13/2016, http://www.investopedia.com/articles/insights/051316/6-successful-companies -are-employeeowned.asp.

Mondragon Corporation: w.p. and references; "About Us," Mondragon Corporation, http://www.mondragon-corporation.com/eng/about-us; Alastair Campbell et al., *Worker-Owners: The Mondragon Achievement: The Caja Laboral Popular and the Mandragon Co-operatives in the Basque Provinces of Spain: A Report* (London: Anglo-German Foundation for the Study of Industrial Society, 1977); Daniel Zwerdling, *Workplace Democracy: A Guide to Workplace Ownership, Participation, and Self-Management Experiments in the United States and Europe* (NY: Harper & Row, 1980), pp. 151ff.; William Foote White and Kathleen King Whyte, *Making Mondragon: The Growth and Dynamics of the Worker Cooperative Complex* (Ithaca, NY and London: ILR Press, 1988); Robert Oakeshott, "Mondragón, Spain's Oasis of Democracy," in Vanek, *Self-Management*, pp. 290–96; Alyssa Davis and Lawrence Mishel, "CEO Pay Continues to Rise as Typical Workers Are Paid Less," Economic Policy Institute Policy Brief #380 (6/12/2014).

Wage differential: The Economic Policy Institute calculated 295:1 in 2013, http://www.epi.org /publication/ceo-pay-continues-to-rise.

Evergreen cooperatives: http://www.evgoh.com; *US News & World Report,* 7/21/2016.

Control: Bertil Gardell, *Psychosocial Aspects of the Working Environment* (Swedish Institute: Stockholm, 1977), p. 15; Ira Brous, *Democracy in the Workplace: Readings on the Implementation of Self-Management in America* (Washington, DC: Strongforce, 1977), p. 39; United States Federation of Worker Cooperatives, https://usworker.coop/home; Seymour Melman, "Industrial Efficiency Under Managerial vs. Cooperative Decision-Making: A Comparative Study of Manufacturing Enterprises in Israel," *Review of Radical Political Economics* 2, no. 1 (April 1970); *Studies in Comparative International Development* (Sage, 1969); Gerry Hunnius et al, *Workers' Control,* Random House, 1973, pp. 252–54; Moberg, *In TheseTimes,* December 21–27, 1977; Rushton, in Zwerdling, *Workplace Democracy,* pp. 31ff.; Traci Hukill, "A World without Bosses?" *Alternet* (website), 7/1/2005, http://www.alternet.org/story/23201/a_world_without _bosses; John Curl, "NoBAWC and Bay Area Regional Cooperative/Solidarity Economics Organizing," Grassroots Economic Organizing (GEO), 6/15/2015, http://www.geo.coop/story /nobawc-and-bay-area-regional-cooperativesolidarity-economics-organizing; Paul Blumberg, *Industrial Democracy: The Sociology of Participation* (NY: Schocken Books, 1974); Vocations for Social Change, *No Bosses Here: A Manual for Working Collectively* (1976), p. 32; Scott Burns, *The Household Economy: Its Shape, Origins, and Future* (Boston: Beacon Press, 1977), p. 96; Sachs, in Brous, *Democracy in the Workplace,* p. 39, and Zwerdling, *Workplace Democracy,* p. 159.

Kibbutzim: Kibbutz, w.p.; Keitha Sapsin Fine, in Hunnius, *Workers' Control;* Haim Barkai, in Vanek, *Self-Management;* Arnold Sherwood Tannenbaum, *Hierarchy in Organizations: An Internal Comparison* (San Francisco: Jossey-Bass Publishers, 1974).

Mondragon: Campbell, *Worker-Owners,* p. 3.

Community: Robert A. Dahl, *After the Revolution?: Authority in Good Society* (New Haven, CT: Yale UP, 1970), p. 64; Lima, McWhinney, in Leften Stavros Stavrianos, *The Promise of the Coming Dark Age* (San Francisco: W. H. Freeman, 1976), p. 63.

Yugoslavia: Workers' Self-Management, w.p.; Saul Estrin, *Self-Management: Economic Theory and Yugoslav Practice* (NY: Cambridge UP, 1983); Hunnius, *Workers' Control,* p. 268ff.; Ichak Adizes, *Industrial Democracy: Yugoslav Style: The Effect of Decentralization on Organizational Behavior* (NY: Free Press, 1971); Blumberg, in ibid., chs. 8 and 9; Vanek, *Self-Management.*

Kibbutz: Melman, in *Studies in Comparative Economic Development* (Thousand Oaks, CA: Sage Publications, 1969); Barkai, in Vanek, *Self-Management.*

Systematic arrangements: British team, in Campbell et al., *Worker-Owners,* p. 51; Schumacher, *Small Is Beautiful,* p. 268ff.; Vanek, *Labor-Managed Economy;* Henry George, *Progress and Poverty* (originally published in 1879; abridged reprint ed., NY: Robert Schalkenbach Foundation, 1970), p. 159; George, *Progress and Poverty,* edited and abridged by Bob Drake (Robert Shalkenbach Foundation, 2006), http://www.henrygeorge.org/pcontents.htm.

Community land trust: Schumacher Center for a New Economics, http://www.centerfornew economics.org; w.p.; National Community Land Trust Network (Portland, OR), http:// cltnetwork.org; *Smithsonian,* June 1978; *Green Revolution,* March 1978; *Organic Gardening,* August 1977; *Communities,* December 1974; John McClaughry, "A Model State Land Trust Act," *Harvard Journal on Legislation* 12 (June 1975), pp. 563–609.

Utopian experiments: List of American Utopian Communities, w.p.; Rosabeth Moss Kanter, *Commitment and Community: Communes and Utopias in Sociological Perspective* (Cambridge, MA: Harvard UP, 1972); Erasmus, *In Search of the Common Good;* German/Austrian cities, Griscom Morgan, *Community Comments* (Yellow Springs, OH, March 1969); *New Republic,* 8/10/62.

Kibbutz: Erasmus, *In Search of the Common Good,* pp. 183, 301.

Spanish Civil War: Sam Dolgoff, *The Anarchist Collectives: Workers' Self-Management in the Spanish Revolution, 1936–1939* (NY: Free Life Editions, 1977); George Orwell, *Homage to Catalonia* (Boston: Beacon Press, 1955); George Woodcock, *Anarchism: A History of*

Libertarian Ideas and Movements (Cleveland: Meridian Books, 1962), ch. 12; Laval, in Dolgoff, *The Anarchist Collectives*, pp. 135ff., 146ff.

Chapter 19: Self-Sufficiency

Paleolithics: Marshall Sahlins, *Stone Age Economics* (Chicago: Aldine-Atherton, 1972); Sale, *After Eden*; Marvin Harris, *Cannibals and Kings: The Origins of Cultures* (NY: Random House, 1977); John E. Pfeiffer, *Emergence of Man*; Rene Dubos, *Beast or Angel? Choices That Make Us Human* (NY: Scribner, 1974), ch. 2.

Life expectancy: Hillred Kaplan et al., "A Theory of Human Life History Evolution: Diet, Intelligence, and Longevity," *Evolutionary Anthropology* 9, no. 4, 2000, pp. 156–85.

Self-sufficiency: Jane Jacobs, *The Economy of Cities* (NY: Random House, 1969), ch. 5; F. Fraser Darling, "The Ecological Approach to the Social Sciences," *American Scientist* 39, no. 2 (April 1951), pp. 244–54; Schumacher, *Small Is Beautiful*, p. 55; Murray Bookchin, *Post-Scarcity Anarchism*, pp. 83ff., 141ff.; Kohr, *The Breakdown of Nations* and *Development without Aid*; Stein, *Size, Efficiency, and Community Enterprise*, pp. 71ff.; Edward Ullman et al., *The Economic Base of American Cities: Profiles for the 101 Metropolitan Areas Over 250,000 Population Based on Minimum Requirements for 1960* (Seattle: University of Washington Press, 1969); Charles Tiebout, *The Community Economic Base Study* (NY: Committee for Economic Development, 1962); Robert E. Dickinson, *City and Region* (London: Routledge & Paul, 1964); Robert Goodman, *The Last Entrepreneurs: America's Regional Wars for Jobs and Dollars* (NY: Simon & Schuster, 1979), chs. 8 and 9; w.p.

Manufacturing statistics: "Top 20 Facts about Manufacturing," National Association of Manufacturers, http://www.nam.org/Newsroom/Top-20-Facts-About-Manufacturing; "Facts about Manufacturing," Manufacturing Institute, http://www.themanufacturing institute.org/Research/Facts-About-Manufacturing/Facts.aspx.

Small towns: Mumford, *The City in History*, p. 126ff.; Fernand Braudel, *Capitalism and Material Life, 1400–1800* (NY: Harper & Row, 1973), pp. 375, 376–79.

Jojoba and guayule: Mother Earth News, November–December 1977; *NYT*, 3/30/1977; National Research Council, *Jojoba: Feasibility for Cultivation on Indian Reservations in the Sonoran Desert Region*, National Academy of Sciences, https://www.nap.edu/catalog/20337; *Guayule: An Alternative Source of Natural Rubber*, National Academy of Sciences, https://www.nap.edu/catalog/19928.

Bookchin: Post-Scarcity Anarchism, p. 111.

Lucca: See, e.g., Kohr, *The Overdeveloped Nations*, esp. ch. 8, and *Development without Aid*, esp. chs. 5, 13, and 14; Schumacher, *Small Is Beautiful*, p. 59ff.

Chapter 20: The Malaise of Citizenship

Voter turnout: w.p.; Voter Participation Data Center, http://data.voterparticipation.org; United States Census Bureau, https://www.census.gov.

Tuchman: "My Turn," *Newsweek*, 7/12/1976.

Loss of citizenship: Robert Paul Wolff, *In Defense of Anarchism* (NY: Harper & Row, 1970), pp. 30–31; *In Defense of Anarchism*, w.p.

$2.1 trillion: "Offshore Shell Games 2015," Citizens for Tax Justice, 10/5/2015, http://ctj.org/ctjreports/2015/10/offshore_shell_games_2015.php.

The Rebel: 2/18/1896, reprinted in *The Match* (Tucson), January 1972, http://www.library.illinois.edu/hpnl/newspapers/results_full.php?bib_id=1252

Chapter 21: The Decentralist Tradition

Decentralism: See, generally, the corpus of Kohr, Schumacher, Mumford, Bookchin, Illich, Kropotkin, Ralph Borsodi, and Paul Goodman; Decentralization, w.p. and references; Jeff Taylor, *Politics on a Human Scale: The American Tradition of Decentralism* (Lanham, MD: Lexington Books, 2013); Bill Kaufman, in Ronald Hamowy, *The Encyclopedia of*

Libertarianism (Thousand Oaks, CA: Sage Publications, 2008); Herbert Agar, *Land of the Free* (Boston: Houghton-Mifflin, 1935); Richard Cornuelle, *De-Managing America: The Final Revolution* (NY: Random House, 1975); Karl Hess, *Dear America* (NY: Morrow, 1975); Thomas Hewes, *Decentralize for Liberty* (NY: E. P. Dutton, 1947); Peter T. Manicus, *Death of the State* (Putnam, 1974); Ioan Bowen Rees, *Government by Community* (London: Charles Knight, 1971); Mark Ivor Satin, *New Age Politics: Healing Self and Society* (NY: Dell Publishing, 1979); Colin Ward, *Anarchy in Action* (NY: Harper & Row, 1973); Ralph Louis Woods, *America Reborn: A Plan for Decentralization of Industry* (NY: Longmans, Green, 1939). And see bibliographies in Satin, *New Age Politics*; Michael Marien, *Societal Directions and Alternatives: A Critical Guide to the Literature* (LaFayette, NY: Information for Policy Design, 1976).

Historical evidence: Hannah Arendt, *On Revolution* (NY: Viking Press, 1965), pp. 254–85; quotes, pp. 260, 267, 252–53; Rudolf Rocker, *Nationalism and Culture* (Los Angeles: Rocker Publications, 1937; Montreal: Black Rose, 1997), ch. 5 and p. 362; Switzerland, Jonathan Steinberg, *Why Switzerland?* (Cambridge, UK: Cambridge UP, 1976), quote, p. 73: Kropotkin, *Mutual Aid* (London: Heinemann, 1902), and "The State" in Miller, *Selected Writings.*

Decentralism in America: Taylor, *Politics on a Human Scale*; David De Leon, *The American as Anarchist: Reflections on Indigenous Radicalism* (Baltimore: Johns Hopkins UP, 1979); Merrill Jensen, *The American Revolution within America* (NY: New York UP, 1976), and *The Articles of Confederation: An Interpretation of the Social-Constitutional History of the American Revolution 1774–1781* (Madison: Wisconsin UP, 1940); Murray Rothbard, *Conceived in Liberty*, vols. 1–4 (New Rochelle, NY: Arlington House, 1975–79); Staughton Lynd, *Intellectual Origins of American Radicalism* (NY: Pantheon Books, 1963); Lawrence Goodwyn, *Democratic Promise: The Populist Movement in America* (NY: Oxford UP, 1976); Howard Zinn, *A People's History of the United States: 1492–2001* (NY: HarperCollins, 2003, 2015); Paine, in Ward, *Anarchy in Action*, p. 65; Cartwright letter, 6/5/1824, Kercheval letters 7/12/1816 and 9/5/1816, Micah Burnett, "Thomas Jefferson," *Our Republic* (website), http://www.ourrepubliconline.com/Quote/451; Arendt, *On Revolution*, pp. 252–59; Merrill Jensen, *The New Nation: A History of the United States during the Confederation, 1781–1789* (NY: Vintage Books, 1965), p. 120; Henry David Thoreau, *Civil Disobedience* (1849), http://xroads.virginia.edu/~hyper2/thoreau/civil.html.

Populists: Goodwyn, *Democratic Promise.*

1920s and '30s: Twelve Southerners, *I'll Take My Stand: The South and the Agrarian Tradition* (NY: Harper, 1930; reprint, NY: Harper & Row, 1962); Herbert Agar and Allen Tate (eds.), *Who Owns America? A New Declaration of Independence* (Boston: Houghton-Mifflin, 1936); Edward S. Shapiro, "Decentralist Intellectuals and the New Deal," *Journal of American History* 58, no. 4 (March 1972), pp. 938–57; *Free America* (magazine), 1937–47.

Port Huron Statement: Sale, *SDS* (NY: Random House, 1972).

Harrington: Nation, 12/23/1978.

Centralization: Woodward, *New York Review of Books*, 4/5/1979.

Number of nations: "How Many Countries Are There in the World in 2016?" *Political Geography Now* (website), 8/1/2016, http://www.polgeonow.com/2011/04/how-many-countries-are-there-in-world.html.

Chapter 22: Society Without the State

Pfeiffer: Emergence of Man, p. 290.

Walter: In Colin Ward, *Anarchy in Action*, p. 50, and *Anarchism: A Very Short Introduction* (NY: Oxford UP, 2004), p. 75.

Societies without states: Aidan Southall, "Stateless Society," *International Encyclopedia of Social Sciences*, vol. 15 (NY: Macmillan, 1968); M. Fortes and E. E. Evans-Pritchard (eds.), *African Political Systems* (London: Oxford UP, 1940); John Middleton and David Tait (eds.) *Tribes without Rulers: Studies in African Segmentary Systems* (London: Routledge & Paul, 1958);

Clastres, *Society Against the State*; Franz Oppenheimer, *The State: Its History and Development Viewed Sociologically* (NY: Free Life Editions, 1975); Edward Goldsmith, *Blueprint for Survival* (Harmondsworth, UK: Penguin Books, 1973), p. 106ff.; Peter Farb, *Humankind* (Boston: Houghton Mifflin, 1978), p. 104.

Dinka: Lienhardt, in Middleton and Tait, *Tribes without Rulers*, quote, p. 114.

Braudel: Capitalism and Material Life, p. 420.

Ireland: Joseph Peden, *The Libertarian Forum* 3, no. 4 (April 1971).

Town meetings: Frank Bryan, *Real Democracy: The New England Town Meeting and How It Works* (Chicago: Chicago UP, 2004); Jane Mansbridge, *Beyond Adversary Democracy* (Chicago: Chicago UP, 1980); Zuckerman, *Peaceable Kingdoms: New England Towns in the Eighteenth Century* (NY: Vintage Books, 1972), quotes, pp. 32, 34, 37, 87, 46, 87, 93,100–02; also see Robert E. Brown, *Middle-Class Democracy and the Revolution in Massachusetts, 1691–1780* (NY: Cornell UP, 1955).

Chapter 23: The "Necessity" of the State

Dahl: After the Revolution?, pp. 146–47, 86.

Simons: Henry Simons, *Economic Policy for a Free Society* (Chicago: Chicago UP, 1948).

Nuclear warheads: Arms Control Association, https://www.armscontrol.org.

Small-society peacefulness: Peter van Dresser, *Free America* (magazine), July 1938; Kohr, *The Breakdown of Nations*, pp. 60ff.

Tiwi: C. W. M. Hart and Arnold R. Pilling, *The Tiwi of North Australia* (NY: Holt, 1960).

Public services: Dahl and Tufte, *Size and Democracy*, pp. 22–24; Michael Taylor, *Anarchism and Cooperation* (NY: Wiley, 1976), pp. 134–35.

Weil: Simone Weil, *The Need for Roots: Prelude to a Declaration of Duties toward Mankind* (NY: Putnam, 1952), p. 43.

Chapter 24: The Importance of Size: Harmony

Dunstable: In Zuckerman, *Peaceable Kingdoms*, p. 121.

Switzerland: Steinberg, *Why Switzerland?*

Crime: https://www.themarshallproject.org.

Size: Jeremy A Sabloff and C. C. Lamberg-Karlovsky, *Ancient Civilization and Trade* (Albuquerque: New Mexico UP, 1975); Pfeiffer, *The Emergence of Society*, p. 467; Padavino, in Steinberg, *Why Switzerland?*, p. 23.

Chapter 25: The Importance of Size: Democracy

Democracy: Rousseau, *Social Contract*, book 3, ch. 15; *Geneva Manuscript*, book 2, ch. 3; *Social Contract*, book 3, ch. 1; Aristotle, *Politics*, book 7, ch. 4; James Madison, *Federalist* No. 10, in Clinton Rossiter (ed.), *The Federalist Papers* (NY: New American Library, 1961); John Stuart Mill, *Considerations on Representative Government*, 1861, 2017 (Create Space); Dahl, *After the Revolution?*, p. 85; Kohr, *The Breakdown of Nations*, pp. 99–100.

Greece: See, e.g., Kathleen Freeman, *Greek City-States* (NY: Norton, 1950); M. I. Finley, *Democracy: Ancient and Modern* (New Brunswick, NJ: Rutgers UP, 1973).

Switzerland: Steinberg, *Why Switzerland?*, pp. 72–73, 190.

Town meetings: Zuckerman, *Peaceable Kingdoms*; Jensen, *The New Nation*; Jane Mansbridge, "Conflict in a New England Town Meeting," *Massachusetts Review* 17, no. 4 (Winter 1976), pp. 631–63; Zimmerman, *NYT*, 3/15/1979.

Size and Democracy: Dahl and Tufte, *Size and Democracy*, pp. 57, 46–51, 87–88, 60; Swedish study, ibid., pp. 62ff.; confirmative studies in Arthur Vidich and Joseph Bensman, *Small Town in Mass Society: Class, Power and Religion in a Rural Community* (Garden City, NY: Doubleday, 1960), and Ritchie P. Lowry and Robert Rankin (eds.), *Sociology: The Science of Society* (Lexington, MA: George Cross Books, 1977).

REFERENCES

Voting paradox: Richard G. Miemi and William H. Riker, "The Choice of Voting Systems," *Scientific American* 234, no. 6 (June 1976); Peter C. Fishburn, *The Theory of Social Choice* (NJ: Princeton UP, 1973).

Consensus: Consensus Decision-Making, w.p.; Consensus Decision-Making, http://www .consensusdecisionmaking.org; Hoffman, "Quaker Dialogue," in Center for the Study of Democratic Institutions, *The Civilization of the Dialogue* (Cincinnati, 1968); Jane Mansbridge, "Conflict in a New England Town Meeting."

Kohr: The Breakdown of Nations, pp. 98–99.

Chapter 26: Parthenogenesis

Kohr: The Breakdown of Nations, pp. 196–97.

Kolakowski: In Rudolf Moos and Robert Brownstein, *Environment and Utopia: A Synthesis* (NY: Plenum Press, 1977), p. 262.

Schelling: In Daly, *Steady-State Economics,* p. 145.

Index

—

Note: Page numbers in *italics* refer to figures.